In contrast to current attempts to formalize the innovation process through standardization, in this excellent book Peter Augsdorfer argues the case for bootlegging, the ultimate example of informal innovation. The book brings together the latest international research and case studies, and represents a refreshing antidote to the institutional pressures to control, structure and stifle the motivations and energy of grassroots innovation.

Professor Joe Tidd
Science Policy Research Unit,
University of Sussex, UK

Bootlegging is one of those hidden secrets in the innovation process — the kind of project that stays out of sight, below the radar screen because it may involve bending or even breaking the rules. We want internal entrepreneurs in our organizations and we want them to experiment and explore — but we don't know too much about them and even less about how they operate. This is why this book is such a valuable addition to our innovation management library; it draws on a wealth of experience from multiple authors to give us helpful insights into how we might understand and support this important activity.

Professor John Bessant
Business School, University of Exeter, UK

This book is amazing and a true eye-opener. The first time that an untapped but crucial source of innovation is explained to a wider audience. A comprehensive and easy-to-read summary of the principles of bootlegging as source of innovation. You can't ignore — another masterpiece of Peter Augsdorfer and his global research team.

Fabian S. Schlage
Head of Ecosystem Engagement,
Nokia Enterprise Solutions, Germany

An interesting whirlwind discussion on bootlegging: from definitional aspects through enabling organizational conditions to psychological characteristics of single individuals apt to bootleg. This book is a must-read for innovation students and practitioners.

Professor Andrea Prencipe
Rector, Luiss University, Rome, Italy

This is an amazing book to read if you want to understand the drivers and results of undeclared innovation within multinational corporations.

Professor Victoire de Margerie
Chief Executive, Rondol, France

The author team behind this book place bootlegging from the underground of innovation to whether it truly belongs: On the main stage as a core mechanism for how organizations can achieve radical innovation.

Professor Frank T. Piller
RWTH Aachen University, Germany

Corporate Underground: Bootleg Innovation and Constructive Deviance serves as an informative resource on many aspects of the theory, research, and practice of bootlegging. The book contains articles from different countries and cultures, allowing researchers and practitioners to gain an understanding of bootlegging for further research or application within their companies.

Melodi Guilbault
Assistant Dean, Martin Tuchman School of Management,
New Jersey Institute of Technology, USA

Innovation, as the art of launching any more or less creative output on the market, often starts with creativity in the underground. Recognizing bootlegging as one major contributor to the dynamic capabilities of companies, the book provides useful tips for managing, enhancing and fostering this unformal practice. A book I do recommend to all managers seeking to generate impact!

Professor Séverine Le Loarne – Lemaire
Grenoble Ecole de Management, France

Corporate Underground

Bootleg Innovation and Constructive Deviance

Series on Technology Management

Series Editor: Joe Tidd (*University of Sussex, UK*) ISSN 0219-9823

The Technology Management Series is dedicated to the advancement of academic research and management practice in the field of technology and innovation management. The series features titles which adopt an interdisciplinary, multifunctional approach to the management of technology and innovation, and includes work which seeks to integrate the management of technological, market and organisational innovation. All titles are based on original empirical research, and includes research monographs and multiauthor edited works. The focus throughout is on the management of technology and innovation at the level of the organisation or firm, rather than on the analysis of sectoral trends or national policy.

Published

Vol. 39 *Corporate Underground: Bootleg Innovation and Constructive Deviance*
edited by Peter Augsdorfer (Technical University Ingolstadt, Germany)

Vol. 38 *Artificial Intelligence and Innovation Management*
edited by Stoyan Tanev (Carleton University, Canada) &
Helena Blackbright (Mälardalen University, Sweden)

Vol. 37 *Managing Knowledge, Absorptive Capacity and Innovation*
edited by Joe Tidd (University of Sussex, UK)

Vol. 36 *Digital Disruptive Innovation*
edited by Joe Tidd (University of Sussex, UK)

Vol. 35 *Developing Holistic Strategic Management in the Advanced ICT Era*
by Mitsuru Kodama (Nihon University, Japan)

Vol. 34 *Managing Innovation: Internationalization of Innovation*
edited by Alexander Brem (Friedrich-Alexander-Universität Erlangen-Nürnberg, Germany & University of Southern Denmark, Denmark), Joe Tidd (University of Sussex, UK) & Tugrul Daim (Portland State University, USA)

Vol. 33 *Managing Innovation: What Do We Know About Innovation Success Factors?*
edited by Alexander Brem (Friedrich-Alexander-Universität Erlangen-Nürnberg, Germany & University of Southern Denmark, Denmark), Joe Tidd (University of Sussex, UK) & Tugrul Daim (Portland State University, USA)

Vol. 32 *Managing Innovation: Understanding and Motivating Crowds*
edited by Alexander Brem (Friedrich-Alexander-Universität Erlangen-Nürnberg, Germany & University of Southern Denmark, Denmark), Joe Tidd (University of Sussex, UK) & Tugrul Daim (Portland State University, USA)

More information on this series can also be found at http://www.worldscientific.com/series/stm

(Continued at the end of the book)

SERIES ON TECHNOLOGY MANAGEMENT – VOL. 39

Corporate Underground

Bootleg Innovation and Constructive Deviance

Editor

Peter Augsdorfer

Technical University Ingolstadt, Germany

World Scientific

NEW JERSEY • LONDON • SINGAPORE • BEIJING • SHANGHAI • HONG KONG • TAIPEI • CHENNAI • TOKYO

Published by

World Scientific Publishing Europe Ltd.
57 Shelton Street, Covent Garden, London WC2H 9HE
Head office: 5 Toh Tuck Link, Singapore 596224
USA office: 27 Warren Street, Suite 401-402, Hackensack, NJ 07601

Library of Congress Cataloging-in-Publication Data
Names: Augsdorfer, Peter, editor.
Title: Corporate underground : bootleg innovation and constructive deviance / editor, Peter Augsdorfer, Technical University Ingolstadt, Germany.
Description: New Jersey : World Scientific, 2023. | Series: Series on technology management, 0219-9823 | Includes bibliographical references and index.
Identifiers: LCCN 2022001502 | ISBN 9781800612259 (hardcover) | ISBN 9781800612266 (ebook) | ISBN 9781800612273 (ebook other)
Subjects: LCSH: Creative ability in business. | Technological innovations.
Classification: LCC HD53 .C6748 2023 | DDC 658.4/063--dc23/eng/20220303
LC record available at https://lccn.loc.gov/2022001502

British Library Cataloguing-in-Publication Data
A catalogue record for this book is available from the British Library.

For any available supplementary material, please visit
https://www.worldscientific.com/worldscibooks/10.1142/Q0361#t=suppl

Desk Editors: Jayanthi Muthuswamy/Adam Binnie/Shi Ying Koe

Typeset by Stallion Press
Email: enquiries@stallionpress.com

https://doi.org/10.1142/9781800612266_fmatter

Preface

This book is about corporate underground creativity, also called "bootlegging." But then, it has many names: slack innovation, underground system, under-the-table work, informal corporate entrepreneurship, autonomous initiatives, underground innovation, stealth innovation, unsponsored innovation, and more recently it has also become popularly known as creative deviance. R&D practitioners also refer to it as: Friday-afternoon work, work behind the fume cupboard, freelance work, under-the-counter work, pet project, discretionary research, intrapreneurship, freewheeling, illicit research, scrounging, and renegades' work. French firms call it *recherche camouflagé*, *recherche caché*, *recherche parallèle*, *recherche libre*, *recherche en perruque*, *recherche sauvage*, or *recherche sous-marine*. German firms call it *U-Boot Forschung* or *graue Projekte*. And, I am sure quite a few companies have their own unique term for it.

This book is a kind of handbook, says the dictionary, is a type of reference work that is intended to provide ready reference. It gives information about facts on a particular topic and should guide the reader. This book has this ambitious goal, and I hope, indeed, that it will serve as an authoritative resource on many aspects of the theory, research, and practice of bootlegging. Ideally, it will become a useful compendium for researchers and practitioners and encourage others to develop an interest in this subject.

There is a growing interest in the subject, far more now than when Donald A. Schon published the first paper about bootlegging in

1963 in the *Harvard Business Review*. The number of publications has increased manifold. So, uniting the research community in a handbook was a logical and long-overdue step.

This book is not an original research contribution but a summary of the state-of-the-art of published knowledge. It hopes to accomplish at least four things. First, to give the reader expert insight into the latest research in the field of bootlegging. Indeed, some of the world's leading specialists agreed to contribute. Second, the book presents many facets of bootlegging including basic information, the sensitive transition from underground to formal disclosure at an organization, as well as psychological factors. This breadth of cover allows the reader to acquire a comprehensive picture of the nature of bootlegging. Third, the reader will develop an astute understanding of what spurs potentially creative and innovative people toward their extraordinary achievements and exceptional performance. Fourth, and perhaps most importantly, the reader will be able to critically apply the insights gained from this book in order to consider how best to manage their own innovative capabilities in their companies.

Handbooks typically lack a detailed methodology section. The focus is on "what we know about" rather than a full description of how the knowledge was gained and with which empirical method. This is not different in this book. However, each chapter is a summary of the state-of-the-art of the contributor's research.

There are many people to thank for helping this handbook come to fruition. First, I would like to thank Saida Biberović, who did a great job formatting the book. Second, many thanks to Joe Tidd for encouraging me to prepare this book. However, most important are the authors: I would like to discharge a debt of gratitude to them for their willingness to undertake the additional task of contributing chapters while being inundated with work.

https://doi.org/10.1142/9781800612266_fmatter

About the Editor

Peter Augsdorfer is professor of technology and innovation management at the Technical University Ingolstadt, Germany. He holds a German engineering degree, a French management degree, and a DPhil from SPRU, England. His research interests include R&D management, evolutionary aspects of early innovation processes, and discontinuous innovation. Bootlegging in corporate R&D is not only his central research focus but a passion since his days when he bootlegged a project during his first job in industry.

https://doi.org/10.1142/9781800612266_fmatter

List of Contributors

Poul Houman Andersen is professor at Aalborg University Business School and head of the PhD School at the faculty of Social Sciences of Aalborg University, Denmark. In addition, he is part-time professor of supply management at the Norwegian University of Science and Technology in Trondheim. His research interests cover research methodology, strategy, operations management, and the organization of buyer–seller relationships.

Erfan Jalali Bidakhavidi holds a master's degree in entrepreneurship from the faculty of entrepreneurship at the University of Tehran, Iran. His main research interests are corporate entrepreneurship, innovation management, and organizational behavior. He has been working in the telecommunications industry for several years and is now a research assistant conducting research on the role of cultural and institutional factors affecting firms in the emerging economies.

Arne Buchwald is associate professor of information systems and digital transformation at the Vlerick Business School, Gent, Belgium.

Matej Černe is associate professor at the University of Ljubljana, School of Economics and Business, Slovenia.

Pauline Fatien Diochon is associate professor at Grenoble Ecole de Management, France. She holds a PhD in management from HEC School of Management, France and has academic experience in France, United States, and Colombia. Her research explores the ethical and political dimensions of organizational phenomena, in contexts such as leadership development (coaching) and collaborative spaces.

Yunzhou Du is professor at the school of economics and management of the Southeast University, China.

Stephan Eicher was a doctoral student of Peter Augsdorfer and Kathrin Möslein at the Universität Erlangen-Nürnberg. He has been working in the semiconductor industry for more than 10 years. He is currently working as head of operations processes at Siltronic AG in Germany. His research interest is primarily focused on bootlegging in an R&D context.

Khatereh Ghasemzadeh is a postdoc fellow at the University of Bologna in Italy. She received her PhD from the University of Udine, Italy, in the field of innovation management in 2020. Her dissertation was mainly focused on the scope of open and user innovation and she has published some scientific articles on this theme. Further, she has experience in researching organizational behavior subjects, namely diversity, creativity and mindfulness. She is also engaged in research on sustainability (agenda 2030) and how higher education institutions are transforming societies through sustainable development.

Dietfried Globocnik is a senior scientist at the Alpen-Adria Universität and the University of Graz, Austria. He holds a PhD in social and economic sciences and a habilitation in business administration. His research interests include innovation marketing, sustainable innovation, corporate entrepreneurship, managing innovation initiatives, and organizing innovation activities in multinational enterprises (MNEs).

Tomislav Hernaus is associate professor at the University of Zagreb, Croatia and visiting professor at the University of Ljubljana, Slovenia.

Wei Huang is a doctoral candidate at the school of business administration of the Zhejiang Gongshang University in Zhejiang, China.

Rudolph Koch is senior manager in global project and strategic controlling at the international automotive supplier Magna Powertrain and a lecturer for finance at the Joanneum University of Applied Science in Graz, Austria. In his previous career, he was a scientist at the Center for Innovation Systems and Policy at the Austrian Institute of Technology where his research focused on new product development from a complexity science perspective. He wrote his dissertation about the role, functions, and dynamics of self-organization in innovation processes.

Alexander Krueger is a senior consultant in energy and utilities at Capgemini Invent. He was a PhD candidate at the EBS Business School, Wiesbaden, Germany.

Linda Nhu Laursen is assistant professor at the department of architecture, design and media technology of Aalborg University, Denmark. Her research interests cover innovation, design, entrepreneurship, open innovation, and renewal in large organizations. In her current research, she studies the innovation, design, intrapreneurial, and agile approaches of leading corporations such as Lego, Unilever, B&O, among others.

Karl-Heinz Leitner is senior scientist at the center for innovation systems and policy at the Austrian Institute of Technology and professor for innovation management at the Center for Entrepreneurship and Applied Business Studies at the University of Graz. His main research interests cover changing innovation processes, industrial transformation, startup ecosystems, foresight, and innovation policy. Karl-Heinz Leitner conducted research and consultancy projects for funding agencies, ministries and the European Commission.

Yang Liu is associate professor at the school of business administration of the South China University of Technology, Guangzhou, China.

Amadou Lô is assistant professor of strategy, entrepreneurship, and innovation at Toulouse Business School (TBS) Education, France. He received his PhD from the University of Lyon. His research focuses on strategic innovation management through a paradoxical lens and the emergence of collaborative spaces. He conducted research projects with Renault-Nissan-Mitsubishi Group on those topics in Paris and in Silicon Valley in the United States.

Yaser Masoudnia was a PhD student and supervised by Marek Szwejczewski at Cranfield University. He is cofounder and CEO of LinqPal, and a serial entrepreneur who founded startups in fintech, cyber-security, enterprise software, and construction. His last startup, NoPassword, was acquired by LogMeIn, who's most famous product is LastPass. Yaser completed his PhD at Cranfield School of Management while he held a research associate position at MIT. His research work focused on bootlegging in large tech companies. For his research, he interviewed teams of scientists and engineers at some of the largest tech giants in the United States. Yaser also holds an MBA and a BA in economics.

Claudia C. Michalik is a business consultant in the financial services sector with a passion for secretive R&D projects leading to ground-breaking innovations. In her day job, she delivers major transformation programs in finance and technology. In her spare time, she happily releases her own inner Gyro Gearloose and tinkers with her innovative ideas. Claudia holds a PhD from Universität Münster, Germany and master degrees in business economics and business science from international alma maters.

Kamal Sakhdari is assistant professor at the faculty of entrepreneurship at the University of Tehran, Iran. He received his PhD in business and entrepreneurship from the Queensland University of Technology (QUT) in Brisbane, Australia. His main research interests are corporate entrepreneurship, innovation management, institutional theory, and international business. He is also a member of the Australian Centre for Entrepreneurship Research (ACE) at the QUT Business School.

Miha Škerlavaj is professor and vice dean at the school of economics and business, University of Ljubljana, Slovenia. He is also adjunct professor at BI Norwegian Business School, Norway.

Anika Stephan-Korus is research fellow and postdoc at the Center for Entrepreneurship and Innovation of the School of Management, Fribourg (HEG-FR). She is also data manager at BMW Group and responsible for different analytic use cases and has contributed to multiple innovation initiatives at the BMW Group headquarters in Munich. Anika is an expert on internal innovation management processes and holds a doctorate from the University of Strasbourg.

Marek Szwejczewski is a senior lecturer at the Sheffield University Management School. Prior to joining Sheffield, he was director of the Best Factory Awards at Cranfield University. Before becoming an academic, he worked in various industry sectors ranging from retail to telecommunications. Marek has authored numerous articles and reports on innovation management, supplier management, and manufacturing strategy. He has advised a wide range of organizations, both public and private. Marek completed his PhD at Cranfield University. His current research interests are innovation management, portfolio management, and international manufacturing strategy.

Helene Tenzer is associate professor of International Business at Tübingen University, Germany. She has earned a master's in international cultural and business studies and a PhD in intercultural communication. Her research focuses on multinational and multilingual teams, innovation management, organizational behavior, international human resource management and leadership in multinational organizations.

Guopeng Xiang is professor at the school of business administration at the Zhejiang Gongshang University in Zhejiang, China.

Philip Yang is associate professor of strategy and organization at Tübingen University, Germany. He obtained a master's in economics and a PhD in labour economics. His research focuses on leadership, diversity, ethics, and innovation in the context of teams.

https://doi.org/10.1142/9781800612266_fmatter

Contents

https://doi.org/10.1142/9781800612266_0001

Introduction

Peter Augsdorfer
Technical University of Ingolstadt, Ingolstadt, Germany
peter.augsdorfer@thi.de

1. Definition of Bootlegging

Originally, "bootlegging" was coined as a term during the American Prohibition when the law made it illegal to produce alcohol. Dodgy moonshiners smuggled whiskey from back country to sell on the black market. Why the contrabandists were called bootleggers is not known. The word seems to originate from the practice of smuggling illicit goods in the leg of tall boots. However, Schon, incidentally a whiskey drinker, first used the term in 1963 for smuggled R&D projects in companies (Schon, 1963). Since then, "bootlegging" has become the predominant term to describe covert R&D projects. The following definition is the result of analysis of previous publications.

Bootlegging in corporate R&D is defined as a nonformalized (no officially allocated resources) and non-declared (secret) bottom-up innovation process that benefits the bootlegger's firm. It goes against — deliberately or not — corporate rules, including explicit management orders.[1]

[1]Bootlegging is not to be confused with skunkworks or permitted bootlegging. For example, Leicht-Deobald and Lins (2017) write about bootlegging, but in reality they mean skunkworks. This becomes clear when reading such sentences as: "A further element is that researchers in bootleg projects are liberated from different organisational

This is a refined version of the definition first published in Augsdorfer (1996).[2] It contains the same elements but importantly includes the moral aspect. The reason is that in some firms tinkering that is undeclared but allowed and experimental is also called "bootlegging."

A number of famous product innovations were bootleg innovations. Table 1 contains a list by Eicher (2020) to which I have added further examples. These examples paint a picture in which bootlegging generally produces radical innovations. Moreover, publications that consider bootlegging as a strong violation of norms, for example, as going against the explicit orders of management, frequently conclude that bootlegging results in radical innovation (Burgelman and Grove, 2007; Mainemelis, 2010). On the other hand, publications that take a softer stance on this aspect find that bootlegging chiefly results in incremental innovation and that therefore it is in line with a corporation's strategy (Masoudnia and Szwejczewsk, 2012; Criscuolo *et al.*, 2014). This raises the question as to different interpretations emerge from different types of bootlegging.

The different types or subclasses of bootlegging given in Fig. 1 are based on Augsdorfer (1996). The decision tree is intended to help researchers identify the different types in academic papers. This should make comparison of papers easier. It will also help researchers structure questions for empirical studies and generate unambiguous contingencies.

Bootlegging is a bottom-up innovation — as the initiative for the idea comes from the R&D staff and not from management. Ideas from management are top-down innovations.

Bootlegging is for the benefit of the firm and not for private purposes. Private handicraft is often referred to as moonlighting.

---

obligations and their day-to-day work" or "... for project 2020+x we put a team together and gave them one year ..." The term "skunkwork" was devised by C.L. Johnson at Lockheed Corporation in 1943. Their spy plane U-2, an airborne surveillance system, was developed through skunkwork (Peters, 1988a). Skunkwork is defined as a group of elite employees who work officially on a parallel project along with the formal organization to solve problems more efficiently (Wolff, 1987).

[2]Bootlegging is research in which motivated individuals secretly organize the innovation process. It usually is a bottom-up, non-programmed activity without the official authorization of management but nonetheless for the benefit of the company. It is not included in the department's action plan nor are there any formal resources allocated to it (Augsdorfer, 1996).

Table 1. List of well-known bootleg innovations, adopted from Eicher (2020).

Development of the first memory disk	IBM	Schon	1963
Sidewinder air-to-air missile		Greenberg	1966
Audi 100 model	Audi	Audi	1968
Pontiac Fiero model	Pontiac	Pinchot	1988
RISC processor developed against company strategy favoring CISC	Intel	Burgelman	1991
Simultaneous spectrometer	Carl-Zeiss	Berke *et al.*	1992
Ciprofloxacin	Bayer	Hoffmann	1994
LCD technology	Merck	Hoffmann	1994
Laser development	Hughes Aircraft	Hoffmann	1994
Filter membrane for the production of clavulanic acid (Augmentin) antibiotics	Beecham	Augsdorfer	1996
Laptop computer	Toshiba	Abetti	1997a
Electrostatic display	HP	Nemeth	1997
Masking tape at 3M	3M	Nicholson	1998
Fuel cell development	Dornier	Eglau *et al.*	2000
Aldara creme	3M	Eglau *et al.*	2000
Blue LED	Nichia	Hara	2001
First laser printer	Xerox	Sutton	2002
Acetylsalicylic acid	Bayer	Michalik	2003
Monitor development	HP	Michalik	2003
BMW 3 Series Touring	BMW	Goeschl	2004
Makrolon	Bayer	Hausschildt	2004
UNIX (developed in the 1970s)	AT&T, Bell Labs	Stefik and Stefik	2004
Pacific Tech's Graphing Calculator in 1985	Apple	Ron Avitzur	2004
Brown Box, the first video game system	Sanders Associates	Stoecker	2006
BMW 12-cylinder engine	BMW	Augsdorfer	2008
Chip pan without oil	SEB	Simond	2008
Fuhrmann 'drawer' engine	Porsche	Schätzl	2010
Tape slitter	3M	Mainemelis	2010
The Godfather movie	Paramount	Mainemelis	2010
Agilent Technologies 1200 series chemical test equipment	Agilent	Masoudnia	2012
Sony SPC700 sound chip	Sony	Zwiener	2014
Audi 80 Quattro 4-wheel drive	Audi	Leicht-Deobald und Lins	2017

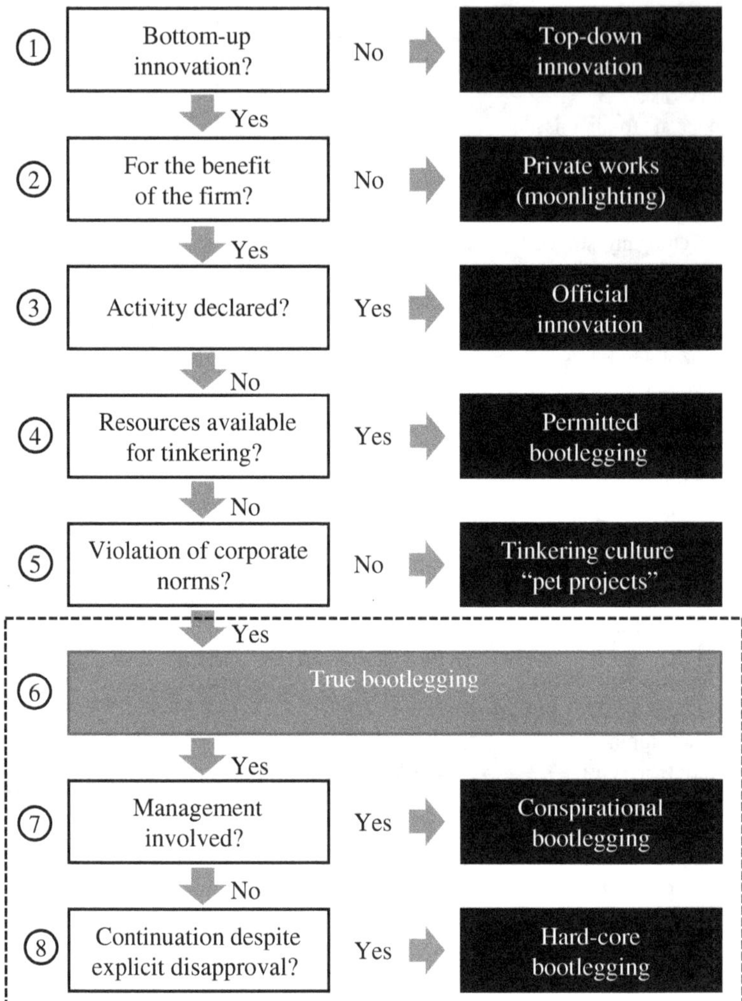

Fig. 1. Decision tree enabling the comparison of different bootlegging research papers.

Bootlegging is an undeclared activity. If the innovation process is formalized, the research is an official project with designated resources.

Bootlegging has no designated resources. Researchers have to find their own resources. If the company allows resources (time and budget) to be used it is called "permitted bootlegging." It is defined as research time when technical staff are allowed to spend a certain amount of their time working on "pet projects" in the hope that it leads to an innovation for the company (N.N., *The Economist*, 1991). Renowned examples of companies that support such initiatives are 3M, Google, and Hewlett Packard (Krogh *et al.*, 1988). They allow 10–15% of working time for own-product interests (Krogh and Nicholson, 1990). A well-known example of a permitted bootleg product is the yellow sticky "post-it notes" developed by Art Fry and Spencer Silver at 3M (N.N., CBI *et al.*, 1993).

Bootlegging is a violation of corporate norms, "... activity that is disguised, if not almost illicit" (Aram, 1973), "... keeping the development undercover from the disapproving power in the organization until it is introduced" (Knight, 1967), "... unauthorized flights of technical fancy" (Roussel *et al.*, 1991). Some companies tolerate tinkering within the corporate culture. An example is BMW where Burkhard Göschel, at the time head of R&D, said on the occasion of the Best Innovator Award 2004 in Berlin, "An important element of our innovation management is a high degree of freedom for our employees and stimulating research conditions. ... we leave free space for work on so-called bootleg projects, about which I have no information."

At times, it is difficult to distinguish between an accepted experimental tinkering culture and true bootlegging in particular at the fuzzy front end. There can be a fine line between what is allowed or tolerated within the corporate culture and what isn't, because the rules are broken only temporarily. Usually, a researcher knows when he has strayed off sound moral ground. However, sometimes, neither researchers nor management are certain whether an activity goes against corporate norms or rules. When asked, they often equate the digression to resources consumed (does it involve a substantial amount of time, money, duration of project, delay of other projects due to bootlegging, ...). In any case, researchers, when in doubt, more than less revert to true bootlegging before they run the risk of being stopped.

This ambivalent situation is reflected in academic research papers. For example, Koch and Leitner found that "up to one-third of all formal NPD projects that successfully ended up in a new product launched on a market had their roots in self-organizational activities outside the formal process." One can assume that their definition of bootlegging is broad.

To sum up, fuzziness makes research into bootlegging difficult. Proper contingencies cannot be established if the corporate culture and its norms are interpreted flexibly. More research is needed about the moral aspects in order to distinguish between "allowed tinkering," "tolerated tinkering," "weak violation of corporate norms," and "true bootlegging" situations with an unambiguous violation of the corporate norms.

True bootlegging is the classic bootleg situation. It is known only to the individual researcher and at some stage a few colleagues but not the management.

However, bootlegging can also be carried out conspiratorially with management. Such a conspiracy may have different degrees of occurrence. It can simply be acknowledged unofficially (actively or passively) by the superior. The manager "turns a blind eye to it." But it can also be substantially financially supported. A good example is the development of the Audi 80 four-wheel-drive by the head of R&D, Ferdinand Piech, in 1977. He kept it covert by simply not assigning a project number to the venture (Leicht-Deobald and Lins, 2017). More research is needed as to why a manager, who is responsible for the management of R&D and its planning processes, undermines the system he represents.

The strongest form of bootlegging is hardcore bootlegging. In this case, the bootleg researcher continues bootlegging despite explicit managerial disapproval. This "violation of orders to stop working on an idea" is precisely what Mainemelis labeled "creative deviance" (2010).[3] One of the most impressive cases of hardcore bootlegging is the Japanese Nichia Corporation versus Shuji Nakamura case. Nakamura, an employee of

[3]It was Mainemelis who in 2010 introduced the term at the Academy of Management (AOM) Conference. Unaware of any previous literature about bootlegging, he discovered the phenomenon. By using Merton's strain theory (1968) and referring to Warren's paper about constructive and destructive deviance in organizations, he named his discovery "creative deviance" (2003). The AOM conference and the Academy of Management Review are important platforms with a broad audience. For a number of inspired researchers, Mainemelis' paper was the starting point of their own research. Unfortunately, as a consequence, there are currently two terms for the same subject.

Nichia, developed the blue LED over four years in the bootleg manner, ignoring several clear management directives to stop. The full story can be found on the internet (e.g., EETimes, 2001).

2. Rationale for the Handbook

Interest is growing in the subject. At a personal level, there is more demand now for my 2005 paper on research policy than at the time of its publication (Augsdorfer, 2005). Moreover, I have recently published a second edition of my book due to an increasing demand (Augsdorfer, 2021). When I started my research in 1991 at SPRU at the University of Sussex (UK), a large number of well-known authors, such as Thompson (1969), Kanter (1983), Burgelman (1986) and Roberts (1991) referred to bootlegging by giving examples or by mentioning it in a paragraph. Occasionally, they drew attention to the possible reasons for its occurrence. However, it was never researched in more detail. This was a surprise to me because from my own experience as an R&D engineer, I realized that it is an essential element of corporate innovation processes and all corporate people know about it. My research led to a number of publications and culminated in a book in 1996 dedicated solely to covert research with the title *Forbidden Fruit* (Augsdorfer, 1993, 1994a, 1994b, 1995, 1996, 2005, 2008, 2012, 2021). It was very much exploratory and qualitative research — as it was very much groundwork.

My book sparked interest in the subject. Allan Pearson from Manchester Business School (UK) presented new research at the NTBF conference in 1994, one year after my presentation at the same conference (Pearson, 1994). Jürgen Hauschildt from University of Kiel (D) in Germany who was a good friend of Alan Pearson and who I met at a PhD summer school encouraged his PhD students to dig deeper into the subject after I gave a presentation at a doctoral seminar. One of his students was Gerhard Schewe, who not long after became a professor at Münster University (D) and suggested to his own PhD student, Claudia Michalik, that she write on the subject. Her 2003 thesis was the second on the topic (Michalik, 2003). A third thesis followed by Yaser Masoudnia of Sheffield University (UK) in 2012. He had read one of my papers and contacted me in 2008. I helped him draft his doctoral research proposal (Masoudnia, 2012). Anika Stephan from BETA Strasbourg University (F) completed her thesis in 2019. Her research interest was creativity within rigidly organized structures. She also stumbled across one of my papers (Stephan, 2019).

Stephan Eicher is my own PhD student. He published his thesis looking at bootlegging in the context of illegitimacy in 2020 at the University Erlangen-Nuremberg (Eicher, 2020). Finally, the latest thesis from 2021 was produced by Wan Shamsul Rezal Wan Salleh at my own alma mater, the University of Sussex. He found my thesis from 1995 in the SPRU library and got inspired to write about bootlegging in service organizations. Therefore, to date there are in total six PhD dissertations that have bootlegging as their sole focus. Please see also Appendix 1.

It is nice to see the topic starting to take off in China as well. We have seen the first publications (Ying Xuan Wunju, 2018; Wei Huang, Guopeng Xiang, Yunzhou Du *et al.*, 2017). And more and more master's theses are dedicated to the subject as well (e.g., Biermann, 2018). I am regularly contacted by master students from the Netherlands, France, and Germany who need advice (Ruijten, 2014). In Fig. 2, I have plotted all papers about bootlegging between 1963 and 2018 in reviewed journals over time (in total 101 scientific publications). I have not differentiated between papers that had their sole focus on bootlegging and those in which

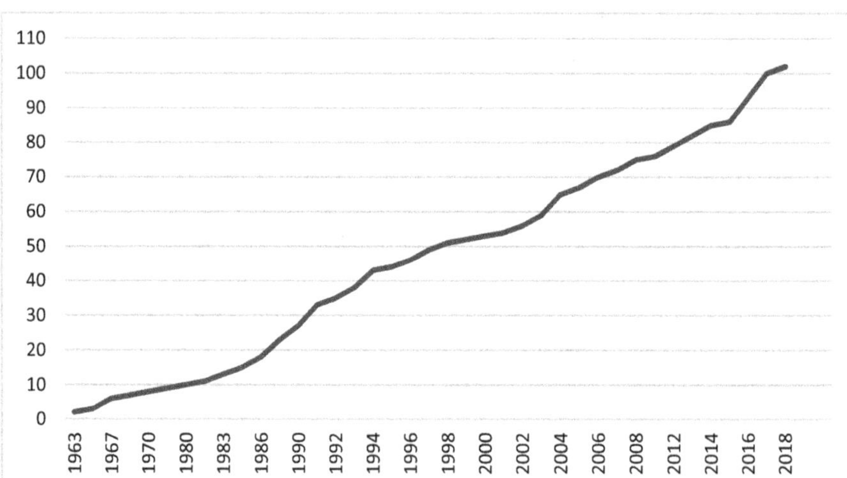

Fig. 2. Accumulated number of publications in reviewed journals.

it was simply mentioned. It shows that we have already learned a lot about the phenomenon.

The quality of papers has changed over time as well. All the papers from 1963 until 1970 were descriptive and not empirically based research. In the majority of papers, bootlegging was mentioned only as a phenomenon. Despite this, we know that one of the reasons for bootlegging is the tension between organizational goals and the interests of the individual researcher, in that it is informal and illicit, and that funds come from slack in planning. The first empirical paper was by La Porte and Wood in 1970. Surprisingly, it was already based on a quantitative study involving 307 questionnaires in three laboratories (La Porte and Wood, 1970). For another 43 years, it remained the only significant quantitative study until in 2014 Criscuolo *et al.* published their paper in *Organization Science*.

The early focus on qualitative instead of quantitative research methodology is easy to explain. Pioneering researchers needed first to explore the dynamics of bootlegging rather than its frequency. The logic is inductive reasoning by generalizing from specific cases. Today, as we have a number of statements about bootlegging, researchers can form deductive logical conclusions from it. In future, we probably can expect more quantitative research papers.

Between 1970 and 1990, there was only one paper with a strong focus on bootlegging. Aram uncovered informal networks in companies (1973). His research is based on an undisclosed number of interviews. Most papers during that period were not empirical and assumed the reason for bootlegging to be excessive bureaucracy that subsequently generated autonomous research. Furthermore, it was assumed that most outcomes of bootlegging were radical innovations (Peters, 1988b).

The 1990s marked the starting point for substantial research on bootlegging with Hoffmann (1991), Augsdorfer (1996), Abetti (1997b), and others. During the 2000s and 2010s, research became even more substantial. Criscuolo *et al.*'s paper was a very good paper with a sound methodology based on 238 questionnaires completed by senior scientists and engineers in a single US firm (Criscuolo *et al.*, 2014). It made inroads in the community. However, the most interesting consequence was that it inspired the interest of a number of young academics in the subject.

There is a relatively small number of individuals around the world who study bootlegging. Most of the important publications during this recent period are included as summaries in this book. My goal in bringing them together is to present a comprehensive picture of bootlegging and to outline directions for further research. In one way or another, each chapter in the handbook adds something new to our existing bootlegging knowledge. This is the main value of the handbook, which is international in scope, reflecting the perspectives of America, Asia, Europe, and the rest of the world. The authors take a number of different approaches, both empirical and theoretical, reflecting a variety of possible perspectives aimed at understanding bootlegging.

3. Road Map

This book is divided into four parts. Part 1 provides a general introduction to bootlegging. It sets the stage for understanding bootlegging. It describes the various approaches used by the authors of this handbook in understanding bootlegging and briefly summarizes the main contents of each chapter. Part 2 consists of seven chapters representing distinctive approaches to understanding the management and organization of bootlegging. Part 3 of the handbook focuses on understanding the disclosure process, which marks the delicate transition from the underground to the official world. Part 4 authors analyze bootlegging from the psychological point of view. Its focus is individuals within the organizational context who enthusiastically dare to bootleg innovations. The success of the innovations depends to a great extent on the activities of such bootleggers.

This introductory chapter discusses some important issues of bootlegging. It started with the definition and then derives a decision tree for a systematic research methodology to identify whether an activity is or is not bootlegging, and if so, which type of bootlegging it is. This should make future empirical work easier. There is also a list of well-known bootleg innovations and data about the growing interest in the subject.

Part 1 contains the basics about bootlegging. Chapter 1 is based on Peter Augsdorfer's 1996 book (Augsdorfer, 1996). Despite its age, it continues to provide a solid foundation for the subject and is as useful now as it was at the time of publication. Recently a second edition was published (Augsdorfer, 2021). It provides data about the prevalence of bootlegging and is descriptive. It includes national and sectoral differences, the percentage of bootleg entrepreneurs, and bootleg time consumption.

Probably most importantly, it establishes that bootlegging is not a major phenomenon either in terms of manpower, or resource consumption but is common during the initial stages of innovation. The three essential resources are materials, tools, or equipment, and time of which the latter is the most important resource.

It also looks at the purpose of bootlegging, its technological stage at disclosure, the bootleg product size, and its technology. Unsurprisingly, most bootleg output is not radical product innovation as most literature might suggest. Bootlegging is usually the incremental improvements made to a technological product or process. From this, bootlegging can be interpreted as part of the continuous learning process that is fundamental to experimental R&D. It also emerges that most companies benefit from bootlegging. The output meets business needs, and any uncertainty caused by bootleg activity is evaluated as relatively low.

Moreover, it shows that firms are guided by the selective logic of path dependency in their innovation processes. Even if management has no part in decisions to invest in a new business idea, new ideas are mostly in line with corporate strategy. Bootlegging emerges as an incremental, continuous, trial-and-error learning process in R&D and its uncertainty is no better or worse than that of "normal" R&D. The fear of some managers that transgression of strategic direction setting and potentially that total anarchy will ensue from bootlegging is unfounded.

Chapter 2 by Marek Szwejczewski and Yaser Masoudnia is a mix of basic information about bootlegging and the disclosure of bootlegging projects. It examines the reasons why employees carry out this underground activity. The reasons range from having to carry out preparatory work on the idea all the way to doing work to be able to show proof of concept. The key explanation of why the interviewees carried out bootlegging was to reduce uncertainty (mainly technical rather than market) surrounding their ideas and thereby improve the chances of it securing management approval for further development. The findings of the research are in line with Augsdorfer's research (1996, 2005), which demonstrated that employees bootleg mainly to prepare ideas for the formal decision process.

Chapter 3 delivers further basic information on bootlegging. Anika Stephan-Korus compares bootlegging processes to regular processes and explores how the characteristics, which often represent challenges, differ between the two. Second, building on the specific and challenging characteristics of bootlegging processes, she lays out what specific support measures are needed. Subsequently, she makes suggestions as to how support measures could be systematically implemented organization-wide through a system of corporate crowdfunding once the transition to the formal world has been made.

Part 2 starts with Chapter 4 by Linda Nhu Laursen and Poul Houman Andersen. They present a typology of entrepreneurial strategies. It responds to recent calls in research to examine the theoretical underpinnings of corporate entrepreneurial strategies. The typology explains underlying structural dimensions of how entrepreneurial strategies, such as bootlegging, skunkwork, bricolage, and guided evolution, differ in respect to the origin of an entrepreneurial initiative and resource availability for an entrepreneurial initiative. The typology is used to examine an exemplary longitudinal case study at Unilever. The Unilever Knorr case shows how, in practice, managers navigate different entrepreneurial strategies to overcome the corporate immune system. It finds that in dynamically evolving situations, where new sources of corporate resistance are continually arising, navigating between corporate entrepreneurship modes could be more a viable approach for understanding the mechanisms of corporate entrepreneurial initiatives. As such, this chapter contributes to understanding how entrepreneurial strategies are an *a priori* choice, and to in situ navigation depending on the organizational context, and furthers discussion on the important underlying structural dimensions for navigating corporate entrepreneurial strategies.

In Chapter 5, Dietfried Globocnik reviews past quantitative research on individual factors such as self-efficacy and risk propensity as well as contextual factors of formal and social control, which were found to affect employees' individual bootlegging tendencies. The article also puts bootlegging in the context of related innovative behaviors to highlight their conceptual similarities and differences. The chapter presents various avenues for future research covering further theoretical refinements, studying organizational-level outcomes of bootlegging, and empirical measurement issues that need to be resolved to facilitate progress in the quantitative stream of bootlegging literature.

In Chapter 6 Rudolph Koch and Karl-Heinz Leitner investigate which organizational and managerial factors foster or hamper self-organized or autonomous innovation activities within firms. The informal bottom-up

NPD projects of six Austrian electronics companies are examined based on a case study approach and on a theoretical framework rooted in complexity science and innovation literature. The analysis focuses mainly on the role of an open communication culture that delivers autonomy for experimentation, the impacts of financial incentive systems, the rigidity of organizational structures and, finally, the formalism of control systems. The authors deliver evidence on how classical formal management systems affect self-organized innovation activities and how they can be designed to promote and harness such bottom-up activities.

Amadou Lô and Pauline Fatien Diochon found that while bootlegging is often reduced to an individual equation, Chapter 7 opens up a spatio-political approach to bootlegging. It depicts how a third space (here a Fab Lab) supports low-power actors' bootlegging through three dimensions of transgression (namely cognitio-cultural, material, and socio-political). In doing so, bootlegging enables them to empower themselves through the triple control of meaning, resources, and processes. It builds on a case study they conducted in the Fab Lab of the French car manufacturer Renault. Importantly, they noticed that innovation doesn't happen in a vacuum but needs physical space. Any managerial encouragement needs to consider the spatial dimension of bootlegging. This empowers the researcher and has a strategic and firm-political dimension. More than ever, employees seek self-fulfillment in their work, which should be acknowledged and fostered by management.

In Chapter 8, Tomislav Hernaus, Matej Černe, and Miha Škerlavaj show that previous meta-analytic evidence has produced several job-design characteristics that are crucial predictors of employee innovativeness. The reality is, however, that individuals are likely to misfit the defined characteristics of their jobs. Discrepancy in job-design characteristics (actual versus wanted) has (paradoxically) the potential to explain employee innovative work behavior. Their particular focus is on task identity and they entertain the possibility that employee engagement in creative bootlegging interacts with incongruent situations between actual and wanted task identity, thereby increasing their creative and innovative performance. The results of moderated polynomial regression analyses from the multisource field study of 233 working professionals and 62 direct supervisors employed by a European bank delivered several interesting findings. First, congruence in actual–wanted task identity at high levels (a high-fit situation) leads to higher levels of innovative work behavior than congruence achieved at low levels (a low-fit situation). Second, they found empirical evidence that task–identity incongruence drives innovative work behaviors more than congruence does. Finally, incongruence in actual–wanted task identity interacts with creative bootlegging in positively predicting innovative work behavior when employees self-report higher levels of underground innovation activities.

Chapter 9, written by Khatereh Ghasemzadeh, discusses the role of creative bootlegging as a bridge between individuals' self-efficacy characteristics and individuals' tendency to become the lead users. Analyzing the mechanism of bootlegging activities among working employees of small and medium enterprises (SMEs) in the blue sector, this chapter shows that bootlegging is a transitional space between individuals' self-beliefs in their abilities and their willingness to generate innovative ideas by providing the opportunity for identity play among employees. The chapter contributes to the bootlegging concept by shedding light on the individuals' self-exploration characteristics, namely self-efficacy that triggers them to perform bootleg activities through which they achieve sufficient confidence and autonomy to participate in innovation-related activities.

Chapter 10 discusses the relationship between bootleg and individual innovation performance and considers the joint moderating effect of status and creativity. Wei Huang, Guopeng Xiang, Yunzhou Du, and Yang Liu found that bootlegging contributes to the improvement of individual innovation performance on the whole, and individuals with high creativity and high status benefit most from bootlegging. In addition, when, and only when, individual creativity and status (formal or informal) are high, bootlegging will have a significant positive impact on individual innovation performance. This chapter contributes to the concept of contingency relationship between bootlegging and individual innovation performance, and explains the complex mechanism of individual-level variables on the effect of bootlegging.

Part 3 includes two chapters on how bootleg researchers disclose their underground innovation projects. As bootleggers innovate in secrecy in the corporate underground without official support from their firm, they are hijacking a state of autonomy by developing and growing their own ideas independently. Bootlegging typically takes place in several stages. The initiation, development, and initial implementation of the projects largely happens in an environment invisible to substantial parts of the organization. At the final and decisive stage of the process, bootleggers disclose their projects and have to convince decision makers to implement their innovations and give them the official stamp of approval. This step — to win legitimacy — ultimately governs the success or failure of the bootlegging. Stephan Eicher's Chapter 11 is based on the qualitative study of 26 cases of bootleg innovation in his doctoral thesis. It applies and extends the legitimacy framework in the context of bootlegging. It shows how the various reports by researchers in this field are actually encompassed by the same overarching and dynamic process. He describes how bootleggers apply specific mechanisms within broader strategies to win legitimacy for their underground product or process innovation project. The results highlight the importance of strategies of manipulation and selection when disclosing such projects. He found seven distinct mechanisms to explain their legitimacy-seeking behavior, of which cognitive and pragmatic legitimacy are the most important ones.

In Chapter 12, Erfan Jalali Bidakhavidi and Kamal Sakhdari show that individuals, as the originators of corporate entrepreneurship and innovation, often resort to undercover activities to develop and elaborate their initial ideas. Although reasons behind such behavior are well documented in the extant literature, less is known about what drives bootleggers to reveal their ideas. Drawing on field data from in-depth interviews with innovators in R&D departments in different industries of Iran, this research identified five groups of factors at the individual, managerial, firm, industrial, and idea level that are at play during the revelation stage of bootlegging behavior.

Part 4 is titled "Psychology of Bootlegging" as it looks at the individuals involved in bootlegging. It starts with Chapter 13 by Alexander Krueger and Arne Buchwald. Innovation ultimately depends on individual employees in organizations who may develop and implement their innovative ideas by adhering to the organization's rules and procedures or by reverting to unofficial means. Previous studies on bootlegging have mostly focused on organizational factors, while recent research acknowledges the important role of the individual employee as a factor in whether or not bootlegging is pursued. Drawing on deviance and motivation theory, they propose that individual motivation is a promising factor that should be investigated in more depth by future research.

In Chapter 14, Claudia Michalik focuses on innovative engagement during bootlegging. The results are based on her doctoral thesis. She observes that many well-known innovations have been solely the result of the enthusiasm and dedication of individuals who continued to tinker in secrecy when things got challenging. These are the “rebels.” Looking at behavioral dimensions and specific levels of the individual innovative personality, she tries to isolate traits, how they can be identified and what makes them stand out. Her findings show that rebels are often at the hierarchical level of a group or team leader. In terms of experience, they have on average 15–29 years of work experience and have been with their current organization for a similar amount of time. Moreover, most bootleggers have been with their firms for an average of 22.38 years. Not surprisingly, they display an above-average level of innovative engagement. And when their activity is discovered, sanctions by management play a rather subordinate role. Closely linked to this is the question of how they can be managed for the benefit of the firm. Like Augsdorfer in Chapter 15, she found that the bootleggers display character traits and capabilities that identify them as important drivers for innovative success. However, there seemed to be two different types of bootleggers. While the first type is predominantly characterized by a pronounced strength of purpose and determination, the latter’s innovative drive is dominated by creative flow, nonconformity, and performance-motivated innovation behavior. Concluding with some implications for practice, she states that management needs to understand that there is no one-size-fits-all incentive system for both types.

Chapter 15 by Peter Augsdorfer examines the proposition that bootlegger-entrepreneurs can be identified by their creativity. This is done with the help of a standard nonverbal psychological test. He found that bootleg researchers can indeed be identified because they are more creative than average people. By applying the test, any R&D manager is able to discourage or encourage employment of potential bootleggers.

Helene Tenzer and Philip Yang dedicate final Chapter 16 to hardcore bootlegging or creative deviance. This is disregarding a managerial order to stop working on a new idea, as an extreme form of bootlegging. Based on a recent article published in the *International Journal of Innovation Management* (Tenzer and Yang, 2019), it complements prior research on the organizational-level determinants of creative deviance by discussing its individual-level antecedents. Analyzing survey data from 457 employees in a German high-tech corporation, Tenzer and Yang demonstrate that risk propensity as a personality trait is positively related, whereas allocentrism as a personal value orientation and organizational commitment as a personal attitude are negatively related to creative deviance. Risk propensity emerged as the strongest predictor, as it affects creative deviance both directly and indirectly through allocentrism and commitment.

In sum, all chapters show the range of knowledge about bootlegging. No wonder, therefore, that they reveal not only aspects but also contradictions and myths about its nature. Bootlegging seems to be a remarkable meeting ground for separate but related disciplines. Psychology, social psychology, sociology, technology, economics, and even philosophy may aid explanation of the phenomenon. However, the contributions provide reasonable arguments to suggest that the corporate organizational context accommodates most parameters associated with bootlegging.

4. Future Research

This handbook is also intended to be useful for a wide range of graduate students as a first source of information. To help them define their research topics, all contributors were invited to provide some text about where they see important research avenues in the future.

To me, most importantly, research on bootlegging should rigorously follow the definition suggested at the beginning of this chapter (Fig. 1). Only then, is a precise knowledge gain possible and comparisons between different publications are made easier. If you look at Criscuolo's paper (Criscuolo *et al.*, 2014) it is a good paper, but they slightly changed the definition by Augsdorfer (1996) by saying "often hidden from senior management." This leaves room for interpretation. When it is not hidden, it might be "permitted tinkering" and not "deviant bootlegging" or it is "conspiracy bootlegging." This is why it is important to follow the decision tree structure in Fig. 1.

Second, although many quantitative papers include a rigorous statistical section, the questionnaires on which the statistics are based are not published. In many papers, it remains unclear how the definition of bootlegging is translated into questions. And the translation is the most delicate part in quantitative research. This is where most misunderstandings can occur rather than in the statistics. As a consequence, we see doubtful generalizations about bootlegging.

Third, bootlegging originally concerned corporate R&D. We have seen from recent publications that bootlegging also appears in other departments of a firm. However, insights stemming, for example, from medical services and banks cannot be the same as from R&D. Mixing the knowledge gain from both dilutes of what we know about bootlegging.

Moreover, what is the actual bootleg product in other corporate departments? I think any quantitative study should be preceded or accompanied by a (small) qualitative study to illustrate the output (product or process innovation) of bootlegging. Again, this helps in the comparison of different research papers and the generalization of results.

Fourth, we need to learn more about the psychological nature of bootlegging. The stream of literature about creative deviance has successfully initiated research in this domain. That's great and should be expanded. Not only with regard to the personally traits of bootleg researcher but also the social psychology of, at times, schizophrenic organizational realities. This includes, in particular, the political bargaining process orchestrated by bootleggers trying to win over the decision maker (Burgelman and Grove, 2012; Eicher, 2020). Moreover, it includes the contingencies of different firm contexts and management actions along the refined definition of bootlegging mentioned above.

Finally, has ever somebody come across a female bootlegger in R&D? I was wondering about this when I referred to bootleggers as "he" and "his." Maybe this is because there are more male researchers than females. Nonetheless, I am sure that there are gender differences we don't know yet about.

Marek Szwejczewski and Yaser Masoudnia's research investigated bootlegging only from the employees' point of view. They suggest that further research should examine bootlegging from a management perspective. For example, it may consider how the different levels of management (senior versus middle management) perceive the existence of bootlegging in their organization, what each management level does to control or promote bootlegging and whether they really consider it beneficial to their organization? Does it feature in their strategic thinking or is it an annoyance that is tolerated because of the desire to keep R&D employees motivated and productive?

Anika Stephan thinks that bootlegging projects have been, are, and will continue to be an important part of organizational innovation aside from the familiar innovation tracks, because they help strike a balance between settled routines and radical, passionate, and open-minded thinking until organizations can renew and transform themselves. Further research should focus on the quality of project development during bootlegging in comparison to official projects, and whether bootlegging projects are more sustainable than other projects, and issues concerning the organizational identification of bootleggers.

Dietfried Globocnik was prolific and has a number of recommendations for future research. Research on bootlegging has progressed over the last years, but what we know about the special innovative behavior of employees is still limited. He quotes Pinchot (1985) who emphasized that "management cannot appoint someone an intrapreneur, tell him to become passionately committed to an idea, and then expect success. Managers will do far better if they simply keep a sharp eye out for intrapreneurs who believe passionately in something and them empower some of them to follow their intuition. In fact, the best candidates have probably already begun without permission." This implies that, from a managerial perspective, both the characteristics of the individual and organizational context factors need to be considered when trying to better understand the emergence of bootlegging. From a research perspective, this requires the inclusion of both an individual's and contextual factors in explanatory models and the theorizing of possible interactions by taking a person–context interactionist view. For empirical research, this implies the investigation of multiple employees from multiple organizations to achieve the necessary variance in both individual and contextual variables. However, there are many additional aspects to explore in order to develop prior research on bootlegging further. Some of them are elaborated.

Another issue is the antecedents of secret versus compliant innovation activities. Whereas prior research has identified several individual characteristics that differentiate bootlegging from non-bootlegging employees, we do not know which personal characteristics drive employees to elaborate their ideas more or less in secret rather than compliant ways within their organizations. This question is rooted in the fact that most characteristics of individuals such as self-efficacy, creativity, and intrinsic motivation have also been identified as attributes to explain compliant innovation behavior (e.g., Oldham and Cummings, 1996; Axtell *et al.*, 2000; Marvel *et al.*, 2007). Similarly, many of the organizational factors investigated cultivate bootlegging, that is, work discretionary rewards and management support are also relevant antecedents of compliant innovations (e.g., Scott and Bruce, 1994; Pearce, Kramer and Robbins, 1997; Hornsby, Kuratko and Montagno, 1999).

It would be interesting to know more about which individual and/or organizational factors drive employees to investigate ideas in the bootlegging style as opposed to compliant ways, or in other terms, develop a tendency toward one of these two styles of innovative behavior. With front-end formality and management support in the form of feedback and resources, past research has already started to identify organizational factors that are facilitators of compliant innovative behavior but reduce the frequency of bootlegging. Future research can develop this thread further. This might require upcoming studies to capture the intensity of both conform and secret innovation activities of individual employees to allow for empirical examination of which factors drive innovation activities toward one of these innovation styles.

Another interesting question refers to organizational dispositions that facilitate individual employees engaging in more bootlegging activities or even predisposing organizations to have a higher tendency toward bootlegging in their employee base. For instance, the organizational characteristics of an organization could play an important role. A relevant foundation could be the competing values framework with its cultural archetypes developed by Cameron and Freeman (1991): clan, adhocracy, hierarchy, and market, which differ in their general leadership style, dominant control mechanisms, goals, and internal and external orientations. It is reasonable to believe that hierarchy cultures with a strong emphasis on internal role clarity, rules, policies, and stable operation within defined boundaries will make it more difficult to engage in bootlegging, whereas adhocracy cultures with their high flexibility, adaptability, entrepreneurial mindset, and growth orientation might provide a more favorable environment for bootlegging.

Another relevant factor might be the business focus of the firm, particularly the relevance of the service business. Service innovation differs significantly from product innovation by close involvement of the customer and further service network partners, heterogeneity of customer needs, and service solutions, their being executed by frontline employees rather than a dedicated R&D department, and often being initiated *ad hoc*. Past research has shown that a firm's business focus has an impact on how effective management practices are (Schultz *et al.*, 2018). Given the characteristics of service innovations, it might well be the case that bootlegging is a more common approach to realizing service innovation compared to product innovation. Such high-order organizational characteristics might help to better understand the type of organization that can expect bootlegging from innovating employees.

With a few exceptions, what eventually happens to bootlegged projects beyond anecdotal evidence of prominent successes has not been investigated. One of these exceptions is a study by Augsdorfer (2005) who finds that most bootleg projects follow a certain path of dependency on organizations' activities and are therefore incremental in nature — and as the majority benefit the organization they are accepted once communicated to organizational decision makers. Criscuolo *et al.* (2014) find that an individual's bootlegging efforts are associated with achieving higher levels of innovation performance. Nevertheless, little is known about the actual commercial value created by successful bootleg projects or the damage created by failed bootlegging activities for the employee and the organization. Compared to compliant innovation activities, there is little known about actual failure rates.

Furthermore, it would be interesting to know, at the portfolio level, whether bootlegging can be seen as a mechanism that can also help the organization to overcome inertia as past authors on bootlegging have suggested (e.g., Koch and Leitner, 2008). Early empirical results of Globocnik *et al.* (2020) indicate that organizations with a higher general tendency to bootlegging among their employees do indeed report higher innovativeness of their innovation project portfolio. This opens the discussion as to whether bootlegging can be seen as one of the mechanisms through which new strategic paths can be explored without undermining the planned innovation strategy and at the same time provide the evidence required for realizing the emergent strategies of an organization.

Research still lacks consensus as to whether bootlegging should be considered desirable or undesirable behavior (Augsdorfer, 2005). On the one hand, bootlegging is supposed to expand an organization's capacity to elaborate more ideas without causing additional costs (Augsdorfer, 2005), to avoid premature rejection of ideas because feasibility or potential has not been demonstrated at the time of its first evaluation, to accelerate innovation by bypassing planning periods and decision cycles (Koch and Leitner, 2008), and to allow radical new ideas to grow, thereby avoiding them being systematically rejected due to their fuzziness, risk, and strategic misfit at the early stage (Ahuja and Lampert, 2001). Bootlegging is thereby a strategy to overcome structural shortcomings such as selection biases and bureaucratic inefficiencies. On the other hand, bootlegging employees might delay their officially assigned projects (Roussel, Saad and Erickson, 1991) and divert resources such as laboratory time or materials from their intended use. Furthermore, bootlegging hampers the efficiency and effectiveness of the innovation management (Burgelman and Grove, 2007) and risks altering the balance of the innovation project portfolio (Kanter, 2000).

These arguments suggest that there may be an optimal level of bootlegging that takes advantage of the benefits associated with bootlegging and at the same time avoids "let[ting] a thousand flowers bloom ... resulting in a garden full of weeds" (Criscuolo *et al.*, 2014). This raises two questions: (i) what the optimal level of bootlegging is and (ii) the measures required to encourage as well as regulate bootlegging to achieve the optimum level. The latter in particular requires deviation from the isolated view on bootlegging dominating past research and to study secret and compliant innovation activities with their antecedents and outcomes in parallel because — as pointed out earlier in this chapter — many antecedents of compliant innovation activities result in bootlegging as a by-product, and using these measures to reduce bootlegging might also result in less compliant innovation activities.

Furthermore, it would be valuable to investigate the long-term effect on the acceptance of bootlegging and formal innovation processes for compliant innovation activities among managers and employees after one or a series of successful bootleg projects. This question draws on the assumption that as the organizational experience with bootlegged outcomes grows, attitudes and responses of managers to bootlegging might shift. Similarly, trust in and acceptance of formal management practices stimulating compliant innovative behavior might also change among employees if peers create successful innovation outside organizational rules and processes. A series of bootlegged successes might have a sustainable impact on how the organization subsequently approaches innovation and so far, it is not clear whether this is to the benefit of the organization or not.

For findings derived from quantitative empirical studies, two measurement issues regarding the phenomenon of bootlegging need to be addressed. The first issue refers to the information source. As bootlegging may not be visible to onlookers, especially if bootleg projects fail and are not communicated to the organization at a later stage, the bootleg entrepreneur is basically the main source when investigating this phenomenon at the individual level of analysis. When studying organizational factors relating to bootlegging, it is easier to collect the corresponding data from someone who is not the bootleg entrepreneur. However, if the research is interested in the impact of individual perceptions, attitudes, and characteristics on this individual's behavior, common source bias becomes almost inevitable. Future research should take all possible measures to reduce the likelihood of such a bias, which includes but are not limited to approaches such as peer ratings, time-delayed assessment of different variables, and masking the actual focus of the study by asking for other innovative behaviors.

The second issue refers to the measure itself. So far, two main approaches can be observed in quantitative research: One that asks for the absolute number of different bootlegging behaviors (Globocnik and Salomo, 2015), and one multi-item scale capturing the general tendency of the individual for creative bootlegging (Criscuolo *et al.*, 2014). The advantage of capturing the absolute frequency of behaviors is to formulate fact-based questions that are less associated with biases and are uniformly and easily understood, and enable a more fine-grained analysis of the effect of antecedents on particular behavioral manifestations of bootlegging. However, as a single-item scale, the assessment of reliability and validity is limited with this operationalization. The multi-item scale captures a general bootlegging tendency or attitude with items that do not necessarily emphasize the secret nature of bootlegging and also captures workplace design-related aspects such as having the flexibility to work on projects other than the assigned ones. However, multi-item scales allow for better scale validity and reliability assessments as opposed to the single-item scales.

However, both operationalizations seem to be valid in capturing the phenomenon of bootlegging because studies analyzing the same antecedents report similar findings. For instance, the positive relationship between self-efficacy and bootlegging is consistently supported by Globocnik and Salomo (2015) and Ghasemzadeh *et al.* (2020) despite using different operationalizations of the dependent variable bootlegging behavior. Similarly, the positive correlation between the benefit expectations of lead userness is consistently supported by Globocnik (2015) and Ghasemzadeh *et al.* (2020).

The third, most frequently used scale refers to creative deviance (Lin *et al.*, 2016) but, as mentioned previously, captures a specific form of bootlegging. The difference between the phenomena captured is supported by the finding that in contrast to the two prior studies that find a positive relationship between self-efficacy and bootlegging, Martin and Ismail (2019) cannot find this effect for creative deviance.

Nevertheless, future research might draw on existing approaches to capture bootlegging behavior and develop a reliable and valid measure of bootlegging behavior following a thorough scale development approach. This would help future quantitative bootlegging research to use a consistent scale and thereby continue field development.

Rudolph Koch and Karl-Heinz Leitner suggest looking for more empirical evidence about the strategic fit and degree of innovativeness (i.e., incremental, radical, disruptive) of self-organized innovation activities. Furthermore, the success rate of self-organized innovations in contrast to top-down imposed innovations would be of interest as well as the occurrence and dynamics of bottom-up activities in other industries.

Khatereh Ghasemzadeh thinks that future research should inspect the boundary conditions of the proposed mediating model in terms of a certain personality characteristic and/or context-specific factors such as management support and organizational climate. Moreover, future research could investigate the relationship between entrepreneurial self-efficacy and user entrepreneurs and investigate how bootleg activities could trigger individuals to push the innovative ideas further and commercialize them and become the users' entrepreneurs.

Wei Huang, Guopeng Xiang, Yunzhou Du, and Yang Liu find that existing studies have confirmed that there is no reverse causal relationship between bootleg and individual innovation performance. Their study used cross-sectional data. Therefore, it is not possible to test further whether there is a reverse causal relationship between bootleg and individual innovation performance. With the help of the quantitative analysis of large samples, the relationship between individual bootleg and performance one could be understood intuitively. Moreover, the internal mechanism of bootlegging affecting individual innovation performance needs more case studies to explore these problems further. The effect of individual bootlegging on performance will be affected by two individual-level variables: individual creativity and status in the organization. Future research can explore whether other individual level variables have similar effects.

Erfan Jalali Bidakhavidi and Kamal Sakhdari recommend an interest in the importance of religiosity and morality in the bootlegging process. As bootlegging is hidden and undercover by nature, it might seem unethical or be against moral and religious beliefs. Therefore, how ethics and religiosity can influence bootlegging behavior and how moral and religious employees interpret, justify, or avoid such conspiracy-like, but constructive, activities need further investigation.

Helene Tenzer and Philip Yang think that given the striking dominance of risk propensity among the three individual-level antecedents to creative deviance, they would particularly encourage future studies relating to the Big Five personality traits (John and Srivastava, 1999) in creative deviance in order to elucidate the impact of personality on deviant behavior in more detail. Similarly, Schwartz's (1992) comprehensive set of individual values and other major job criteria such as satisfaction and engagement could be tested as predictors of creative deviance. Creative self-efficacy (Tierney and Farmer, 2002), thrill-seeking (Self *et al.*, 2006), status-seeking (Bowers *et al.*, 2017), intrinsic motivation (Cerasoli *et al.*, 2014), curiosity (Grossnickle, 2016), or attitudes to rules, products, and the supervisor could also be studied as individual-level predictors of deviant behaviors in organizations. In addition, it would be insightful to study the interaction between the organizational framework covered by previous work and the psychological basis we added to creative deviance research.

To sum up, one can see that there is still plenty of work to do and exciting new knowledge to generate. I believe that there will be another edition to this book before too long, perhaps within two or three years. Let's get to work, colleagues!

References

Abetti, P. A. (1997a). The birth and growth of Toshiba's laptop and notebook computers: A case study in Japanese corporate venturing. *Journal of Business Venturing*, **12**: 6.

Abetti, P. A. (1997b). Underground innovation in Japan: The development of Toshiba's word processor and laptop computer. *Creativity and Innovation Management*, **6**(3): 127–139.

Abetti, P. A. (1999). The birth and growth of the Japanese language word processor: Internal venturing in Toshiba corporation. *International Journal of Technology Management,* **18**(1–2): 114–132.

Abetti, P. A. (2004). Informal corporate entrepreneurship: Implications from the failure of the concord alloy foundry and the success of the Toshiba laptop. *International Journal of Entrepreneurship and Innovation Management*, **4**(6): 529–545.

Ahmad, N. H., Nasurdin, A. M. and Zainal, S. R. (2012). Nurturing intrapreneurship to enhance job performance: The role of pro-intrapreneurship organizational architecture. *Journal of Innovation Management in Small and Medium Enterprises*, 1–9.

Ahuja, G. and Lampert, C. M. (2001). Entrepreneurship in the large corporation: A longitudinal study of how established firms create breakthrough inventions. *Strategic Management Journal*, **22**(6/7): 521–543.

Aldrich, H. E. and Fiol, C. M. (1994). Fools rush in? The institutional context of industry creation. *Academy of Management Review*, **19**(4): 645–670.

Alexy, O., Criscuolo, P., Salter, A. and Sharapov, D. (2016). Going off-piste: The role of status in launching unsponsored R&D projects. In *Academy of Management Annual Meeting Proceedings — 2016.*

Allmendinger, M. (2019). *Towards Asymmetric Partnership Management Against the Background of Corporate Entrepreneurship and Open Innovation Literature.* Dissertation at University of Hohenheim.

Amabile, T. M. (1996). *Creativity in Context: Update to the Social Psychology of Creativity*. Boulder: Westview Press.

Amabile, T. M. and Khaire, M. (2008). Creativity and the role of the leader. *Harvard Business Review*. October.

Andersson, H. and Berggren, C. (2007). Individual inventors in the R&D factory. *Creativity and Innovation Management*, **16**(4): 437–446.

Andersson, M., Baltzopoulos, A. and Lööf, H. (2012). R&D strategies and entrepreneurial spawning. *Research Policy*, **41**: 54–68.

Aram, J. D. (1973). Innovation via the R&D underground. *Research Technology Management,* **16**(6): 24–26.

Asendorf, D. (2004). Der gefeierte Verräter. *Die Zeit*, **18**(40). April 22nd.

Augsdorfer, P. (1994a). Taxonomy of management attitudes bootlegging and uncertainty. In Oakey, R. (Ed.), *New Technology-Based Firms in the 1990s*. London: Sage.

Augsdorfer, P. (1994b). The manager as pirate: An inspection of the gentle art of bootlegging. *Creativity and Innovation Management*, **3**(2): 91–95.

Augsdorfer, P. (1996). *Forbidden Fruit - An Analysis of Bootlegging, Uncertainty and Learning in Corporate R&D*. Aldershot: Avebury.

Augsdorfer, P. (2005). Bootlegging and path dependency. *Research Policy*, **34**(1): 1–11.

Augsdorfer, P. (2008). Managing the unmanageable. *Research Technology Management*, **51**(4): 41–47.

Augsdorfer, P. (2012). A diagnostic personality test to identify likely corporate bootleg researchers. *International Journal of Innovation Management*, **16**(1): 1–18.

Augsdorfer, P. (2021). *Forbidden Fruit - An Analysis of Bootlegging, Uncertainty and Learning in Corporate R&D* (2nd edn.). Gold & Apple Transfers Publishing.

Avitzur, R. (2004). http://www.pacifict.com/Story/.Accessed13.03.2021.

Axtell, C. M. and Parker, S. K. (2003). Promoting role breadth self-efficacy through involvement, work redesign and training. *Human Relations*, **56**: 113–131.

Bailyn, L. (1985). Autonomy in the industrial R&D lab. *Human Resource Management*, **24**(2): 12–146.

Bart, C. K. (1993). Controlling new product R&D projects. *R&D Management*, **23**(3): 187–197.

Beath, C. M. (1991). Supporting the information technology champion. *MIS Quarterly*, **15**(3): 355–372.

Berends, H., Vanhaverbeke, W. and Kirschbaum, R. (2004). Knowledge management challenges in new business development: Case study observations. *Journal of Engineering and Technology Management*, **24**(4): 314–328.

Berke, J. (1992). INNOVATIONSKLIMA: Die konspirativen Tricks der Pioniere Geheimbund der Genies. *Wirtschaftswoche*, **31**: 52–54.

Berke, J., Böndel, B., Röthig, I. and Wichmann, S. (1993). Todesurteil auf Raten. *Wirtschaftswoche*, **49**.

Bessant, J. R. and Tidd, J. (2007). *Innovation and Entrepreneurship* (2nd edn.). Hoboken: John Wiley and Sons.

Bonoma, T. (1986). Marketing subversives. *Harvard Business Review*, **64**(6): 113–118.

Bowers, A. H., Greve, H. R. and Mitsuhashi, H. (2017). Look at me: Overt status-seeking behaviour and competitive emergence among securities analysts. In Seidel, M.-D. L. and Greve, H. R. (Eds.), *Emergence*. Research in the Sociology of Organizations (Vol. 50, pp. 351–382). Bingley: Emerald Publishing Limited.

Brockhoff, K. (1990). Stärken und Schwächen industrieller Forschung und Entwicklung. Stuttgart: Poeschel.

Brockhoff, K. (1993). Zur Erfolgsbeurteilung von Forschungs- und Enwicklungsprojekten. *Zeitschrift für Betriebswirtschaft*, **63**(7): 643–662.

Brown, A. D. and Toyoki, S. (2013). Identity work and legitimacy. *Organization Studies*, **34**(7): 875–896.

Brown, J. S. (1991). Research that reinvents the corporation. *Harvard Business Review*, 101–111. August 2002.

Burchart, A., Knudsen, M. P. and Sondergaard, H. A. (2016). The role of employee autonomy for open innovation performance. *Business Process Management Journal*, **23**(6): 1245–1269.

Burcharth, A. *et al.* (2017). The role of employee autonomy for open innovation performance. *Business Process Management Journal*, **23**(6): 1245–1269.

Bürgel, H. D. (1989). *Controlling von Forschung und Entwicklung*. München: Vahlen.

Burgelman, R. A. (1983). A process model of internal corporate venturing in the diversified major firm. *Administrative Science Quarterly*, **28**: 223–244.

Burgelman, R. A. (1988). Strategy making as a social learning process: The case of internal corporate venturing. *Interface,* **18**(3): 74–85.

Burgelman, R. A. (1991). Intra-organizational ecology of strategy making and organizational adaptation: Theory and field research. *Organization and Science*, **2**(3): 239–262.

Burgelman, R. A. and Sayles, L. T. (1986). *Inside Corporate Innovation.* New York: Free Press.

Burgelman, R. A. and Grove, A. S. (2007). Let chaos reign, then rein in chaos — Repeatedly: Managing strategic dynamics for corporate longevity. *Strategic Management Journal,* **28**: 965–979.

Burns, G. and Stalker, M. (1961). *The Management of Innovation.* London: Tavistock.

Cameron, K. S. and Freeman, S. J. (1991). Cultural congruence, strength, and type: Relationships to effectiveness. *Research in Organizational Change and Development,* **5**: 23–58.

Cardim de Carvalho, F. J. (1988). Keynes on probability, uncertainty, and decision making. *Journal of Post Keynesian Economics*, **9**(1): 66–81.

Castellacci, F. *et al.* (2018). Functional centrality and innovation intensity: Employee-level analysis of the Telenor group. *Research Policy*, **47**(9): 1674–1687.

Cerasoli, C. P., Nicklin, J. M. and Ford, M. T. (2014). Intrinsic motivation and extrinsic incentives jointly predict performance: A 40-year meta-analysis. *Psychological Bulletin*, **140**(4): 980.

Cheng, Y. and Van de Ven, A. H. (1996). Learning the innovation journey: Order out of Chaos? *Organization Science*, **7**: 593–614.

Cohen, A. and Ehrlich, S. (2019). Exchange variables, organizational culture and their relationship with constructive deviance. *Management Research Review.*

Coleman, J. W. and Ramos, L. L. (1998). Subcultures and deviant behaviour in the organizational context. *Research in the Sociology of Organizations*, **15**: 3–34.

Corsten, H., Gössinger, R., Müller-Seitz, G., and Schneider, H. (2016). *Grundlagen des Technologie- und Innovationsmanagements.* München: Vahlen.

Courpasson, D. and Younes, D. (2017). Double or quits: Understanding the links between secrecy and creativity in a project development process. *Organization Studies.* September 2017.

Criscuolo, P., Salter, A. and Ter Wal, A. L. J. (2013). Going underground: Bootlegging and individual innovative performance. *Organization Science.* October 2013.

Criscuolo, P., Salter, A. and Ter Wal, A. L. J. (2014). Going underground: Bootlegging and innovative performance. *Organization Science*, **25**(5): 1287–1305.

Cyert, M. C. and March, J. G. (1963). *A Behavioral Theory of the Firm.* Englewood Cliffs, NJ: Prentice Hall.

D'Aujourd'hui, V. Y. (2015). *Projektentstehungsmuster im zentralen Forschungsbereich.* Wiesbaden: Springer Gabler.

Daft, R. L. (1978). A dual-core model of organizational innovation. *Academy of Management Journal,* **21**(2): 193–210.

Danneels, E. *et al.* (2018). Overcoming the inertia of organizational competence: Olivetti's transition from mechanical to electronic technology. *Industrial and Corporate Change,* **27**(3): 595–618.

Darban, M. *et al.* (2021). Social network strategies and innovative performance: Formation and interplay of latent ties. *Knowledge Management Practice and Research Practice.* Published online: 08 Apr 2021.

Daskalopoulou, A. *et al.* (2019). Discretionary technology bootlegging tensions in institutional healthcare work. *New Technology, Work and Employment*, **34**(1): 73–89.
Davis, L. N., Davis, J. and Hoisl, K. (2008). Leisure time invention — Waste of effort, or wellspring of breakthrough ideas? In *25th DRUID Celebration Conference 2008*, Copenhagen, Denmark.
Debackere, K., Clarysse, B., Wijnberg, N. M. and Rappa, M. A. (1994). Science and Industry: A story of networks and paradigms. *Technology Analysis & Strategic Management*, **6**(1): 21–37.
Deci, E. L. and Ryan, R. M. (1985). The general causality orientations scale: Self-determination in personality. *Journal of Research in Personality*, **19**: 109–134.
Deci, E. L. and Ryan, R. M. (1987). The support of autonomy and the control of behaviour. *Journal of Personality and Social Psychology*, **53**: 1024–1037.
Dickson, K., Smith, H. L. and Smith, S. L. (1991). Bridge over the troubled waters? Problems and opportunities in inter firm research collaboration. *Technology Analysis & Strategic Management*, **3**(2): 143–157.
Dougherty, D. (1992). A practice-centered model of organizational renewal through product innovation. *Strategic Management Journal*, **13**: 77–92.
Drucker, P. F. (1985). *Innovation and Entrepreneurship*. London: Heinemann.
Duncan, W. J., Ginter P. M., Rucks, A. C. and Jacobs, T. D. (1988). Intrapreneurship and the reinvention of the corporation. *Business Horizons*, **31**(3): 16–21.
Edison, H., Wang, X. and Abrahamsson, P. (2017). Innovation initiatives in large software companies: A systematic mapping study. *Information and Software Technology*, **95**: 1–24.
Eglau, H. O., Kluge, J., Meffert, J. and Stein, L. (2000). *Durchstarten zur Spitze: McKinsey Strategien für mehr Innovation*. Frankfurt/New York: Campus Verlag.
Eicher, S. (2021). *Uncovering Covert Innovation*. Wiesbaden: Springer Gabler Verlag.
Ekvall, G. (1996). Organizational climate for creativity and innovation. *European Journal of Work and Organizational Psychology*, **5**(1): 105–123.
Ekvall, G. (1997). Organizational conditions and levels of creativity. *Creativity and Innovation Management*, **6**(4): 195–205.
Epitropaki, O. and Mainemelis, C. (2016). The "genre bender": The creative leadership of Kathryn Bigelow. In *Academy of Management Annual Meeting Proceedings*, January.
Evink, J. R. and Beam, H. H. (1999). Just what is an ideation group. *Business Horizons*. January–February.
Flynn, M., Dooley, L., O'Sullivan, D. and Cormican, K. (2003). Idea management for organisational learning. *International Journal of Innovation Management*, **7**(4): 417–442.
Fosfuri, A. and Ronde, T. (2007). Leveraging resistance to change and the skunk works model of innovation. In *Corporate Intellectual Property (RIPE). Conference, 7–8 December*, Copenhagen, Denmark.
Freeman, C. (1974). *The Economics of Industrial Innovation* (1st edn.). London: Printer.
Frese, M., Kring, W., Soose, A. and Zempel, J. (1996). Personal initiative at work: Difference between west and east Germany. *Academy of Management Journal*, **39**(1): 37–63.

Galbraith, J. R. (1973). *Designing Complex Organizations.* Boston: Addison-Wesley Longman Publishing Company.

Galbraith, J. R. (1982). Designing the Innovation Organization. *Organization Dynamics*, 202–223. Winter 1982.

Garud, R., Gehman, J. and Kumaraswami, A. (2011). Complexity arrangements for sustained innovation: Lessons from 3M corporation. *Organization Studies*, **32**(6): 737–767.

Gaynor, G. H. (2002). *Innovation by Design: What it Takes to Keep your Company on the Cutting Edge.* New York: Amacom.

George, J. M. (2007). Creativity in organizations. *Academy of Management Annals*, **1**: 439–477.

Ghasemzadeh, K., Bunjak, A., Bortoluzzi, G. and Černe, M. (2020). Efficaciously smuggling ideas: Untangling the relationship between entrepreneurial self-efficacy, creative bootlegging and embedded lead users. *International Journal of Innovation Management*, 2150032, p. 23.

Gilbertson, D. (2002). *Public Service Innovation Concepts.* Innovative Processes, Ltd.

Gläser, J., Laudel, G., and Whitley, R. (2016). The Impact of changing funding and authority relationships on scientific innovations. *Minerva*, **56**(1): 109–134.

Ghasemzadeh, K. *et al.* (2021). Efficaciously smuggling ideas: Untangling the relationship between entrepreneurial self-efficacy, creative bootlegging and embedded lead users. *International Journal of Innovation Management*, 2150032.

Gleicher, D. B. (1967). *Product Innovation: A Learning Process.* New York: Reinhold Publishing Corporation.

Globocnik, D. and Salomo, S. (2014). Kreative Devianz — Innovationsinitiativen von Mitarbeitern abseits legitimierender Innovationspfade. In Schultz, C. and Hölzle, K. (Eds.), *Motoren der Innovation.* Wiesbaden: Springer Gabler.

Globocnik, D. and Salomo, S. (2015). Do formal management practices impact the emergence of bootlegging behaviour? *Journal of Product Innovation Management*, **32**(4): 505–521.

Globocnik, D., Peña Häufler, B. and Salomo, S. (2020). Opportunities for radical innovation through bootlegging — An investigation of antecedents and outcomes. In *Proceedings of the 27th IPDMC Innovation & Product Development Management Conference* (pp. 1–21).

Götz, M. *et al.* (2019). Contextual undertow of workplace deviance by and within units: A systematic review. *Small Group Research*, **50**(1): 39–80.

Grantham, A. and Readman, J. (2005). Comparing quality and business improvement methodologies for collaborative working in the product development of SMEs. In *CI Net 2005, 5–6 September* (pp. 249–260).

Greenberg, D. S. (1966). "Bootlegging": It holds a firm place in conduct of research. *Science*, **153**: 848–849.

Grimpe, C. (2006). Making use of the unused: Shelf warmer technologies in research and development. *Technovation*, **26**(7): 770–774.

Grossnickle, E. M. (2016). Disentangling curiosity: Dimensionality, definitions, and distinctions from interest in educational contexts. *Educational Psychology Review*, **28**(1): 23–60.

Grote, G. (2009). *Management of Uncertainty: Theory and Application in the Design of Systems and Organizations.* Berlin: Springer.

Grundling, E. and Porras, J. I. (2000). *The 3M Way of Innovation: Balancing People and Profit.* New York: Kodansha International

Hamel, G. (2007). *The Future of Management.* Boston: Harvard Business School Press.

Hannan, M. T. and Freeman, J. H. (1977). The population ecology of organizations. *American Journal of Sociology,* **82**: 929–964.

Hara, Y. (2001a). Available from: https://www.eetimes.com/researcher-sues-nichia-over-blue-led-patent-rights/. Accessed 13.03.2021.

Hara, Y. (2001b). Researcher sues Nichia over blue LED patent rights. [Online] Available from: https://www.eetimes.com/document.asp?doc\textunderscoreid$=$1143754{\#}.

Hausschildt, J. (2004). *Innovationsmanagment* (3. Auflage). München: Vahlen.

Henderson, R. (1994). Managing innovation in the information age. *Harvard Business Review.* January/February.

Hernandez, M. (2019). Unveiling international new ventures' success: Employee's entrepreneurial behavior. *Administrative Sciences*, **9**(3): 56.

Hirota, T. (1986). Technology development of American and Japanese companies. *Kansai University Review of Economics and Business*, **14**(1/2).

Hoffmann, D., Müller, T. and Ahlemann, F. (2017). Balancing alignment, adaptivity, and effectiveness: Design principles for sustainable IT project portfolio management. In *ECIS 2017 Proceedings.*

Hoffmann, L. (1991). Innovation durch Konspiration. *Harvard Business Manager*, **13**(1): 121–127.

Hoffmann, L. (1994). Bootlegging Innovationen — Geniestreich oder Schurkenstück? *gdi-impuls*, **4**: 19–28.

Hornsby, J. S., Kuratko, D. F. and Zahra, S. A. (2002). Middle managers' perception of the internal environment for corporate entrepreneurship: Assessing a measurement scale. *Journal of Business Venturing*, **17**(3): 253–273.

Houman Andersen, P. and Laursen, L. N. (2020). Entrepreneurial strategies for MNCs: A typology. *International Journal of Entrepreneurship and Innovation.*

Howell, J. M. and Higgins, C. A. (1990). Champions of technological innovation. *Administrative Science Quarterly*, **35**(2): 317–341.

Iyer, B. and Davenport, T. H. (2008). Reverse engineering Google's innovation machine. *Harvard Business Review*, **86**(4): 64.

Jenssen, J. I. and Jorgensen, G. (2004). How do corporate champions promote innovations. *International Journal of Management*, **8**(1): 63–86.

John, O. P. and Srivastava, S. (1999). The big five trait taxonomy: History, measurement, and theoretical perspectives. In *Handbook of Personality: Theory and Research* (Vol. 2, pp. 102–138).

Kannan-Narasimhan, R. (2014). Organizational ingenuity in nascent innovations: Gaining resources and legitimacy through unconventional actions. *Organization Studies*, **35**(4): 483–509.

Kanter, R. M. (1983). *The Change Masters.* New York: Simon & Schuster.

Kanter, R. M. (2000). *When a Thousand Flowers Bloom: Structural, Collective, and Social Conditions for Innovation in Organizations.* New York: Oxford University Press.

Keltner, D., Gruenfeld, D. H. and Anderson, C. (2003). Power, approach, and inhibition. *Psychological Review*, **110**: 265–284.

Kline, J. and Rosenberg, N. (1986). An overview of innovation. In Landau, R. and Rosenberg, N. (Eds.), *The Positive Sum of Strategy: Harnessing Technology for Economic Growth*. Washington, D.C.: National Academy Press.

Knight, K. E. (1940). *Risk, Uncertainty and Profit* (5th impression, no. 16). London School of Economics and Political Science.

Knight, K. E. (1967). A descriptive model of the intra-firm innovation process. *The Journal of Business,* **40**(4): 478–496.

Koch, R. and Leitner, K. H. (2008). The dynamics and functions of self-organization in the fuzzy front end: Empirical evidence from the Austrian semiconductor industry. *Creativity and Innovation Management*, **17**(3): 216–226.

Konegen, N. and Sondergeld, K. (1985).*Wissenschaftstheorie für Sozialwissenschaftler: eine problemorientierte Einfhrung*. Leske und Budrich, Opladen.

Krogh, L. C. and Nicholson, G. C. (1990). 3M's international experience. *Research — Technology Management*, **33**(5): 23–27.

La Porte, T. R. and Wood, J. L. (1970). Functional contributions of bootlegging and entrepreneurship in research organizations. *Human Organizations*, **29**(4): 273–288.

Laudel, G. (2006). The art of getting funded: How scientists adapt to their funding conditions. *Science and Public Policy*, **33**(7): 489–504.

Leicht-Deobald, U. and Lins, N. (2017). Innovation im Verborgenen. *Organisations Entwicklung*, Nr. 1, 2017.

Lengnick-Hall, C. A. (1992). Innovation and competitive advantage: What we know and what we need to learn. *Journal of Management*, **18**(2): 399–429.

Lenka, S. *et al.* (2018). Exploring the microfoundations of servitization: How individual actions overcome organizational resistance. *Journal of Business Research*, **88**(C): 328–336.

Li, K and Yan, E. (2019). Are NIH-funded publications fulfilling the proposed research? An examination of concept-matchedness between NIH research grants and their supported publications. *Journal of Informetrics*, **13**(1): 226–237.

Lin, B., Mainemelis, C. and Kark, R. (2016). Leader's responses to creative deviance: Differential effects on subsequent creative deviance and creative performance. *The Leadership Quarterly*, **27**: 537–556.

Lo, A. and Diochon, F. (2020). Rethinking contextual ambidexterity through parallel structures. *R & D Management*, **50**(4): 522–534.

Ma, H. (2002). Competitive advantage: What's luck got to do with it? *Management Decision*, **40**(6): 525–536.

MacAulay, S. C., Steen, J. and Kastelle, T. (2017). The search environment is not (always). Benign: Reassessing the risks of organizational search. *Industrial and Corporate Change*, 1–23.

Mahringer, C. and Renzl, B. (2018). Entrepreneurial initiatives as a microfoundation of dynamic capabilities. *Journal of Accounting and Organizational Change*, **14**(1): 61–79.

Mainemelis, C. (2010). Stealing fire: Creative deviance in the evolution of new ideas. *Academy of Management Review*, **35**(4): 558–578.

Mannucci, P. V. and Perry-Smith, J. E. (2021). "Who are you going to call?" Network activation in creative idea generation and elaboration. *Academy of Management Journal.* Available from: https://doi.org/10.5465/amj.2019.0333.

March, J. G. (1991). Exploration and exploitation in organizational learning. *Organizational Science*, **2**(1): 71–87.

Martin, F. F. and Ismail, R. (2019). The role of openness to experiences, conscientiousness and creative self-efficacy in predicting creative deviance. In *E-Proceedings of UKM-GSB I c-Rise* (pp. 76–89).

Marvel, M. R., Griffin, A., Hebda, J. and Vojak, B. A. (2007). Examining the technical corporate entrepreneurs' motivation: Voices from the field. *Entrepreneurship Theory and Practice*, **31**(5): 753–768.

Masoudnia, Y. and Szwejczewski, M. (2012). Bootlegging in the R&D departments of high-technology firms. *Research Technology Management*, **55**(5).

Masoudnia, Y. (2012). *Bootlegging in High Technology R&D Departments: From Initiation to Disclosure*. Dissertation at Cranfield University. Available from: https://dspace.lib.cranfield.ac.uk/handle/1826/7919.

Meyer, J. W. and Rowan, B. (1977). Institutionalized organizations: Formal structure as myth and ceremony. *American Journal of Sociology*, **83**(2): 340–363.

Mezias, S. J. and Glynn, M. A. (1993). The three faces of corporate renewal: Institution, revolution, and evolution. *Strategic Management Journal*, **14**(2): 77–101.

Michalik, C. (2003). *Innovatives Engagement*. Wiesbaden: Gabler.

Miller, P. and Wedell-Wedellsborg, T. (2013). The case for stealth innovation. *Harvard Business Review*, **91**(3): 90–97.

Mintzberg, H. (1990). The manager's job: Folklore and fact. *Harvard Business Review*. July–August 1975.

Miyazaki, K. (1995). *Building Competencies in the Firm: Lessons from European and Japanese Optoelectronics*. Basingstoke: Palgrave Macmillan.

Muhdi, L. and Boutellier, R. (2011). Motivational factors affecting participation and contribution of members in two different Swiss innovation communities. *International Journal of Innovation Management*, **15**(3): 543–562.

N.N. Available from: https://en.wikipedia.org/wiki/Shuji_Nakamura. Accessed 13.03. 2021.

N.N. Available from: https://www.coursehero.com/tutors-problems/Management/9056528-Case-51-Nichia Corporation-Versus-Shuji-Nakamura-The-Blue-LED-Dispu/.

N.N. (1991). 60.000 and counting. *The Economist*, November 30th, pp. 86–89.

N.N. (2011). *Das ist Piech's exclusive Privatgarage*. [Online] Available from: http://www.auto-motor-und-sport.de/videos/auto-patriarch-ferdinand-piech-das-ist-piechs-exklusive-privatgarage-2781943.html.

N.N. (2015). http://www.auto-motor-und-sport.de/news/auto-patriarch-ferdinand-piech-das-ist-piechs-exklusive-privatgarage-2781943.html. [20/04/2015 15:43:23].

N.N., CBI and DTI, Technology Group. (1993). *Innovation the Best Practice*. London.

Nelson, R. R. and Winter, S. G. (1982). In search of useful theory of innovation. *Research Policy*, **6**: 36–76.

Nemeth, C. (1997). Managing innovation: When less is more. *California Management Review*, **40**(1): 59–74.

Nicholson, G. C. (1998). Keeping innovation alive. *Research Technology Management*, **41**(3): 34–40.

Niemann, C. (2020). *Essays on the Antecedents and Effects of Corporate Entrepreneurship*. Dissertation at Christian-Albrechts-Universität zu Kiel.

Nilsson, L., Elg, M. and Bergman, B. (2002). Managing ideas for the development of new products. *International Journal of Technology Management*, **24**(5–6): 489–513.

Nohria, N. and Gulati, R. (1996). Is slack good or bad for innovation? *Academy of Management Journal*, **39**(5): 1245–1264.

Nongo, E. S. and Ikyanyon, D. N. (2012). The influence of corporate culture on employee commitment to the organization. *International Journal of Business and Management,* **7**(22): 21–28.

O'Connor, G. C. and McDermott, C. M. (2004). The human side of radical innovation. *Journal of Engineering and Technology Management*, **21**(1–2): 11–30.

Oakey, R. P. (2014). Schumpeterian economics: Some observations on the relevance of his theoretical contributions to the management of industrial research and development. *R&D Management*, **45**(4): 386–396.

Oldham, G. R. and Cummings, A. (1996). Employee creativity. *The Academy of Management Journal,* **39**(3): 607–634.

Owen, H. (1990). *Leadership Is.* Potomac, USA: Abbott Publishing.

Ozcan, P. and Eisenhardt, K. M. (2009). Origin of alliance portfolios: Entrepreneurs, network strategies, and firm performance. *Academy of Management Journal*, **52**(2): 246–279.

Parker, R. C. (1985). *Going for Growth.* New York: John Wiley and Sons Ltd.

Pavitt, K. (1990). What makes basic research economically useful? *Research Policy*, **19**: 1–11.

Paxton, L. J. (2006). Managing innovative space missions: Lessons from NASA. *Journal of Knowledge Management*, **10**(2): 8–21.

Pearce, J. A., Kramer, T. R. and Robbins, D. K. (1997). Effects of managers' entrepreneurial behavior on subordinates. *Journal of Business Venturing*, **12**(2): 147–160.

Pearson, A. W. (1990). Innovation strategy. *Technovation*, **10**(3): 185–192.

Pearson, A. W. (1994). Bootlegging, small firms and innovation management. In *Paper for the Second NTBF Conference at Manchester.*

Pearson, A. W. (1997). Innovation management - Is there still a role for "Bootlegging"? *International Journal of Innovation Management*, **1**(2): 191–200.

Pelz, D. C. and Andrews, F. M. (1966). Autonomy, coordination, and stimulation in relation to scientific achievement. *Behavioral Science*, **11**(2): 89–97.

Peters, T. J. (1988a). A skunkworks tale. In Katz, R. (Ed.), *Managing Professionals in Innovative Organizations.* Cambridge, MA: Ballinger Publishing Company.

Peters, T. J. (1988b). *Thriving on Chaos: Handbook for Management Revolution.* New York: Harper Perennial.

Peters, T. J. and Waterman, R. H. (2003). *Auf der Suche nach Spitzenleistungen 9. Auflage.* Frankfurt: Redline Wirtschaft.

Petrou, P. *et al.* (2020a). Rebel with a cause: When does employee rebelliousness relate to creativity? *Journal of Occupational and Organizational Psychology*, **93**(4): 811–833.

Petrou, P. *et al.* (2020b). When breaking the rules relates to creativity: The role of creative problem-solving demands and organizational constraints. *Journal of Creative Behavior*, **54**(1): 184–195.

Pinchot, G. (1985). *Intrapreneuring: Why You Don't Have to Leave the Corporation to Become an Entrepreneur.* New York, NY: Harper & Row.

Pinchot, G. (1988). *Intrapreneuring. Mitarbeiter als Unternehmer.* Wiesbaden: Gabler.

Pittaway, L., Robertson, M., Munir, K., Denyer, D. and Neely, A. (2004). Networking and innovation: A systematic review of the evidence. *International Journal of Management Reviews,* **5**(6): 137–68.

Puech, L. and Durand, T. (2017). Classification of time spent in the intrapreneurial process. *Creativity and Innovation Management*, **26**(2): 142–151.

Quinn, J. B. (1985). Managing innovation: Controlled chaos. *Harvard Business Review*, **63**(3): 73–84.

Randall, M. (2014). Innovationen aus der Box. *Harvard Business Manager.* Nov 2014.

Rich, B. R. and Janos, L. (1994). *Skunk Works: A Personal Memoir of My Years at Lockhead.* New York: Little, Brown & Co.

Richtner, A. and Ahlstrom, P. (2006). Influences on organisational slack in new product development projects. *International Journal of Innovation Management*, **10**(4): 375–406.

Robbins, P. and O'Gorman, C. (2014). Innovating the innovation process: An organizational experiment in global pharma pursuing radical innovation. *R&D Management*, **45**(1): 76–93.

Roberts, E. B. (1991). The technological base of the new enterprise. *Research Policy*, **20**(4): 283–298.

Robins, S. P. and Judge, T. A. (2013). *Organizational Behavior* (15th edn.). London: Pearson.

Rosenberg, N. (1990). Why do firms do basic research (with their own money)? *Research Policy*, **19**: 165–174.

Roussel, P. A., Saad, K. N. and Erickson, T. J. (1991). *Third Generation of R&D.* Boston: Harvard Business School Press.

Ruba, R. (2019). Organizational antecedents and intrapreneurial intensity of SOEs after the structural adjustment policy. *International Journal of Innovative Science, Engineering & Technology*, **6**(9): 447–463.

Ruijten, B. (2014). Thesis, Radboud University in Nijmegen, The Netherlands.

Ryan, B. (2005). The problematic nature of organization culture and a changing control context. *Strategic Change*, **14**(8): 431–440.

Sakhdari, K. and Bidakhavidi, E. J. (2016). Underground innovation: How to encourage bootlegging employees to disclose their good ideas. *Technology Innovation Management Review*, **6**(3): 5–12.

Salomo, S. and Mensel, N. (2001). Front-end idea generation for innovation: Empirical evidence from German industrial corporations. In *International Conference on Management of Engineering and Technology PICMET* (Vol. 2).

Sarpong, D., Appiah, G., Bi, J. and Botchie, D. (2018). In direct breach of managerial edicts: A practice approach to creative deviance in professional service firms. *R&D Management*, January.

Saul, C. and Gebauer, H. (2018). Born solution providers — Dynamic capabilities for providing solutions. *Industrial Marketing Management*, **73**: 31–46.

Schätzl, A. (2010). Kleiner Bastard. *Süddeutschen Zeitung.* [Online] Available from: https://www.sueddeutsche.de/auto/porsche-550-spyder-kleiner-bastard-1.559754.22.04.2021.

Schein, E. H. (1992). *Organizational Culture and Leadership*. San Fransisco, CA: Jossey-Bass Publishers.

Schlapp, J., Oraiopoulos, N. and Mak, V. (2015). Effizienter Forschen. *Harvard Business Review*. July.

Schon, D. A. (1963). Champions for radical new inventions. *Harvard Business Review*, **41**(2): 77–86.

Schon, D. A. (1969). The fear of innovation. In Hainer, R. M., Kingsbury, S. and Gleicher, D. B. (Eds.), *Uncertainty in Research, Management and New Product Development* (pp. 11–25).

Schultz, C., Globocnik, D., Kock, A. and Salomo, S. (2019). Application and performance impact of stage–gate systems — The role services in the firm's business focus. *R&D Management*, **49**(4): 534–554.

Schwartz, S. H. (1992). Universals in the content and structure of values: Theoretical advances and empirical tests in 20 countries. In Zanna, M. (Ed.), *Advances in Experimental Social Psychology* (Vol. 25, pp. 1–65). New York: Academic, Press.

Scott, S. G. and Bruce, R. A. (1994). Determinants of innovative behaviour: A path model of individual innovation in the workplace. *Academy of Management Journal*, **37**: 580–607.

Scott, W. R. and Meyer, J. W. (1991). The organization of societal sectors. In Powell, W. W. and DiMaggio, P. J. (Eds.), *The New Institutionalism in Organizational Analysis* (pp. 108–140). Chicago: University of Chicago Press.

Secord, P. F. and Backman, C. W. (1964). *Social Psychology*. New York: McGraw Hill.

Segarra-Ciprés, M. *et al.* (2019). Employees' proactive behaviour and innovation performance: Examining the moderating role of informal and formal controls. *European Journal of Innovation Management*, **22**(5): 866–888.

Self, D. R., De Vries, H. E., Findley, C. S. and Reilly, E. (2006). Thrill seeking: The type T personality and extreme sports. *International Journal of Sport Management and Marketing*, **2**(1–2): 175–190.

Shapero, A. (1985). *Managing Professional People*. New York: Free Press.

Shapero, A. (1988). *Managing Creative Professionals*. Harlow: Longman Higher Education.

Shepard, H. A. (1967). Innovation-resisting and innovation-producing organizations. *The Journal of Business*, **40**(4); 470–477.

Shils, E. (1956). *Torment of Secrecy*. Melbourne: William Heinemann Ltd.

Sjödin, D. *et al.* (2019). How individuals engage in the absorption of new external knowledge: A process model of absorptive capacity. *Journal of Product Innovation Management*, **36**(3): 356–380.

Škerlavaj, M., Cerne, M., Dysvik, A. and Carlsen, A. (2016). *Capitalizing on Creativity at Work: Fostering the Implementation of Creative Ideas in Organizations*. Cheltenham: Edward Elgar Publishing.

Slocum, J. W. and Hellriegel, D. (2011). *Principles of Organizational Behavior*. Nachville, TN: South-Western.

Smith, S. M. (2003). *The Constraining Effect of Initial Ideas*. New York: Oxford University Press.

Stanley, B., Sieber, J. and Melton, G. (1987). Empirical studies of ethical issues in research: A research agenda. *American Psychologist*, **42**(7): 735–741.

Stefani, U. *et al.* (2019). New tools and practices for financing novelty: A research agenda. *European Journal of Innovation Management.*

Sutton, R. I. (2002). Der Kreativität den Boden bereiten. *Harvard Business Manager*, **2**: 2–12.

Talke, K., Salomo, S. and Mensel, N. (2006). A competence-based model initiatives for innovations. *Creativity and Innovation Management*, **15**(4): 373–384.

Tenzer, H. and Yang, P. (2020). The impact of organizational support and individual achievement orientation on creative deviance. *International Journal of Innovation Management*, **24**(2): 20–28.

Thom, N. (1980). *Grundlagen des betrieblichen Innovationsmanagement* (2nd edn.). Königstein: Hanstein.

Thompson, V. A. (1965). Bureaucracy and innovation. *Administrative Science Quarterly*, **10**(1): 1–20.

Thompson, V. A. (1969). *Bureaucracy and Innovation.* Alabama: University of Alabama Press.

Tierney, P. and Farmer, S. M. (2002). Creative self-efficacy: Its potential antecedents and relationship to creative performance. *Academy of Management Journal*, **45**(6): 1137–1148.

Trott, P. (1998). *Innovation Management and New Product Development.* London: Financial Times Pitman Publishing.

Tushman, M. E. and Romanelli, E. (1985). Organizing for innovation. *California Management Review*, **28**(3): 74–92.

Un, C. A., Cuervo-Cazurra, A. and Asawaka, K. (2010). R&D collaborations and product innovation. *Journal of Product Innovation Management*, **27**(5): 673–689.

Unsworth, K. (2001). Unpacking creativity. *Academy of Management Review*, **26**(2): 289–297.

Vesper, K. H. (1984). Three faces of corporate entrepreneurship: A pilot study. In Hornaday, J. A., Tarpley, F. Jr., Timmons, J. A. and Vesper, K. H. (Eds.), *Frontiers of Entrepreneurship Research* (pp. 294–320). Wellesley, MA: Babsen College.

Wan Shamsul Rezal and Wan Salleh. (2020). The study of bootlegging initiatives in a service organization. Unpublished thesis, SPRU, University of Sussex, UK.

Warren, C. and Laslett, B. (1977). Privacy and secrecy: A conceptual comparison. *Social Issues*, **33**(3): 43–51.

Warren, D. E. (2003). Constructive and destructive deviance in organizations. *Academy of Management Review*, **28**(4): 622–632.

Weber, M. (1978). *Economy and Society: An Outline of Interpretive Sociology.* Berkeley: University of California Press.

Weick, K. E. (1979). *The Social Psychology of Organizing* (2nd edn.). New York: McGraw-Hill.

Weiss, E. (1989). *Management diskontinuierlicher Technologie-Übergänge.* Göttingen: Vandenhoek & Ruprecht.

Wendelken, A., Danzinger, F., Rau, C. and Moeslein, K. (2014). Innovation without me: Why employees do (not) participate in organizational innovation communities. *R&D Management,* **44**(2): 217–236.

Westphal, J. D., Gulati, R. and Shortell, S. M. (1997). Customization or conformity? An institutional and network perspective on the content and consequences of TQM adoption. *Administrative Science Quarterly*, **42**: 366–394.

Whitley, R., Gläser, J. and Laudel, G. (2018). The impact of changing funding and authority relationships on scientific innovations. *Minerva*, **56**(1): 109–134.

Williams, L. (1966). Bootlegging. *Research Science*, **153**.

Wolff, M. F. (1987). To innovate faster: Try the skunk works. *Research Technology Management,* **30**(5): 7–8.

Wood, D. J. (1991). Corporate social performance revisited. *Academy of Management Review*, **16**: 691.

Wu, C. *et al.* (2020). Work process-related lead userness as an antecedent of innovative behaviour and user innovation in organizations. *Research Policy*, **49**: 103986.

Yi, M. and Wang, S. (2020). Empowering leadership and bootlegging: The counterbalancing effect of directive leadership. *Academy of Management Proceedings.*

Appendix 1: Related Literature Review

The table summarizes the shortlisted publications of the literature analysis. It lists authors, the applied research method, the contributions to defining bootlegging, which of the categories listed in literature review they contribute to, and whether bootlegging is the primary focus of the publication.

Appendix 1. Shortlisted publications of the literature analysis.

Author/Year	Research Method	Definition of Bootlegging	Focus
	no/e/r = no empirical research; qual = qualitative; quant = quantitative; lit rev = literature review; case = case study		Focus = focus on bootlegging; Side = bootlegging is mentioned
Cyert, M. C. and March, J. G. (1963)	no/e/r	The term "slack innovation" is introduced, describing innovation stemming from slack resources	Focus
Schon, D. A. (1963)	no/e/r	Provides earliest definition of bootlegging as "funded by sums detoured"	Focus
Greenberg, D. S. (1966)	no/e/r	Bootlegging is "a catchall term that covers much territory but that generally means you're doing one thing and calling it something else"	Focus
Gleicher, D. B. (1967)	no/e/r	NA	Side
Knight, K. E. (1967)	no/e/r	"keeping the development undercover from the disapproving power in the organization until it is introduced"	Focus
Shepard, H. A. (1967)	no/e/r	NA	Side
Thompson, V. A. (1969)	no/e/r	"using resources budgeted for another project or purpose on problems of the researcher's own choice"	Side
La Porte, T. R. and Wood, J. L. (1970)	quant (307 responses, 3 laboratories)	"Bootlegging is engaging in research projects not formally specified in the contract or grant funding the organization's work"	Focus

(Continued)

Appendix 1. (*Continued*)

Author/Year	Research Method	Definition of Bootlegging	Focus
Aram, J. D. (1973)	qual (no details provided)	Introduction of the term "underground system," which is "activity that was disguised, if not almost illicit"	Focus
Freeman, C. (1974)	no/e/r	NA	Side
Thom, N. (1980)	no/e/r	NA	Side
Galbraith, J. R. (1982)	no/e/r	NA	Side
Peters, T. J. and Waterman, R. H. (1982)	no/e/r	NA	Side
Burgelman, R. A. (1983)	qual (longitudinal study of 6 internal corporate ventures)	Describes "initiatives" that ignore the bureaucratic system at the innovators own risk	Focus
Kanter, R. M. (1983)	no/e/r	NA	Side
Drucker, P. F. (1985)	no/e/r	NA	Side
Pinchot, G. (1985)	case	Subsumes it under the notion of "intrapreneuring"	Side
Quinn, J. B. (1985)	no details provided	NA	Side
Bonoma, T. (1986)	qual (1000 interview, 30 companies)	Article refers to "marketing subversives" who ignore internal rules	Focus
Burgelman, R. A. and Sayles, L. T. (1986)	qual (no further details provided)	Bootleg projects are "projects that are carried out by researchers but that are 'informal' insofar as they are not formally authorized in the department's action plans and resource allocation"	Focus
Hirota, T. (1986)	quant (500 largest firms in Japan and US)	Article mentions "underground research" but does not define it	Side

Burgelman, R A. (1988)	qual (3 internal corporate ventures)	NA	Focus
Duncan, W. J., Ginter P. M., Rucks, A. C., and Jacobs, T. D. (1988)	no/e/r	NA	Focus
Peters, T. J. (1988a)	no/e/r	NA	Side
Peters, T. J. (1988b)	no/e/r	NA	Side
Pinchot, G. (1988)	case	"It is easier to ask for forgiveness than permission" work in the underground	Side
Shapero, A. (1988)	no/e/r	NA	Side
Bürgel, H. D. (1989)	no/e/r	Lead the controlling up the garden path	
Weiss, E. (1989)	no/e/r	NA	Side
Alter, N. (1990)	no/e/r	NA	Side
Brockhoff, K. (1990)	no/e/r	NA	Side
Mintzberg, H. (1990)	no/e/r	NA	Side
Owen, H. (1990)	no/e/r	NA	Side
Pearson, A. W. (1990)	no/e/r	NA	Side
Beath, C. M. (1991)	qual (15 cases)	"IT Champions" ignore internal processes that are in their way	Focus
Brown, J. S. (1991)	qual (1 case)	Article talks about informal work practices that ignore procedures or guidelines	Focus
Burgelman, R. A. (1991)	qual (several cases at Intel)	Article mentions "autonomous initiatives," which challenge prevailing corporate strategies	Focus
Dickson, K., Smith, H. L., and Smith, S. L. (1991)	no/e/r	NA	Side

(Continued)

Appendix 1. (*Continued*)

Author/Year	Research Method	Definition of Bootlegging	Focus
Hoffmann, L. (1991)	qual (5 cases)	Describes bootlegging as consciously breaking internal rules	Focus
Roberts, E. B. (1991)	no/e/r	NA	Side
Dougherty, D. and Heller, F. (1991)	no/e/r	Illegitimate research	Side
Roussel, P. A., Saad, K. N., and Erickson, T. J. (1991)	no/e/r	Bootlegging is "unauthorized flights of technical fancy," "hidden from the transparency of broader scrutiny"	Side
Lengnick-Hall, C. A. (1992)	no/e/r	NA	Side
Augsdorfer, P. (1993)	qual (interviews in 25 firms)	"It is research in which motivated individuals secretly organise the innovation process, in other words, research which does not appear on project sheets drawn up by the management of the firms"	Focus
Berke, J. *et al.* (1993)	no/e/r	NA	Side
Brockhoff, K. (1993)	no/e/r	NA	Side
Mezias, S. J. and Glynn, M. A. (1993)	lit rev	NA	Side
Augsdorfer, P. (1994a)	qual (cases from 24 firms)	"It is research in which motivated individuals secretly organise the innovation process, in other words, research which does not appear on project sheets drawn up by the management of firms"	Focus

Augsdorfer, P. (1994b)	qual (cases from 24 firms)	"Bootlegging is a special type of innovation because it is covert research without the explicit approval of the responsible manager. It incorporates the dimension of secrecy . . ."	Focus
Debackere, K., Clarysse, B., Wijnberg, N. M., and Rappa, M. A. (1994)	no/e/r	NA	Side
Hoffmann, L. (1994)	qual (5 cases)	"Irregular practices"	Focus
Pearson, A. W. (1994)	lit rev	Refers to bootlegging as "secret"	Focus
Miyazaki, K. (1995)	no/e/r	NA	Side
Augsdorfer, P. (1996)	qual (cases from 57 European firms)	"Bootlegging is research in which motivated individuals secretly organize the innovation process. It usually is a bottom-up, non-programmed activity, without the official authorization of the responsible management, but for the benefit of the company. It is not in the department's action plan nor are there any formal resources allocated toward it"	Focus
Nohria, N. and Gulati R. (1996)	quant (256 responses from 2 firms)	NA	Side

(*Continued*)

Appendix 1. (*Continued*)

Author/Year	**Research Method**	**Definition of Bootlegging**	**Focus**
Abetti, P. A. (1997a)	qual (20 interviews at Toshiba)	Article about "under the table development." This refers to secret and unofficial projects. Some of these projects also pose a violation of norms and are therefore bootlegging (laptop case). Others do not because they are authorized by management (notebook case)	Focus
Abetti, P. A. (1997b)	qual (2 cases at Toshiba)	"Under the table development." Some examples are bootlegging (laptop case) others are not (word processor case)	Focus
Pearson, A. W. (1997)	no/e/r	NA	Side
Nicholson, G. C. (1998)	qual (case study of 3M)	3M case study. Covers a permitted bootlegging example (post-it note) and a hard-core bootlegging case (masking tape)	Side
Trott, P. (1998)	no/e/r	NA	Side
Abetti, P. A. (1999)	qual (1 Toshiba case)	"Under the table development." The presented case is officially tolerated by management	Focus
Eglau, H. O., Kluge, J., Meffert, J., and Stein, L. (2000)	no/e/r	NA	Side

Salomo, S. and Mensel, N. (2001)	quant (responses from 101 German firms)	"Bootlegging generally describes intensive new product development activities performed by employees parallel to their formal job assignment and without knowledge to the organization"	Side
Gaynor, G. H. (2002)	no/e/r	NA	Side
Sutton, R. I. (2002)	no/e/r	NA	Side
Hatakenaka, S. (2003)	qual (300 interviews at 3 universities)	No explicit definition but cases encompass a violation of norms	Side
Michalik, C. (2003)	qual (174 cases in 4 German firms)	Uses definitions by La Porte and Wood (1970) and Augsdorfer (1996). Outlines that bootlegging represents a violation of corporate norms. However, method does not specify how bootlegging was distinguished from non-bootlegging	Focus
Abetti, P.A. (2004)	qual (2 cases)	Refers to "informal corporate entrepreneurship" and "underground innovation." The "laptop" case is hard-core bootlegging	Focus
Berends, H., Vanhaverbeke, W., and Kirschbaum, R. (2004)	no/e/r	NA	Side
Hausschildt, J. (2004)	no/e/r	NA	Side
Jenssen, J. I. and **Jorgensen, G. (2004)**	lit rev	NA	Side

(Continued)

Appendix 1. (*Continued*)

Author/Year	**Research Method**	**Definition of Bootlegging**	**Focus**
O'Connor, G. C. and McDermott, C. M. (2004)	qual (longitudinal study of 13 projects in 11 US based firms)	Only reference to the underground of innovation but do not define it	Side
Stefik, M. (2004)	qual (multiple cases)	NA	Side
Augsdorfer, P. (2005)	qual (cases from 57 European firms)	Uses Augsdorfer's (1994b) definition	Focus
Grantham, A. and Readman, J. (2005)	lit rev	Reference to the definition of Augsdorfer (1996)	Side
Laudel, G. (2006)	qual (66 interviews with university researchers)	"Rearranged money" to fund projects of own interest	Side
Richtner, A. and Ahlstrom, P. (2006)	no/e/r	NA	Side
Talke, K., Salomo, S., and Mensel, N. (2006)	no/e/r	NA	Side
Bessant, J. R. and Tidd, J. (2007)	no/e/r	Bootlegging is "employees working on innovation projects in their own time and often accessing resources in an informal way," "get around the system" according to Augsdorfer (1996)	Side
Burgelman, R. A. and Grove, A. S. (2007)	qual (longitudinal study at Intel)	Article about "autonomous initiatives," which are not controlled by management. Some autonomous initiatives violate corporate norms (RISC processor development at Intel), but it is not a defining element of "autonomous initiatives"	Focus
Augsdorfer, P. (2008)	qual (cases from 70 European firms)	Follows Augsdorfer's (1996) definition	Focus

Iyer, B. and Davenport, T. H. (2008)	qual (long-term observation of Google)	NA	Side
Koch, R. and Leitner, K. H. (2008)	qual (24 interviews in 5 Austrian firms)	Article about "self-organized innovation." "Self-organization means that new structures, patterns, or properties emerge spontaneously without being externally imposed on the system." Some cases violate corporate norms, some even pursued again explicit orders by management, others however do not violate norms	Focus
Mainemelis, C. (2010)	lit rev	Provides definition for "creative deviance." Creative deviance ignores explicit orders to stop projects. It is a synonym for Augsdorfer's (1994b) hardcore bootlegging	Focus
Augsdorfer, P. (2012)	quant (49 responses from 12 German firms)	Uses Augsdorfer's (1994a) definition	Focus
Masoudnia Y. and Szwejczewski M. (2012)	qual (55 interviews at 34 firms)	Same as below	Focus
Masoudnia, Y. (2012)	qual (55 interviews at 34 firms)	Uses "unofficial, informal, independent" as synonyms for bootlegging. Bootlegging starts when resources are spent that go beyond initial pre-research activities	Focus

(*Continued*)

Appendix 1. *(Continued)*

Author/Year	Research Method	Definition of Bootlegging	Focus
Criscuolo, P., Salter, A., and Ter Wal, A. (2014)	quant (238 responses from 1 British firm)	"We define bootlegging as the process by which individuals take the initiative to work on ideas that have no formal organizational support and are often hidden from the sight of senior management, but are undertaken with the aim of **producing innovations that will benefit the company" (Augsdorfer, 2005)**	Focus
Miller, P. and Wedell-Wedellsborg, T. (2013)	qual (4 cases)	The term "stealth innovation" is introduced. Innovations are intentionally hidden from the organization	Focus
Globocnik, D. and Salomo, S. (2014)	quant (109 responses from 39 Austrian firms)	Same as above	Focus
Globocnik, D. and Salomo, S. (2015)	quant (109 responses from 39 Austrian firms)	"Bootlegging activities occur when employees engage in predevelopment activities without official mandates or supervisory control"	Focus
Kannan-Narasimhan, R. (2014)	qual (99 interviews at 9 Silicon Valley firms)	NA	Side
D'Aujourd'hui, V. Y. (2015)	qual (8 research projects in 1 firm)	Bootlegging mentioned as one pattern of development activities. No definition provided	Side

Sakhdari, K. and Bidakhavidi, E. J. (2016)	qual (33 interviews in 15 Iranian firms)	"The process by which employees secretly work on ideas which are not formally supported by their organizations"	Focus
Epitropaki, O. and Mainemelis, C. (2016)	qual (analysis of 43 published interviews with movie director Kathryn Bigelow)	Refers to creative deviance	Side
Lin, B., Mainemelis, C., and Kark, R. (2016)	quant (226 responses from 2 Chinese firms)	Creative deviance and bootlegging are both explained as deviant behavior. Creative deviance is considered as one form of bootlegging, where explicit orders to stop working on a project are ignored	Focus
Škerlavaj, M., Černe, M., Dysvik, A., and Carlsen, A. (2016)	lit rev	NA	Side
Alexy, O., Criscuolo, P., Salter, A., and Sharapov, D. (2016)	quant (analysis of 40000 innovations)	Article on "unsponsored innovation," which are innovations that are not officially managed. Some of them may be bootlegging, but in general the extent of the overlap between unsponsored innovations and bootlegging is unclear	Focus
Corsten, H., Gössinger, R., Müller-Seitz, G., and Schneider, H. (2016)	no/e/r	Describe bootlegging as working without official approval or even against the explicit will of management	Side

(*Continued*)

Appendix 1. (*Continued*)

Author/Year	Research Method	Definition of Bootlegging	Focus
Burcharth, A. *et al.* (2017)	quant (survey results from 307 firms)	States that constructive creative deviance is bootlegging behavior and defines it as an employee's attempt to pursue an idea in an illegitimate manner (Augsdorfer, 2005). Bootlegging includes engaging in underground market-related and business-planning tasks, as well as making efforts to communicate with potential customers outside of official channels (Globocnik and Salomo, 2015)	Side
Leicht-Deobald, U. and Lins, N. (2017)	qual (20 interviews at Audi)	Referring to Mainemelis' (2010) definition of creative deviance as interchangeable with bootlegging	Focus
Hoffmann, D., Müller, T., and Ahlemann, F. (2017)	no/e/r	NA	Side
Courpasson, D. and Younes, D. (2017)	qual (60 interviews in 1 firm)	No definition of bootlegging provided but descriptions of the case study make it clear that it violates corporate norms	Focus
Puech, L. and Durand, T. (2017)	qual (47 interviews in 1 firm)	NA	Side
Lenka, S., Parida, V., Sjödin, D.R., and Wincent, J. (2017)	qual (35 interviews)	No explicit definition provided. Term "bootlegging" used as synonym for "unofficial" and "undeclared"	Side

MacAulay, S. C., Steen, J., and Kastelle, T. (2017)	qual (38 interviews)	NA	Side
Edison, H., Wang, X., and Abrahamsson, P. (2017)	qual (4 interviews)	"In some cases, bootlegging is carried out without approval from management"	Side
Sarpong, D., Appiah, G., Bi, J., and Botchie, D. (2018)	qual (14 interviews)	Refers to creative deviance as defined by Mainemelis (2010)	Focus
Petrou, P. *et al.* (2018)	quant (83 pairs of employees working in various occupational sectors in the Netherlands)	Refers to Mainemelis (2010); creative employees are not given what they need in order to be creative, the only route to creativity is being deviant	Focus
Castellacci, F. *et al.* (2018)	case (Telenor)	Refers to Criscuolo *et al.*'s (2014) informal R&D and underground exploration activities to develop new ideas that are not formally accepted by the firm's management	Side
Mahringer, C. and Renzl, B. (2018)	lit rev	Bootlegging as entrepreneurial initiative; refers to Augsdorfer (2005)	Side
Danneels E. *et al.* (2018)	case (Olivetti)	Bootlegging is active resistance and defined as illicit diversion of resources to work on new technology and a way to overcome inertia	Side
Whitley, R., Gläser, J., and Laudel, G. (2018)	qual (3 scientific innovations)	No definition provided but bootlegging viewed as diverting official funds for projects of personal interest	Side
Saul, C. and Gebauer, H. (2018)	qual (16 interviews)	Refer to Lenka *et al.* (2017); routines for overcoming organizational resistance to providing advanced services	Side

(*Continued*)

Appendix 1. (*Continued*)

Author/Year	**Research Method**	**Definition of Bootlegging**	**Focus**
Globocnik, D. (2019)	quant (sample size 92)	Innovation projects autonomously without the knowledge of or permission from their organization (definition according to Burgelman, 1983; Vesper, 1984; Kanter, 2000)	Focus
Krueger A. and Buchwald A. (2019)	no/e/r	NA	Focus
Daskalopoulou, A. *et al.* (2019)	qual (32 in-depth interviews)	NA	Focus
Sjödin, D. *et al.* (2019)	qual (37 interviews)	Illicit behaviors; refers to Criscuolo *et al.* (2013)	Side
Götz, M. *et al.* (2019)	lit rev	Criscuolo and colleagues (2014) offered a very intriguing approach to workplace deviance by studying bootlegging behavior in research and development units. Here, bootlegging is the process by which individuals take the initiative to work on ideas that have no formal organizational support and are often hidden from the sight of senior management but are undertaken with the aim or producing innovations that will benefit the company (p. 1288)	Focus
Allmendinger, M. (2019)	case	Refers to Augsdorfer (2005) as the corporate entrepreneur	Side

Cohen, A. and Ehrlich, S. (2019)	quant (602 sample size)	Constructive deviance related to Criscuolo *et al.* (2013)	Side
Hernandez, M. (2019)	qual (30 interviews)	Refers to developing an entrepreneurial action in the employee (Globocnik and Salomo, 2015)	Side
Ruba, R. (2019)	quant (71 sample size)	Definition of bootlegging referred to Gilbertson (2002) and Ahmad *et al.* (2012)	Side
Li, K. and Yan, E. (2019)	quant (Lit)	Bootlegging is defined as researchers use grant money under a specific project to try new research ideas or even changing the research trial (Gläser *et al.*, 2016; Hackett, 1987; Laudel, 2006)	Side
Stefani, U. *et al.* (2019)	no/e/r	Bootlegging among other novel techniques advocates that the battle for internal finance is strategic and reckless	Side
Houman Andersen P. and Laursen L. N. (2020)	lit rev	Entrepreneurial strategy where "individuals take the initiative to work on ideas that have no formal organizational support and are often hidden from the sight of senior management but are undertaken to produce innovations, that benefits the organization" (Criscuolo *et al.*, 2014: 1288)	Focus

(*Continued*)

Appendix 1. (*Continued*)

Author/Year	Research Method	Definition of Bootlegging	Focus
Lô, A. and Diochon F. (2020)	case	"Underground" behaviors seeking to benefit a company's innovation processes; refers to Augsdorfer (1996)	Focus
Yi, M. and Wang, S. (2020)	quant	NA	Focus
Tenzer, H. and Yang, Ph. (2020)	quant (659 sample size)	Refer to creative deviance.as the "violation of a managerial order to **stop working on a new idea" (Mainemelis, 2010, p. 558)**	Focus
Niemann, C. (2020)	**several**	**Refers to Globocnik und Salomo** (2015), Criscuolo *et al.* (2013); Augsdorfer (2005)	**Side**
Petrou, P. *et al.* (2020a)	quant (156 sample size)	Employee's creative efforts that are secretive and noncompliant to organizational rules and policies (refers to Mainemelis *et al.*, 2016, 2010)	Focus
Petrou, P. *et al.* (2020b)	quant (83 pairs of employees)	Creative deviance (i.e., "the violation of a managerial order to stop working on a new idea"; (Mainemelis, 2010; p. 560), and bootlegging (i.e., working on ideas with no formal organization support with the aim of producing innovations; Criscuolo *et al.*, 2014)	Focus

Wu, Ch. *et al* (2020)	quant	Employees sometimes deliberately hide innovation projects to "prototype first, reveal later" and (partly) use their free time to innovate, a phenomenon known as bootlegging (Criscuolo *et al.*, 2013). They may even engage in creative deviance, that is, violate managerial/organizational instructions, to keep working on innovative ideas (Mainemelis, 2010)	Focus
Ghasemzadeh, K. *et al.* (2021)	quant (sample size 554)	Deviate behavior hidden from senior managers whereby organizational time and resources are used for pursuing innovative ideas that are mainly in line with organizational goals and benefits; refer to (Sakhdariand and Bidakhavidi, 2016, p. 6)	Focus
Eicher S. (2021)	several	Definition is based on Augsdorfer (1996). Bootlegging is a nonformalized and non-declared bottom-up innovation process for the benefit of the bootlegger's firm. It violates — deliberately or not — corporate norms and is in this respect immoral behavior	Focus

(*Continued*)

Appendix 1. (*Continued*)

Author/Year	Research Method	Definition of Bootlegging	Focus
Augsdorfer, P. (2021)	qual	Definition is based on Augsdorfer (1996). Bootlegging in corporate R&D is defined as a nonformalized and non-declared (secret) bottom-up innovation process for the benefit of the bootlegger's firm. It violates — deliberately or not — corporate norms, including explicit management orders	Focus
Wan Shamsul Rezal and Wan Salleh (2021)	mixed methods	Definition is based on Augsdorfer (1996). Individual self-initiative and bottom-up process that emerges outside management's formal innovation framework and thus has no management authorization and support while nonetheless aiming to deliver positive impacts or benefit to the company	Focus

Part 1

General Information About Bootlegging

https://doi.org/10.1142/9781800612266_0002

Chapter 1

The Basics of Bootlegging

Peter Augsdorfer
Technical University of Ingolstadt, Ingolstadt, Germany
peter.augsdorfer@thi.de

Abstract

This chapter discusses the prevalence of "bootlegging." It looks at national and sectoral differences, the percentage of bootleg entrepreneurs, and the time consumed by bootlegging. Probably most importantly, it establishes that bootlegging is not a major phenomenon, either in terms of manpower or resource consumption but an activity common to the initial stages of innovation. The three essential resources involved in bootlegging are materials, tools or equipment, and time, the latter of which is the most important. The purpose of bootlegging is specified, the technological stage associated with disclosure, the size of the bootleg product, and the technology involved. Unsurprisingly, most bootleg output is not radical product innovation as most literature suggests. Bootlegging is mainly incremental technological product or process improvement. It is a continuous learning process and a natural part of experimental R&D. Most companies do benefit from bootlegging. The output meets business needs, and any uncertainty caused by bootleg activity is evaluated as relatively low.

1.1. Introduction

This chapter discusses the prevalence of "bootlegging." It looks at the national and sectoral differences, the percentage of bootleg entrepreneurs, and the time consumed by bootlegging. Most importantly, it establishes that bootlegging is not a major phenomenon, either in terms of manpower or resource consumption but an activity common to the initial stages of innovation. The three essential resources involved in bootlegging are materials, tools or equipment, and time, with the last mentioned being the most important.

This chapter is about the purpose of bootlegging, the technological stage associated with disclosure, the size of the bootleg product, and the technology involved. Unsurprisingly, most bootleg output is not radical product innovation as most literature suggests. Bootlegging involves an incremental technological product or process improvement. It is a continuous learning process and a natural part of experimental R&D.

Is there a tangible value for the firm? In other words, does bootlegging meet business needs? What happens to bootleg products after disclosure? Are they rejected or accepted? What emerges is that most companies do benefit from bootlegging. The output meets business needs, and any uncertainty caused by bootleg activity is evaluated to be relatively low. This chapter is based on a study by Augsdorfer (1996).

1.2. Prevalence of Bootlegging

Over 80% of a sample of 57 companies admitted to the existence of bootleg activities. It can be safely assumed that the actual percentage is higher than that because bottom-up projects often start as covert research.[1] It is found in many industrial sectors (software, telecommunication,

[1]This statement might be a little philosophical. Is "thinking time" about innovations, which is not agreed with management, already broaching bootlegging? In the early stages of a bottom-up innovation process, there is usually little difference between bootleg projects and "normal" projects, if ever there is a "normal" start to an innovation project. Does a project become a bootlegging project after the transition from thinking to physical activity? Is it a question of resources spent, and, if so, how much money needs to be spent? Only when it is more than the R&D kitty allows? Research is a cumulative and continuous learning process (Dosi, 1991). Therefore, it is often impossible to single out bootlegging, because it is difficult to identify whether a new research idea is part of an official ongoing project or already a completely separate underground project. To sum up, the early stage of bootlegging is fuzzy. The best indicator of bootlegging, it seems, is if the research is within or outside of what is morally allowed within the organization of the firm. Interpretation of "bootlegging" carries with it a degree of uncertainty. Bootlegging concerns both early and late innovative activity. However, early-stage bootlegging has unveiled a major insight. A plausible explanation is that it is the phase between creativity and the formal beginning of a new research project. In this sense, bootleg innovation can be interpreted as the antecedent of the formal innovation process.

electronics, chemicals, mechanical engineering, materials, health care). One would expect to find bootlegging in all industries. There are no national differences between the bootleg cultures of England, Germany, and France (Augsdorfer, 1996). Looking at the wider literature on bootlegging, there seems to be no significant difference in other national cultures such as those of Austria (Globocnik, 2019), Greece (Mainemelis, 2010), Iran (Sakhdari and Bidakhavidi, 2016), China (Han Yi *et al.*, 2007), the United States (Burgelman, 1988), Canada (Mintzberg, 1990), and Japan (Miyazaki, 1994).

The knowledge about ongoing bootlegging activities is relative. Sometimes, everybody in a laboratory knows about it, but nobody would admit to it. Bootlegging may be combined with or followed by a period of discussion with peers or other trusted individuals. Such discussions are useful for the "distillation" and quality of an idea. Discussions may even include a customer. There are cases where a customer knew about the product before management was informed. In one case, 40 products had been sold before the product became an official product of the company. In another case, the bootleg innovation was even exhibited at a trade fair. Secrecy is an important factor in the development of bootleg products. Although their development does not follow formal procedures, bootleg entrepreneurs are supervised to a certain extent by friends, colleagues, customers, and other peers. This is important to know, because it is actually these indirect checks that prevents bootleg output from being totally blue sky.

It is estimated that on average, 5–10% of the researchers in an R&D laboratory are bootleg entrepreneurs. Eighty percent of the survey sample supplied information about the numbers of bootleg entrepreneurs. However, two factors unsettle the precision of these figures. Firstly, the number of bootleggers involved can vary over time. Bootleg projects are usually initiated by one person but can slowly develop into conspiracies involving entire laboratories working under cover. For example, in one company, over a certain period, nearly the whole laboratory was involved in the undercover development of a fire-resistant cable.[2] A second source of uncertainty lies

[2] An even more extreme case occurred in a company where the "whole" company was involved in bootlegging at a political level. This was obviously a special case and of no further significance for this chapter but interesting nevertheless. The European

in the interpretation of when is a project a true bootleg project. The term can be interpreted broadly or narrowly. During the research, it became obvious that overstatements generally outweighed understatements. In other words, people liked to "show off" by exaggerating. This, as a fact, reduces the actual number of bootleg researchers.

Bootleg time accounted for approximately 10% of annual working hours. This was the average for the year and confirmed by Eicher (2020). Forty-six percent of the total sample supplied data about the extent of covert research. Again, the average value of bootleg time is subject to imprecision and statistical error. The reasons for inaccuracy are similar to those concerning the number of bootleg entrepreneurs. The definition of bootlegging is blurred, the definition of working time is blurred, and the extent of bootlegging varies over time.

As a result, it is difficult to determine the precise amount of bootleg time as a percentage of working hours. For a start, it is difficult to determine exactly what is working time as opposed to paid or unpaid overtime, and most researchers do overtime anyway. Secondly, as pointed out earlier, the amount of time dedicated to bootlegging time varies over time. Times of increased bootleg activity follow times of no bootlegging. It is possible to distinguish between periodical, occasional, or continual bootleg activity. There are researchers who set aside regular time for bootlegging activities. In one such company, the researchers used Friday afternoons for their bootleg projects. Friday afternoon is much quieter than the rest of the week. Most colleagues, and maybe also the boss, have already gone home. In most of the cases, the researchers pursued bootlegging full-time for a short period. In one case, bootleg research was carried out by two people over a period of three years. Their research was built into the laboratory scheduling and approved by the head of the department. In rare cases, some creative individuals work on bootleg ideas almost continuously. The full-time bootleg entrepreneur must be concealed and supported by his team members. They often do this by doing his officially allocated

---

Union (EU)-funded research project undermined a political decision of the European Parliament but was backed by the French government. The managing director of the company involved ordered the development of certain competencies, which the company was not supposed to acquire as this was the task of the partner firm in another European country. He feared not keeping pace with certain technological advances. Obviously, the work never appeared in the book-keeping records.

work for him. The result of conspiracies like this is a symbiosis between bootlegger and his team. While laboratory colleagues aid the bootleg entrepreneur, he, in turn, supplies valuable ideas to the laboratory and thus contributes to its overall success.

Serendipities, spin-offs of current research projects, or other unforeseen events initiate bootleg activity. This also includes sudden doubts about decisions of the head of the R&D department, or significant personal interest in a specific popular topic. Increased bootleg activity usually comes at the end or the beginning of a formal research project. This is when researchers are under less pressure and have time to look around and let their thoughts wander. This seems logical as it is well known that an absence of free-thinking time is a creativity killer.

The focus of bootlegging in literature is predominantly on radical product innovation (Hoffman, 1991). This produces a distorted picture. Radical innovations, as the work by Peters and Waterman (1982) or Knight (1967) suggests, are rare. Bootlegging emerges as an incremental, continuous R&D learning process. In total, the reasons to bootleg fall into five main activities (these percentages are for one firm in the engineering industry and cannot be transferred to other industries): pre-research (40%), product and process improvements (34%), troubleshooting (20%), new product and process innovation (5%), and purely scientific research (1%) (Augsdorfer 1996).

Pre-research is defined as research in which the objectives for the annual planning system are researched. In other words, the feasibility of objectives to be proposed is verified by means of minor experiments. Verification of both new objectives and continued objectives of the preceding year's research is addressed. Smart people do pre-research to work out what to put in the objectives in order to avoid failure to meet those objectives.

Bootlegging was frequently undertaken to improve existing products or processes. Improvements can either introduce a new or different technology, or simplify the product or process. The overall design of a product generally does not change and therefore this sort of work can be defined as incremental improvement. Mostly, it concerns technological solutions to key parts of products or processes. The improvements are not always developed through to implementation. The pre-stages rank from preliminary data collection, to the feasibility stage showing the basic principle of an idea, to the prototype stage of the final product.

Troubleshooting as a reason for bootlegging was only found in certain laboratories. However, when it occurred, it accounted for a significant amount of bootleg time. "Troubleshooting" is usually carried out as a favor for a colleague or another department within the company. Usually, help is urgently required because damages, delays or losses are likely to occur. The cause of the problem is often human error. Troubleshooting covers up errors to avoid criticism. Most of the time, it is a mutual favor in the sense of "if you scratch my back, I'll scratch yours."

Most case studies on bootlegging concern new product developments. However, this is deceptive. Bootlegging rarely covers the complete development process of a new product or process. More frequently, but nonetheless rare, it is the development of early or advanced stages of new products.

Bootlegging as pure scientific research does not primarily result in direct benefits for the company. Indirectly of course, a company always has an advantage if the competencies of its employees are broadened. Sometimes an academic paper results from such research that then has a public relations benefit for the company.

The distribution of these five categories varies across companies and time. It also seems to be associated with the industrial sector. For example, troubleshooting was not found in research laboratories focusing on new materials. As far as this data is concerned, troubleshooting was primarily found in the engineering and software industries. Pre-research was also found in the same industries. But the percentage of pre-research varied. In some corporate organizations work pressure was, at times, too intense for it to be carried out. Finally, pure scientific research was more often found in "basic research" laboratories.

Most interesting is the question of when researchers choose to declare their bootleg innovations. Is the disclosure deliberate or triggered by external pressure? In 60% of the sample, researchers stopped their research when they could demonstrate the feasibility of their project and 17% when the stage of prototyping was reached. Another 17% stopped bootlegging when additional resources were needed in order to continue developing the product. These figures lead to the belief that a lack of financial resources in bootleg research is only a minor obstacle in developing innovations to a degree where feasibility can be proven. Moreover, it seems that progressing beyond the feasibility stage seems not be in the researcher's interest either.

Also, it could be that progressing beyond that stage is not easy because it would drastically exceed the resources accessible. In general, researchers confirmed that they prefer to disclose their innovations too early than too late, and it has to be done diplomatically.

What do we know about the technology of bootleg innovations? The vast majority of the companies categorized the average bootleg innovation as a technological improvement. Existing products were improved either by adding functionality or eliminating "technological imperfections." Often, it is experimentation with new technology. Less often, the technology can also be a spin-off from previous research or continuation of technology from an abandoned project. Not unusually, researchers are still enthralled by the technology of previous projects. Sometimes, they try to keep their knowledge up-to-date with bootleg research. It might become useful again for a further, similar project. In rare cases, technology concerns fun and cool topics (such as "artificial intelligence" or "small computer gimmicks") or a novel application of an existing technology.

However, there is evidence that despite being technological improvements, bootleg ideas are "ingenious" solutions. "Researchers think all the time about things and how they could improve them ... it is experimenting ...," as one researcher put it.

The nature of technological improvements can be illustrated by an example. This example comes from the Swiss machine tool company, Rieter. Rotor spinning was invented in 1967. The crucial element for technical progress in this industry was a bearing in the spinning machines. The rotor can reach up to 60,000 rotations per minute with direct bearings. This technology was standard in the 1960s. The indirect bearings, developed in the 1970s, increased the speed to 120,000 rotations per minute. If the bearing is an oil-based lubricant, up to 140,000 rotations per minute can be reached. This was a barrier of sorts until the 1980s. In 1987, a researcher proposed an aero-static bearing with the potential for a speed beyond 140,000 rotations per minute. The idea was rejected until 1991 when the researcher was able to produce enough technical evidence from bootleg research to support his idea. The reason for rejection for this brilliant idea was apparently the "short-sightedness" of two decision takers. Technical drawings in Fig. 1.1 illustrate the idea.

The complexity of products and technologies is increasing steadily. As a result, time and knowledge constraints make it impossible to develop

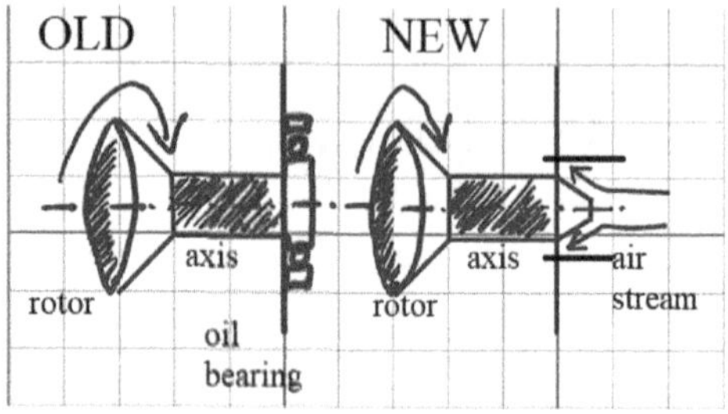

Fig. 1.1. Lubricant and aero-static bearing for rotor spinning.

whole products or completely new technologies single-handedly. For more than any other type of bootleg project, improvements seem to lie within the limits of what is possible for a researcher in terms of money, time, and expertise. Also, the physical size of an innovation can be a constraint for bootleg research. However, researchers are resourceful and often work on miniature models. The easiest bootleg product to hide is software.

1.3. Valuable for the Firm?

The purpose of this section is to get a vague idea of the usefulness of bootlegging for a company. "Vague idea" may be an unscientific term, but it makes sense at this point. The benefits of bootleg innovation for a company cannot be measured fully. In addition, the value of an individual innovation is always specific and cannot be justified in a general way (Jewkes *et al.*, 1969: 25). Nonetheless, some literature assumes that bootleg innovation is more successful than normal innovation. Three attempts to "measure" the approximate value of bootlegging are discussed. Firstly, does bootlegging meet business needs in general? Secondly, are the bootleg innovations adopted by the firm? And thirdly, from the cost point of view, does the consumption of the resource justify this type of research?

It is unsurprising to find that most bootleg products are considered to be commercially valuable by firms. Most bootlegging concerns incremental improvements to an existing product range, that is, products already officially approved by management. By inference, improvements to approved products should also meet business needs. In only about 10% of all cases was the value of bootlegging questioned. So, it seems that, in general, covert activity has some value for a company.

The unexpectedly high acceptance of bootleg products after disclosure produces an even clearer picture of the positive recognition gained for bootlegging. A study has shown that the majority of bootleg innovations are developed further or are expected to be developed further by firms. Sometimes only parts or modified versions of the bootleg innovation were considered useful by the company.

Bootlegging causes no or only minor additional cost in terms of the number of bootleg entrepreneurs, time consumption, tools, material, and equipment. This is easy to demonstrate. The number of bootleg entrepreneurs multiplied by numbers of hours spent for bootlegging in comparison to total manpower in R&D. So, 5–10% of bootleg entrepreneurs multiplied by 10% of their working time equals less than 1% of the total working force. As one R&D manager confessed, "Bootlegging is peanuts in comparison to the enormous money spent in R&D." Material, equipment, and tools are mostly already available in the laboratory. The expenses for materials are usually low as bootleg researchers are known to be masters of improvisation. Thus, by far the biggest danger for all the companies interviewed was that official projects could be jeopardized by bootleg activity. Generally, bootleg researchers use their resources carefully simply because they are scarce.

Companies usually evaluate the resource consumption of equipment, tools, and materials as being less important than time. A simple calculation can show why this is the case. If a researcher earns a salary of €60,000 per year, an average bootleg time of 10% equates to €6,000. Accessibility of tools, material, and laboratory equipment is not considered an obstacle to bootlegging. For example, the new alloy engine parts of one company were produced alongside standard engine parts simply by adding another row to the assembly line. In other cases, the materials used were either low-cost materials that were available anyway in the laboratory or they were acquired by other means such as mutually beneficial favor swap inside or outside of the company. Some laboratories were permitted to spend a certain amount of money for "general expenses." Any material that exceeds this budget is difficult to get. Besides, "a lot of people would be nervous about ordering tools which are not connected to the company's current research."

Bootlegging draws heavily on the availability of overhead slack. That is presumably the reason why scholars like Cyert and March (1963) or Knight (1967) discuss the topic of "bootlegging" under the heading of "resource planning." Slack resources exist because of uncertainty in planning R&D resources. Eighty-five percent of 40 laboratories, which provided information on slack, admitted to having slack in their laboratory budget. Thirty of those could quantify the amount of slack. Average overheads were 13%, but the trend seems to be that slack is in decline. The highest value acknowledged was 30%. Figure 1.2 shows the clustered average slack for the companies.

Researchers are generally overworked and if they do not want to jeopardize projects already in progress, they have to work harder. The consequence is a smaller amount of slack. It has been observed that researchers voluntarily work harder when idiosyncratic identification with the research project is high. As a result, they seem to be less interested in bootlegging.

A number of factors directly determine the amount of slack in R&D. For example, cross-responsibilities in the organizational structure, a generous funding body, efficient work performance, lack of control, and high task uncertainty appear to facilitate the creation of slack resources. It seems that the researcher has some control over slack resources. Control has a natural origin: "researchers want to be on the safe side" and demand more time than is necessary for the implementation of the research task. The logic is that if the budget is overdrawn, it can be justified, if the budget is too high it is simply not declared and provides slack resources.

Slack in the form of bootlegging is usually limited by both non-delivery of normal work and careful control by management. As soon as projects

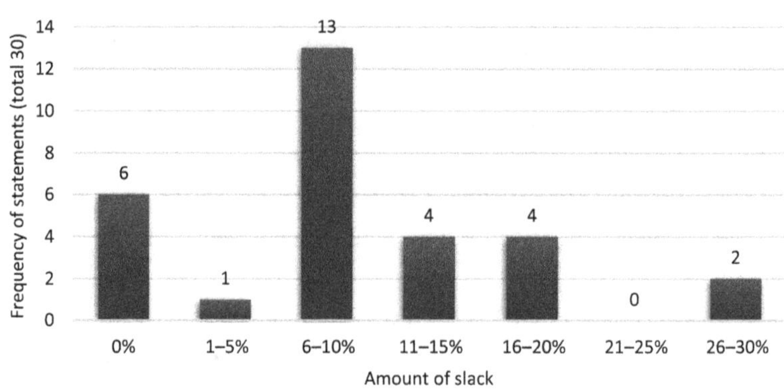

Fig. 1.2. Distribution of slack.

are jeopardized and the researcher "does not meet his targets," bootlegging becomes detectable. Sometimes, management is aware of the existence of slack without really having the means to control it, apart from exerting pressure. As a countermeasure, management can try to make cuts across the board. However, there are researchers clever enough anticipate this and build it into their budgets. Companies were not worried about the disappearance of slack resources. "If something which does not exist officially (slack) is used for something which does not exist officially (bootlegging), where is the problem?" as one firm expressed it.

Slack is not the only source for bootleg time. Researchers also "dig for time" elsewhere. Additional resources are found, for example, by reallocating money from other projects, investing spare time, or via "dubious channels." The average researcher spends only two-thirds of his working time in the laboratory. The rest is needed for administrative tasks, meetings, educational training, conferences, and other purposes. These figures vary over time and are dependent on the firm, position, and the function of the researcher. This non-research time can be redirected and used for bootlegging. There is enough elbow room to cheat. For example, one company permits 10 days per year of educational training. This is time to be used for courses, for further education, or professional training. Some researchers carry out their bootleg projects during this time.

On average, researchers work between 10 and 15% overtime. This is the result found from data gained from 18 companies. However, all the people interviewed pointed out that it is hard to distinguish between what is "normal work" and what is "overtime." Interestingly, it seems that the amount of overtime has experienced a major shrinkage since health and safety laws were introduced in the countries investigated. Working late nights was quite common in some laboratories before the 1970s. Today, it is prohibited or only allowed under exceptional circumstances. Now, it is strictly controlled by work councils. Bootleg researchers use overtime for their covert projects. They seem to work even more than the average researcher's 15% overtime. Often, they work at the weekends, at home and during the night. Thus, spare time and overtime, which are generally not paid, are a very important source of time. In fact, some researchers consider this their only source of "slack."

Last but not least, research time can be gained through a variety of "dubious channels." "As a matter of fact, it is possible to change the purpose of budgets, for example, up to 10%," to intentionally overspend, or to "borrow" time from other departments and projects. Thompson, in his research, paid tribute to this behavior and called it "fund juggling" (1969). It includes piggybacking projects and misallocating hours to other projects. For example, in one particular case, over half a million pounds was found "somewhere in the system," which made possible employment of some additional researchers on a research project. This kind of "swamp-funding," as the company named it, is only done when there is a direct need for it. No information could be obtained about the average amount possible and the exact mechanism in place, except that "friends in key positions" can be helpful.

This chapter introduced the nature of bootlegging. Firstly, it showed that it is a common phenomenon found in over 80% of the companies. However, only 5–10% of researchers carry out bootlegging using only 10% of their working time. Without the availability of some slack resources, bootlegging decreases or might stop completely. Other resources, such as materials, tools, and equipment do not play an important role. No drastic differences could be found among the nationalities investigated.

Secondly, most bootleg output concerns pre-research for objective setting, and incremental product or process improvements incorporating clever technological solutions. As a result, bootlegging generally meets business needs, and the uncertainty for the company in terms of resource consumption is low. This contradicts most literature, which points toward bootlegging as a way of overcoming corporate constraints on major and radical innovations.

Thirdly, bootlegging is mostly used to demonstrate the feasibility of innovative ideas. In this way, bootlegging bridges the creative stage of experimental R&D and its formal acceptance. During this phase, researchers are often informally overseen by colleagues discussing the results of their research. In this early stage of bottom-up innovation, bootlegging can hardly be distinguished from "normal" innovation. In fact, the research seems to suggest that, at this stage, bootlegging is normal innovation. All these findings point toward bootlegging as a continuous learning mode of R&D.

1.4. Implications for Theory and Management

Firstly, bootlegging emerges as the link between creativity and formal innovation. In traditional descriptions of innovation processes, ideas are usually considered "deus ex machina" (Bradbury, 1989). This perspective both ignores and excludes the importance of creative trial-and-error research. The formulation of an idea requires oscillation between theoretical (thinking) and practical search (experimenting). The information gathering process may subsequently result in a proposal for a formal research project. In this research, bootlegging's main function crystallized as the provision of "free space" for (mostly incremental) bottom-up innovation. As such it provides an excellent explanation for the knowledge gap because it describes the covert trial-and-error period as a transition from creativity to innovation.

Secondly, it allows some conclusions about self-regulating mechanisms in corporate organizations. Organization has its limits. Focusing on the formal and informal world, Weltz (1990a, 1990b, 1990c) argues that informal organization "corrects" and compensates for the weaknesses of formal organizational systems. He also points out that the more the accent is on formal procedures the more important informal organization becomes. He quotes Attwell (1986), who pointed out the irony that the search for rationality sometimes leads to more irrationality (Weltz, 1990b: 56). In this respect, bootlegging can be regarded as an irrational but an important, informal, self-regulating element in the complexity of corporate innovative activity. This imposes a certain amount of legitimacy on bootlegging. It reflects the basic axiom of the evolutionary perspective: change and creativity are reliant upon elements of redundancy, waste, and inefficiency (Metcalf, 1994: 159).

Management afraid of losing control can be assured that there is nothing to fear. A kind of self-organizing mechanism is in place, which concerns the technological projection of uncontrolled innovative advances. The "blind variation" (Cambell, 1987 in Metcalf, 1994: 160) of bootleg innovation, which *a priori* is considered independent of a managerial selective advantage, is not that blind. In other words, innovations are not of all sorts of things. The findings confirm, to a certain extent, the selective logic of technological path dependency: bootlegging is mostly incremental and not radical and thus follows directions set in the past.

Thirdly, some authors are skeptical about benefits for the company. They refer to the occasional success that became public against the countless failures that were never made public (Roussel *et al.*, 1991). However, the results of this chapter point toward tolerance of bootlegging. The main arguments in this regard are the low degree of investment uncertainty and its value for its tangible, and even more importantly, its intangible competence-building output.

Finally, a number of scholars have tried to identify the corporate entrepreneur (Schon, 1973). Some authors are convinced that the bootleg researcher is the corporate Schumpeterian entrepreneur (Hoffman, 1991; Peters and Waterman, 1982). However, according to Schumpeter, the entrepreneur exploits an invention but is not the inventor of "untried technological possibilities" (Schumpeter, 1954). His capitalistic behavior is opportunistic in particular markets. The findings indicate that the bootleg researcher has, by and large, no commercial ambitions at all. Nonetheless, it seems that the bootleg entrepreneur has some important characteristics in common with the Schumpeterian entrepreneur. Both are restless personalities, "see the new possibility," and show heroic behavior in coping "with resistance and difficulties." Furthermore, both "get things done!" (Schumpeter, 1954). In this respect, the bootleg researcher can be considered an entrepreneur in his particular work environment: the firm organization. Bootleg entrepreneurs are actively creative researchers and are able to produce ideas autonomously. Two implications follow directly from this. Companies wanting to foster bootlegging would be ill-advised to simply give free time to everybody because not every researcher is capable of unguided research. The second implication is that a company that tries to exclude bootlegging altogether should rightly fear that most of its actively creative people will leave. Thus, bootlegging seems to be a necessary condition for in-house creativity. Bottom-up ideas are not "free of charge," but the company should accept bootleg research as a "biotope" for actively creative people. This requires a flexible management style and the acceptance of the "tumultuous realities of innovation" (Quinn, 1985). From all this, it can be concluded that variety among research staff is important. For example, curiosity, the ability to "network," and political bargaining determines the selection and existence of bottom-up innovation.

The competence to organize innovation despite organizational uncertainties in the form of innovation barriers could be called the "social competencies" of a firm. In this sense, it is not solely technological competencies that allow firms to progress along their trajectory but also soft factors such as social competencies. Their catalytic function is part of what Teece described as "complementary assets" (Teece, 1986) or Pavitt meant by introducing the notion "firm specific competencies" (Patel and Pavitt, 1994).

References

Attwell, G. (1986). In Weltz (1990b).

Augsdorfer, P. (1996). *Forbidden Fruit: An Analysis of Bootlegging, Uncertainty, and Learning in Corporate R&D*. Aldershot: Avebury.

Augsdorfer, P. (2021). *Forbidden Fruit: An Analysis of Bootlegging, Uncertainty, and Learning in Corporate R&D* (2nd edn.). Gold&Apple Transfers Publishers.

Bradbury, J. A. A. (1989). *Product Innovation: Idea to Exploitation*. New York: John Wiley & Sons.

Burgelman, R. A. (1988). Strategy making as a social learning process: The case of internal corporate venturing. *Interfaces*, **18**(3): 74–85.

Cambell. (1987). In Metcalf (1994, p. 160).

Cyert, M. C. and March, J. G. (1963). *A Behavioral Theory of the Firm*. Prentice Hall: Englewood Cliffs, N.J.

Dosi, G. (1991). Perspectives on evolutionary theory. *Science and Public Policy*, **18**(6): 353–361.

Eicher, S. (2020). *Uncovering Covert Innovation: Bootlegging, Illegitimacy, and Management's Attitude*. Berlin: Springer Gabler Verlag.

Globocnik, D. (2019). Taking or avoiding risk through secret innovation activities — the relationship among employee's risk propensity, bootlegging, and management support. *International Journal of Innovation Management*, 1950022.

Han Y., Liao, J. and Long, L. (2007). Employee work performance structure model construction and empirical research. *Journal of Management Science*, **10**(5): 62–77.

Hoffmann, L. (1991). Innovation durch Konspiration. *Harvard Manager*, (13): 121–127.

Jewkes, J., Sawers, D. and Stillerman, R. (1969). *The Sources of Invention* (2nd edn.). London: Macmillan.

Knight, K. E. (1967). A descriptive model of the intra-firm innovation process. *The Journal of Business*, **40**: 478–496.

Mainemelis, C. (2010). Stealing fire: Creative deviance in the evolution of new ideas. *Academy of Management Review*, **35**(4): 558–578.

Metcalf, J. S. (1994). *Technology Policy and Small Firms: An Evolutionary Perspective*. In Oakey, R. (Ed.), *New Technology-Based Firms in the 1990s* (pp. 157–168). London: Paul Chapman.

Mintzberg, H. (1990). The manager's job: Folklore and fact. *Harvard Business Review*, (March-April): 163–176. Reprint of HBR July–August 1975.

Miyazaki, K. (1994). *Building Competencies in the Firm: Lessons from European and Japanese Opto-electronics*. London: Macmillan.

Patel, P. and Pavitt, K. (1994). *Technological Competencies in the World's Largest Firms: Characteristics, Constraints and Scope for Managerial Choice*. Brighton: Mimeo, SPRU, Sussex University.

Peters, T. and Waterman, R. W. (1982). *In Search of Excellence*. New York: Harper and Row.

Quinn, J. B. (1985). Managing innovation: Controlled chaos. *Harvard Business Review*, **63**(May–June): 73–84.

Roussel, P. A., Saad, K. N. and Erickson, T. J. (1991). *Third Generation of R&D*. USA: Arthur D. Little, Inc.

Sakhdari, K. and Bidakhavidi, E. (2016). Underground innovation: How to encourage bootlegging employees to disclose their good ideas. *Technology Innovation Management Review*, **6**(3) (March).

Schon, D. A. (1963). Champions for radical new inventions. *Harvard Business Review*, **41**(2): 77–86.

Schumpeter, J. (1954). *Capitalism, Socialism, and Democracy* (3rd edn.). Boston: George Allen & Unwin.

Teece, D. J. (1986). Profiting from technological innovation. In Teece, D. J. (Ed.), *The Competitive Challenge*. Cambridge, Mass.: Ballinger.

Thompson, V. A. (1969). *Bureaucracy and Innovation*. Alabama: University of Alabama Press.

Weltz, F. (1990a). Management by Potemkin. *Technische Rundschau*, **33**: 10–12.

Weltz, F. (1990b). Die Herrschaft der Zahlen. *Technische Rundschau*, **42**: 52–57.

Weltz, F. (1990c). Der Traum von der absoluten Ordnung und die doppelte Wirklichkeit der Unternehmen. *Technische Rundschau*, **45**: 10–13.

https://doi.org/10.1142/9781800612266_0003

Chapter 2

The Presence of Bootlegging Activity in the R&D Department of High-Technology Firms

Marek Szwejczewski* and Yaser Masoudnia†
University of Sheffield, Sheffield, UK
**m.szwejczewski@sheffield.ac.uk*
†yaser_m@mit.edu

Abstract

This chapter presents some of the major findings from a study of bootlegging. A large group of R&D employees (all serial bootleggers) were interviewed in-depth about various aspects of their clandestine work. The interviews explored the type of innovations (product, process, radical, incremental) that resulted from bootlegging as stated by the respondents. The research examined the reasons behind why the employees carried out this illicit activity. In the interviews, the bootleggers were asked about how they managed their time so they could work on covert projects. The research also examined how these employees went about the crucial activity of revealing the clandestine projects to the wider organization.

2.1. Introduction

Management literature recommends the use of structured models of innovation by companies. This includes Cooper's (1990) stage and gate approach or Kline and Rosenberg's (1986) chain-linked model. However, there is a growing view that organizations should place their emphasis on giving employees more freedom as an effective way of increasing the number of innovations (Gaynor, 2002; Iyer and Davenport, 2008) and developing radical innovation (Grantham and Readman, 2005; Berends *et al.*, 2007). This emphasis can be found in various areas such as the fuzzy front end of innovation (e.g., Boeddrich, 2004), creativity (e.g., Amabile and Khaire, 2008), and ambidexterity (Gibson and Birkinshaw, 2004; Raisch *et al.*, 2009).

In the past years, managers have formalized the research and development process in order to achieve greater control, reduce risks of failure, and decrease costs. The greater restrictions that have been placed on research and development (R&D) employees has meant that some have worked outside the imposed structures in order to develop their innovative ideas, to protect them from the "disapproving power of the organization" (Knight 1976: 493). Employees undertake bootlegging activity, developing their innovations in a clandestine manner.

Bootlegging is predominantly a bottom-up activity carried out by an individual at the lower levels of the organization (Daft, 1978; Knight, 1967). The employee who undertakes bootlegging avoids the formal rules and bureaucracy that constrains creativity, allowing them to be free to explore new ideas. It is an underground activity (Aram, 1973) that is unofficial, not budgeted for and as such not featured in any company plans (Augsdorfer, 1996).

Innovations emerge from the unrestrained environment that the bootlegger operates in (Augsdorfer, 2008). This clandestine endeavor is considered by Augsdorfer (2008) and Peters and Waterman (1982) to be a "quick" method that delivers brilliant innovations. The clandestine activities of individuals have resulted in important innovations over the years, for example the BMW 12-cylinder engine (Augsdorfer, 2008), Toshiba's first laptop (Abetti, 1997a), and the Agilent Technologies' 1200 series chemical test equipment. These innovations proved to be critical and helped the companies improve their competitive position.

Bootlegging is considered to be a significant source of bottom-up innovation (Augsdorfer, 1996, 2005, 2008; Iyer and Davenport, 2008). Bootlegging may deliver benefits for the organization in terms of innovations, but it may also cause problem. This clandestine activity is a concern for managers because it is hidden and consequently not under their control. Officially sanctioned projects may be delayed because employees are developing their own ideas and so cannot cope with their assigned workload (Roussel *et al.*, 1991). Individuals who carry out this secret work use company resources in order to develop their ideas. If laboratory equipment and materials are being used on bootlegging projects, then efficiency losses are likely (Globocnik and Salomo, 2015). Bootleggers can shift organization time and resources to their secret projects, which will impact the firm's organizational priorities (Abetti, 1997a, 1997b, 1999a).

The bootlegging activities of employees can facilitate innovations that can potentially benefit the organization. However, the existence of this clandestine action casts doubts on the manageability of innovation in an organization (Augsdorfer, 2008). Therefore, it is important to understand if the activity is really for the benefit of the organization or the bootlegger. In order to understand the true nature of the activity, it is important to understand the rational and purpose. This chapter presents some of the findings of a research study into bootlegging in R&D departments of high-technology companies.

2.2. Literature Review

2.2.1. Background to bootlegging

The term "bootlegging" originates from the illegal production, transport, and sales of alcohol, particularly whiskey in the United States (Augsdorfer, 1996). The term was first introduced in management literature by Schon (1963) who defined it as the covert development of new ideas by innovators in order to protect themselves from the disapproving power in organizations. Bootlegging projects are normally clandestine, unbudgeted, unofficial, and not programmed (Augsdorfer, 1996). Such projects are also "bottom-up" because they are initiated by an individual low down the hierarchy (Daft, 1978) with the company's time and resources being utilized without management approval. In the case of this research project, bootlegging is defined as unauthorized projects initiated by an employee and directed toward innovation for the benefit of their organization.

In the management literature, the term "underground innovation" is used as an alternative term for bootlegging (Aram, 1973). Other terms are also used to refer to bootlegging in the literature. These include: under the counter work, work behind the fume cupboard, illicit research, renegade work, work in the shadows (Augsdorfer, 1996), pet-projects (Nohria and Gulati, 1996), under the table work (Abetti, 1997a), Friday afternoon work (Grimpe, 2006), and self-organization (Koch and Leitner, 2008).

The activity of bootlegging should not be confused with the activity of "skunkworks," a concept defined by Kelly Johnson in the Lockheed

Martin Corporation to refer to a secret, company-sanctioned research project (Rich and Janos, 1994; Pace, 1992). While a skunkworks project is clandestine in that it may be hidden from part of the organization, it has explicit management approval and support, unlike bootlegging.

Bootlegging should also not be confused with the concept of "permitted bootlegging," which refers to the type of project pursued by some designated employees (usually in R&D) who have been allowed to pursue personal interests and ideas (with the permission granted to do so by management) (Augsdorfer, 1996). Firms such as 3M (Krogh *et al.*, 1988) and Google (Iyer and Davenport, 2008) allow their researchers to spend a specific amount of time working on personal projects. It is important to distinguish this activity from bootlegging because it is authorized by management and not clandestine (Augsdorfer, 1996).

It is also important to differentiate bootlegging from other clandestine activities, especially moonlighting, where employees use organization time and resources for personal gain. Although it is a secret activity, bootlegging may actually serve the organization's interests in ways that moonlighting and similar practices do not.

2.2.2. Bootlegging research

The term "bootlegging" was first used by Schon (1963) in a paper examining the process of innovation. He suggested that bootlegging challenged the current situation in the organization and gave rise to change. He was also of the view that weak or lack of managerial control was the basis for bootlegging taking place in the organization.

One of the significant early studies of bootlegging was undertaken by Augsdorfer (1994, 1996, 2005, 2008). He found that more than 80% of the firms studied confirmed that bootlegging was taking place among their workforce. His analysis indicated that most bootlegging served organizational interests because it resulted in the application of new technology or resulted in technological improvement. In addition, he suggests that bootlegging is not necessarily in conflict with a company's strategy (Augsdorfer, 1996, 2005). This observation runs contrary to the claim made by other researchers who expounded that it does directly challenge the organization's strategy (Roberts, 1991; Ma, 2002) or cause disruption within the company (Roussel *et al.*, 1991).

Research by Augsdorfer (1996, 2005), in which he performed 57 case studies of companies, identified that R&D researchers needed permission to develop their ideas. However, in order to attain this, they needed to first thoroughly prepare these ideas. They had to undertake it clandestinely and so consequently the researchers had to bootleg. In a later study, he pinpointed several other reasons for bootlegging (Augsdorfer, 2008). Firstly, organization R&D budgets were planned on a periodic basis and resources assigned to particular objectives. The inflexibility of this planning system means that ideas emerging between planning periods are unlikely to be supported and so the must be pursued underground if they stand a chance of realization. Secondly, even if the organization had a contingency budget that is available to support the development of new ideas that appear between budget cycles, projects to develop them further may go underground to maintain independence, and to avoid the psychological pressure to produce a quick result.

The research undertaken by Abetti (1997a, 1997b, 1999a, 1999b) into underground innovations at Toshiba pointed to the rejection of an idea by management as the main reason behind employees carrying out clandestine development work. Pearson (1997) also proposes that one of the reasons behind bootlegging is disagreement with management about the value of the product being proposed. Abetti also suggested that employees carry out bootlegging in order to overcome bureaucratic barriers (Abetti, 1999a) or to protect their project from managerial disapproval or interruptions during the early stages of its development (Abetti, 1997a).

Research carried out by Koch and Leitner (2008) discovered that clandestine development was undertaken in order to avoid ideas being terminated as a result of management being presented with unfinished work. Echoing Abetti's earlier findings, Koch and Leitner (2008) found that employees bootleg to circumvent cumbersome, time-consuming formal procedures. They identified that some development was being carried out secretly because the idea was outside the company strategy or because individuals were working outside their permitted field of activity, and therefore, any request to progress work on an idea would have been rejected by management. Interestingly, they also found that somc individuals carried out clandestine work in order to reduce worry about the possible failure of their innovation. It has also been suggested that bootleggers may work clandestinely to establish legitimacy and thereby acquire the needed resources to help them develop and refine their ideas (Kannan-Narasimhan, 2014).

A few researchers have tried to specify the characteristics of the employee who undertake bootlegging (Augsdorfer, 1996; Abetti, 1997b, 2004). Augsdorfer says 5–10% of researchers who initiate bootlegging are a "*special species.*" These employees are very motivated and creative individuals who are willing to undertake the risk of pursuing an emerging idea, especially clandestinely (Augsdorfer, 1996; Abetti, 1999b, Abetti 2004, and Andersson and Berggren, 2007). They are considered to have entrepreneurial characteristics and are called entrepreneurs by Augsdorfer (1994, 1996, 2005, 2008), Abetti (1997a, 1997b, 1999a, 1999b, 2004), Hellström and Malmquist (2000), Andersson and Berggren (2007), and Koch and Leitner (2008). Among these papers, only Augsdorfer (1994, 1996, 2005, 2008), Abetti (1997a, 1997b, 1999a, 1999b, 2004), and Koch and Leitner (2008) are papers that are based on empirical evidence.

In terms of how bootleggers operate clandestinely and how they acquire resources and time to work, different researchers have offered their views that are often contradictory. The majority of writers — Augsdorfer (1996, 2005, 2008), Abetti (1997a, 1997b, 1999a, 1999b), Thompson (1969), Pinchot (1985); Trott (1998), Kanter (2000); Ma (2002), Richtner and Ahlstrom (2006), Bessant and Tidd (2007) — agree that slack resources are vital for any underground activities. However, Pearson (1997) theorizes that slack resources are not important and Nijhof *et al.* (2002) report that slack resources were not necessary to undertake this activity. In addition, Abetti (1997b, 1999a) and Debackere *et al.* (1994) seem to be concerned about limitations in acquiring resources, as Abetti even claims that if bootleggers need to, they may steal the required resources for bootlegging. In contrast, Augsdorfer (1996) claims the most crucial limitation for bootlegging is time. Unofficial networks of bootleggers are highlighted as the main path for getting the expertise required for underground projects (Augsdorfer, 1996; Abetti, 1997b, 1999a; Hellström and Malmquist, 2000; Koch and Leitner, 2008).

There has been some initial research into the issue of when the bootlegger reveals their project to the wide organization. According to Augsdorfer (1996, 2005), very few bootleg projects remain underground once the feasibility of the idea has been proven. While Burgelman (1983) says that disclosure occurs when the bootlegger reaches the point when the benefits can be proven to the organization. In contrast, Abetti (1997a, 1997b, 1999a) indicates that projects will be taken nearly all the way through the new product development process and only revealed to management at the final stage.

The results of employees bootlegging activities have been studies by some researcher. The investigation carried out by Augsdorfer (1996, 2005) suggests that in the majority of cases the activity results in incremental innovation, while on the other hand, Abetti (1997a, 1997b, 1999a, 2004) and also Knight (1967) both put forward projects that resulted in radical innovations. The literature lacks some degree of consensus as to the type of innovations that result from bootlegging.

2.2.3. Bootlegging research gaps

Researchers investigating bootlegging has identified numerous reasons for employees undertaking this secret activity. Some of the various reasons behind bootlegging include: lack of managerial control (Knight, 1967); disagreement with management (Abetti, 1999b; Pearson, 1997); funding system that does not allow for experimental trials (Augsdorfer, 1996); time to develop an idea (Augsdorfer, 1996, 2005); to protect underdeveloped ideas (Koch and Leitner, 2008; Cyert and March, 1992); and to avoid psychological pressure to come up with results (Augsdorfer, 2008). Researchers have suggested there are numerous reasons for why individuals undertake bootlegging; however, given the wide and varied reasons, it is not clear which are the main ones and there is little empirical evidence to support the existence of particular factors. This shows a clear gap in our comprehension of the reasons for bootlegging.

There are various other areas where the current research does not provide a conclusive picture of the dynamics of bootlegging. It is important to understand whether bootleggers carry out their activities in work time or if their activities are carried out outside of normal working hours. It is also of interest as to their use of company resources. Since all these arguments are either theoretical arguments or based on limited data gathered by the means of few case studies, it is essential to undertake further investigations about how time and resources are acquired by bootleggers, and in particular, the role of slack resources in bootlegging.

Another area of interest that has not been sufficiently explored is the issue of when and how does the bootlegger go about revealing their project to the organization. Thus, the dynamic of bootlegging still remains a gap in our knowledge and the question of how bootleggers operate underground remains unanswered. The research outlined in this chapter examined various aspects of how the bootleggers operate underground, in particular, how they find the time and resources to carry out the work, how long they carry out this underground activity, and what the outcome of their bootlegging are.

2.3. Methodology

In order to investigate the issue of bootlegging, a qualitative research approach was used. This method is the most appropriate when the researcher wants to gain a deeper understanding of the phenomenon under investigation (Bell *et al.*, 2018). It was decided to investigate the bootlegging activities of R&D employees in high-technology industries. These were chosen because they were dynamic with demand for high rates of innovation and so likely to have more active bootleggers compared to other sectors.

An employee undertaking bootlegging may be carrying out activities in work time and may be using company resources without permission. Given the illegal nature of their activities, the employee will be reluctant to discuss their secret activities for fear of punishment or sanctions by the organization. Bootlegging is essentially a clandestine endeavor. Therefore, research into such an activity needs to be undertaken using a different approach to that used in mainstream management research.

Research into bootlegging has a lot in common with research into sensitive subjects in the social sciences. In the social sciences, sensitive areas are those areas that may potentially have an adverse effect on the participant or a specific group of individuals (Stanley *et al.*, 1987). The investigation of sensitive issues is rare in the innovation management discipline. However, it is more common in social science; for example, studies have been carried out examining the shadow economy (Schneider and Enste, 2000; Schneider, 2005), tax evasion (Slemrod, 2007), and HIV and nursing (Faugier and Sargeant, 1997; Polit and Beck, 2008).

An examination of the methods used by researchers investing sensitive issues suggested that survey, interviews, and ethnography were possible approaches that could be used (Lee and Renzett, 1990). It was decided that for this type of research, face-to-face interviews were the most appropriate technique of data collection (Lee, 1993). The interviews were carried out using a semistructured questionnaire, which allowed the researcher to explore in more detail an answer the respondent provided or to clarify a point that had been made. Following the advice of various researchers, care was taken with the design of the questionnaire, in particular the wording of the questions was reviewed so that phrasing did not cause any potential distress (Lee, 1993; McPhee and Terry, 2007).

2.3.1. Sample

The use of the traditional approach to sampling, probability sampling, was not possible because the individuals under investigation could be considered to be a rare and divergent group, and consequently difficult to sample (Lee, 1993; Faugier and Sargeant, 1997). Therefore, it was necessary to adopt the snowball approach in order to be able to undertake the research (Faugier and Sargeant, 1997). Snowball sampling is commonly used when it is difficult to identify members of a desired population, for example, individuals who are working while claiming unemployment benefit (Saunders *et al.*, 2007).

Using personal contact, it was possible to find individuals who had been involved in bootlegging. Then through a process of asking them to recommend other individuals who they knew had carried out bootlegging, it was possible to grow the sample of individuals interviewed. Through this process of snowball sampling, it was possible to complete 55 in-depth face-to-face interviews with individuals who were undertaking bootleg activities. While this approach helped to arrive at a relatively large sample of respondents it took several months to achieve — it took time to build trust and arrange each interview. The focus of the research was on serial bootleggers and therefore not all individuals recommended fitted the profile and in addition the researchers were interested in individuals working in high-technology sectors. This need to interview certain types of individuals also helped to slow down the research projects progress.

2.3.2. Interview

Each interview started with an introduction by the interviewer and then an explanation that the interview was confidential and that the interviewees anonymity would be preserved (this meant that all transcripts did not include the real name of the respondent or the company they worked for — code names were used). The interviewee was reminded that they free to decline to answer any question and could ask the recording machine to be switched off at any point. After this introduction, the interview started.

The interview commenced with a few general questions about the interviewee and their organization (size, industry sector, etc.). They were then asked about the R&D or product development group they worked in and department structure. Prior to the interview, the researcher had collected background information about the company the interviewee worked for, so this reduced the amount of time spent asking the respondent questions about their company.

The interview then moved onto the main focus of the research and covered the more sensitive issues. The first set of questions related to what the respondent did when they came up with an idea that they then pursued as a bootleg project. They were asked about how many bootleg projects they had undertaken during the last two years, and the degree to which they were clandestine. They were then asked to choose a particular bootleg project (that they had completed recently) and explain in detail what happened from the start to the completion of the project when they disclosed it to the organization. The outcome of the chosen project was also covered. The interview finished with a discussion of the outcomes of all the bootleg projects that the interviewee had worked on over the two-year period.

2.3.3. Data analysis

After the interviews, the audio recordings were transcribed, and notes and any additional information (e.g., company background information) were added to the transcripts. During the transcription process, the anonymity of the participants was maintained through the use of codes names to refer to the interviewees and the organizations they worked for. The transcripts were also checked for any information that might identify the company and the individuals, and again code names were used to ensure anonymity.

All the data (interview transcripts and notes) were then entered into NVivo 8 software, which was used to aid the analysis. This software allows the user to code the data and then analyze it for patterns and possible relationships. The data analysis that was carried out followed the approach recommended by King (2004). Each transcript was read and re-read to gain familiarity with the data. The analysis started with open coding of the data. As the process progressed hierarchical coding was applied to enable deeper analysis. Each interview was coded separately and analyzed individually. Then cross-case analysis was carried out across the whole sample to compare participants and identify the common themes that emerged from the data. Pattern and cluster coding that highlights the repetition and common patterns in the data was also applied. Peer review was undertaken to discuss and confirm the codes and relationships.

2.4. Results

2.4.1. Respondent profile

The respondents who were interviewed were all company employees who regularly carried out bootlegging. They were all highly experienced with the vast majority of them (84%) having 10 or more years' experience working in research and development. In addition, they had attained a high level of education with 41 of the 55 interviewees having a PhD or equivalent qualification.

The interviewees came from 34 different companies, all of which can be considered to fall into the high-technology sector. The industry sector where the respondents currently worked are shown in Fig. 2.1.

The majority (72%) of the interviewees worked for North American companies, around 22% worked for European companies and a small minority (6%) worked for Asian companies. The vast majority of the 55 interviewees worked for large companies (based on turnover and number of employees).

The respondents were a mix of senior and junior roles, with 24% having a middle management position (see Table 2.1). None of those interviewed had the authority to make critical decisions, such as stopping or approving projects or allocating large budgets to development projects. In the majority of cases, the interviewee commented that their direct manager (the person they reported to) could not make such major decisions

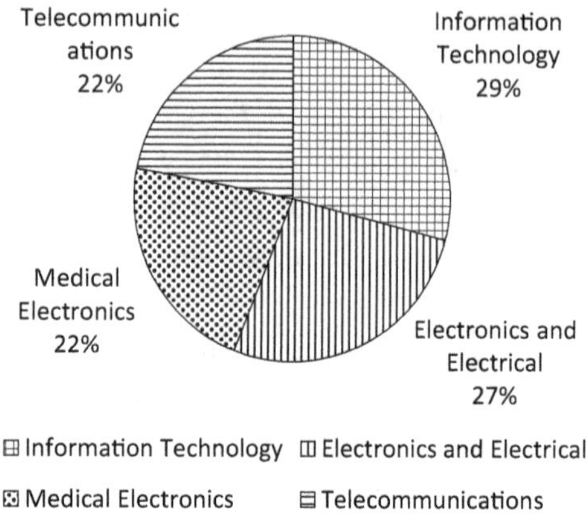

Fig. 2.1. Respondents — Industry sector.

Table 2.1. Respondent job position.

Staff (Scientist, engineer, researcher)	49%
Senior Staff (Senior scientist, senior engineer)	27%
Middle Management (R&D manager, manager)	24%

(stopping or approving large projects) independently, due to the fact that they worked for large organizations with four to five management levels.

The respondents' responsibilities covered the working on research projects, developing technology, or new product development. They were engaged in working on more than one project at a time and were free to prioritizing their own time on a daily basis. Their responsibilities also included attending meetings, preparing reports, giving presentations, attending conferences, etc. Since the interviewees were in charge of managing their time across different projects and responsibilities, this gave them a degree of flexibility in terms of how they spent their working hours.

2.4.2. Bootlegging outcomes

The interviews covered the issue of what was the outcome of the respondents' bootlegging activity. During the interview, they were asked to discuss a recently completed bootlegging project. Of the 55 bootleg

Table 2.2. Outcome of bootlegging activity.

Product innovation	63.6%
Process innovation	7.3%
Knowledge creation and learning	10.9%
Invention	9.1%
No benefit to organization	9.1%
Total	100%

projects that were discussed, 35 projects (63.6%) resulted in a product innovation that was launched onto the market (see Table 2.2).

While most of the clandestine activity produced a product innovation, only four (7.3%) of the projects resulted in a process innovation. The remaining 16 projects resulted in three outcomes and five projects produced what we can consider an invention (the outcome produced a patent, but this had not been implemented by the organization). Six projects resulted in what was considered to be knowledge creation and learning (the outcomes were published in conference proceedings). Of the 55 bootlegging projects, there were only five that did not have an outcome which could be considered to be a benefit for the organization — of which four were discontinued by the bootlegger before they were revealed.

The interviews probed into the types of innovations the projects were. The 35 product innovations consisted of 19 significant product improvements and the remaining 16 could be considered to be incremental product improvements. Only three bootleg projects resulted in what could be considered to be radical innovations — products that were new to the company and which also included new technology. The four process innovations led to changes in production processes and resulted in improved quality, reduced manufacturing lead times, and production cost improvements.

2.4.3. Reasons for bootlegging

The research helped to reveal the reasons why the respondents carried out bootlegging. When interviewees discussed why they chose to use the clandestine method they gave very practical reasons (see Table 2.3).

Table 2.3. Reasons for bootlegging.

Decision maker will not understand the initial idea	29.1%
Immature idea	27.3%
Pre-research needed to be carried out	27.3%
Show feasibility or proof of concept	25.5%
Avoid psychological pressure	3.6%
Show market demand	3.6%

Table 2.3 indicates that 16 of the interviewees mentioned that a difference in the background (education and scientific experience) between them and the management (decision makers) meant that they had different perceptions and understanding of the benefits of certain solutions and technologies. The interviewees were of the opinion that the decision makers (who had the authority to fund further development) would not be able to grasp their ideas when they were in an early stage of development. They were of the view that they would not be able convince the decision makers into approving their ideas because they would not understand and comprehend the embryonic idea. The level of uncertainty is high for the decision makers if they had trouble understanding the idea. In this situation, bootlegging seems a viable option to collect enough evidence to reduce the uncertainty for the decision makers. A product development engineer commented that it was difficult to convince somebody of the merits of a concept if they don't understand the basic idea, it is easier to show a working product and then they will see the benefits.

Fourteen of the interviewees decided to bootleg because their ideas were too immature and the chances of them being seriously considered for funding were very low. So, bootlegging was a way of incubating a newly emerged ideas to the point where they have been developed enough to be approved. As one interviewee concluded, you would never get management approval for raw ideas, hence the need to go underground to develop it further.

Of the 55 interviewees, 14 said that when they presented their ideas to the decision makers, they would need to show some form of proof of concept or demonstrate its feasibility and so consequently they would carry out bootlegging. This reason appeared to be more common among those individuals who focused on product development as opposed to basic research.

Some of the respondents were of the view that they needed to carry out pre-research activities. In their situation, they did not necessarily need to show proof of concept or feasibility of the idea but because there was technical uncertainty about their innovation they felt that the probability of getting official approval was low. Consequently, they would go underground to work on the idea and reduce any technical uncertainty by undertaking pre-research activities. By going underground, they would have time to identify the ways of solving the main problems with their idea. As one respondent explained, during the interview, they had come up with a great innovation, however, the problem was how to manufacture it. The interviewee had identified two possible solutions but were not sure which would work and so needed time to determine which was the best route to adopt. Pearson (1997) refers to this as uncertainty about the means, which he considers to be one of the elements that causes bootlegging.

Some researchers have suggested that bootlegging is prompted by disagreement with the management (Pearson, 1997) or rejection by the management (Knight, 1967; Dickson *et al.*, 1991). The findings from this research project suggest that disagreement or rejection was not a reason for bootlegging nor was attempting to prove them wrong for rejecting the idea. It is interesting to observe that no interviewee said that they had pursued a bootlegging project just to prove management wrong.

2.4.4. Motivation

An analysis of the interview data suggested that the primary motive behind bootlegging was to benefit the organization. The respondents were very experienced scientists and engineers. And when they saw an opportunity, they would try to make the best use of it for their colleagues and the company. As one interviewee commented, when they come up with an innovation they always consider what benefit it will be for the colleagues and the company before they start exploring it in more detail.

The respondents did not initially mention any personal benefits they may gain as a result of bootlegging. However, this issue was probed further during the interview and this revealed some interesting personal benefits that they said they had gained from the clandestine activity.

The large proportion of the interviewees concentrated on the intangible benefits, which included enhanced reputation and personal satisfaction

Table 2.4. Motivation for bootlegging.

Learning and experience	29.1%
Satisfaction from innovation	29.1%
Respect and recognition	27.3%
Patent applications	10.9%
Research papers	10.9%
Personal financial benefit	9.1%

(see Table 2.4). A number of the respondents (27.3%) indicated that one of the benefits of bootlegging is the recognition and reputation that is gained when they succeeded in delivering an innovation they had clandestinely developed. This then resulted in gaining the trust of management and greater authority in the eyes of the colleagues.

Another intangible benefit was the chance to learn new things and gain experience. Bootlegging projects often require experimentation and the methods the bootlegger may not necessary employ as part of working on official projects. So, working on clandestine projects provided the interviewees with unique learning and opportunities. As one of the respondents (researcher) commented, they learned a lot of new things from carrying out bootlegging and that the activity was always a learning experience for this individual. The final benefit that the interviewees gained from bootlegging was the satisfaction that they were developing an innovation that functioned as they intended and benefited the organization.

During the interview, only a small proportion of the respondents mentioned tangible benefits as a motivating factor. In general, the tangible benefits of bootlegging were only pointed out by 13 of the interviewees. Only five of the interviewees benefited financially from the result of their bootlegging activities. While six respondents mentioned that they would get a patent application, six others mentioned they would be able to publish research papers based on their innovation.

2.4.5. The use of time to bootleg

Given the clandestine nature of bootlegging, there were questions about the use of time. When do employees work on their bootleg projects? If they spend their working hours on bootleg projects, how do they manage their time given they have to work on several company projects? How long do bootleg projects last underground?

In order to try to answer these questions, the researcher investigated how the bootlegger operated on a daily basis: the different tasks they need to do, how loosely their time is structured, among other tasks. The first question to be answered is whether bootleggers use their working time to bootleg or do they use their own time. The interviews indicated that most worked on clandestine projects during the work hours. Of the 55 interviewees, 54 admitted that they worked on their bootleg projects during the normal working hours (e.g., 8 am to 5 pm) and they would also work outside of the normal working hours at the office (extra hours in the office). The majority of the respondents mixed their bootleg projects with their official work. They would often bootleg in normal working hours and then spend the extra hours (after 5 pm) to catch up on their official work. They would also spend extra hours and weekends at their office working on bootleg projects while pretending to be working on official projects.

It is interesting to note that only one interviewee denied using the organization's time for the bootleg work. This individual claimed that they only worked on their clandestine projects at home or while commuting to work. They mainly carried out software development and so this allowed them to do the clandestine work away from the office.

The interviews revealed that in addition to their primary work of research and development activities, the interviewees were normally required to perform different tasks such as writing reports, attending meetings, and giving papers and presentations. Thus, they needed to prioritize their time to be able to work on different projects concurrently and to complete additional tasks. This gave them a great opportunity to bootleg during working hours by mixing their official work with their clandestine projects and thereby hide them from management.

Those individuals whose work involves software development, algorithm development, computer coding, and work that could be done on a simple computer were not restricted to only working in the office. They are able to work on their bootleg projects while they are away from the workplace. This is in line with Pearson's (1997) theory that the opportunity for bootlegging varies from one industry to another. Those individuals whose work is concerned with materials and hardware are not able to pursue their bootleg projects away from their working environment. Thus, their work on clandestine project will be limited to work hours and the extra hours they can spend at work.

In general, since all interviewees were experienced employees who were involved in complicated technological research and development, they were in charge of managing and prioritizing their time, unless there was an emergency to be addressed or a deadline coming up. Being in charge of their own time, working on more than one project and having a number of other duties gave the interviewees a little freedom and flexibility they require to work on their own ideas and projects without anyone else noticing. Bearing in mind that their work is highly specialized, it is not easy for other people in the organization — not even their direct manager — to determine whether interviewees are working on an official project or something else. Thus, they can create the pretense that they are working on official projects while in fact they are working on their bootleg projects. Even when the interviewees were under pressure to meet a deadline, bootlegging was not completely impossible and some revealed that they could still find the time to work on their ideas.

However, the interviewees were of the opinion that bootlegging activities must not be allowed to get in the way of official projects as this can lead to difficulties with their manager. This could result in being monitored more and a reduction in freedom to manage their time as they consider appropriate.

In large organizations, time is not usually precisely budgeted, particularly for those in research and technology development. Those interviewees who work in large organizations therefore have more freedom to bootleg, especially if they are senior staff or middle managers. In organizations with relatively modest R&D units, time is often budgeted to specific projects. This is particularly true in product development units, especially for relatively less experienced staff. In such circumstances, bootleggers would carry out their bootleg projects by finding an official project to charge their bootleg time against.

A few interviewees stated that they had no spare time since all their time was budget to specific projects but were able to create some time for themselves to pursue their clandestine projects by charging their bootlegging time to official projects.

The interviews revealed that some respondents took advantage of the slack time between the end of one project and the beginning of the next to carry out their clandestine activities. Once one project had been completed, they are normally able to find some slack time to bootleg until the next project deadline was due. This may be a few days or a week and provided a perfect opportunity for bootlegging.

2.4.6. Time spent working on a bootleg project

The interview covered how long the respondents spent working on a clandestine project. Table 2.5 shows the length of time they had spent on a recently completed project. The majority of bootleg projects lasted between one and nine months underground. On average, bootleg projects last over five months and interviewees spend 26% of their time on bootleg projects. There were five exceptions for some projects that took between one and two years.

The data analysis suggested that the average number of months spent on clandestine projects by senior staff and middle managers was higher than the time taken by those in more junior roles. The senior staff had more responsibilities and greater demands on their time and therefore it made it more difficult for them to find enough time to work on clandestine projects.

2.4.7. Use of resources

Figure 2.2 shows the various sources from which the interviewees obtained their resources. Of the 55 interviewees, 14 described working on projects that needed no resources to begin with. This was often because the initial stages of these projects were computer-based tasks such as design, visualization, developing algorithms, and writing software. However, the need for resources such as machines, test equipment, and raw materials became an issue when interviewees need resources to pursue their bootleg projects. The main source, as mentioned by 33 interviewees, is the slack

Table 2.5. Time spent working on bootleg project.

1 to 3 months	38.2%
4 to 6 months	38.2%
7 to 9 months	12.7%
10 to 12 months	5.4%
More than 12 months	5.4%
Total	100.0%

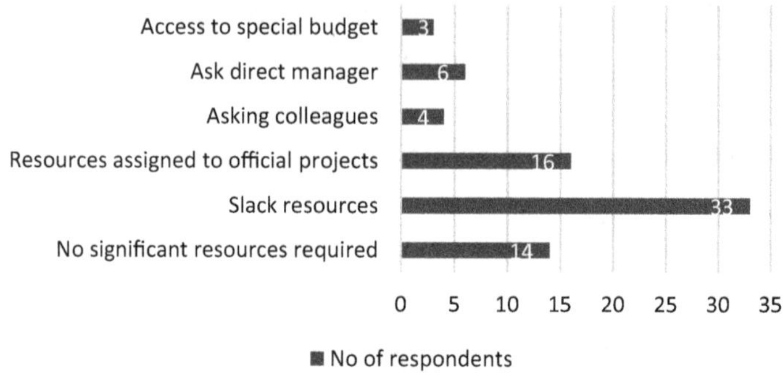

Fig. 2.2. Use of various types of resources.

resources available in their laboratory and work environment. The slack resources refer to raw material, machinery, and equipment that already exists in their lab. These resources are not tied to any special project.

The second most important source that is used by the interviewees to gather required resources for their bootleg projects are the resources that are assigned to official projects. Around 16 interviewees admitted that they used resources assigned to official resources or have charged their bootleg projects' costs to official projects. They often mix their bootleg projects with official projects in order to use resources assigned to official projects.

A further way of acquiring resources is to approach those colleagues who have access to the required resources and take them on board. However, this method was only used by four interviewees. Among the bootleggers, there was a reluctance to draw in other colleagues since it would become more difficult to keep the project secret.

2.4.8. Revealing the project

Another area that was explored in detail was the disclosure of the bootlegging project to the organization and especially to the decision maker who would provide funding and support for the full development of the innovation. The analysis of the interview data indicated that the disclosure of the bootlegging project in the majority of cases happened in two steps.

- *Step 1*: This involved the bootlegger approaching their direct manager and indicating that they had been working on an innovation, the main intention being to make them aware of the project. This move can be considered to be one of transition from true bootlegging to quasi-bootlegging.

- *Step 2*: This second step involved the bootlegger presenting their project to the decision maker to get official approval and support for further development.

Before they approached their manager, the interviewee ensured that their idea was sufficiently developed and had produced satisfactory results that could help prove that their organization would benefit from the adopting the project and developing it further.

The interviews revealed that there were a number of reasons for revealing the project to their manager. Firstly, the bootlegger wanted to maintain a good relationship with their manager and at some point, they would need to be made aware of what development activities were taking place. Secondly, the manager would be in a position to shield the bootlegger from interruptions by senior management, and thereby allow the completion of the clandestine development. By approaching the manager, the bootlegger was hoping to obtain greater freedom to be able to spend more time working on the project. Another reason for approaching their manager was to acquire more resources (machinery, test equipment) to pursue the project. Also, an important reason for revealing the project to their direct manager is because they have an important role to play in supporting the project when it was finally revealed to the decision makers. The manager will help with the presentation to the decision maker, and they can help prepare the ground before the presentation so the audience is more receptive to the idea.

The bootlegger approaching their manager did not mark the end of their clandestine activity since they were rarely the key decision makers. Most individuals would continue to work underground in a quasi-bootlegging environment until they are ready to make the final step and reveal the project to the decision makers who can approve further development.

The analysis of the interviews revealed the elements that caused the interviewees to inform their projects to the organization and more importantly to the decision maker was in order for them to become official projects. The interviews indicate that the fundamental reason for going underground is to reduce the uncertainty of an idea and so improve the chances of it getting official approval for further development. Therefore, once the bootlegger is sure they are likely to get official approval, then there is no reason to continue working underground. Another reason is that often a project reaches a natural point where no further progress can be made with its development unless the project becomes official and has the support of the senior management.

The interviews revealed the fact that the bootlegger also takes into consideration when would be a good time to reveal their work. They usually wait for the right moment to present their project. The right moment could be before budgets are being agreed upon or when the CEO is visiting the department. Each project decision has its own circumstance but what is apparent is that bootlegger does take time to think about the events that are happening around them and when would be a beneficial time to reveal the project.

2.5. Discussion

The research described in this chapter examined the nature of bootlegging in high-technology organizations. A large group of employees who were serial bootleggers were interviewed in depth about various aspects of their clandestine activities. The interviews explored the type of innovations that resulted from the respondents' bootlegging activities. The majority of the clandestine projects that had been completed by the respondents had resulted in product innovation, but only a small proportion of these were considered to be radical product innovations. The underground activity also produced a small number of process innovations. The research results indicate that bootlegging produces an outcome that is beneficial to the organization, although it does not produce as much radical innovation as some researchers have suggested.

The research examined the reason behind why the employees carried out this underground activity. The main reasons provided ranged from having to carry out preparatory work on the idea all the way through to doing work to be able to show proof of concept. The fundamental reason that the interviewees carried out bootlegging was to reduce the uncertainty (mainly technical rather than market) surrounding their ideas and thereby improve the chances of it securing management approval for further development. The findings of the research are in line with Augsdorfer's research (1996, 2005), which demonstrated that employees bootlegged in order to prepare their ideas for entry into the formal development process. Moreover, the interview transcripts did not indicate that bootlegging was prompted by the rejection of the employee's idea by management, as suggested by Knight (1967) and Dickson *et al.* (1991) in their work.

The research also examined the forces that motivation employees to bootleg. The interview data suggested that the primary motivation for the activity appeared to be pursuing work that would benefit the organization. An important secondary motivation was intangible benefits, such as respect, recognition, learning, and personal satisfaction from successful innovation. Financial benefits such as monetary rewards, bonuses, or patent incentives were found to be minor motivators. The findings suggest that bootleggers are focused on developing ideas that meet organizational goals, rather than on their own personal objectives. This suggests that bootlegging is more likely to support an organization's overall strategy than to undermine it.

The research revealed that the disclosure of the clandestine projects by the bootleggers did not happen in one easy step; on the contrary, it tended to consist of two steps. The employee would first approach their direct manager and reveal the idea to them and then present their bootleg project to the decision maker. The research suggests that the process of revealing the project to the organization is not a simple one and it takes times and preparation.

Managers typically have concerns about the impact of bootlegging, in particular with regard to the impact on cost and time management. Our research suggests that these concerns may be overstated. The interview data suggests that the clandestine work involved mainly the preliminary development of an idea — they were only working on demonstrating the feasibility of their concept rather than producing a fully working prototype. This would suggest that the cost would be relatively low. With respect to time management, the interviews suggest that the respondents had an awareness of the need to manage their time sensibly, both to preserve the secrecy of their clandestine projects and to avoid underperforming on their official work. Hence, they mixed bootleg work with official project work with official projects taking priority.

The research suggests that allowing bootlegging can deliver benefits to the organization; however, it is important for managers to be conscious of possible drawbacks. Too many bootlegging projects taking place can create distraction, dilute the organization's strategic focus, and siphon resources away from official projects. Not every employee be relied on to bootleg productively; not everyone is capable of producing and developing innovative ideas independently. Also, some individuals may work on ideas that are no longer the main focus of the firm, wasting time and resources developing an idea that is ultimately likely to be rejected.

The challenge for management is how to promote bootlegging behavior in a way that delivers the benefits but without losing the focus and control of R&D. The following principles may help to achieve a productive approach to bootlegging:

- To stop employees going underground with an idea, managers should avoid dismissing it when it is first presented. Management should set up a clear process for assessing bottom-up ideas, and as part of this they need to provide clear and consistent feedback about the potential for such ideas to win official approval for further development. Having a transparent approach to assessing ideas will ensure that individuals do not carry out bootlegging working on an idea unlikely to win approval. In addition, substantive feedback should be provided; this will help employees improve their ideas.
- The research suggested that bootleggers were motivated more by recognition and respect than by the possible financial reward. So, to encourage productive bootlegging managers should create an environment that respects and rewards innovation efforts. Those employees who willingly go beyond their official responsibilities to benefit the organization should be formally acknowledged to show that their efforts are appreciated. This signals that the company favors innovation among its employees even if sometimes this activity is a failure.
- The research identified that bootleggers typically reveal their projects to managers in order to get support for further development of their ideas. Therefore, managers should be given access to a small amount of money specifically allocated to support such projects. Having access to funding will allow bootleggers to swiftly refine their ideas, speeding development and bringing the idea out into the open more quickly.
- The interviewees reported struggling to balance their underground work with their official work. If the organization is to benefit from bootlegging,

employees must have time for this activity. So, managers should avoid monitoring employee activities too closely and also allow them to have some slack time this will give the bootleggers an opportunity to work on their unofficial projects (and reduce the psychological pressure to produce results quickly).

The research only investigated the activities of bootleggers in high-technology companies. Further research in other sectors such as engineering is warranted. This will help to determine if the findings from this study apply in other industrial sectors. Further research should be carried out involving a larger sample. This would allow the investigation of some issues that the current study only touched on. In particular, a larger number of interviews would allow for the investigation into the nature of clandestine projects pursued by bootleggers with different positions (and responsibilities) in the organization, for example, a comparison of engineers and managers.

2.6. Conclusion

It is known that bootlegging provides an important complement to officially approved innovation activities. Through allowing employees to break free of the constraints of the innovation system, this clandestine activity can nurture unexpected innovations. Therefore, companies need to find a balance between allowing some bootlegging to take place and also maintain control over R&D activities. If they are able to strike that balance, then bootlegging can become a valuable activity that will produce important innovations.

References

Abetti, P. A. (1997). Underground innovation in Japan: The development of Toshiba's word processor and laptop computer. *Creativity and Innovation Management*, **6**(3): 127–139.

Abetti, P. A. (1999a). The birth and growth of the Japanese language word processor: Internal venturing in Toshiba corporation. *International Journal of Technology Management*, **18**(1–2): 114–132.

Abetti, P. A. (1999b). Underground innovation in USA, Europe, and Japan. In *Portland International Conference on Management of Engineering and Technology, July 1999, Portland, OR, USA*, (1): 91. Available from: https://

www.picmet.org/conferences/1999/picmet99.pdf page 65, session WB-04.3 on Wednesday, July 28, 1999.

Abetti, P. A. (2004). Informal corporate entrepreneurship: Implications from the failure of the concord alloy foundry and the success of the Toshiba laptop. *Entrepreneurship and Innovation Management*, **4**(6): 529–545.

Amabile, T. M. and Khaire, M. (2008). Creativity and the role of the leader. *Harvard Business Review*, **86**(10): 100–109.

Andersson, H. and Berggren, C. (2007). Individual inventors in the R&D factory. *Creativity and Innovation Management*, **16**(4): 437–446.

Aram, J. (1973). Innovation via the R&D underground. *Research Management* **16**(November): 24–26.

Augsdorfer, P. (1994). The manager as pirate: An inspection of the gentle art of bootlegging. *Creativity and Innovation Management*, **3**(2): 91–95.

Augsdorfer, P. (1996) *Forbidden Fruit: An Analysis of Bootlegging, Uncertainty, and Learning in Corporate R&D*. Aldershot: Avebury.

Augsdorfer, P. (2005). Bootlegging and path dependency. *Research Policy*, **34**(1): 1–11.

Augsdorfer, P. (2008). Managing the unmanageable. *Research-Technology Management*, **51**(4): 41–47.

Bell, E., Bryman, A. and Harley, B. (2018) *Business Research Methods*. Oxford: Oxford University Press.

Berends, H., Vanhaverbeke, W. and Kirschbaum, R. (2007). Knowledge management challenges in new business development: Case study observations. *Journal of Engineering and Technology Management*, **24**(4): 314–328.

Bessant, J. R. and Tidd, J. (2007) *Innovation and Entrepreneurship*. Hoboken: John Wiley and Sons.

Birkinshaw, J. and Gibson, C. (2004). Building ambidexterity into an organization. MIT *Sloan Management Review*, **45**(4): 47–55.

Boeddrich, H. (2004). Ideas in the workplace: A new approach towards organizing the fuzzy front end of the innovation process. *Creativity and Innovation Management*, **13**(4): 274–285.

Brannen, J. (1988). The study of sensitive subjects. *Sociological Review*, **36**(3): 552–563.

Burgelman, R. A. (1983). A process model of internal corporate venturing in the diversified major firm. *Administrative Science Quarterly*, 223–244.

Cooper, R. G. (1990). Stage gate system: A new tool for managing new products. *Business Horizons*, **33**(3): 44–53.

Cyert, R. M. and March, J. G. (1992). *A Behavioral Theory of the Firm* (pp.1–53).

Debackere, K., Clarysse, B., Wijnberg, N. M. and Rappa, M. A. (1994). Science and industry: A theory of networks and paradigms. *Technology Analysis & Strategic Management,* **6**(1): 21–38.

Dickson, K., Smith, H. L. and Smith, S. L. (1991). Bridge over troubled waters? Problems and opportunities in interfirm research collaboration. *Technology Analysis & Strategic Management,* **3**(2): 143–155.

Faugier, J. and Sargeant, M. (1997). Sampling hard to reach populations. *Journal of Advanced Nursing*, **26**(4):790–797.

Gaynor, G. H. (2002) *Innovation by Design: What It Takes to Keep Your Company on the Cutting Edge*. New York: AMACOM.

Gibson, C. and Birkinshaw, J. (2004). The antecedents, consequences, and mediating role of organizational ambidexterity. *Academy of Management Journal*, **47**(2): 209–226.

Globocnik, D. and Salomo, S. (2015). Do formal management practices impact the emergence of bootlegging behavior? *Journal of Product Innovation Management*, **32**(4): 505–521.

Grantham, A. and Readman, J. (2005). Comparing quality and business improvement methodologies for collaborative working in the product development process of SMEs. In *Proceedings of the 5th International CINet Conference* (pp. 249–260).

Grimpe, C. (2006). Making use of the unused: Shelf warmer technologies in research and development. *Technovation*, **26**(7): 770–774.

Hellström, T. and Malmquist, U. (2000). Networked innovation: Developing the Axe110 "Mini-Exchange" at Ericsson. *European Journal of Innovation Management*, **3**(4): 181–189.

Iyer, B. and Davenport, T. H. (2008). Reverse engineering Google's innovation machine. *Harvard Business Review*, **86**(4): 58–68.

Kannan-Narasimhan, R. (2014). Organizational ingenuity in nascent innovations: Gaining resources and legitimacy through unconventional actions. *Organization Studies*, **35**(4); 483–509.

Kanter, R. M. (2000). When a thousand flowers bloom: Structural, collective, and social conditions for innovation in organization. In Swedberg, R. (Ed.), *Entrepreneurship: The Social Science View* (pp. 167–211). Oxford: Oxford University Press.

King, N. (2004). Essential guide to qualitative methods in organizational research. In Cassell, C. and Symins, G. (Eds.), *Essential Guide to Qualitative Methods in Organizational Research* (pp. 256–270). London: Sage Publications.

Kline, J. and Rosenberg N. (1986). An overview of innovation. In Landau, R. and Rosenberg, N. (Eds.), *The Positive Sum Strategy: Harnessing Technology for Economic Growth* (pp. 275–305). Washington, D.C: National Academy Press.

Knight, K. (1967). A descriptive model of the intra-firm innovation process. *The Journal of Business*, **40**(4): 478–496.

Koch, R. and Leitner, K. H. (2008). The dynamics and functions of self-organization in the fuzzy front end: Empirical evidence from the Austrian semiconductor industry. *Creativity and Innovation Management*, **17**(3): 216–226.

Krogh, L. C., Prager, J. H., Sorensen, D. P. and Tomlinson, J. D. (1988). How 3M evaluates its R&D programs. *Research-Technology Management*, **31**(6): 10–14.

Lee, R. (1993). *Doing Research on Sensitive Topics*. London: Sage Publications Ltd.

Lee, R. and Renzetti C. (1990). The problems of researching sensitive topics: An overview and introduction. *American Behavioral Scientist*, **33**(5): 510–528.

Ma, H. (2002). Competitive advantage: What's luck got to do with it? *Management Decision,* **40**(6): 525–536.

Masoudnia, Y. and Szwejczewski, M. (2012). Bootlegging in the R&D departments of high-technology firms. *Research Technology Management*, **55**(5): 35–43.

McCracken, G. (1988). *The Long Interview*. Newbury Park, CA: Sage.

McPhee, N. and Terry, R. (2007). *The Hidden Art of Interviewing People*. Chichester: John Wiley & Sons.

Nijhof, A., Krabbendam, K. and Looise, J. C. (2002). Innovation through exemptions: Building upon the existing creativity of employees. *Technovation*, **22**(11): 675–683.

Nohria, N. and Gulati, R. (1996). Is slack good or bad for innovation? *Academy of Management Journal*, **39**(5): 1245–1264.

Pace, S. (1992). *Lockheed Skunk Works*. Osceola, WI: Motorbooks International.

Pearson, A. (1997). Innovation management – is there still a role for "Bootlegging"? *International Journal of Technology Management*, **1**(2): 191–200.

Peters, T. J. and Waterman, R. H. (1982). *In Search of Excellence: Lessons from America's Best-Run Companies*. London: Harper and Row.

Pinchot, G. (1985). *Intrapreneuring: Why You Don't Have to Leave the Corporation to Become an Entrepreneur*. New York: Harper & Row.

Polit, D.F. and Beck, C.T. (2008). *Nursing Research: Generating and Assessing Evidence for Nursing Practice*. Philadelphia: Lippincott Williams & Wilkins.

Raisch, S., Birkinshaw, J., Probst, G. and Tushman M. L. (2009). Organizational ambidexterity: Balancing exploitation and exploration for sustained performance. *Organization Science*, **20**(4): 685–695.

Rich, B. R. and Janos, L. (1994). *Skunk Works: A Personal Memoir of My Years at Lockheed*. Boston, MA: Little Brown & Company.

Richtner, A. and Ahlstrom, P. (2006). Influences on organisational slack in new product development projects. *International Journal of Innovation Management*, **10**(4): 375–406.

Roberts, E. B. (1991). The technological base of the new enterprise. *Research Policy*, **20**(4): 283–298.

Rosenau, M. D. (1988). From experience: Faster new product development. *Journal of Product Innovation Management*, **5**(2): 150–153.

Roussel, P. A. Saad, K. N. and Erickson, T. J. (1991). *Third Generation R&D: Managing the Link to Corporate Strategy*. Boston, MA: Harvard Business School Press.

Saunders, M., Lewis, P.H. and Thornhill, A.D. (2007). *Research Methods* (4th edn.). England: Pearson Education Limited.

Schneider, F. (2005). Shadow economies around the world: What do we really know? *European Journal of Political Economy*, **21**(3): 598–642.

Schneider, F. and Enste, D.H. (2000). Shadow economies: Size, causes, and consequences. *Journal of Economic Literature*, **38**(1): 77–114.

Slemrod, J. (2007). Cheating ourselves: The economics of tax evasion. *Journal of Economic Perspectives*, **21**(1): 25–48.

Stanley, B., Sieber J. and Melton G. (1987). Empirical studies of ethical issues in research: A research agenda. *American Psychologist*, **42**(7): 735–741.

Thompson, V. A. (1969). *Bureaucracy and Innovation*. Alabama: University of Alabama Press.

Trott, P. (1998). *Innovation Management and New Product Development*. London: Financial Times Pitman.

https://doi.org/10.1142/9781800612266_0004

Chapter 3

Bootlegging in a Technology-Driven Organization: Process, Challenges, and Opportunities*

Anika Stephan-Korus
School of Management Fribourg, Fribourg, Switzerland
anika.stephan@hefr.ch

Abstract

This chapter focuses on three aspects of the bootlegging process summarizing our prior research: First, we compare bootlegging processes to regular processes and explore how the characteristics, which often represent challenges, differ between both. Second, building on the specific and challenging characteristics of bootlegging processes, we lay out what specific support measures are needed. Third, we suggest how selected support measures could be systematically implemented organization-wide via a system of corporate crowdfunding. Before summarizing our findings and propositions in these three areas, we describe the methods by which they have been developed.

3.1. Introduction

While innovations are widely taken for granted as important sources of competitive advantage (Crossan and Apaydin, 2010; Tushman and O'Reilly, 1996), organizational members differ as to how open and supportive they are when innovations are radical: While managers may hesitate or often outright refuse radical innovation ideas (Mainemelis, 2010; Ahuja and Lampert, 2001; March, 1991), their subordinate members

*This chapter summarizes parts of the author's cumulative dissertation that were largely not yet presented elsewhere.

may often continue believing in them. These members may then choose to develop their radical innovative ideas secretly, shielded from management to avoid official development "hurdles" until tangible results can be shown (Criscuolo *et al.*, 2014). First, Schon in 1963 mentioned about "smuggled R&D projects" in companies followed by Knight in 1967. Knight described this phenomenon as "bootlegging" as follows: "in some instances the innovator may be able to implement a new idea by keeping the development under cover from the disapproving power in the organization until it is introduced. At that time, it may be impossible for the organization to reverse itself" (Knight, 1967: 493). More recently, Criscuolo and colleagues (2014) defined bootlegging as "the process by which individuals take the initiative to work on ideas that have no formal organizational support and are often hidden from the sight of senior management but are undertaken with the aim of producing innovations that will benefit the company" (Criscuolo *et al.*, 2014: 1288). If bootlegging generally represents a form of deviance from legitimate behavior in organizations (Mainemelis, 2010; Merton, 1968), bootlegging projects have often proven highly profitable for the organization. For example, the BMW Series 3 touring vehicle (Augsdorfer, 2008) and the Agilent Technologies 1200 series chemical test equipment (Masoudnia and Szwejczewski, 2012) found their way to market success only after unapproved secret development, that is, bootlegging.

Extant research on bootlegging is scarce and has particularly focused on reasons and motivations to start a bootlegging project (e.g., Masoudnia and Szwejczewski, 2012, see Appendix 1), on managerial regulations to prevent bootlegging (Criscuolo *et al.*, 2014), on process steps during surfacing (e.g., Masoudnia and Szwejczewski, 2012), and the individual-level attributes of bootleggers (Alexy *et al.*, 2016; Criscuolo *et al.*, 2014) or status considerations (Alexy *et al.*, 2015). While prior research has thus provided initial descriptions of the phenomenon and suggested some of its antecedents, an understanding of the *process* of bootlegging as a project is largely missing.

This chapter focuses on three aspects of the bootlegging process summarizing our prior research: First, we *compare bootlegging processes to regular processes* and explore how the characteristics, which often represent challenges, differ between both. Second, building on the specific and challenging characteristics of bootlegging processes, we lay out what *specific support measures* are needed. Third, we suggest how selected support measures could be systematically implemented organization-wide via a *system of corporate crowdfunding*. Before summarizing our findings and propositions in these three areas, we describe the methods by which they have been developed.

3.1.1. Participative budgeting and crowdfunding

In an organization, the decision-making process is normally defined in a structured process with internal process descriptions and steps that reduce uncertainty and the risk of failure and allow the organization to maintain control of decisions and resources. These process steps can also include decisions regarding project budgeting. Generally, in an organization, the budgeting procedure is decided in one-year intervals (the annual budget), although budgeting can be organized over a shorter period (Ziegenbein, 2001; Küpper *et al.*, 2013; Horváth, 2011). These budgeting and decision-making processes are hierarchically organized to maintain budgetary control (Otley, 1999). Therefore, "budgeting has traditionally been a central plank of most organizations' control mechanisms, as it is one of the few techniques capable of integrating the whole gamut of organizational activity into a single coherent summary" (Otley, 1999: 370). Additionally, the budgeting process in an established organization typically has a central coordinating mechanism function, the existence of which does have a justification; however, certain business areas must become more flexible (Otley, 1999) by improving the R&D process to be more readily for market launches and for competitive advantage. Therefore, the term "participative budgeting" (PB) is noted by Shields and Shields (1998) as a process in which managers or employees are involved in the internal budgeting process to be more flexible. This practice is also termed "participatory budgeting" and belongs to the so-called bottom-up budgeting processes (Shields and Shields, 1998). In budgeting and management research, the questions of how budgeting influences employee motivation, decisions, and organizational performance are still being investigated (Covaleski *et al.*, 2007; Sandalgaard *et al.*, 2001). The budget also has motivational aspects for the employees (Küpper *et al.*, 2013) as it helps R&D projects attain the desired degree of maturity for an intra-organizational transfer and allowing the project to be more seriously considered. Sandalgaard and colleagues (2001) found that "budget participation interacts with motivation profile to affect budget goal commitment which implies that the effect of this increased influence is largest for subordinate managers that are motivated by having influence (i.e., high need for power)" (Sandalgaard *et al.*, 2001: 17). In addition, a fixed amount of money can provide employees some degree of participation in decision-making and project autonomy (Gemünden *et al.*, 2005). Hence, the engagement of employees in an organization's R&D planning and budget processes can help to achieve a project's goals and contribute to organizational performance.

As an example of engagement in the budget process, be it external or internal, the phenomenon of crowdfunding has become a popular subject, for both, participants and academic researchers over the past decade. Crowdfunding is rooted in the concept of crowdsourcing and microfinance (Morduch, 1999), which refers to using the crowd to obtain ideas, feedbacks, and solutions to develop corporate activities (Bayus, 2013; Howe, 2008). Mollick (2014: 2) found a definition, which focus more entrepreneurial aspect, as following quote shows: "Crowdfunding refers to the efforts by entrepreneurial individuals and groups — cultural, social, and for-profit — to fund their ventures by drawing on relatively small contributions from a relatively large number of individuals using the internet, without standard financial intermediaries." Therefore, crowdfunding obtains a platform to fund projects, ideas, and personal tasks. In recent years, funding and collecting money from the crowd to invest in novel ideas in the startup scene, as well as for private projects and foundations, has become increasingly popular. Crowdfunding is inspired by concepts such as microfinance, in which a large number of individuals is represented by the crowd as opposed to specialized investors (Mollick, 2014). Mollick (2014) has stated that the most critical resource for new ventures is financing, but many difficulties are often faced securing funding. To overcome these difficulties and barriers and to start new ventures or projects, ambitious persons have used internet-based platforms as a new source of financing. The so-called crowdfunding approach provides new founders and private persons with a means with which to request the crowd to fund their projects and ideas (Belleflamme *et al.*, 2014). By presenting projects on a platform before their final release and the end of funding, other developers can also write applications for these products, which helps to improve the idea or product and thereby increase a project's competitive advantage before it is even released to the consumers (Belleflamme *et al.*, 2014; Mollick, 2014). Thus, tendencies for products, services, and new venture creations can be mapped. Crowdfunding therefore helps entrepreneurs to adopt new approaches to undertaking entrepreneurial projects and managing ventures, which in turn leads to new forms of business development in which the "ordinary" public is more closely involved in these firms, either as active consumers or, investors, or both (Belleflamme *et al.*, 2014). Both the entrepreneurs and the public crowd are thus involved in the budgeting process.

Nevertheless, the concept of crowdfunding has already found its way into an organizational context. In early 2013, IBM was one of the first organizations to implement CCF with the internal name "iFundIT" (Muller *et al.*, 2013b). Muller and colleagues (2013b) and Feldmann and colleagues (2013, 2014) have published results from IBM studies on this approach, which appears to be promising for the internal use of crowdfunding. Feldmann and colleagues (2014) mentioned that this mechanism can improve the management of large idea portfolios, with the use of collective intelligence for decisions.

However, as a relatively young research field, the concept of CCF is still at its infancy with regard to empirical evidence and practical implementation. Further empirical research and theoretical assumption are currently missing, especially about the necessities for crowd supporting measures for those creative employees, who generally make use of "gray zones" to develop innovative projects. Therefore, this research draws on a qualitative and longitudinal data collection within a technology-driven to answer the previous research question and to present empirical and theoretical assumptions.

3.1.2. Methods

We studied bootlegging processes in a leading technology-driven organization in Germany[1] as an embedded case study (Eisenhardt and Graebner, 2007). The chosen organization was particularly suitable to study bootlegging projects for three reasons. Firstly, cases of bootlegging have been known as "U-Boot Projekte"[2] for many decades within this organization.

---

[1]The organization is not named due to of confidential reasons. The name XY is used in the chapter, for example, if the organization was named in the quotations.

[2](See Augsdorfer, 2005). Other names for bootlegging exist, which include firm-specific ones: Friday afternoon work, work behind the fume cupboard, freelance work, under-the-counter work, under-the-table work, pet-project, discretionary research, intrapreneurship,

While this bottom-up approach is sometimes practiced by members, it is not official allowed or desired by management. To the contrary, management actively tries to prevent it, because bootleggers normally make use of resources and staff capacity that were earmarked for other projects. Secondly, in the organization under study, a high pressure for new, innovative ideas by senior management as well as the R&D development department had raised the probability to find active bootlegging projects. Thirdly, a formal stage-gate innovation process (Cooper, 1990) had been practiced for many years and thus provided a well-established "baseline" for the comparison between bootlegging and regular projects.

The formal stage-gate process for regular innovation projects aims at assisting innovative employees in their daily work and facilitating the implementation of their innovative ideas. The process is structured in three phases. The first phase of a call for novel ideas and ideation takes place in April. Ideas are then suggested and prioritized from April to October. This second phase concludes with the final determination by a committee. The third phase includes financing, which is provided from the new fiscal year in January of the following year to develop the novel project further. In order to achieve successful development and launch, it is necessary to succeed across each of these mandatory process phases and their respective gates. We had privileged access to gather firsthand observations with one of the authors being fully embedded in the company over several years as a member of the corporate doctoral program. This represented a form of engaged scholarship (Van de Ven, 2005), which can be broadly understood as "a participative form of research for obtaining the different perspectives of key stakeholders (. . .) in studying complex problems" (Van de Ven, 2007: 9). Engaged scholarship helped increase background knowledge for the internal processes of this complex, multinational organization. In addition to interview data, multiple quantitative or qualitative data were collected, such as organizational field observation, project documents,

---

freewheeling, illicit research, scrounging, renegades work, work in the shadow, or underworld. The French have an imaginative term, research under the wick and the Germans, because a new product suddenly emerges as submarines breaking through the water on to the "commercial surface" call it U-Boot project, which translates as submarine project.

project briefs, presentations, and business plans in order to triangulate and validate results (Gioia *et al.*, 2013; Jick, 1979).

The following approach was used for data collection, coding, and analysis (Eisenhardt and Graebner, 2007): (i) bootlegging cases were searched and selected by using "pyramiding" (von Hippel *et al.*, 2009); (ii) interviews with the identified bootleggers were conducted; (iii) the interviews were transcribed and coded, with different rounds of coding to avoid bias, to ensure data relevance, and a steady buildup of theoretical insights, (iv) internal experts were consulted to rate the bootlegging projects along a certain number of dimensions, for example, to assess the innovativeness of the project; (v) a second round of interviews was conducted with each bootlegger; (vi) employees from different departments were surveyed in order to cross check information collected from the bootleggers; (vii) documents and material from the bootlegging projects such as presentations and prototypes were sifted; (viii) data was reviewed and coded regarding requested supporting measures and CCF were selected after informal exchanges with innovation managers and innovation process documents were reviewed; and (ix) data was collected to validate the current internal crowd platform approach and acceptance by users (Appendix 6). The following section summarizes selected findings from our analyses that have not yet been presented elsewhere or are in the process of being published.

3.2. Summary of the Findings

3.2.1. Bootlegging process versus regular projects (Stephan and Bubenzer, 2019)

To better understand bootlegging projects, we first compare them with regular internal official projects to answer the question of how bootlegging projects differ from official projects. Differences are categorized based on the *starting point*, *initial network*, *social skills*, *duration*, *final networks*, *target department*, and *project maturity* (see Appendix 2).

In an official innovation project, the employee needs to wait until one or several committees approve the project and give permission for it to *start*. Committees can be composed of members with different expectations and incentives. For instance, in the process of our case company, employees must adhere to the official project specifications and directions from both unit management and the strategy department. Projects must thus be described in project briefs in a way that meets expectations in each of the innovation committee's decision rounds. Further, the opportunity to pass certain stage-gates only presents itself once a year. In contrast, our data reveals that while there is a certain gestation period before the bootlegging decision is made, a bootlegging project can start immediately after this decision-making. Thus, bootlegging projects can start much faster than regular projects. This is not surprising but represents a critical first difference that can prove consequential in fast-paced and highly competitive markets.

Second, an *initial network,* which includes knowledgeable, known and trusted colleagues, is typically involved at the start of a bootlegging project. In most cases, this network will have been developed in prior regular or bootlegging projects from which a trustful relationship has been built over time. In contrast, official projects use a dedicated network that consists of official interface partners for the scheduled official project. These networks mostly involve colleagues from specialized departments who are directly responsible for the series production afterward or are necessary for technical expertise, booking of machinery, funding, and access to the steering committee. In regular innovation projects, trust and the strength of personal ties are much less at the center of the initial network.

Third, *social skills* also seem to play a different role in bootlegging than they do in a regular project. Social skills are here defined as the "ability to perceive interpersonal or social cues, integrate these cues with current motivations, generate responses, and enact responses that will satisfy motives and goals" (Norton and Hope, 2001: 60). The data reveals that the ability to perceive social cues is helpful during critical project phases for discussions on project problems, such as during the transfer phase and project development. Additionally, within successful bootlegging projects, aspects like using the right social cues to generate response for support and to convince others were found to be enabling factors and to generate success.

Fourth, differences were also revealed for *duration.* During regular project development, the project time is largely determined by the different phases of the innovation management process within an organization. This includes more administration time in the form of preparation for committee meetings involving all relevant stakeholders. In contrast, the duration of bootlegging projects is less constrained by the stage-gate system and is largely driven by the right time to surface. The right time to surface for radical bootlegging projects can be influenced by several factors, such as internal negotiations for new solutions or external awareness of new customer needs or similar moves by the competition.

Fifth, *final networks*, that is, networks at the moment of transferring a project to the next department differ between official projects and bootlegging (see Appendix 2). An example of a bootlegging project is described in more detailed in the appendixes (see Appendix 4) to reflect the difference from official projects. While official projects have typically been communicated within a broad network prior to transfer to seek acceptance across the organization, bootlegging projects are known within very limited and focused networks owing to the secret nature of the project. It can be dangerous to communicate bootlegging projects too broadly too early because of internal project competition, risk of rejection for immaturity, and the not-invented-here (NIH) syndrome (Katz and Allen, 1982; Antons and Piller, 2015). This occurs particularly during the transfer of bootlegging projects. Bootleggers use a less broad but more trustful and focused network during the transfer than that used in regular projects.

Sixth, the *target department* to which a regular project is transferred for scale-up can already be identified and integrated in the early development stage, and regular projects do not need to establish particular legitimacy and relationships. It is only important to identify and know the target department's requirements, particularly if the project is to be integrated into a product derivative. For bootlegging projects, however, establishing trustful relationships with a target department is key, as the bootlegging project is fraught with uncertainty and risk. These relationships must include an influential mentor or promoter who will support the transfer against potential resistance.

Seventh, *project maturity* differs. For regular projects, the degree of maturity at transfer is agreed upon from the beginning — and thus a lower maturity can be acceptable. In contrast, the maturity of bootlegging projects needs to be high at transfer in order to convince decision makers of the viability of the solution. Therefore, bootleggers typically develop their project up to a prototype or a minimum viable product (MVP).

Interestingly, relatively immature bootlegging outcomes may still be acceptable to decision makers when they are under pressure from external competitive preannouncements to launch similar products (Su and Rao, 2010).

Eighth, *resource allocation* and related efforts were found to differ. For regular projects, resources are allocated and determined by official entities such as the controlling department. Hence, when an innovation project is officially launched within the organization, it is also a prerequisite to have internal resources like manpower, machinery, and budget for external support or project location. In comparison, bootlegging projects have to find creative ways to generate and allocate resources. A typical way for bootleggers to allocate resources is to use an official project to donate some of resources for bootlegging projects. Therefore, the bootleggers use an official project number to book the bootlegging project time on an official project. Bootleggers also accelerate official projects to have more time to work on bootlegging projects. Time that could be used for other new official projects is used to be creative for the bootlegging project. Furthermore, if the bootlegging project requires additional expertise from coworkers from different departments, the bootleggers used their personal trusted networks. Employees who are serial bootleggers (with numerous different bootlegging projects in the past) normally have established a broad and trustful network within the organization, or they know experts within the organization and trust them when requesting support for a bootlegging project.

In sum, bootleggers engage with much effort in projects that bear particularly challenging characteristics and may put their careers at risk because of their passion for and identification with their projects:

> *You have to believe 100% in the idea, you have to be there with enthusiasm and be fully convinced that this is the right thing. And only then, so, only if you get up every day and think and believe in this thing, only then you bring the energy to bear against all these resistances. This is of course the most important factor.* (INT 15)

If bootlegging projects *differ significantly* from regular projects in multiple dimensions but can be highly valuable to the organization and very important to the bootleggers' passion and motivation, how can an organization create an institutional framework that supports bootlegging projects? We asked bootleggers which supporting measures they would wish for and summarize their insights in the next section.

3.2.2. Bootlegging process and support measures

This section focuses on identifying the support measures that bootleggers themselves request to improve their working situation and to produce successful results (see Appendix 5). Some organizations offer certain, often minimal, support to projects outside the regular task domain, such as Google's 20% slack time (Walker, 2011). However, organizations have developed and implemented only a few systems and tools to support bootlegging indirectly (Gundling and Porras, 2000; Steiber and Alänge, 2013; Augsdorfer, 2008). From our data, we identified five aggregate dimensions of requested support measures (see Appendix 5): (i) new regulation of financial support; (ii) secured free working space and time; (iii) process improvement; (iv) evaluation of external options; and (v) innovation culture improvement.

First, financial support (or an absence thereof) was an important issue to interviewees. As mentioned above, radical projects often fail to receive the necessary budget from dedicated "innovation pots"[3] because they lack approval for further official development. Support from alternative "innovation pots," a split of the budget, or a prioritization process for radical and disruptive ideas were mentioned as currently missing. The dimension *(i) new regulation of financial support* could thus be conceived.

Second, in the organization under study, employees often used official working hours or leisure time to develop bootlegging projects because they were fascinated by the project idea and wanted to innovate for the benefit of the organization. Hence, the dimension *(ii) secured free working space and time* is currently lacking, making it difficult to develop bootlegging ideas.

Third, it was observed that the existing innovation process limits rapid idea development, and innovators indicated their expectations for improving this innovation process. These requests were aggregated as the *(iii) process improvement* dimension.

[3]Internal proposed budget share for innovative projects.

Fourth, interviewees requested more open innovation initiatives within the organization (Enkel, Gassmann and Chesbrough, 2009) in the sense of *(iv) evaluation of external options*. Interview partners mentioned that implementing more open innovation approaches could be helpful for receiving feedback at an early stage from externals. Examples of these initiatives include customer workshops, supplier technology days, and co-creation of innovative projects with startups. These different initiatives to evaluate external options can be supportive and contribute to (a) increase technology know-how within the organization; (b) gather customer feedback from the beginning as market voice; (c) reduce internal human resource costs; and (d) decrease the development time for a product, service, or process to reach the market.

Fifth, the dimension *(v) innovation culture improvement* was aggregated from our data. A pro-innovation climate was seen as important for adopting new knowledge and behavior according to new customer expectations and external events, especially within branches and organizations that have been established for a long time and focus on the same processes and steps. Establishing different transformation workshops within the organization could be helpful, as could open discussion rounds about new technologies and testing within projects apart from official pathways. Additionally, organizations should think about a more open culture regarding failure and reduce the rejection of novel, more disruptive ideas. Establishing a culture of open trial-and-error can signal employees to try more, which can also be supportive for organization-level innovation, as mentioned in the literature (Jung *et al.*, 2008; Patterson *et al.*, 2005).

In sum, the analyses revealed high demand for changing current processes in order to encourage innovation at a faster rate within the organizations. The requested support measures would affect internal processes or programs that already exist. None of the interviewees refused to give an answer, and most of them mentioned additional ideas to solve the current situations and challenges they were facing or had faced in the past. Hence, the results presented here provide a foundation for further in-depth analysis, as well as offering suggestions for dedicated and pragmatic support systems to enhance financial resources, provide flexible time to focus on innovative ideas, open the innovation process, renew innovation and culture processes, and allow bootlegging projects to be official innovation projects in their own right. These components could encourage organizational innovativeness.

While various supporting measures were requested, the three most requested, and thus potentially most promising, dimensions were *(i) new regulation of financial support*; *(iii) process improvement*; and *(v) innovation culture improvement*. As a first step toward addressing these requests and providing a concrete solution for enabling bootlegging-type innovation projects, we subsequently explore the concept of corporate crowdfunding (CCF). We also discuss how a pilot study of CCF was received by employees in terms of providing more degrees of participation in decision-making and innovation project autonomy (Gemünden *et al.*, 2005) to support successful intra-organizational project transfer and enhance the innovation culture by using a collaborative approach to allocate more resources to radical ideas.

3.2.3. Bootlegging process and corporate crowdfunding

The promising concept of CCF, also known as enterprise crowdfunding or internal crowdfunding implemented in organization (Feldmann *et al.*, 2014). As a new way of funding projects internally this approach can perform with a separate "innovation pot" for project funding. It is a type of PB process, for the funding of novel ideas and project which are selected by an internal crowd (Mollick, 2014).

As a new way of financing internally with the voice of the internal employee crowd, we thus propose CCF as a financial support measure for bootleggers addressing the request of a *(i) new regulation of financial support*. The use of CCF for the financial support of bootleggers could be beneficial for "speeding development and bringing the idea out of the underground more quickly" (Masoudnia and Szwejczewski, 2012: 41). The benefits to introducing this form of participation may thus have a positive impact on the transferability of a bootlegging project because bootlegging can be funded at an early stage and during transfer and also be more visible for other interested employees and management. Additionally, if bootlegging projects can be encouraged with a democratically allotted budget, the acceptance of the transferable specialized department can increase because, for instance, the specialized department employees will recognize the willingness and demand from the internal crowd for such an innovation. Furthermore, the recognition of the willingness and demand from internal crowd can be an important signal for other department and reduce indications of NIH syndrome due to transparency on an internal platform. Crowd commitment in the form of a budget allocation to a novel idea can also convince management to approve further project development because they see commitment and positive voting in the form of budget allocation by experts and employees. However, it is important for the intra-organizational transfer that projects to receive a given maturity level for acceptance by the specialized departments. Thus, the implementation of CCF in organizations can be supportive for the transfer and can accelerate the development of bootlegging projects by using the budget allocation to develop projects further and to reach a presentable maturity. The budget can be used, for example, for internal resources like developer or external supports, which are helping projects in the early stage to accelerate.

CCF can thus be a useful internal supporting system in terms of allocating ideas and especially funding to vote for potential ideas via a digital platform. These factors also emphasize the idea of PB, mechanisms that can have an impact that translates into greater internal transparency in the internal innovation process, positive feelings related to job performance, and increased job satisfaction. As mentioned in literature budget participation interaction "has motivational aspects ... and its influence is largest for subordinate managers that are motivated by having influence (i.e., high need for power)" (Sandalgaard *et al.*, 2001: 17). Additionally, a fixed amount of budget providesi motivated employees some degree of participation in decision-making and project autonomy (Gemünden *et al.*, 2005).

In addition, CCF can help employees who normally struggle with face-to-face idea presentation in the internal R&D and innovation process, by presenting the idea on the internal platform with the upload of project description or self-made video to the crowd. They can also help to secure internal supporters; however, the usability of the systems must be ensured. To use CCF, a functional, intuitive, user-friendly digital platform must be established on which to upload projects with idea content in a descriptive form and to visualize the ideas that the internal crowd can then rate regarding market value and customer need. Nevertheless, by introducing CCF through PB, the internal budget approval and decision-making process can become more democratic and decentralized, thus becoming a system for democratic decision-making (Niemeyer *et al.*, 2015), which has been found to have a significant positive impact on job performance (Chong and Chong, 2002).

To summarize, it is important to understand internal possibilities and needs for creative employees to support supporting system and tools such as CCF. The benefits of such an approach are the allocation of ideas and opinions for decision-making and budget allocation on a digital platform within an organization.

3.3. Discussion and Conclusion

3.3.1. Contributions to literature

Since being named by Knight for the first time in 1967, bootlegging has received attention as a special case of project development within an organization.

We found that bootleggers must wisely choose those with whom they cooperate in order to receive the necessary resources, which must then be handled with care because of their scarcity. The study adds findings to the literature concerning project management by comparing official and unofficial projects. As stated by Masoudnia and Szwejczewski (2012: 41), "bootlegging provides an important complement to official innovation activities," and this study was conducted to demonstrate this extreme case of project management and to contribute to bootlegging literature and project management literature. To the best of our knowledge, this study is the first to compare official projects to bootlegging projects, and the data shows clear differences regarding the *starting point*, *initial network*, *social skills*, *duration*, *final networks*, *target department*, and *project maturity* of these two types of projects (see Appendices 2 and 3).

This chapter makes three contributions. First, we contribute to the literature on project management and bootlegging transfer (Criscuolo *et al.*, 2014).

We found that bootlegging projects differ from official projects in aspects such as the starting point. As an extreme case of project management, bootlegging projects must be differentiated from official projects as they use different allocation forms to gather resources. We clearly indicated which factors differentiate bootlegging from official projects. This research contributes a new perspective on how projects are established as self-organized vehicles in larger organizations. Our results also support the research by Criscuolo and colleagues, who assert the autonomy that individuals proactively perform (Criscuolo *et al.*, 2014).

Additionally, bootlegging projects must be able to attract other internal stakeholders during the transfer stage, yet due to their secretive nature, bootleggers must carefully consider with whom they communicate until the final successful transfer stage. The communication and network used are more focused in comparison with official projects. In particular, a trusted network is used because communicating too broadly can be of high risk for the following reasons: internal project competition; rejection because a radical or disruptive idea is not sufficiently developed to present to management; and NIH syndrome (Katz and Allen, 1982; Antons and Piller, 2015). NIH dynamics can also occur for official projects but are often found in the accumulated data. It is hence widespread within respective bootlegging projects since other departments or teams could fear cannibalization of an official project.

Furthermore, this research contributes to the bootlegging literature regarding the establishment of CCF as a supporting system for nascent bootleggers and as a way to reduce the parallel process in the underground for management. CCF can be valuable, therefore, in improving the current innovation process and innovation culture and in finding a new financial mechanism for more radical and disruptive ideas. In line with previous researchers, we found that substantive feedback can offer good guidance to improve ideas, which is helpful for original and creative thinkers. Therefore, a small amount of funding as an internal startup budget can be advantageous for employees to refine their ideas and accelerate the development. As a consequence, bootlegging can be reduced, and trust and transparency can be increased to display innovative ideas with more internal crowd involvement (Masoudnia and Szwejczewski, 2012).

In summary, as previous results have shown, it is beneficial to have innovative employees and creative thinkers within a company. In addition, our findings have implications for the methods of supporting these employees with an entrepreneurial mindset when their ideas are put into practice as novel insights. These methods improve innovation processes and innovation culture and increase organizational welfare and innovativeness.

3.3.2. Managerial implications

This research has implications for practitioners and organizations to better understand bootlegging and find structures and measures for supporting it.

Regarding participation and decision-making, Wilkinson, Gollan and Marchingtion (2010) have reflected that "the concept of industry democracy ... see[s] participation as a fundamental democratic right for workers to extend a degree of control over managerial decision-making in an organization" (169). However, the right to participate in organizational decisions regarding ideation and idea implementation is still absent in some organizations and displays a lack of democracy within an organizational structure. Management should address this topic, especially as the findings show strong requests by the current and new generation of employees for new working methods and processes. Several steps in this direction have already been established in organizations and have been growing in recent years, including the open innovation approach, lean startup methods (Furr and Dyer, 2014), and internal skunkworks or speedboats, which increase the speed of projects with a dedicated team (Rich and Janos, 1994; Fosfuri and Rønde, 2009). Moreover, the new generation of employees, known as Generation Y and born between 1982 and 2000, are described as preferring to take action in a collective manner and valuing input in decisions and actions (see Wong *et al.*, 2008, for a review).

In addition, reaching market launch at a faster pace plays an important role in retaining creative and passionate employees. Management should be aware of these creative thinkers as they use reduced and specific internal resources to accelerate ideas. Compared to official projects, bootlegging projects also reduce the amount of interaction with official bureaucratic measures, saving time that could otherwise be invested in innovative ideas. These could also be factors for management to consider as it implements the appropriate supporting systems. Bootlegging projects can start sooner and accelerate at a faster rate than official projects because they do not have to follow official stage-gate processes or internal innovation processes. In contrast, official projects are normally organized according to a prefabricated innovation process, established and proven over the years. Bootlegging projects bypass such processes to push ideas due to a strong sense of passion for the project.

In the case of bootlegging as a vehicle for radical or ground-breaking project ideas, the open innovation approach can be beneficial for developing ideas outside of the normal innovation processes with a partner willing to explore new avenues and take risks in an environment of organizational flexibility. Therefore, management should focus on finding a balance between internal innovation and external cooperation to outperform the competition and increase innovation within the firm. However, this should not just be limited as a supporting strategy for bootlegging projects. In line with Hornsby and colleagues, this chapter argues that an "important dimension is management support, which indicates the willingness of managers to facilitate and promote entrepreneurial activity in the firm" (Hornsby *et al.*, 2002: 259). In doing so, internal processes must first be analyzed, and employees who have displayed entrepreneurial activity should be approached to begin restructuring and rethinking organizational processes.

In summary, management should be aware of employees' tendency to cultivate creative and novel ideas and their drive to develop them further. It is important for organizations to embody both exploitation and exploration tendencies to increase the loyalty and satisfaction of both their employees and customers.

3.3.3. Conclusion

Bootleggers often try to develop smart and novel ideas faster and more efficiently, but it is not uncommon for them to face obstacles in the form of organizational routines, NIH syndromes, reluctance toward new ideas, or managerial decisions based on hidden agendas. Nevertheless, bootlegging projects have been, are, and will continue to be an important part of organizational innovation aside from the familiar innovation tracks because they help strike a balance between settled routines and radical, passionate, and open-minded thinking until organizations can renew and transform themselves. However, empowering bootleggers and out-of-the-box thinkers by implementing organizational support systems to welcome a new spirit of work seems to benefit the company. The empirical findings and contributions presented in this chapter can lead to a better understanding of this organizational phenomenon.

This chapter concludes with a quote from US Naval Officer Grace Hopper, a developer of the first compiler for a computer programming language, who stipulated, "If it's a good idea, go ahead and do it. It is much easier to apologize than it is to get permission." (Purington, Butler and Fister Gale, 2003). While this mindset was also shared by interviewees within this work, such out-of-the-box thinkers nevertheless need support during the development and transfer stage and to enhance their intrinsic motivation when they face barriers to ensure a stable and high level of organizational identification.

References

Abetti, P. A. (1997a). The birth and growth of Toshiba's laptop and notebook computers: A case study in Japanese corporate venturing. *Journal of Business Venturing*, **12**: 507–529.

Abetti, P. A. (1997b). Underground innovation in Japan: The development of Toshiba's word processor and laptop computer. *Creativity and Innovation Management*, **6**: 127–139.

Adams, R., Bessant, J. and Phelps, R. (2006). Innovation management measurement: A review. *International Journal of Management Reviews*, **8**: 21–47.

Ahuja, G. and Lampert, C. M. (2001). Entrepreneurship in the large corporation: A longitudinal study of how established firms create breakthrough inventions. *Strategic Management Journal*, **22**: 521–543.

Alexy, O., Salter, A., Sharapov, D. and Criscuolo, P. (2016). Going off-piste: The role of status in launching unsponsored R&D projects. In *Academy of Management Annual Meeting Proceedings*.

Antons, D. and F. T. Piller. (2015). Opening the black box of 'Not Invented Here': Attitudes, decision biases, and behavioral consequences. *Academy of Management Perspectives*, **29**(2): 193 217.

Augsdorfer, P. (2005). Bootlegging and path dependency. *Research Policy*, **34**: 1–11.

Augsdorfer, P. (2008). Managing the unmanageable. *Research Technology Management*, **51**: 41–47.

Augsdorfer, P. (2012). A diagnostic personality test to identify likely corporate bootleg researchers. *International Journal of Innovation Management*, **16**(1): 1–18.

Belleflamme, P., Lambert, T. and Schwienbacher, A. (2014). Crowdfunding: Tapping the right crowd. *Journal of Business Venturing*, **29**(5): 585–609.

Benner, M. J. and Tushman, M. L. (2003). Exploitation, exploration, and process management: The productivity dilemma revisited. *Academy of Management Review*, **2**: 238–256.

Chen, M. H., Chang, Y. C. and Hung, S. C. (2008). Social capital and creativity in R&D project teams. *R&D Management*, **38**: 21–34.

Chesbrough, H. (2003a). *Open Innovation: The New Imperative for Creating and Profiting from Technology*. Boston, MA: Harvard Business School Press.

Chesbrough, H. (2003b). The logic of open innovation: Managing intellectual property. *California Management Review*, **45**(3): 33–58.

Chong, V. K. and Chong, K. M. (2002). Budget goal commitment and informal effects of budget participation on performance: A structural equation modelling approach. *Behavioral Research in Accounting,* **14**: 65–86.

Cooper, R. G. (1990). Stage-gate systems: A new tool for managing new products. *Business Horizons,* **33**: 44–56.

Criscuolo, P., Salter, A. and Ter Wal, A. L. J. (2012). Going underground: Bootlegging and individual innovative performance. In *DRUID 2012*.

Criscuolo, P., Salter, A. and Ter Wal, A. L. J. (2014). Going underground: Bootlegging and innovative performance. *Organization Science*, **25**: 1287–1305.

Crossan, M. M. and Apaydin, M. (2010). A multi-dimensional framework of organizational innovation: A systematic review of the literature. *Journal of Management Studies*, **47**(6): 1154–1191.

Eisenhardt, K. M. and Graebner, M. E. (2007). Theory building from cases: Opportunities and challenges. *Academy of Management Journal*, **50**: 25–32.

Enkel, E., Gassmann, O. and Chesbrough, H. (2009). Open R&D and open innovation: Exploring the phenomenon. *R & D Management*, **39**(4): 311–316.

Fosfuri, A. and Rønde, T. (2009). Leveraging resistance to change and the skunk works model of innovation. *Journal of Economic Behavior and Organization*, **72**: 274–289.

Furr, N. and Dyer, J. (2014). *The Innovator's Method: Bringing the Lean Startup Into Your Organization.* Boston, MA: Harvard Business Press.

Gemünden, H. G., Salomo, S. and Krieger, A. (2005). The influence of project autonomy on project success. *International Journal of Project Management*, **235**: 366–373.

George, J. M. (2007). Creativity in organizations. *Academy of Management Annals*, **1**: 439–477.

Gioia, D. A., Corley, C. G. and Hamilton, A. M. (2013). Seeking qualitative rigor in inductive research: Notes on the Gioia methodology. *Organizational Research Methods,* **16**(1): 15–31.

Globocnik, D. and Salomo, S. (2015). Do formal management practices impact the emergence of bootlegging behavior? *Journal Product Innovation Management*, **32**: 505–521.

Gundling, E. and Porras, J. (2000). *The 3M Way to Innovation: Balancing People and Profit*. Boston: Kodansha International.

Hienerth, C., Keinz, P. and Lettl, C. (2011). Exploring the nature and implementation process of user-centric business models. *Long Range Planning*, **44**(5–6): 344–374.

Hornsby, J. S., Kuratko, D. F. and Zahra, S. A. (2002). Middle managers' perception of the internal environment for corporate entrepreneurship: Assessing a measurement scale. *Journal of Business Venturing*, **17**: 253–273.

Jick, T. D. (1979). Mixing qualitative and quantitative research methods: Triangulation in action. *Administrative Sciences Quarterly*, **24**(4): 602–611.

Jung, D., Wu, A. and Chow, C. W. (2008). Towards understanding the direct and indirect effects of CEOs' transformational leadership on firm innovation. *The Leadership Quarterly,* **19**: 582–594.

Katz, R. and Allen, T. J. (1982). Investigating the not invented here (NIH) syndrome: A look at the performance, tenure, and communication patterns of 50 R&D project groups. *R&D Management*, **12**: 7–19.

Knight, K. (1967). A descriptive model of the intra-firm innovation process. *The Journal of Business,* **40**(4): 478–496.

Koch, R. and Leitner, K. H. (2008). The dynamics and functions of self-organization in the fuzzy front end: Empirical evidence from the Austrian semiconductor industry. *Creativity and Innovation Management*, **17**: 216–226.

Koschatzky, K. (2001). Networks in innovation research and innovation policy — An introduction. In Koschatzky, K., Kulicke, M. and Zenker, A. (Eds.), *Innovation Networks: Concepts and Challenges in the European Perspective*. Heidelberg: Physica Verlag.

Langfred, C. W. and Moye, N. A. (2004). Effects of task autonomy on performance: An extended model considering motivational, informational, and structural mechanisms. *Journal of Applied Psychology*, **89**: 934–945.

Mainemelis, C. (2010). Stealing fire: Creative deviance in the evolution of new ideas. *Academy of Management Review*, **35**: 558–578.

March, J. G. (1991). Exploration and exploitation in organizational learning. *Organization Science,* **2**: 71–87.

Masoudnia, Y. (2012). *Bootlegging in High Technology R&D Departments: From Initiation to Disclosure*. PhD, DBA, and MSc by Research theses (School of Management).

Masoudnia, Y. and Szwejczewski, M. (2012). Bootlegging in the R&D departments of high-technology firms. *Research Technology Management*, **55**: 35–42.

Merton, R. K. (1968). *Social Theory and Social Structure*. New York: Free Press. *International Journal of Project Management*, **25**: 21–32.

Mollick, E. R. (2014a). The dynamics of crowdfunding: Determinants of success and failure. *Journal of Business Venturing*, **29**: 1–16.

Norton, P. and Hope, D. (2001). Analogue observational methods in the assessment of social functioning in adults. *Psychological Assessment,* **13**: 59–72.

Patterson, M. G., West, M. A., Shackleton, V. J., Dawson, J. F., Lawthom, R., Maitlis, S., Robinson, D. L. and Wallace, A. M. (2005). Validating the organizational climate measure: Links to managerial practices, productivity and innovation. *Journal of Organizational Behavior*, **26**: 379–408.

Purington, C., Butler, C. and Fister Gale. (2003). *Built to Learn: The Inside Story of How Rockwell Collins Became a True Learning Organization* (p. 171).

Rich, B. R. and Janos, L. (1994). *Skunk Works: A Personal Memoir of My Years at Lockheed*. Boston, MA: Little Brown & Company.

Robinson, S. and Bennett, R. J. (1995). A typology of deviant workplace behaviors: A multidimensional scaling study. *Academy of Management Journal*, **38**(2): 555–572.

Schon, D. A. (1963). Champions for radical new inventions. *Harvard Business Review*, **41**(2): 77–86.

Steiber, A. and Alänge, S. (2013). A corporate system for continuous innovation: The case of Google Inc. *European Journal of Innovation Management*, **16**(2): 243–264.

Stephan, A. and Bubenzer, P. (2019). Ex tenebris: Challenges and strategies for surfacing and reintegrating secret innovation projects. *Academy of Management Proceedings*, **1**: 18836. Academy of Management.

Su, M. and Rao, V. R. (2010). New product preannouncement as a signaling strategy: An audience-specific review and analysis. *Journal of Product Innovation Management*, **27**(5): 658–672.

Surowiecki, J. (2005). *The Wisdom of Crowds*. New York: Anchor.

Teece, D. J., Pisano, G. and Shuen, A. (1997). Dynamic capabilities and strategic management. *Strategic Management Journal*, **18**(7): 509–533.

Tushman, M. L. and O'Reilly C. A. (1996). Ambidextrous organizations: Managing evolutionary and revolutionary change. *California Management Review*, **38**(4): 8–30.

Van de Ven, A. H. (1986). Central problems in the management of innovation. *Management Science,* **32**: 590–607.

Van de Ven, A. H. (2007). *Engaged Scholarship: Creating Knowledge for Science and Practice*. Oxford: Oxford University Press.

Van Dijk, C. and Van den Ende, J. (2002). Suggestion systems: Transferring employee creativity into practicable ideas. *R&D Management*, **32**: 387–395.

Von Hippel, E., Franke, N. and Prügl, R. W. (2009). Pyramiding: Efficient search for rare subjects. *Research Policy*, **38**: 1397–1406.

Walker, A. (2011). Creativity loves constraints: The paradox of Google's twenty percent time. *Ephemera: Theory and Politics in Organization*, **11**: 369–386.

Appendices

Appendix 1

Management	• Idea was outside the organizational strategy or individuals were working outside their permitted field of work (Masoudnia and Szwejczewski, 2012) • The rejection of an idea by management (Abetti, 1997a; 1997h; 1999a; 1999b) • Management asked for data to support the idea and employees bootlegged to compile required data (Masoudnia and Szwejczewski, 2012) • To protect the project from managerial interruptions and disapproval during the early stages (Abetti, 1997a) • To avoid having ideas written off as a result of presenting unfinished work (Koch and Leitner, 2008) • To get permission from management, employees must first thoroughly prepare ideas (Augsdorfer, 1996; 2005) • Differences in background between bootlegger and management by having different understandings of the benefits of certain solutions or technologies (Masoudnia and Szwejczewski, 2012) • The chance of acceptance for immature ideas too low (Masoudnia and Szwejczewski, 2012) • Disagreement with management about the eventual value of the product or service being proposed (Pearson, 1997)

Appendix 1. (*Continued*)

Process	• R&D budgets are planned on a periodic basis and assigned to particular objectives, so ideas emerging between planning periods must be pursued underground (Augsdorfer, 2008) • Just as budget is available for ideas between budget cycles, projects went underground to maintain independence and avoid psychological pressure to produce a result quickly (Masoudnia and Szwejczewski, 2012) • To overcome bureaucratic barriers (Abetti, 1999a) • Bypass time-consuming and cumbersome formal procedures (Koch and Leitner, 2008) • Formal process and organization impede creativity (Augsdorfer, 2008)
Uncertainty	• Market uncertainty exist and underground activity was directed to prove market demand (Masoudnia and Szwejczewski, 2012) • Pre-research activities intended to reduce technical uncertainty about their projects (Masoudnia and Szwejczewski, 2012) • Reduce apprehension about failure (Masoudnia and Szwejczewski, 2012)

Note: Reasons and motivations to start a bootlegging project.

Appendix 2

Differences	Official Project	Bootlegging Project
• **Start point**	Starting after official approval from management or committee	Staring after decision from bootleggers and team members. Mostly before an intervening condition is progressing
• **Networking at the beginning**	Dedicated official project network/official interface partners	Trusted network, when exist from former projects
• **Social skills**	Less or not needed during development. Helpful in critical development phase and for negotiation	More, to convince others, build bonds and social cues to generate response and convince others for support
• **Duration**	Slow, because of the official project phase steps within the innovation process	Fast, because less steps are needed. Mostly driven by right time to surface and it can be influenced by several factors, e.g., internal negotiations

(*Continued*)

Appendix 2. (*Continued*)

Differences	Official Project	Bootlegging Project
• **Final networks**	Communicated in a broad network	Known, limited, and focused network. Dangerous to communicate too broadly and too early because of internal project competition
• **Target department**	Mostly identified and integrated in the early development stage. Important to identify and know the target department's requirements	Unknown, visible during transfer. Important to use trustworthy relationships with a target department. Necessary to have a relationships to influential mentor or promotor who will support the transfer against potential resistance
• **Project maturity**	A lower maturity can be acceptable	High at transfer to convince decision makers. MVP or prototype has to be developed
• **Resources allocation**	Less effort are used to allocate resources, because mainly dedicated/official resources are already authorized	High effort to allocate the needed resources from: (a) Official project which are in the same team/department or (b) Co-workers in the trustful network

Note: Comparison of official and bootleg projects.

Appendix 3

Differences	Official Project (Exchanges with Experts)	Bootlegging Project (Data Revealed)
How to (a) use network, and (b) communicate about the project	Broader: (a) Use of network within the official project alignment mostly. If needed the network are extended (b) Broadly communicating about one's project is useful, to convince internal stakeholders and to place the project in the official innovation process	Focused: (a) Use of personal network and just with trustful co-workers (b) It can be dangerous to communicate too broadly, because of internal project competition, rejection because (radical/disruptive) idea is not fully developed to present, and NIH syndrome

Appendix 3. (*Continued*)

Differences	Official Project (Exchanges with Experts)	Bootlegging Project (Data Revealed)
When to establish "customer" relationships and search for an internal customer	Late: Mostly the dedicated department for the transfer is known or already integrated in the early development stage, but to build a relationship is mostly not necessary because project is officially announced by committee for transfer. Hence, it is sufficient to identify and know the target department for transfer: (a) To check existing requirements if it is a project to be integrated into a product derivatives (b) The project management is certain about the project success and transfer	It depends: (a) Bootlegger already has a trustworthy relationship (b) Project has already reached a presentable maturity stage and prototype to convince colleagues (c) Mentor supports the transfer in the specialized department Hence: It is sometimes critical to establish relationships and convince the target department early to maintain the idea and benefit of the idea and on the other side it is sometimes advisable to gather first results and wait for the "right time" to present the idea/project
What level of maturity is needed at transfer	(a) Low — If the official project is already approvable for launch by senior management (b) High — If the official project has competitive similar projects in the organizations	Mostly high with an MVP and/or prototype to: (a) Visualize the idea (b) Communicate emotions (c) To convince other stakeholders about the value of the project

Note: Comparison between official projects and bootlegging project transfer.

Appendix 4

Description of the ZZ[4] bootlegging project (RI_10):
The ZZ project was developed to support internal services for employees. Initially, the project was intended for use by employees but with the perspective of designing something for market entry. The project idea emerged in discussions with the interviewee's network. During an internal exchange with a department in which comparable concepts are already being carried out, the interview participant developed thoughts about new

(*Continued*)

[4]For confidentiality reasons the name of the project is not disclosed but named ZZ in the text.

Appendix 4. (*Continued*)

Description of the ZZ[4] bootlegging project (RI_10):
concepts supporting the departmental goals. From partaking in the discussions, the bootlegger devised ideas to produce a solution and to reach the departmental goals. To find a solution, the interviewee considered the requirements during the idea generation phase. After the initial ideation phase at the beginning of 2013, the project began as a bootlegging project and surfaced with a pilot scheme, where the concept really became visible and tangible. This was in May 2014. The interviewee also knew that the colleagues who were responsible for developing and implementing these internal concepts had no additional budget to work with. From their formal position, the interviewee also had no budget, and those in the organization whose formal function it was to develop a product solution for market entry "*were not amused*" by this. For this purpose, the project was developed with resources available on the sidelines, such as creating synergies or hiring students through other projects. First, the entire technical development process was initiated to launch the project through backend enabling, among other things. This also happened in the underground because the backend was not intended to undertake this in productive mode. In order to keep the project alive and shielded and to obtain support for the backend consultation, the project was titled as a research project: *So officially, it was only allowed to be a research project and thus be a bit under the radar. This also helped me even due it was claimed: "Oh yes, it is only a research project". Because the people who would have had such a potential problem were a little soothed.* (INT 10) The renaming temporarily appeased potential critics and reduced upcoming barriers from other departments. Nevertheless, during this bootlegging project, financial funds and silo thinking were the biggest barriers, as the interviewee mentioned: *So, funding was a huge obstacle, and from my point of view, the biggest obstacle was this "flowerpot thinking." And we kept it under this research cover...because they saw me as an internal competitor... So, there was one party in the company that really wanted to prevent this and also tried to escalate into higher levels of hierarchical management. We just ignored it. We just kept going.* (INT 10) The interviewee handled resistance by ignoring it. Even when escalations into higher levels of hierarchical management were attempted by other departments, the interviewee received support. This was especially the case in regard to their immediate supervisor: *I believed in it, and the immediate supervisor thought it was great. So this is really important. In this case, it was important to integrate him, because he was or is a confidant...This depends so much on the personal relationship and the immediate supervisor.* (INT 10)

Appendix 4. (*Continued*)

Description of the ZZ[4] bootlegging project (RI_10):

During the project phase, the interviewee attempted to develop alternative solutions to achieving important advances in the development of the prototype, such as its technical development. Due to the bootlegger's lack of previous technical knowledge, colleagues were asked for assistance. Additionally, the interviewee strove to inspire trusted coworkers and "*to get them onboard*" the project, and this was ultimately successful. To test the concept under real conditions, the first testing began after one year:

> *And of course, we also wanted it to be tested under real conditions and so decided to also reach out to the potential (internal) users or to their managers. They were approached and asked: "Here we have a pilot and do you want to get involved?" And they said: "Yes, and super cool, and we support [it]." And within the first few days, half of the staff that we had ever contemplated were logged.* (INT 10)

After the successful testing and piloting phase, the interviewee was required to hand the project over to the dedicated department because of a departmental change. As the pilot had just started, the project was in a "hot phase" during the handover; the internal reactions and feedback were very good, and acceptance was increasing. The interviewee wanted to continue to be responsible for the product until its launch. However, the status of the research project ultimately had to change for the next steps to occur. The project still runs internally, and the external use of the concept as a product market launch was never further developed or discussed by decision makers.

Overall, the interviewee was convinced that bootlegging projects are an important part of novel ideas and their initial testing period:

> *Absolutely, so I believe many things, especially when it comes to newer topics or topics that are a bit further away from the core business. I think bootlegging projects are necessary for many reasons. Firstly, the potential of the project is not always initially recognized — this depends on when you get into it, and there it can make sense to develop something first and then to test it and when it comes to the feedback of users or whatever, it can initially take time to convince others because the potential is just not seen immediately. And I think it is also very important for the motivation of the employees.* (INT 10)

Appendix 5

(i) New regulation of financial support	(i) Free competence budget within the organization
	(ii) In-year financial support for radical ideas
(ii) Secured free working space and time	(i) Internal project space for temporary booking
	(ii) External project space
	(iii) One week exempted from official projects for creative development of new ideas
(iii) Process improvement	(i) Less committee presentation during development phase and instead faster development of radical ideas
	(ii) Decoupling from official process steps and budget innovation pots
	(iii) Flexibility within organization for new technologies/innovation
(iv) Evaluation of external options	(i) Cooperation with small innovative firms (start-ups)
	(ii) Spin-offs
	(iii) Joint ventures
(v) Innovation mentality improvement	(i) Open innovation culture and acceptance to make faults
	(ii) Freedom to work on radical ideas without constraints
	(iii) Recognition for extra-mile work by management
	(iv) Expectation for novel and radical ideas
	(v) Expectation not set too high for new ideas, so on the idea can be developed without pressure

Note: Theoretical aggregate dimensions requested supporting measure.

Appendix 6

A	I felt that I could contribute more through CCS	Participants	(%)
1.	Fully applies	45	40.2
2.	Largely applies	39	34.8
3.	Partially applies	19	17.0
4.	Does rather not apply	6	5.4
5.	Does not apply at all	1	0.9
		110	98.3

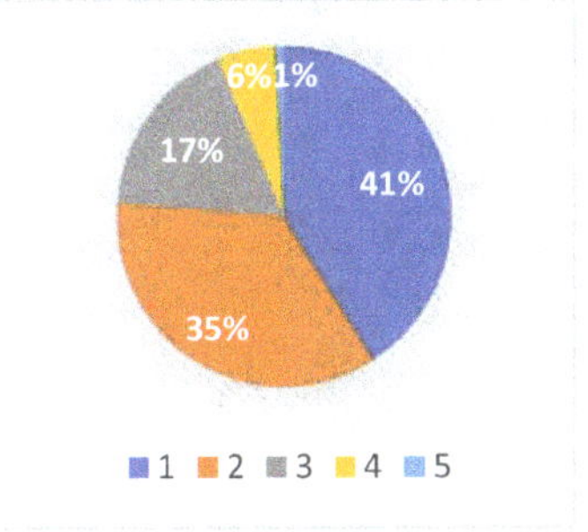

B	The platform supports the innovation power of the company	Participants	(%)
1.	Fully applies	53	47.3
2.	Largely applies	36	32.1
3.	Partially applies	12	10.7
4.	Does rather not apply	6	5.4
5.	Does not apply at all	3	2.7
		110	98.2

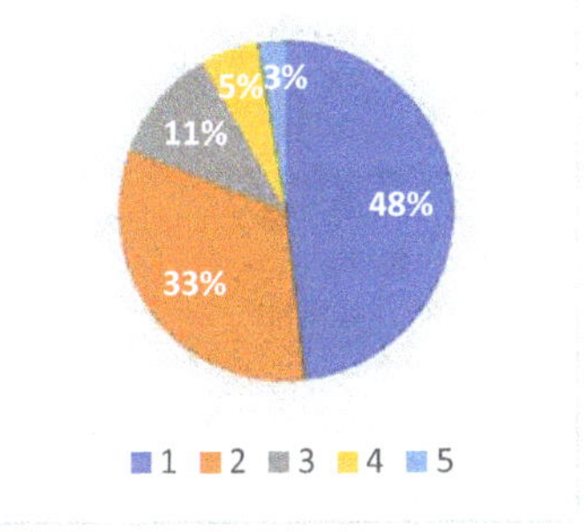

C	It was easy to ask coworkers for their support on the platform	Participants	(%)
1.	Fully applies	19	17.4
2.	Largely applies	21	19.3
3.	Partially applies	26	23.9
4.	Does rather not apply	17	15.6
5.	Does not apply at all	11	10.1
		94	86.3

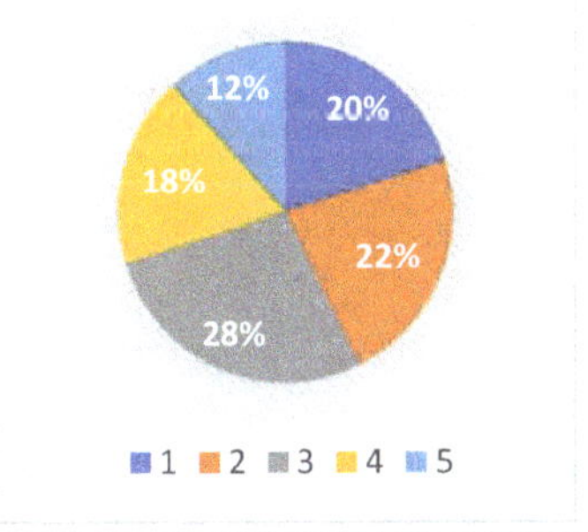

(*Continued*)

Appendix 6. (*Continued*)

D	**The feedback I received on the CCS platform was helpful for my idea**	**Participants**	**(%)**
1.	Fully applies	12	11.0
2.	Largely applies	26	23.9
3.	Partially applies	29	26.6
4.	Does rather not apply	14	12.8
5.	Does not apply at all	0	0.0
		81	74.3

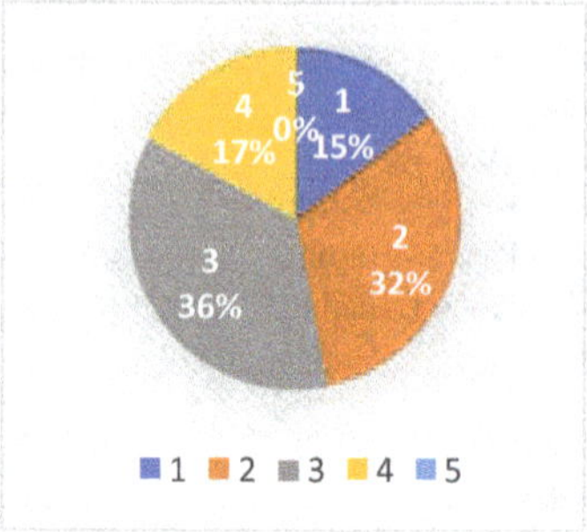

E	**The platform helps to establish interdisciplinary relations between departments**	**Participants**	**(%)**
1.	Fully applies	28	25.7
2.	Largely applies	35	32.1
3.	Partially applies	19	17.4
4.	Does rather not apply	14	12.8
5.	Does not apply at all	7	6.4
		103	94.4

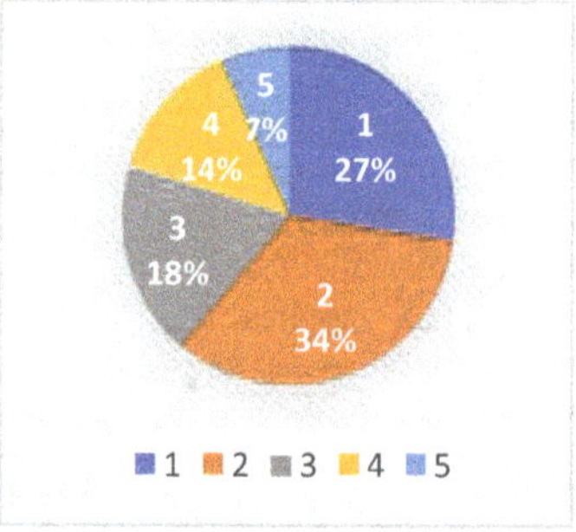

Note: Internal survey after a CCS challenge, May 2018.

Part 2

Management and Organization of Bootlegging

https://doi.org/10.1142/9781800612266_0005

Chapter 4

Navigating a Typology of Corporate Entrepreneurial Strategies: The Case of Unilever

Linda Nhu Laursen* and Poul Houman Andersen†
Aalborg University, Aalborg, Denmark
**linda@create.aau.dk*
†*poa@business.aau.dk*

Abstract

This chapter presents a typology of entrepreneurial strategies. It responds to recent calls in research to examine the theoretical underpinnings of corporate entrepreneurial strategies. The typology explains underlying structural dimensions of how entrepreneurial strategies, such as bootlegging, skunkwork, bricolage, and guided evolution, differ, in respect to the origin of an entrepreneurial initiative and the resource availability for an entrepreneurial initiative. In the chapter, the typology is used to examine an exemplary longitudinal case study at Unilever. The Unilever Knorr case exemplifies how managers in practice navigate different entrepreneurial strategies to overcome the corporate immune system. It finds dynamically evolving situations, where new sources of corporate resistance continually arise, navigating between corporate entrepreneurship modes could be more a viable approach for understanding the mechanisms of corporate entrepreneurial initiatives. As such, this chapter contributes to the understanding of how entrepreneurial strategies are *a priori* choice and *in situ* navigation depending on the organizational context and furthers the discussion of important underlying structural dimensions for navigating corporate entrepreneurial strategies.

4.1. Introduction

A manifold of different corporate entrepreneurial strategies exists, including bootlegging, skunkwork, bricolage, and guided evolution (Castellaci *et al.*, 2018; Fisher, 2012; Fosfuri and Rønde, 2009; Augsdorfer, 2005). However, they exist in disparate literature streams with limited oversight in understanding, choosing, and navigating between these diverse approaches. This chapter responds to calls for examining the theoretical underpinnings of corporate entrepreneurial strategies (cf. Yang, 2018; Kilenthong *et al.*, 2016; Miles and Darroch, 2006). Hence, when referring to entrepreneurship in this chapter, we consistently mean corporate entrepreneurship, which is defined as creating new business activities within an existing organization (Burgelman, 1983). We build on a typology of entrepreneurial strategies that highlight critical underlying dimensions of how entrepreneurial strategies differ, respectively, the origin of an entrepreneurial initiative and the resource availability for an entrepreneurial initiative. We use this typology to present an exemplary longitudinal case study at Unilever in order to examine *how managers navigate different entrepreneurial strategies to overcome the corporate immune system.* The case provides data on how different entrepreneurial strategies dynamically unfold to complement one another on a project level, adapting to a corporate context with emergent and shift organizational resistance sources. Specifically, the focus is on how skunkwork and guided evolution (formalized strategies) substitute one another in this process, whereas bootlegging and bricolage (informal, organic strategies) surface parallel to other entrepreneurial strategies.

This chapter contributes to the understanding of how entrepreneurial strategies are an *a priori* choice and *in situ* navigation. In dynamically evolving situations, where new sources of corporate resistance continually arise, navigating between corporate entrepreneurship modes could be more a viable approach for understanding the mechanisms of corporate entrepreneurial initiatives. Rather than contributing to one grand theory of corporate entrepreneurship, we agree that mid-range theories offer a more pragmatic way forward in entrepreneurship research (Jennings *et al.*, 2013). Thus, through our research, we add to the existing understanding of research traditions and how they reflect the underlying structural dimensions that are essential for navigating different entrepreneurial strategies. For managers, this chapter provides insights into the intricacies of navigating corporate entrepreneurship in complex organizational contexts. The presented case illustrates how Unilever managers use different entrepreneurial strategies at different time points as they navigate to overcome different sources of resistance and enable different support levels. Hopefully, the chapter will raise the managers' awareness of the organizational context and teach them to understand that successful managerial practices differ across corporate entrepreneurship modes. Being able to adjust between these modes when navigating corporate entrepreneurship ventures is a critical managerial skill.

4.2. Entrepreneurial Strategies

Different strands of business literature discuss strategic renewal in companies for fostering corporate entrepreneurship and refreshing or replacing existing critical resources and practices in order to ensure long-term survival (Agarwal and Helfat, 2009). Corporate strategic renewal processes that aim to replace or refresh existing practices are often described as entrepreneurial efforts that call for innovation champions and corporate venturing (Burgelman, 1983). In this chapter, building on previous studies, we argue that when large established firms adopt entrepreneurial strategies, they face a somewhat different task than their smaller startup counterparts. In established corporations, entrepreneurial initiatives have a multifaceted and ambiguous internal structure that typically differs from the context of smaller, often resource-restrained firms (Zahra and Garvis, 2000). On the one hand, they may have access to resources from within established organizational structures, capabilities and practices. On the other hand, existing organizational structures and management practices may offer resistance to such renewing initiatives — having a tendency to limit and keep initiatives at incremental levels and within the realm of existing operational requirements (Birkinshaw, 1997). As entrepreneurial initiatives typically seek to change the existing order, they are not supported by default in established organizational structures and cultures in many cases (Lauring *et al.*, 2017; Birkinshaw and Ridderstråle, 1999). Thus, approaches to accessing resources are a matter of critical concern for entrepreneurial strategies within established firms.

The current research on entrepreneurial strategies incorporates various entrepreneurial strategies, such as bootlegging, skunkwork, bricolage, and guided evolution (Castellaci *et al.*, 2018; Fisher, 2012; Fosfuri and Rønde, 2009; Augsdorfer, 2005). However, the literature provides a limited overview of how these labels and concepts differ (Schindehutte *et al.*, 2018). Moreover, as pointed out by some scholars, there is a gap in understanding how such different entrepreneurial strategies unfold in a corporate context (Yang, 2018). This study examines entrepreneurial strategies, including bootlegging, bricolage, skunkworks, and guided evolution, in order to explain how they unfold in the organizational context of larger corporations. To do so, we build on a recent contribution that brings forward two underlying structural dimensions of entrepreneurship. When referring to structural dimensions, we take a systems view on organizations and invoke the sociological notion of underlying social structures as being important for understanding the distribution of power, influence, functioning, and differences in organizational systems (Pfeffer, 1997). We refer to these, respectively, as the origin of such entrepreneurial initiatives and the resource rigidity that such strategic renewal initiatives may face in a corporate organizational setting (Andersen and Laursen, 2020). Both these assumptions appear in discussions about the process of corporate strategic renewal in large complex organizations (Schmitt *et al.*, 2016; Agarwal and Helfat, 2009; Huff and Huff, 1992). In the following, we build on these underlying assumptions and on the characteristic entrepreneurial strategies within the typology in order to then deploy it as a framework for examining an exemplary case of Unilever's entrepreneurial initiative.

4.2.1. Resources: Enablers or rigidities?

The first central underlying structural dimension concerns the role and distribution of existing resources. Whether resources may serve as enablers or, conversely, as rigidities for corporate entrepreneurial initiatives is a matter for debate. While a corporation's resources are usually perceived as supporting and enabling entrepreneurial initiatives, Leonard-Barton (1992) showed how a company's core competencies are associated with its existing management belief system, which may also inhibit and reject development initiatives. He argued that core competencies entail core rigidities. Since core competencies entail knowledge-sets that are optimized and deeply embedded for supporting existing procedures, they may, in return, act as rigidities that could hinder renewal initiatives (Leonard-Barton, 1992). Hamel and Ruben (2000) developed a similar argument relating to the role of resources as rigidities in corporate innovation.

The above perspectives suggest that an existing resource structure may provide either organizational resistance or support for an entrepreneurial initiative. The role of resources as enablers or obstacles for entrepreneurial efforts is a well-known problem in the literature on organizational transition and corporate entrepreneurship (Stopford and Baden-Fuller, 1994). By resources, in this chapter, we broadly refer to corporate resources, such as materials, labor, time, money, skills, and institutional domains (Yang, 2018). Resources may be both physical (such as research lab facilities) and nonphysical (such as organizational routines) (Mahoney, 1995). Existing internal resources, in the form of structures, practices, and capabilities, may provide resistance and constraints for entrepreneurial initiatives in organizations (Birkinshaw and Ridderstråle, 1999; Williams and Lee, 2009). They focus on and are configured to support existing organizational procedures and may provide internal resistance toward transformative initiatives (Hamel *et al.*, 2015). Large established corporations are better at retaining existing practices than at learning new ones and, therefore, tend to resist internal initiatives that call for significant deviations (Birkinshaw and Ridderstråle, 1999; Dörrenbacher and Gammelgaard, 2016). Hence, the resource base of large firms can either enable or reject their entrepreneurial initiatives.

Furthermore, this double role of resources additionally addresses the organizational tension between exploration and exploitation (March, 1991). Because entrepreneurial attempts that call for organizational change frequently meet both internal and external resistance, large established organizations traditionally tend to limit search efforts and keep initiatives at incremental levels and within the realm of existing operational requirements (Fecher *et al.*, 2020). Balancing these issues is a central matter of corporate renewal (Hamel, 1996; Christensen *et al.*, 2003; Chesborough, 2003). Some researchers even suggest that decision-making in large corporations unfolds in a field of tension, resistance, and power, which may stifle efforts of resource leverage for renewal (Markides and Geroski, 2003).

4.2.2. Origin: Formal or informal?

The second underlying assumption deals with the organizational origin of a corporate entrepreneurial initiative. Since a corporation typically entails large and complex hierarchical structures, it is significant to distinguish between the origins of entrepreneurial initiatives within a multileveled and complex organization. In other words, whether an entrepreneurial initiative emerges formally or informally is essential for the mandate for the initiative and for the way in which the strategy unfolds. The formal or informal origin of renewal initiatives undoubtedly affects how entrepreneurial initiatives can interface with the corporate context.

The formal–informal discussion stems from Weber's classic organizational theories (2009), which argued that formal structures (clearly defined hierarchies, roles, and work divisions) lead to higher organizational performance. Later, Burns and Stalker (1967) proposed a contingent relation, arguing that formal organizations work well in static environments, whereas informal organizations respond better to dynamic environments. The formal–informal dichotomy, without a doubt, matters for the outcome of corporate entrepreneurial processes because it directly affects its internal legitimacy in large organizations (Balogun *et al.*, 2011). Formal structures, such as clearly defined hierarchies, roles, and work divisions, characterize large organizations. However, often, entrepreneurial strategies are responses to a dynamically evolving environment.

Corporate entrepreneurship typically strives to transform existing formalized practices that, in many cases, are imposed by top management (e.g., in the headquarters of multinationals). However, corporate entrepreneurial initiatives may either emanate formally top-down or originate informally from anywhere in the organization (Yuan *et al.*, 2017; Laukannen *et al.*, 2017; Covin and Slevin, 1991; Laursen and Andersen, 2016). Some scholars have shown that certain corporate entrepreneurial initiatives emanate top-down, such as a formalized initiative with increased internal mandate (Birkinshaw, 1997; Yuan *et al.*, 2017). Other scholars have shown that corporate entrepreneurial initiatives increasingly emerge informally from the "middle" of the organizational hierarchy (O'Brien *et al.*, 2013). When initiatives are driven by middle management — as an informal, organically developing bottom-up process — organizational strategies are assumed to play a minor role (Hornsby *et al.*, 2002). Middle managers who drive entrepreneurial initiatives find themselves in an increasingly complicated context, where legitimacy and resources may be challenging to unlock.

Thus, discussions call for different initiatives, both formal and informal, from different organizational levels in order to allow us to go beyond the reactive resistance of the corporate "immune" system (Birkinshaw and Ridderstråle, 1999; Williams and Lee, 2009).

4.3. A Typology for Categorizing Entrepreneurial Strategies

Following the current debates, Andersen and Laursen (2020) contributed to a typology (see Fig. 4.1) in which the "formal or informal" origins of an entrepreneurial initiative and the "enabler or rigidity" roles of existing resources act as critical dimensions for understanding how entrepreneurial strategies interface with a corporate context. Typologies propose a set of dimensions that capture and distinguish different types or classes (Mayr, 1969, cited in Rich, 1992). They condense the diversity of reality into clearly defined types, capturing the main features in order to distinguish one type from another (Tangpong *et al.*, 2008; Enright and Subramanian, 2007).

Origin of Initiative	*Role of Resources*	**Enablers**	**Rigidities**
	Informal	**Cf. Bricolage, Effectuation** Corporate entrepreneurs identify, combine and utilize available neglected resources with reshaped purpose.	**Cf. Bootlegging** Corporate entrepreneurs ignore and hide initiatives from formal structures to avoid organizational resistance.
	Formal	**Cf. Guided Evolution** Strategic initiatives that are nurtured and developed with resources provided by senior management.	**Cf. Skunkworks** Initiatives are strategically originated and shielded from organizational resistance.

Fig. 4.1. A typology of corporate entrepreneurial strategies (Andersen and Laursen, 2020).

4.3.1. Informal strategy for avoiding resource rigidities: Bootlegging

In its pure form, bootlegging concerns informal innovation activities in organizations, which illegitimately uses resources of organizations to develop new products and ideas that are later acknowledged as path-breaking or even as defining for a company's future (Augsdorfer, 2005). Consequently, bootlegging is defined as an entrepreneurial strategy in which "individuals take the initiative to work on ideas that have no formal organizational support and are often hidden from the sight of senior management but are undertaken to produce innovations, that benefits the organization" (cf. Criscuolo *et al.*, 2014, p. 1288). It is an informal and hidden process because it sometimes runs counter to formal policies to continue entrepreneurial projects, which would have otherwise stopped (Knudsen and Levinthal, 2007). Sometimes, this even means countering direct orders or using resources in ways deemed to be illegitimate. Hence, it constitutes a "specific deviant form of employees' entrepreneurship behavior" (Globocnik and Salomo, 2015, p. 505), where initiatives are kept under the radar to mature an idea early on because an organization is expected to be resistant to or even to block the initiative (Burgelman, 1983; Kanter, 2000). The literature has several well-known bootlegging examples, including the development of the adhesive material that has created 3M's post-it success (Garud and Karnøe, 2005).

However, in reality, in complex organizations, organizational bootlegging is often more muddled. Top management gives a mandate for product development but meets organizational resistance from internal stakeholders as innovation champions try to unfold them (Burgelmann, 1983). We argue that this suggests that innovation champions must counter organizational resistance in many forms or fight to obtain appropriate attendance and release access to resources, which have formally already been granted. This type of innovation activity also consists of several bootlegging elements, although corporate innovation is not "flying under the radar." Multinational corporations (MNCs) are complex organizations that face many intricate and complex strategic aims at the same time. Managers across MNC national entities, departments, and divisions interpret and prioritize this complexity differently. Hence, even when innovation activities are formally endorsed by top management, navigating the MNCs' complex resource ecology can give rise to bootlegging practices. Bootlegging pays attention to processes whereby individuals address and overcome organizational resistance toward entrepreneurial initiatives.

Bootlegging behavior is either partly or wholly illegitimate, bypassing formal organizational channels and operational procedures (Globocnik and Salomo, 2015). Thus, bootlegging's core element lies in convincing a formal organization to embrace bootlegged initiatives. Studies have shown that bootleggers, in this quest, for instance, bypass custom communication channels (Howell and Higgins, 1990).

4.3.2. Informal resource enabling strategy: Bricolage

Bricolage is "a process of combining various available resources to find workable solutions to problems and seize opportunities" (Yang, 2018, p. 2). It is an entrepreneurial strategy that focuses on "making do with what is at hand." While bricolage is also informally initiated, it differs from bootlegging by not perceiving resources or structures as rigidities (Andersen and Laursen, 2020). In contrast to gathering specific resources for a particular intended goal, it utilizes any resources available (Levi-Strauss, 1967). The goal is driven and defined by the present available resource opportunities (Di Domenico *et al.*, 2010; Garud and Karnøe, 2005). Thus, it is a dynamically driven strategy in which the resource constellation is the primary focus and shaper of an initiative.

Consequently, bricolage represents a distinct strategy for resource mobilization, identifying relevant resources for reintegrating and reshaping purposes (Duymedjian and Rueling, 2010). It builds on a particular world view, where the resource environment is perceived as being socially constructed. Hence, managers enacting bricolage do not follow the resource environment's prevailing perceptions. Instead of embracing the usual perceptions or resource limitations, they identify, unlock, and recombine resources that have been perceived as unreachable by others or whose potential value has been overlooked (Baker and Nelson, 2005). For example, accessing free work from internal and external network partners, as well as utilizing self-taught skills, provides unique customized offerings (Yang, 2018). Thus, in contrast to bootlegging, the focus is not on "keeping it under the radar" to avoid rigidities of and rejection from the corporate system; instead, resources are perceived as being available and as enablers for anyone who can unlock them. It addresses the creative leveraging of heterogeneous resources in a resource-based view (Barney, 2001; Kogut and Zander, 1993).

A field study of 29 resource-limited firms showed that companies utilizing bricolage do not adopt the predominant logic from their resource environments (Baker and Nelson, 2005). It is a resource-driven approach, where the goal is co-shaped by the means and partners. Managers carrying out bricolage collect and store resources (in some cases without knowing their potential usage) in order to creatively combine and apply them for new purposes later on (Fisher, 2012). Studies have shown that bricolage is applied as a bottom-up strategy in dynamic and uncertain environments in which forecasting is not possible, utilizing available (and sometimes neglected) resources and recombining these to create new markets (Yang, 2018).

4.3.3. Formalized protection strategy: Skunkworks

Skunkworks is a strategy in which entrepreneurial initiatives are isolated in order to avoid any influence or resistance from leading organizational stakeholders (Gwynne, 1997). Central to implementing skunkworks as a formal idea for protecting a corporate entrepreneurship initiative is to avoid rigidity and resistance, which established corporate systems and structures may provide. Managers often perceive entrepreneurial initiatives as costly. They risk losing recognition or support by employing existing practices (Fosfuri and Rønde, 2009). Since entrepreneurial attempts can have powerful status redistribution effects within organizations, internal resources are perceived as a rigidity that may sabotage an initiative. Rather than being perceived as supporting, internal resources represent vested interests that may hinder or reject an entrepreneurial initiative in a not-invented-here format (Colakoglu *et al.*, 2014).

In these aspects, skunkworks resembles bootlegging. It expects rigidities and hides entrepreneurial initiatives in order to protect them against influences in an organization that may hinder, reject, or even sabotage them. However, it differs from bootlegging by being a formalized, typically top-down approach. Top management supports and legitimatizes such initiatives and separates them from the rest of the organization to protect them. The process builds on either a self-contained or a physically and organizationally independent setup with specific resources being dedicated, in many cases secretly, to the majority of the organization. The label "skunkworks" originated from the case of a windowless facility for carrying out secret military projects at the Burbank Airport during the Cold War (Fosfuri and Rønde, 2009).

Many large firms have adopted skunkworks as their entrepreneurial strategy to overcome inertia and rigidity disadvantages of being a large corporation. These include Apple's efforts to design the Macintosh computer (Linzmayer, 2004), Motorola's development of the Razr phone, and LEGO's development of LEGO House (Laursen and Haase, 2020).

4.3.4. Formalized facilitated development: Guided evolution

Guided evolution is a formalized entrepreneurial strategy, where top management is both passively and actively involved in an entrepreneurial initiative (Laukkanen *et al.*, 2017). Entrepreneurial efforts evolve through an interplay between an organization's strategic and operational levels, representing a guided evolution across several organization layers. In comparison to the formalized skunkworks approach, in a guided evolution strategy, top management is much more actively involved in facilitating the selection of environment. Top management actively sponsors and supports an entrepreneurial initiative. They set strategic aims, partake in risk-taking, and use their influence to assign resources.

The guided evolution model builds on the idea that top management must nurture entrepreneurial initiatives and internally and externally influence prospects in the corporate environment (Burgelman, 1991; Lovas and Ghoshal, 2000). Hence, facilitation may entail initiating and motivating entrepreneurial efforts, such as actively providing new projects or nurturing existing ones, both external and internal (Lovas and Ghoshal, 2000). For example, Nokia, when developing the N95 phone model, tended to use a guided evolution process, where the development of the strategy, business, and product occurred in parallel, across different layers of the organization — and, as aspect developed in parallel, they informed and influenced one another (Laukkanen *et al.*, 2017). In this manner, guided evolution initiatives develop in an existing corporation and take a reciprocal view of the interplay between levels and functions.

4.3.5. A dynamic perspective on entrepreneurial strategies

While this typology of entrepreneurial strategies contributes by highlighting and furthering the understanding of critical underlying differences between its various strategies, we argue that the reality of organizational bootlegging, bricolage, skunkworks, and guided evolution processes is often more muddled in complex organizations. We recognize that it is essential to understand, compare, and categorize different entrepreneurial approaches. However, we also argue that it is crucial to take a situated, dynamic view on the corporate entrepreneurial process. We aim to corroborate this typology with an exemplary case study, where we examine the entrepreneurial process in messy reality. Through the case study, we examine how organizational attitudes and forms of support may dynamically emerge or fade in this process. An entrepreneurial initiative may transform an organization's situation but the situation, in return, may respond, deeming new types of entrepreneurial strategies as being relevant for navigating the new circumstances. In other words, we intend to show how changing conditions, as a result of entrepreneurial initiatives, entail new entrepreneurial strategies that are relevant or useful for different stages of the entrepreneurial process.

For instance, innovative mandates for product development that are formally given by top management can also meet organizational resistance from internal stakeholders as innovation champions try to unfold them (Burgelmann, 1983). This phenomenon suggests that innovation champions must counter organizational resistance in many forms or must fight to obtain appropriate attendance and release access to formally granted resources. This type of innovation activity also considers several bootlegging elements, although corporate innovation does not fly under the radar.

Different entrepreneurial strategies may be relevant both in sequence and in parallel as the process unfolds in different parts of an organization, depending on the functions and different stakeholders' attitudes and agendas toward a project. Large corporations are complex organizations that face many intricate strategic agendas at the same time. Managers across entities, departments, and divisions interpret and prioritize such complexity differently. Hence, even when innovation activities are formally endorsed by top management, navigating a corporation's complex resource ecology may simultaneously give rise to bootlegging, bricolage, skunkworks, and guided evolution practices.

We use this typology and the descriptions of entrepreneurial strategy archetypes, including bootlegging, bricolage, guided evolution, and skunk-works, as a theoretical framework through which we study Unilever as an exemplary corporate entrepreneurship case.

4.4. Methodology

4.4.1. Case background and selection

Unilever represents a relevant case for following the corporate entrepreneurial process in complex organizations for several reasons. It is a large multinational organization that has a complex divisional structure and is currently in a challenging market position, which drives its significant entrepreneurial efforts (Laursen, 2017). Subsequently, we briefly present Unilever and describe its market position in order to provide our case selection background.

Unilever is the fourth largest fast-moving consumer goods company (FMCG) in the world. It operates in multiple consumer goods categories, including foods and refreshments as well as personal and home care. Unilever comprises more than 400 consumer brands, some of which are leading in their product categories, such as Magnum Ice Cream and Knorr. In 2017, Unilever's revenue amounted to €53.2 billion, with the company currently employing more than 160,000 people in 190 countries. In the case study, we primarily focused on Unilever's foods and refreshments division. More specifically, we chose to examine an entrepreneurial initiative at Knorr because of significant challenges that face this category and brand regarding a new consumer group.

Unilever (along with many other leading companies in the FMCG sector) has experienced challenging times since the aftermath of the 2008–2009 financial crisis (Bain, 2018). Despite the lengthy period of dependable annual revenue and operating profit growth, Unilever's market situation (as that of many established FMCG) has been challenged. Brands like Knorr consistently lose market shares to local incumbents, private label brands, and upcoming small firms worldwide due to changing consumer preferences. An essential factor that several industry experts have singled out relates to an underlying change in consumer preferences and habits, as the so-called millennials (consumers born between 1980 and 2000) are becoming increasingly more influential as a consumer group

(US Census Bureau, 2015). These differences include a lower consumption of meat products, less time spent on food preparation and consumption, and less time spent on shopping in traditional retailer outlets (USDA, 2017). Millennials spend more on products and brands but have less brand loyalty than previous generations (Ng *et al.*, 2010; Eastman *et al.*, 2013). The millennial challenge has pushed the leading industry actors, including Unilever, to search for new ways to initiate entrepreneurial initiatives that can strategically disrupt their existing efforts while maintaining their existing management operations (Lee and Evans, 2012).

4.5. The Unilever Case

4.5.1. Background: Market challenges of Unilever

Unilever decided to look for entrepreneurial strategies that would renew and capture market shares following an otherwise successful period and a successful corporate reinvention process and consolidation. In 2005, Unilever began developing functional excellence and standardization of processes in order to create a globally driven organization that is capable of utilizing its advantageous scale and scope across national operations. This initiative reflected problems that were experienced earlier, as top management in the industry regarded Unilever to be too loosely structured and inefficient in the 1990s and early 2000s. Consequently, the organization became increasingly more centralized, applying globally uniform management principles across marketplaces. The functional excellence project was finalized in 2009 and Unilever succeeded in penetrating emerging markets and becoming an increasingly more sustainable and profitable company.

However, this new organizational model that honed functional excellence had weaknesses when catering to organizational actions that require a cross-functional business response. From 2011, it became increasingly clear that Unilever had problems with marshaling adequate responses to new venture companies and other entrants. In several market segments, competitors have been faster at developing new FMCG products, at inventing product categories, or at inventing/utilizing new market channels and market offerings — thus, in effect, chipping away at the market shares. It was hard for brand managers at the subsidiary level to respond to this. Unilever's well-oiled functional excellence model more or less automatically sorted out projects that were not created to be big business projects and launchable on a global scale. As pointed out by one informant, "back then, in Unilever, you could only launch big projects if you had a big business case" (R&D director, Unilever). Another informant concurred: "Small competitors find small niches. This used to be a no-go area for Unilever as it would create much complexity in our supply chain" (Marketing director, Unilever).

Emergent small-scale projects for countering more entrepreneurial and niche-oriented marketers were simply stopped by the Unilever procedures or delayed. It would take any market champion a long time to build a convincing business case and unlock sufficient resources for product development, testing, and launch. Product ideation, test, brand policy, and market ramp-up were well-described and carefully managed processes, which would take no less than 18 months, sometimes longer, to complete internally at Unilever. This model worked well if one could anticipate a steady stream of more or less incremental product and market adjustments — however, it worked less well for brands experiencing disruptive, innovative competition and unforeseeable market trends.

4.5.2. Tending to entrepreneurial strategies: A formalized guided evolution approach

As a response to the challenging market conditions, many initiatives were taken at both corporate and divisional levels to change Unilever's organizational strategies, structures, and processes concerning the rejuvenation of current innovation and business practices. In Unilever's foods division, a traditional Unilever R&D foods center, which was located in the small town of Vlaardingen, Netherlands, was moved to an R&D center at the campus of the Wageningen University, a food science university. The innovation headquarters not only aimed to change the physical location and building but, by partnering up and moving closer to Wageningen University, the intent was to create a food innovation ecosystem of suppliers, startups, and academics.

In the summer of 2017, following up on the Wageningen initiative, the president of the R&D division of Unilever foods selected 40 dedicated senior employees to be pioneers in transforming the Unilever foods' R&D division at the campus in Wageningen. This group of employees, the "transformers," was selected to drive the transformation of the R&D center into an innovation center. As explained by one manager, this decision was made "not only to move the people, but actually to change the way we innovate... we are kind of taking the opportunity of the refresh also to reinvent how we do innovation... it maximizes the idea of working as much as possible with the outside world" (Innovation director, Unilever). They were set on a journey to renew Unilever. Another top manager from Unilever's foods division explains their mission as follows: "There is a general belief in Unilever that other market actors will disrupt us at some point. However, the question came about: how can we disrupt ourselves before someone does it for us?" (R&D director, Unilever).

Individually, these transformers self-divided and self-selected into so-called workstreams with different strategic focuses — for example, transforming the culture, the personal skills, and competencies needed for a future way of organizing innovation and the ways of working with innovation. The group, which volunteered to put effort into transforming and simplifying "how we innovate," included eight senior R&D people with daily functions in different parts of the Unilever organization, one global marketer and one externally assigned researcher.

4.5.3. Utilizing an informal bricolage approach for collecting resources

With both endorsement and expectation from division management to experiment and drive new innovation approaches — but with no particular projects, resources, or mandates assigned — this group of senior R&D people searched across the organization for opportunities to endorse. The ambition was to initiate, drive, and discuss the progress on experiments, to provide knowledge and new approaches to innovation and to disseminate these in order to drive the broader transformation of the Unilever foods community. Requested to take an entrepreneurial approach and to have a lean mindset in which experiments that provide knowledge are valued, they sought to initiate, develop, and execute their experiments. However, finding a place and commitment for renewal in Unilever's established structures was not straightforward. A primary challenge was that this initiative demanded thought and resource mobilization processes that were outside of Unilever's existing functional focus. As pointed out by one of the group members:

> It is essential to say that the moment the work started, I think most of the people invited into this space to talk about how we will innovate quickly said: yes, you know how we will innovate is not an R&D problem. It is more of a business issue. This initiative very explicitly requires a different way of collaborating with marketing ... and that touches on the issue of silos and whatever.
>
> (Innovation director, Unilever)

Simultaneously, the marketing division equally underwent strategic changes. The foods marketing headquarters announced a move from London to Rotterdam. Furthermore, top management emphasized the role of the local region-/country-based marketing units in global success. They encouraged and provided the local marketing units (CCBTs) with the authority to drive local product innovation efforts in order to grow in their respective regions. As their counterparts in several other industries, all of whom also face being disrupted by agile moving startups, Unilever also adopted agile innovation approaches, such as scrum and lean startups, in order to move much more quickly from the idea to the market launch stages. A general manager at Unilever said: "We saw that there are opportunities for us to do some things the way they do and that we can do that with a much smaller focus on some of the things that we do."

These strategic changes created opportunities for new initiatives. There were a total of three strategic initiatives: (1) transforming innovation in R&D, (2) inducing agile approaches in Unilever, and (3) the opening needs of local marketing units. The global director of foods marketing, who was the only marketing specialist and who participated in all three of the above initiatives, connected the dots. He used his influence to orchestrate key project startup meetings between various local marketing units and selected members of the R&D innovation team to oversee all three strategic initiatives. In one of these meetings, he met informally with the manager of food brands at Unilever's Nordic subsidiary, based in Stockholm (Sweden). During this meeting, it turned out that the Nordic subsidiary manager (who also attended the workshop) had certain potential branding and product development issues in relation to the relaunching of some of the more traditional brands geared toward the millennial generation population in the Nordic countries. Since Nordic millennials are seen as being ahead in the food trend from the rest of Europe and, possibly, the world, an interesting possible test case surfaced. The global director took these ideas back to the workgroup and pitched them. It was decided to start with this as a test-case project, labeling it the Knorr Nordic Initiative.

4.5.4. Combining guided evolution and bricolage: Starting the Knorr Nordic initiative

In August 2017, the global marketing director from Unilever initiated a kick-off meeting. The objective was to build collaboration in order "to scope which are the potential areas of collaboration we can find to innovate in Nordics" (quote from the meeting invite). The Nordics marketing unit was asked to present a review of consumer insights in the Nordic region and the selected members of the R&D innovation team were asked to draft ideas about how to collaborate in order to serve the local marketing unit's needs. In the meeting, the selected members of the R&D innovation transformers team participated, along with one global marketer and two members of local marketing teams. The aim was to create an opening for the foods division R&D into the local Nordic food marketing unit, thus combining local initiative with global effort. The global marketing manager saw an opportunity to connect and combine units and resources in new ways across traditional functional areas, thus establishing a concurrent approach in which R&D, local marketing, branding, and packaging would work together in a new way. The aim was to use the resources and the strategic openings available to lay the foundation for new opportunities A task force was established with representatives from each of these functions having a responsibility for execution. Each person on this workforce had a senior management person in a sponsor group, whose role it was to pave the way and place sufficient weight on the existing organization by, for example, providing access to resources. A senior marketing manager suggested this design. As he explains:

> We have done that because, in organizations, there is always a large immune system that tries to defend the existing organization. We said, 'Look, if we are to come up with a real push, we need to change how we do things, such as consumer tests.' We wanted to infect the organization with a virus. In a positive sense. Just seed a bit here and there and let's see what happens.
>
> (Marketing director, Unilever)

4.5.5. Further resistance leads to a bootlegging strategy

After the initial meeting, the team (R&D team, local and global marketing) began scoping for an ideal collaboration opportunity that could catch the interests (and make use of the resources) of both parties. The team had several startup and scoping meetings with different Nordic product category marketing managers in order to identify a fruitful collaboration opportunity. However, the R&D's attempt to assist the local marketing efforts in strategic renewal was met with more skepticism and resistance than first anticipated. Even though the local Nordic head of food marketing was supportive, the managers who drove and managed the brand categories (spreads and soups) in different countries (Denmark, Sweden, and Norway) were reluctant to engage. Crossing functional and regional boundaries and, in this sense, entering foreign territory, as well as facing skepticism regarding the required amount of resources requested, meant that the initiative experienced everything — from passive ignoring to direct resistance from the Nordic brand managers.

The project reached an initial roadblock in September 2017; however, the team and Unilever's Nordic local manager still endorsed it. In September and October 2017, the R&D team decided to push one project forward based on the Knorr brand team's initial local marketing challenges. The first phase of the project took an underground approach, not asking for resources, commitments, or permissions from the local marketing unit. Instead, the R&D team worked with their resources and located external resources to produce something of value for the Nordic marketing managers. This initiative was taken to convince the Nordic marketing unit of the value such initiative could offer if they commit to further involvement. The R&D team leveraged free external resources. In this case, the external researcher on the team gathered their resources and staged two rounds of user-driven innovation workshops. Design students at Aalborg University (Denmark), who also happened to be millennials, were asked to develop new product concepts with themselves as the target group. This task was given as a class assignment. The task centered on solving Nordic marketing's strategic agenda — to increase the use of Knorr products by Nordic millennials. The millennial design students were asked to create a concept for a product that they would buy weekly (Fig. 4.2). The idea was to unlock their tacit knowledge about their own generation's consumer expectations in designing and developing an attractive concept.

Fig. 4.2. Pictures from the design students' workshop.

After two months of work with different Nordic millennial design students and several different product concept proposals, a total of 15 different product ideas were ready by the end of November 2017. From this selection, the global R&D unit chose three main concepts that aligned with the values and lifestyles of millennials and brought renewal to the current portfolio within the Knorr product range. These products were a vegan snack, a breakfast snack, and a mash snack, respectively.

4.5.6. Going from a bootlegging to a skunkworks workshop

The team's next step was to present the prototypes to the Nordic subsidiary, hoping to get them to commit to the project. To do so, a prototyping workshop was organized by the team in collaboration with the subsidiary's Knorr brand manager. The workshop aimed to embrace a closer to market development approach and to combine resources in order to drive a faster and more agile product development process. In addition to local brand managers from Unilever Nordic, representatives from global processing, global packaging, global innovation, local marketing, and external packaging teams, as well as local chefs, millennials, and researchers, were invited as well. The two-day workshop (Fig. 4.3) was meant to enhance cross-functional and cross-hierarchical collaboration

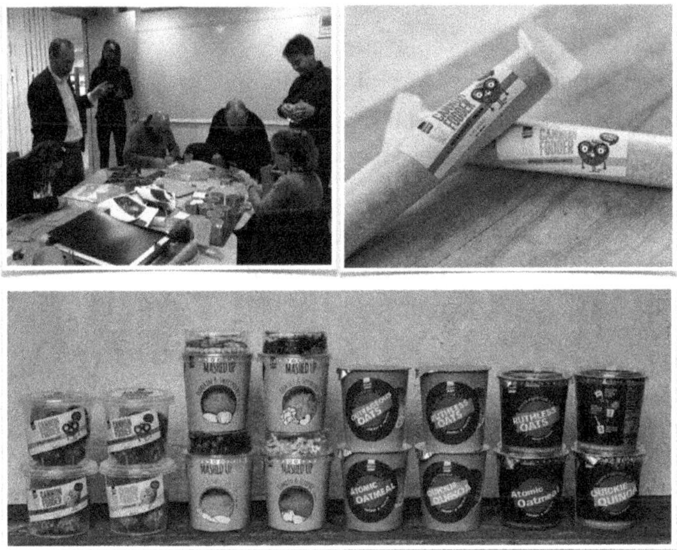

Fig. 4.3. Pictures from the Unilever workshop in Stockholm.

and support further prototype maturation and organizational buy-in to the new form of collaboration. Everyone participated in developing real-life prototypes on the first day. These were then tested by a millennial consumer panel on the second day in a setting organized by the local Knorr brand manager.

4.5.7. Announcing it back into the central organization: Trying a bricolage approach

Since the workshop resulted in renewing the prototypes of product concepts, which the Nordic marketing unit wanted, the R&D and marketing team announced the projects for the broader Unilever organization — including R&D, global marketing and marketing divisions in other regions. The project received great attention and interest within the Unilever organization. The main reason for this surge in interest was the fact that the project had demonstrated that it was possible to develop a product prototype within a few months — something that typically takes much longer and involves more complex market testing, development and quality assurance processes. The Nordic subsidiary of Unilever eventually decided to buy into the project and the key account manager, Hemköp, also engaged.

This local urban retail chain was willing to launch the new product series on a trial basis in the Stockholm area in May 2018.

Unilever's management formally endorsed the project in November 2017 and the local Nordic Knorr brand manager was appointed as the main project manager. He took over this responsibility from the strategic task force to finally release and scale up the project in order for the retailer to be able to launch the product on the set date. This initiative was a new type of responsibility for the local brand manager and it differed from the traditional way of doing things.

> We had the tradition of ... brand building. That is like ... executing the plans in the countries — and brand development. For example, I worked on Magnum (a Unilever ice cream brand). Then it was an evident and precise package to execute.
>
> (Marketing manager, Unilever)

The new responsibility entailed several unknowns for the Nordic Knorr brand manager: "This new project was something else entirely ... the ideas presented at the workshop triggered me. We said, now we are going to do this in an entirely new way" (Marketing manager, Unilever).

A Knorr Nordic core team was organized, consisting of the people involved in executing the process. However, it also engaged a senior executive sponsor team, which was intended to help unlock resources and remove organizational roadblocks. The core project team arranged weekly status meetings, while the sponsor team was supposed to have monthly stakeholder meetings. Each member of the sponsor team was a senior member of R&D or a marketing director.

4.5.8. Facing the corporate immune system: Bootlegging in order to survive

The Nordic team soon realized that, despite the initial success and formal backing from Unilever, effectively shortcutting the existing functional structure and pushing for a more agile product launch was not an easy task. Adopting the renewal project into the global hierarchical, functional, and regional structures of an MNC led to tension and outright resistance. When using established Unilever resources to further develop the product — for example, to develop branding, formulation, processing, and packaging — the team learned that the other departments that controlled these resources did not provide them willingly. Senior stakeholders resisted the renewal initiative in different functions. They did not have control over the Nordic initiative and could not see any reason why they should contribute their support, people, and resources. Consequently, the development of the project was either delayed or stalled. Another issue that arose was that this project competed with other projects for resources. It received attention initially and continued to be monitored by several internal stakeholders; however, it entered into rivalry with other projects to obtain the attention and internal resources it needed.

Finally, the inert established business practices also played a role. One manager, recalling what he described as technical difficulties with providing resources to the Knorr Nordic Project, said:

> We wanted to keep it on a tiny scale. The scale is one of the drivers of the costs of such products. Technically, it is then doable. However, when you produce on a tiny scale, nobody wants to work on your project because they would not see any profits. What will be the outputs and the way forward with the innovation rather than the technical complexity? If we go to complexity, you can always crack the code if you have enough scale or enough resources, and then you have a business case that is good enough, then money is not a problem usually. So, I was not so much bothered with technical difficulties. I am just saying that is what we have to be careful and be decent. We have to be careful with that because that will bring certain complexity.
>
> (R&D manager, Unilever)

Another example of resistance came from the traditional R&D division responsible for product safety and quality issues. Launching a Unilever product requires rigorous testing in order to ensure that shelf life is within acceptable standards and that dangerous products are avoided.

> This test was difficult to accomplish because chilled products mean that you work with short shelf life. You need to make sure that your hygienic standards and quality systems are excellent. So, this was the difficult one... Uh, we had somebody from quality assurance that was involved in this. Moreover, we have done a risk assessment. OK. What kind of ingredients are we talking about? What could be the shelf life if we follow the right procedures?
>
> (Innovation manager, Unilever)

The quality assurance team found the speedy product launch process to be risky and demanded that products were either withdrawn for further testing or launched with the shortest shelf life possible.

One of the informants from the core team explained the encountered resistance in the following way:

> Because we are a big company. Because we are an . . . I think because the entrepreneurial spirit has waned over the years. After all, we are stuck in our processes and these processes were not set up for nothing. Over the years, people realized that we need processes. If something goes wrong, you know we immediately have everybody around our necks. That is why you want to follow all the rules and for good reasons. We have had problems over the years, so that is why you have us in the process. Nevertheless, I also think that people do not understand why the process is there at a particular moment in time, why the rules are there. They stick to the rules and hide behind the process and say no, you do not follow the process. I am not doing anything.
>
> (Innovation manager, Unilever)

The stakeholder sponsor team prioritized negotiating the tension, persuading others and, sometimes, even ignoring organizational resistance in order to overcome it. The core project team members, who had different functions, took different strategies to overcome structural resistance. Some of them, whose superiors told them not to provide resources, volunteered to do this "on the side" as a spare-time hobby. Others, who were more senior, offered the resources they had to help gathered external resources and allow the project to progress. For example, to create a fail-safe strategy, one global packaging director assigned an additional budget line and requested an external Nordic graphic designer to create a conservative version of the new Knorr brand. This version tightly followed the global Knorr brand manual if/when the global branding community attempted to stop the progress of the initiative. The global marketing director continuously supported the project. He pitched for and committed to a budget for an external Nordic graphic designer to create a locally renewing version of the Knorr brand, which all three products were to be launched under. However, global Knorr brand management strongly questioned these brand renewal efforts because they believed that this initiative would confuse customers.

Finally, on May 7, 2018, the three new products were first launched through five Swedish retailers. Based on favorable response to the products,

Fig. 4.4. Products on display at Hemköp's refrigerated counter (Stockholm).

a second launch of these products under the Knorr brand label was decided on in 2019, broadening the brand category to include some of the product ideas that were deselected during the first launch. This product series was launched on a national scale and offered in several additional retail chains (Fig. 4.4).

4.6. Implications for Management and Research

In the FMCG context, continuous transitions in and adjustments to dynamic and complex business conditions are inevitable aspects of organizational life. Furthermore, these processes seem to unfold as part of an ongoing conversation among organizational constituents, seeking to either contribute to these processes or avoid them if their consequences are perceived to oppose other critical strategic priorities. From the findings presented here, there are several useful lessons that can be learned in relation to the perspective of managers who take entrepreneurial marketing initiatives and pursue these processes in an FMCG MNC, such as Unilever.

First, our study suggests that the effectiveness of linear or action-oriented mental models of corporate entrepreneurship is limited because they provide an overly simplistic picture of the challenges that corporate entrepreneurs are likely to meet. Attempts to change things within organizations are frequently and understandably met with rigidity or even resistance, meaning that planned sequences of actions, deadlines, and goals cannot minutely be followed but must be negotiated and renegotiated with both internal and external stakeholders. Goals and deadlines set in informal planning may, indeed, play a role as internal and external signifiers of change. However, both managers and resources often resist the roles that such plans assign to them. Most managers are typically responsible for multiple organizational priorities and processes, which differ from those of the change agents.

Furthermore, making resources available for one purpose usually means that the availability of these resources could potentially be challenging for other purposes. Hence, resources may be "sticky" and difficult to use in other contexts. Breakdowns and deviations are bound to occur, which may not be solved merely by forging ahead. Action toward renewal of marketing efforts must be complemented with attention toward the roots of organizational resistance, as well as how these forces of resistance can be accounted for and, if possible, enrolled or avoided. Resistance acts often have emergent properties — they unfold with and occur because of the attempted change as it unfolds over time. Constituents and their acts of resistance cannot be neutralized or dealt with in advance. However, they must be negotiated en route, often through intensive organizational canvassing and face-to-face meetings with resource holders and influential managers. Sometimes, this leads to new insights and changes the perspective of managers who are responsible for change activities, making them deviate from and piggy-back on other strategic initiatives for shorter and longer periods of time. Consequently, the success or failure of entrepreneurial marketing attempts is seldom categorical and the unintended consequences of change attempts may be as valuable as the intended ones.

A second lesson that can be learned is that it is important to recognize the significance and fleeting nature of top management support. A mandate from top management is often limited and depends on rivaling agendas. Various dynamics can influence whether an entrepreneurial initiative currently operates in a benevolent or hostile context and can navigate accordingly. It is frequently the case — as shown in the Unilever case study — that a strategic initiative ties in with several other strategic initiatives, competing for managerial attention and resources.

Change initiatives may either wane or grow in importance over time. They may be sacrificed or even forgotten about in an influx of events and changes affecting managerial decision-making. There is a continuous challenge for the team involved in keeping abreast with how their initiative ties in with the current priorities of critical constituents in an FMCG MNC. Garbage can model of decision-making.

In terms of research contributions, our study shows that there is room for expanding our insights into the interplay between corporate entrepreneurial initiatives and MNC decision-making. Existing research, such as subsidiary initiative research (Birkinshaw, 1997) and the research of MNC ecology students, often seem to host very static beliefs about the nature of the structures and corresponding social mechanisms that influence corporate entrepreneurship. Adding more theoretical lenses — and understanding under what circumstances each theoretical lens provides a more compelling storyline for understanding unfolding events than another one — provides an important insight that needs further development. This finding echoes Morgan's (2000) call for further research to investigate multiple theoretical metaphors in order to advance both management theory and practice.

In addition, the initial research in this area can benefit from addressing and combining various theoretical approaches regarding how resources and managerial efforts can affect entrepreneurial mar initiatives.

References

Agarwal, R. and Helfat, C. E. (2009). Strategic renewal of organizations. *Organization Science*, **20**(2): 281–293.

Andersen, P. H. and Laursen, L. N. (2020). Entrepreneurial strategies for MNCs: A typology. *The International Journal of Entrepreneurship and Innovation*. Available from: https://doi.org/10.1177/1465750320983156.

Augsdorfer, P. (2005). Bootlegging and path dependency. *Research Policy*, **34**(1): 1–11.

Baker, T. and Nelson, R. E. (2005). Creating something from nothing: Resource construction through entrepreneurial bricolage. *Administrative Science Quarterly*, **50**(3): 329–366.

Balogun, J., Jarzabkowski, P. and Vaara, E. (2011). Selling, resistance, and reconciliation: A critical discursive approach to subsidiary role evolution in MNEs. *Journal of International Business Studies*, **42**(6): 765–786.

Barney, J. B. (2001). Resource-based theories of competitive advantage: A ten-year retrospective on the resource-based view. *Journal of management*, **27**(6): 643–650.

Birkinshaw, J. (1997). Entrepreneurship in multinational corporations: The characteristics of subsidiary initiatives. *Strategic Management Journal*, **18**(3): 207–229.

Birkinshaw, J. and Ridderstråle, J. (1999). Fighting the corporate immune system: A process study of subsidiary initiatives in multinational corporations. *International Business Review,* **8**: 2.

Burgelman, R. A. (1983). A process model of internal corporate venturing in the diversified major firm. *Administrative Science Quarterly*, **28**(2): 223–244.

Burgelman, R. A. (1991). Intraorganizational ecology of strategy making and organizational adaption: Theory and field research. *Organization Science*, **2**(3): 239–262.

Burns, T. and Stalker, G. M. (1961). *The Management of Innovation.* London: Tavistock.

Castellacci, F., Gulbrandsen, M., Hildrum, J., *et al.* (2018). Functional centrality and innovation intensity: Employee-level analysis of the Telenor Group. *Research Policy*, **47**: 1674–1687.

Chesborough, H. (2003). Open Innovation: The New Imperative for Creating and Profiting from Technology. Boston, MA: Harvard Business School Press.

Christensen, C. M., Raynor, M. E. and Anthony, S. D. (2003). Six keys to building new markets by unleashing disruptive innovation. *Harvard Management*. EEUU.

Colakoglu, S., Yamao, S. and Lepak, D. P. (2014). Knowledge creation capability in MNC subsidiaries: Examining the roles of global and local knowledge inflows and subsidiary knowledge stocks. *International Business Review*, **23**(1): 91–101.

Covin, J. G. and Slevin, D. P. (1991). A conceptual model of entrepreneurship as firm behavior. *Entrepreneurship Theory and Practice*, **16**(1): 7–26.

Criscuolo, P., Salter, A. and Ter Wal, A. L. (2014). Going underground: Bootlegging and individual innovative performance. *Organization Science*, **25**(5): 1287–1305.

Di Domenico, M., Haugh, H. and Tracey, P. (2010). Social bricolage: Theorizing social value creation in social enterprises. *Entrepreneurship Theory and Practice,* **34**(4): 681–703.

Dörrenbächer, C. and Gammelgaard, J. (2016). Subsidiary initiative taking in multinational corporations: The relationship between power and issue selling. *Organization Studies*, **37**(9): 1249–1270.

Duymedjian, R. and Rüling, C. C. (2010). Towards a foundation of bricolage in organization and management theory. *Organization Studies*, **31**(2): 133–151.

Eastman, *et al.* (2013). *The Marketing Management Journal*, **23**(1): 57–73.

Enright, M. J. and Subramanian, V. (2007). An organizing framework for MNC subsidiary typologies. *Management International Review*, **47**(6): 895–924.

Fecher, F., Winding, J., Hutter, K., *et al.* (2020). Innovation labs from a participants' perspective. *Journal of Business Research*, **110**: 567–576.

Fisher, G. (2012). Effectuation, causation, and bricolage: A behavioral comparison of emerging theories in entrepreneurship research. *Entrepreneurship Theory and Practice*, **36**(5): 1019–1051.

Fosfuri, A. and Rønde, T. (2009). Leveraging resistance to change and the skunkworks model of innovation. *Journal of Economic Behavior & Organization*, **72**(1): 274–289.

Garud, R. and Karnøe, P. (2005). Distributed agency and interactive emergence. In *Innovating Strategy Process* (pp. 88–96). Hoboken: John Wiley & Sons.

Globocnik, D. and Salomo, S. (2015). Do formal management practices impact the emergence of bootlegging behavior? *Journal of Product Innovation Management*, **32**(4): 505–521.

Gwynne, P. (1997). Skunkworks, 1990s-style. *Research Technology Management*, **40**(4): 18–23.

Hamel, G. (1996). Strategy as revolution. *Harvard Business Review*, **74**(4): 69–82.

Hamel, G. and Ruben, P. (2000). *Leading the Revolution* (Vol. 286). Boston, MA: Harvard Business School Press.

Hamel, G. and Tennant, N. (2015). The 5 requirements of a truly innovative company. *Harvard Business Review*, **27**.

Hornsby, J. S., Kuratko, D. F. and Zahra, S. A. (2002). Middle managers' perception of the internal environment for corporate entrepreneurship: Assessing a measurement scale, *Journal of Business Venturing*, **17**(3): 253–273.

Howell, J. M. and Higgins, C. A. (1990). Champions of technological innovation. *Administrative Science Quarterly*, **35**(2): 317–341.

Huff, J. O., Huff, A. S. and Thomas, H. (1992). Strategic renewal and the interaction of cumulative stress and inertia. *Strategic Management Journal*, **13**(S1): 55–75.

Jennings, P. D., Greenwood, R., Lounsbury, M. D. and Suddaby, R. (2013). Institutions, entrepreneurs, and communities: A special issue on entrepreneurship. *Journal of Business Venturing,* **28**(1), 1–9.

Kanter, R. M. (1988). When a thousand flowers bloom: Structural, collective, and social conditions for innovation in organizations. *Knowledge Management and Organisational Design,* **10**: 93–131.

Kilenthong, P., Hultman, C. M. and Hills, G. E. (2016). Entrepreneurial orientation as the determinant of entrepreneurial marketing behaviors. *Journal of Small Business Strategy*, **26**(2), 1–22.

Knudsen, T. and Levinthal, D. A. (2007). Two faces of search: Alternative generation and alternative evaluation. *Organization Science*, **18**(1): 39–54.

Kogut, B. and Zander, U. (1993). Knowledge of the firm and the evolutionary theory of the multinational corporation. *Journal of International Business Studies*, **24**(4): 625–645.

Laukkanen, S., Lindell, M. and Vanjoki, A. (2017). Corporate entrepreneurship in a large company: Skunkworks or guided. In Gabrielsson, J. (Ed.), *Handbook of Research on Corporate Governance and Entrepreneurship* (pp. 397–434). Cheltenham: Edward Elgar Publishing.

Lauring, J., Andersen, P. H., Storgaard, M., *et al.* (2017). Low-intensity conflict in multinational corporations. *Multinational Business Review,* **25**: 11–27.

Laursen, L. N. (2017). *Matching to openly innovate with suppliers: The phenomenon of innovation summits*. Ph.D.-serien for Det Ingenioer-og Naturvidenskabelige Fakultet. Aalborg, Denmark: Aalborg Universitet.

Laursen, L. N. and Andersen, P. H. (2016). Innovation summits: Comparison and conceptualization. *European Journal of Marketing*, **50**: 2249–2268.

Laursen, L. N. and Haase, L. M. (2020). Reinterpreting tradition to digitalize: Framing the design DNA of LEGO house. In *Synergy: DRS International Conference 2020* (pp. 2011–2022). Design Society.

Lee, Y. and Evans, D. M. (2012). What drives organizations to employ design-driven approaches? A study of fast-moving consumer goods brand development. *Design Management Journal*, **7**(1): 74–88.

Leonard-Barton, D. (1992). Core capabilities and core rigidities: A paradox in managing new product development. *Strategic Management Journal*, **13**(S1): 111–125.

Lévi-Strauss, C. (1967). *The Savage Mind*. Chicago: University of Chicago Press.

Linzmayer, O. W. (2004). Apple confidential 2.0: The definitive history of the world's most colorful company. San Francisco: No Starch Press.

Lovas, B. and Ghoshal, S. (2000). Strategy as guided evolution. *Strategic Management Journal*, **21**: 875–896.

Mahoney, J. T. (1995). The management of resources and the resource of management. *Journal of Business Research*, **33**(2): 91–101.

March, J. G. (1991). Exploration and exploitation in organizational learning. *Organization Science*, **2**(1): 71–87.

Markides, C. and Geroski, P. (2003). Teaching elephants how to dance and other silly ideas. *Business Strategy Review*, **14**(3): 49–53.

Meacham, M., Faelli, F., Giménez, E. and Blasberg, J. (2018). *Overcoming the Existential Crisis in Consumer Goods*. Boston: Bain & Company.

Miles, M. P. and Darroch, J. (2006). Large firms, entrepreneurial marketing processes, and the cycle of competitive advantage. *European Journal of Marketing*, **40**(5/6): 485–501.

Morgan, G. (2000). *Images of Organization* (2nd ed.). California: Sage Publications.

Ng, E. S., Schweitzer, L. and Lyons, S. T. (2010). New generation, great expectations: A field study of the millennial generation. *Journal of Business and Psychology*, **25**(2), 281–292.

O'Brien, D., Scott, P. S. and Gibbons, P. (2013). Developing strategy from the middle: Subsidiary strategy and the role of the subsidiary general manager. *Irish Journal of Management*, **32**(2): 109.

Pfeffer, J. (1997). New directions for organization theory: Problems and prospects. Oxford: Oxford University Press on Demand.

Rich, P. (1992). The organizational taxonomy: Definition and design. *Academy of Management Review*, **17**(4): 758–781.

Schindehutte, M., Morris, M. H., Kuratko, D. F., *et al.* (2018). Unpacking corporate entrepreneurship: A critique and extension. In Kuratko, D. F., Hoskinson, S. (Eds.), *The Challenges of Corporate Entrepreneurship in the Disruptive Age* (Vol. 28, pp. 11–35). Bingley: Emerald Publishing Limited.

Schmitt, A., Raisch, S. and Volberda, H. W. (2018). Strategic renewal: Past research, theoretical tensions and future challenges. *International Journal of Management Reviews*, **20**(1), 81–98.

Stopford, J. M. and Baden-Fuller, C. W. (1994). Creating corporate entrepreneurship. *Strategic Management Journal*, **15**(7): 521–536.

Tangpong, C., Michalisin, M. D. and Melcher, A. J. (2008). Toward a typology of buyer–supplier relationships: A study of the computer industry. *Decision Sciences*, **39**(3): 571–593.

Weber, M. (2009). *The Theory of Social and Economic Organization*. New York, NY: Simon and Schuster.

Williams, C. and Lee, S. H. (2009). International management, political arena and dispersed entrepreneurship in the MNC. *Journal of World Business*, **44**(3): 287–299.

Yang, M. (2018). International entrepreneurial marketing strategies of MNCs: Bricolage as practiced by marketing managers. *International Business Review*, **25**(5): 1045–1056.

Yuan, W., Bao, Y. and Olson, B. J. (2017). CEOs' ambivalent interpretations, organizational market capabilities, and corporate entrepreneurship as responses to strategic issues. *Journal of World Business*, **52**(2): 312–326.

Zahra, S. A. and Garvis, D. M. (2000). International corporate entrepreneurship and firm performance: The moderating effect of international environmental hostility. *Journal of Business Venturing,* **15**(5–6): 469–492.

https://doi.org/10.1142/9781800612266_0006

Chapter 5

Individual and Contextual Factors Affecting Employees' Inclination to Bootlegging

Dietfried Globocnik
Alpen-Adria Universitaet Klagenfurt, Klagenfurt, Austria
dietfried.globocnik@aau.at

Abstract

This chapter reviews past quantitative research on individual factors such as self-efficacy and risk propensity as well as contextual factors of formal and social control, which were found to affect employees' individual bootlegging tendencies. The chapter also puts bootlegging in the context of related innovative behaviors to highlight their conceptual similarities and differences. The chapter also presents various avenues for future research covering further theoretical refinements, studying organizational-level outcomes of bootlegging, and empirical measurement issues that need to be resolved to facilitate progress in the quantitative stream of the bootlegging literature.

5.1. Introduction

To motivate employees to innovate and contribute proactively to the organization's renewal of its scope and further growth, managers facilitate their employees' innovative behavior with various measures aiming at providing innovation guidance and creating structures and a climate for innovation (e.g., Zahra and Covin, 1995; Hornsby *et al.*, 2002; Kuratko *et al.*, 2005; Antoncic, 2007; Bart, 2002). However, this view on innovation outcomes being solely a product of management-induced organizational design neglects the capacity of the individual employee to create his or her own space for innovation in and around the structures of the focal organization to realize innovation (Rindova *et al.*, 2009; Courpasson *et al.*, 2016), sometimes even ignoring or undermining established rules (Aldrich and Fiol, 1994). One of these autonomous innovative behaviors of employees is bootlegging, which shifts the perspective from a managerial view on how to design for innovativeness of an organization to how employees take charge of innovation within the organization but outside managerial control.

The concept of bootlegging describes bottom-up, non-programmed innovation activities of employees, through which they informally initiate and take first steps toward realization of their own innovation ideas without the knowledge or authorization of their management (Augsdorfer, 1996). From a more activity-based perspective (Globocnik and Salomo, 2015), the defining elements of bootlegging involve:

(i) *Secret creation and elaboration of new ideas*, which are developed independently and not necessarily comply with the current scope of the organization, although they usually benefit the organization; employees disclose their bootlegged ideas only once feasibility and potential can be shown whereas when the attempt fails, they can stop it without the need for justification or informing a manager (Koch and Leitner, 2008).

(ii) *Self-organized sourcing of resources* to carry bootlegging activities out; due to the secrecy, bootlegging employees lack officially committed resources and have to invest their private time, gathering hidden or forgotten resources within their organizations, or divert resources of legitimized projects from their intended use (Burgelman, 1983; Roussel *et al.*, 1991).

(iii) *Bypassing formal communication channels*, formal communication channels are frequently avoided during bootlegging activities (e.g., when reaching out to potential customers, suppliers, or experts) and when promoting a successful bootlegged outcome to achieve management buy-in by reaching out directly to those who are supposed to be most receptive to new ideas even if the bootleg employee is not under their supervision (Howell and Higgins, 1990; Masoudnia and Szwejczewski, 2012; Globocnik and Salomo, 2015).

This book chapter aims to differentiate bootlegging from other related behaviors helping to identify core individual characteristics that explain the emergence of this deviant behavior. Furthermore, contextual factors are elaborated that facilitate these individual characteristics to manifest in more or less bootlegging of the employee. Thereby, the focus is on findings validated by quantitative empirical research. Finally, avenues for future research are discussed to develop our limited knowledge about bootlegging further.

5.2. Bootlegging and Related Behaviors

More recently, the theory of creative deviance (Mainemelis, 2010) has frequently been used as the theoretical foundation to explain antecedents and consequences of bootlegging. However, bootlegging and creative deviance are not synonyms. *Creative deviance* describes the behavior of employees to strive for legitimate innovation goals through illegitimate means when they develop their own idea in violation of explicit managerial orders to stop pursuing the idea (Mainemelis, 2010). Bootlegging is closely related to creative deviance but represents a broader concept that is not narrowed to situations in which employees elaborate ideas that have formally been rejected, but also entails situations in which employees secretly innovate without permission regardless of whether the idea has been rejected by management before or not (Lin *et al.*, 2016). Thus, creative deviance might be an act of bootlegging, but not vice versa.

The literature also mentions other innovative behaviors that share some characteristics of bootlegging but need to be treated separately as they differ in one or several defining elements.

Unsponsored inventions (Alexy *et al.*, 2016) also describe innovation activities that are not part of an official innovation program with assigned resources, but these activities are not necessarily performed in secret or outside formal structures.

Permitted bootlegging explicitly allows privileged employees to dedicate a specific amount of work time to develop their own ideas and thereby differs from traditional bootlegging by the provided resources and the lack of secrecy (Augsdorfer, 2008).

Moonlighting describes secret activities, for which an employee uses organizational resources and work time. However, moonlighting serves purely personal interests and harms the organization (Masoudnia and Szwejczewski, 2012).

Bricolage subsumes activities to create something new by applying recombinations of the resources that are already at hand (Baker and Nelson, 2005). *Improvisation* is a behavior that is characterized by simultaneous design and execution of activities aimed at finding a novel approach to address an opportunity. Typically, there is no action plan, and intuition is the initial stimulus. In contrast to bricolage, this behavior is not limited to applying preexisting resources and its novelty goes beyond recombinations of existing elements (Moorman and Miner, 1998). Bootlegging may involve bricolage and improvisation, but they are not inherently happening in secret. New resources might also be gathered from external sources to realize bootleg projects and it is self-organizing of resources rather than the reuse of existing ones that defines bootlegging.

Skunkworks is another concept that also describes isolated, hidden innovation activities that take place outside the operational organizational structure without the knowledge of the rest of the organization. However, employees (or typically a team of experts) of such projects are explicitly assigned by top management, receive legitimized resources for their activities, and directly report to top management (Tushman and O'Reilly, 1999). Thus, skunkwork is not hidden from management.

Finally, *user innovation* describes a self-initiated, voluntary, and often uncompensated innovative behavior independent from the manufacturer (von Hippel, 1986). Users also deploy their own resources such as time, materials, and knowledge to realize their own ideas. However, users are typically located outside the organizational boundaries, and their activities do not benefit manufacturers if users do not share their innovations.

5.3. Individual Characteristics Driving Bootlegging Behavior

In the context of corporate innovation, the investigation of individual characteristics of employees is important to better understand how to achieve innovative outcomes because it is not the organization itself but the individuals within that organization that innovate (Krueger, 2000). This applies especially to employees who temporarily ignore formal rules, procedures, and monitoring systems established by the organization as it is the case for bootlegging employees.

In search for individual differences that might explain why some employees engage in bootlegging whereas others do not, a first start is drawing on the main attributes of this behavior: self-initiated and secret, autonomous, and violating organizational norms. Individual differences might therefore be grounded in the bootlegging employee's self-beliefs of having what it takes to micromanage innovation themselves and independently, and also in their inclination to cope with risks. This section presents corresponding findings of research projects that focused on the relevance of self-efficacy and risk propensity.

5.3.1. Self-efficacy

Research has identified employees' self-efficacy as an important antecedent of various compliant manifestations of innovative and proactive behaviors such as idea submissions (Axtell *et al.*, 2000), taking charge (Morrison and Phelps, 1999) and personal initiative (Speier and Frese, 1997). Thereby, the intensity of employees' bootlegging behavior might also be dependent upon their feeling to be capable and motivated to engage in this deviant behavior. Self-efficacy refers to one's self-beliefs in the ability to exercise control over events, to overcome challenges, and to achieve goals independently (Bandura, 1986). Higher self-efficacy comes along with higher intrinsic motivation for a task resulting from setting higher goals and having firmer commitment to them. It is also associated with exerting greater effort to master challenges and being more persistent when facing obstacles and barriers (Wood and Bandura, 1989). Higher self-efficacy also affects perceptions in such a way that opportunities are framed more positively, risks become less salient, and success rather than failure scenarios are anticipated (Krueger and Dickson, 1994; Mohammed and Billings, 2002; Mitchell and Shepherd, 2010).

Self-efficacy is always task specific, that is, an individual can have different levels of self-efficacy in different domains (Bandura, 1997). In the particular context of bootlegging, the self beliefs in one's capabilities to perform refer to tasks associated with innovation initiatives in the early entrepreneurial stage of the innovation process within an organizational context, which Globocnik and Salomo (2015) refer to as intrapreneurial self-efficacy. Employees with high intrapreneurial self-efficacy are more likely to engage in bootlegging because they believe in having what it takes to successfully develop ideas without their organization's support, accept the risk associated with their unorthodox and secret approach to innovation, and anticipate to later succeed in obtaining buy-in from managerial decision makers. High self-efficacious employees are also more successful in their underground endeavors due to their stronger goal commitment, intrinsic motivation, and greater efforts invested into their innovation activities. The quantitative empirical findings provide ample support that employees with higher intrapreneurial self-efficacy initiate more bootleg projects, more often organize resources necessary for their secret innovation activities themselves, and also more frequently bypass formal communication channels than their peers with lower self-efficacy.

Later quantitative research by Ghasemzadeh *et al.* (2020) replicated the finding that self-efficacy makes employees more proactive and likely to engage in bootlegging activities within their organization. They further report that this higher bootlegging intensity fosters their lead userness, that is, facilitates them to be more willing to think of problems associated with products or services of their focal organization and to provide appropriate new ideas and solutions.

Related research on creative deviance, which refers to the particular bootlegging situation in which employees continue to elaborate their idea despite explicit order of their managers to stop working on that idea. Interestingly, self-efficacy has no impact on creative deviance. This does not necessarily contradict prior findings (Globocnik and Salomo, 2015; Ghasemzadeh *et al.*, 2020) but rather emphasizes the difference between creative deviance and bootlegging. Because creative or intrapreneurial self-efficacy refer to beliefs in one's abilities to generate and realize ideas, it fosters the motivation for independent innovation activities but not necessarily to take it up with managers and the involved power dynamics when disobeying managerial orders and breaking with managerial expectations as in the case of creative deviance.

5.3.2. Risk propensity

Innovation activities are inherently risky due to uncertainties regarding market response and technical feasibility as well as potential internal barriers and conflicts when challenging the established status quo protected by the organization (Ahuja and Lampert, 2001; Klein and Knight, 2005), especially when the degree of innovation is high (O'Connor and Veryzer, 2001). As employees usually fear failure (Zhou and George, 2001), they require a certain risk tolerance to engage in innovation activities (Telusk *et al.*, 1997).

Under this premise, labeling bootlegging as a risk-taking or risk-avoiding behavior of employees is difficult. Bootlegging employees benefit from gaining recognition in case of success and from broadening their knowledge, and the organization benefits from accelerated innovation activities through bypassing bureaucratic processes and the additional value created by the bootlegged outcome itself (Burgelman, 1983; Abetti, 1997; Pearson, 1997; Augsdorfer, 2005; Koch and Leitner, 2008; Masoudnia and Szwejczewski, 2012). The secret nature of bootlegging further reduces certain risks for the employee. Failure does not become visible to others and thereby bootlegging protects employees from status and reputation loss. Also, the psychological pressure to deliver results is lower. Furthermore, innovating without the knowledge of the supervisor allows employees to engage in these activities even if they are not part of the official job description, and protects ideas that are outside the current strategic scope of the firm without the fear of being rejected or stopped by higher authorities (Pearson, 1997; Kanter, 2000; Koch and Leitner, 2008; Augsdorfer, 2008). Nevertheless, bootlegging is a deviant behavior and ignores formal structures, norms, and policies of the organization. Diverting organizational resources from their intended use for own innovation activities and bypassing communication channels might also come along with potential negative consequences if observed by the responsible supervisors. To better understand who engages in bootlegging activities, it is thereby valuable to investigate whether bootlegging is a behavioral strategy of risk-affine or risk-averse employees.

Risk propensity describes a relatively stable tendency of an individual to take or avoid risks (Sitikin and Pablo, 1992) that affects behavior through making upside or downside potential of decision options more or less salient (Lopes, 1987). The study of Globocnik (2019) argues and finds empirical evidence that employees with higher risk propensity are more likely to engage in different bootlegging behaviors than employees with lower risk propensity. Risk-affine employees are more focused on and anticipate a higher likelihood of achieving positive outcomes of their bootlegging activities such as the reputation gains, broadening one's knowledge, and the value created for the organization. Simultaneously, they underweight risks associated with bootlegging such as the loss of the resources they invest in case of failure and the negative consequences when going against organizational norms. In contrast, these threats are more salient for risk-averse employees and the positive outcomes less likely to be achieved, which makes bootlegging less favorable for them. Related research on creative deviance also finds risk propensity to be a strong predictor of this specific form of bootlegging in which employees continue to work on their ideas despite explicit order from their management to stop (Tenzer and Young, 2020).

5.3.3. Related individual characteristics

Bootlegging research has identified various other personal characteristics. Bootlegging employees are characterized by high ambition, intrinsic motivation, extensive working hours, obsession with their ideas, and being unconventional, among the best and brightest employees, nonconformists, and uneasy to supervise (Augsdorfer, 1996; Michalik, 2003). A few studies provide quantitative empirical evidence, which are also related to the discussed characteristics of self-efficacy and risk propensity and use established psychometric tests and scales to assess individual characteristics that separate bootleg entrepreneurs from their nonbootlegging peers.

One characteristic is *individual creativity*. Creativity is closely related to intrinsic task motivation, problem-solving abilities, and task commitment (Amabile, 1988, 1996). Using the *Test zum Schöpferischen Denken – Zeichnerisch* (TSD-Z) creativity test, Augsdorfer (2012) demonstrates that bootlegging employees indeed score higher in this test.

Another interesting connection prior literature has made is the connection between (embedded) user innovation, lead userness, and bootlegging. Indeed, there are many similarities between innovating users and bootleg entrepreneurs, such as the self-starting innovative behavior based on personally perceived deficits or opportunities, the independence of these activities, and the necessity to gather own resources (Globocnik, 2015). Ghasemzadeh *et al.* (2020) find a positive relationship between bootlegging and the *benefit expectation*-related dimension of lead userness of employees and argue that bootlegging facilitates their willingness to identify and solve problems with the products and services of their focal firm. Globocnik (2015) takes a different approach by conceptualizing and empirically demonstrating that employees' lead userness in terms of their *benefit expectations* from better solutions and their *ahead of the trend position* predisposes them to engage more frequently in bootlegging activities. In addition, a superior *network position*, that is, being a central hub within the department and being well connected within people located in other departments, is supported as a strong driver of bootlegging activities.

Related research on creative deviance also finds that a higher mastery achievement orientation (Tenzer and Yang, 2019), risk propensity, allocentrism, organizational commitment (Tenzer and Yang, 2020), openness to experiences, and conscientiousness (Martin and Ismail, 2019) foster this specific form of bootlegging.

5.4. Contextual Factors Affecting Bootlegging Behavior

Bootlegging activities take place "underground" and thereby are difficult to control through managerial measures. Despite their autonomous actions, however, bootlegging employees do not operate in an organizational vacuum like independent entrepreneurs (Luchsinger and Bagby, 1987). Thereby, the emergence of bootlegging behavior is also affected by the organizational context in which this behavior takes place. This is also in line with the theory of creative deviance (Mainemelis, 2010), which is located at the organizational level and argues that organizational constraints — innovation goals, their reinforcement, and limited resources — are the actual causing factors of creative deviance emerging in organizations.

The first quantitative studies relevant for identifying organizational antecedents of individual bootlegging did not focus on bootlegging but corporate entrepreneurial behaviors in general, and the investigated behaviors also include bootlegging-related aspects. Hornsby, Kuratko and Montagno (1999) and Kuratko, Hornsby and Bishop (2005) found that the number of employees' unofficial improvements without organizational approval increases with higher management support for innovation, higher levels of work discretion, and higher organizational boundaries in terms of clear goals and process guidelines. Furthermore, the frequency with which procedures are bypassed to pursue ideas increases with more management support, higher work discretion, and more rewards.

Quantitative research that investigated the impact of organizational factors on the emergence of bootlegging in particular is rare. Furthermore, scholars call for taking a person-context interactionist perspective to better understand the behavior of employees in organizations that sees employee behavior as a function of personal and environmental factors (Zhou and Hoever, 2014). This fits with the future research avenues for creative deviance proposed by Mainemelis (2010), who pointed out that the theory explains the organizational setting facilitating deviance but that individual factors need to be considered to understand why within the same organization some employees engage in creative deviant whereas others do not. Thus, organizational factors might determine individual behavior but also influence behavioral choice indirectly by shaping perceptions or motivations of the individual resulting in certain behaviors.

For the subsequent discussion of organizational factors relevant for the emergence of bootlegging behavior, they are categorized into formal and social controls. This classification follows organizational control theory (Ouchi, 1979), which deals with the different mechanisms and principles the organization can apply to align its members with the organizational goals.

5.4.1. Formal controls

Formal controls involve the specification of goals and tasks to support coordination and reduce information asymmetries within the organization (Jaworski and Macinnis, 1989). Therefore, behavioral (or process) controls determine for employees how certain tasks are to be executed whereas output controls refer to the defined interim and final outcomes of such tasks as desired and monitored by the organization (Ouchi, 1979; Eisenhardt, 1985; Turner and Makhija, 2006). For the particular case of bootlegging behavior, the formal controls refer to management practices that are directly related to employees' execution of front-end activities. Four formal controls have been investigated in the quantitative research of Globocnik and Salomo (2015), who also applied a person-context interactionist perspective by considering the effects of formal controls on and through the individual employees' intrapreneurial self-efficacy.

Strategic autonomy describes the degree of independence and discretion that employees have in their jobs (Bailyn, 1985). "Strategic" refers to the freedom to engage in activities that might even be outside the organization's strategic scope without supervisory approval, which provides them with the necessary practical and psychological requirements to do so (Mainemelis, 2010). From a practical perspective, employees with higher autonomy can allocate their own resources and have better access to organizational resources to realize their innovations (Keltner, Gruenfeld and Anderson, 2003). Their work discretion also comes along with being less tightly monitored, which makes it easier to engage in activities outside organizational norms (George, 2007). From a psychological perspective, work discretion means the ability to choose what to work on (Marvel *et al.*, 2007), which results in the employee developing psychological ownership of decisions they make (Parker, Williams and Turner, 2006) and builds commitment and intrinsic motivation for the involved tasks (Amabile, 1996). Autonomy also facilitates perceiving more potential returns and taking more risk (Keltner, Gruenfeld and Anderson, 2003). Thus, higher strategic autonomy helps employees to develop motivation and commitment to bootlegging activities that are uncertain regarding their outcomes, violate organizational norms, and involve personal risk. Indeed, the empirical findings support that strategic autonomy is associated with more bootlegged projects, more frequently bypassing official communication channels, and more often gathering own resources to realize secret projects.

Furthermore, strategic autonomy also fosters bootlegging indirectly by improving employees' intrapreneurial self-beliefs. Self-efficacy is affected by the degree to which a situation is perceived as being controllable, which in turn depends on the level of independence (Gist and Mitchell, 1992). Higher autonomy over core aspects of tasks creates a feeling of having control over future outcomes (Bandura, 1997) and of having the capability to influence others to see things in a desired way (Lee and Ofshe, 1981). Similar to prior research in the context of compliant innovative behaviors (Speier and Frese, 1997; Axtell and Parker, 2003; Parker, Williams and Turner, 2006), research on bootlegging finds empirical evidence that strategic autonomy strengthens employees' intrapreneurial self-efficacy (Globocnik and Salomo, 2015).

Front-end formality refers to the level of process and output controls by which ideas for innovations are explored, developed, and selected (Burgelman and Sayles, 1986). In innovation management they are typically implemented in some forms of stage-and-gate-type systems (Cooper, 2006; Schultz *et al.*,

2019). Front-end formality does not affect the general emergence of bootleg projects but reduces the frequency with which bootlegging employees bypass official channels and provide their own resources (Globocnik and Salomo, 2015). The reasons behind this observation is less clear. One explanation is that the formal position established by the formal structure that is receptive to new ideas make bypassing communication channels obsolete. Alternatively, the formally established place to go for ideas could make it less likely that bypassing official channels is tolerated (Criscuolo, Salter and Ter Wal, 2014). The limiting effect on independent resource gathering efforts for bootleg projects might be caused by formal processes already providing sufficient slack resources for secret innovation activities. Alternatively, the formalization could just make it more difficult to divert resources as they are assigned to official projects and closely monitored. However, this does not imply that formal processes prevent bootlegging behavior in general but the negative impact of higher levels of innovation process formality on bootlegging intensity has been supported in different empirical study contexts (Globocnik and Salomo, 2015; Globocnik, 2015).

Besides this regulating role of front-end formality for bootlegging behaviors, formality also has an indirect positive impact through self-efficacy (Globocnik and Salomo, 2015). Self-efficacy depends on the availability of action strategies, that is, the knowledge about how to perform a task (Bandura, 1986). By clearly outlining the necessary tasks and deliveries for innovation activities, formal innovation processes provide guidelines how to execute innovation (Goodale *et al.*, 2011) — even if this happens in secret — and thereby increase employees' intrapreneurial self-efficacy, which in turn is a driving force behind bootlegging behavior. This suggests an ambivalent role of front-end formality for the emergence of bootlegging.

Rewards describe financial or nonfinancial consequences provided by the organization following the accomplishment of an agreed goal (Griffin, 1997; Feldman, 1996). Rewards enhance intrinsic motivation and deviating from established routines by increasing the desirability of a behavior, which strengthens goal commitment and self-imposed performance pressure (Eisenberger and Aselage, 2009). Rewards also signal which behavior is of particular value for the organization and affects individuals' attitudes toward that behavior (Bandura, 1986). Rewards for innovative outcomes direct employees' attention toward the organization's desire for innovation (Scott and Bruce, 1994), and employees will strive for innovation even if it requires illegitimate means such as bootlegging. Indeed, rewards are positively associated with engaging in more bootleg projects, more often bypassing communication channels, and more frequently gathering own resources to realize innovation (Globocnik and Salomo, 2015).

Sanctions, which refer to negative consequences such as degradation or status loss following failure, has a limited impact on bootlegging behavior (Globocnik and Salomo, 2015). Potential negative consequences limit the intensity by which bootleg employees provide their own resources for their secret innovation activities as a means to reduce their exposure and risk in case they fail. However, potential sanctions do not result in more or less bootleg projects suggesting that bootlegging employees do not see this secret behavior as an action strategy to avoid risk in case of failure but also not as bearing additional risks. Potential sanctions also do not affect how often employees bypass the organizational channels. This might be grounded in addressing those in the organization that are more likely to be open to new ideas and from whom no consequences in case of failure can be expected.

5.4.2. Social controls

Social controls guide and influence employee behavior to achieve congruency with organizational goals through socialization processes (Ouchi, 1979; Turner and Makhija, 2006). Shared and internalized norms, values, and visions align employee decisions and behaviors with the organization (Jaworski, 1988). Hierarchical social controls describe senior managers becoming actively involved at lower levels to demonstrate their solidarity with all employees and to achieve a mutual commitment to common organizational objectives. In contrast, lateral social controls influence the behavior and decisions of employees through norms and values shared among peers. The common understanding about what is appropriate and expected in the organization facilitates peer pressure on the individual employee to align his or her behavior with the desired organizational goals and to coordinate with peers to achieve such goals (Kirsch *et al.*, 2010). Social controls are especially useful in situations in which tasks are difficult to program (e.g., when tasks are novel and uncertain or when managers lack knowledge about how tasks are executed) and outcomes are difficult to measure (Ouchi, 1979; Kirsch, 2004).

For the particular case of bootlegging behavior, social controls refer to different forms of direct management interventions, which are related to employees' innovation activities. In the quantitative research of Globocnik (2019), this concept was investigated for four aspects of managerial support for innovation. He also applied a person-context interactionist perspective by considering the interactions between risk propensity and different forms of management support. In other terms, social controls are not only seen as impacting bootlegging behavior directly but also indirectly by shaping employees' risk and return perceptions.

Management support — Encouragement of innovation refers to verbal support, openness to new ideas, and motivation to take initiative (Amabile, 1996; Tesluk *et al.*, 1997; Tierney *et al.*, 1999; Scott and Bruce, 1994). Encouragement for innovation strengthens the positive relationship between risk propensity and the frequency by which own resources are provided for bootlegging activities. Thus, managers who emphasize the benefit of innovation and taking initiative in their organization achieve that employees are more willing to invest into their secret activities, but only by those who are willing to take more risks and who see more benefits in bootlegging.

Management support — Providing resources refers to managerial measures to provide employees with time and funds to elaborate their ideas, thus, resources they personally have the power to assign as they see fit (Drazin *et al.*, 1999; Judge *et al.*, 1997; Nijhof *et al.*, 2002; Mumford *et al.*, 2002). By providing additional resources for innovation activities, managers can reduce the tendency of risk-affine employees to gather their own resources for secret innovation activities. Managers unlock additional means for willing employees to pursue innovation activities and thereby reduce the necessity for them to secretly search for the time and materials required to realize their ideas.

Management support — Giving feedback subsumes behaviors of managers by which they value employees' contributions, listen to concerns, and provide space for open discussions (Oldham and Cummings, 1996; Scott and Bruce, 1994; Pearce *et al.*, 1997). Establishing an open, trustful communication about new ideas, reduces the perceived necessity of employees to engage in bootlegging as the only mean to overcome the status quo of the organization. A climate of psychological safety created by open and honest feedback and exchange between manager and employee reduces the frequency of bootlegging.

Management support — Sponsoring refers to management behavior helping employees to overcome internal barriers and pass the organizational red tape (Pearce *et al.*, 1997; Hornsby *et al.*, 2005). Sponsoring does not really change the opportunities and threats associated with bootlegging behavior for the employee, and sponsoring managers also do not establish a deviant role model for bending the organizational rules with this form of support. However, sponsoring reduced the frequency by which employees bypass the official communication channels to pursue their ideas. This suggests that sponsoring provides employees with an action strategy to overcome obstacles located within the formal process and bypass the official chain of communication in a still legitimated way through coalition with their sponsoring manager.

What is particularly interesting about the studies of Globocnik and Salomo (2015) and Globocnik (2020) is that they provide managerial measures that qualify to regulate, that is, reduce, bootlegging and simultaneously foster compliant innovation activities: front-end formality, management support in form of providing resources and giving feedback. In contrast, the organizational factors investigated before such as rewards or autonomy foster both compliant and secret innovation activities. Thereby, using these organizational factors to reduce bootlegging, for example, less autonomy for employees or less rewards for innovation accomplishments, is also likely to hamper compliant innovation activities. In other words, these organizational factors used to stimulate compliant innovation activities are likely to come along with more bootlegging behavior as — from a managerial view — unintended by-product.

References

Abetti, P. A. (1997). The birth and growth of Toshiba's laptop and notebook computers: A case study in Japanese corporate venturing. *Journal of Business Venturing*, **12**(6): 507–529.

Ahuja, G. and Lampert, C. M. (2001). Entrepreneurship in the large corporation: A longitudinal study of how established firms create breakthrough inventions. *Strategic Management Journal*, **22**(6/7): 521–543.

Aldrich, H. E. and Fiol, C. M. (1994). Fools rush in? The institutional context of industry creation. *Academy of Management Review*, **19**(4): 645–670.

Alexy, O., Salter, A., Sharapov, D. and Criscuolo, P. (2016). Going off-piste: The role of status in launching unsponsored R&D projects. In *Academy of Management Proceedings (Best Paper Proceedings)* (pp. 1006–1011). DOI:10.5465/AMBPP.2016.259.

Amabile, T. M. (1988). From individual creativity to organizational innovation. In Grønhaug, K. and Kaufmann, G. (Eds.), *Innovation: A Cross-Disciplinary Perspective* (p. 139). Cambridge, UK: Oxford University Press.

Amabile, T. M. (1996). Creativity in the context: Update to the social psychology of creativity. Boulder, CO: Westview.

Antoncic, B. (2007). Intrapreneurship: A comparative structural equation modeling study. *Industrial Management and Data Systems*, **107**(3): 309–325.

Augsdorfer, P. (1996). *Forbidden Fruit: An Analysis of Bootlegging, Uncertainty, and Learning in Corporate R and D.* Aldershot: Avebury.

Augsdorfer, P. (2005). Bootlegging and path dependency. *Research Policy*, **34**(1): 1–11.

Augsdorfer, P. (2008). Managing the unmanageable. *Research-Technology Management*, **51**(4): 41–47.

Augsdorfer, P. (2012). A diagnostic personality test to identify likely corporate bootleg researchers. *International Journal of Innovation Management*, **16**(1): 1–18.

Axtell, C. M. and Parker, S. K. (2003). Promoting role breadth self-efficacy through involvement, work redesign and training. *Human Relations*, **56**: 113–131.

Axtell, C. M., Holman, D. J., Unsworth, K. L., Wall, T. D., Waterson, P. E. and Harrington, E. (2000). Shop-floor innovation: Facilitating the suggestion and implementation of ideas. *Journal of Occupational and Organizational Psychology,* **73**: 265–285.

Bailyn, L. (1985). Autonomy in the industrial R&D lab. *Human Resources Management*, **24**(2): 129–146.

Baker, T. and Nelson, R. E. (2005). Creating something from nothing: Resource construction through entrepreneurial bricolage. *Administrative Science Quarterly*, **50**(3): 329–366.

Bandura, A. (1986). *Social Foundations of Thought and Action: A Social Cognitive Theory*. Englewood Cliffs, NJ: Prentice Hall.

Bandura, A. (1997). *Self-Efficacy: The Exercise of Control*. New York: Freeman.

Bart, C. K. (2002). Product innovation charters: Mission statements for new products. *R&D Management*, **32**(1): 23–34.

Burgelman, R. A. (1983). A process model of internal corporate venturing in the diversified major firm. *Administrative Science Quarterly*, **28**(2): 223–244.

Burgelman, R. A. and Sayles, L. R. (1986). *Inside Corporate Innovation: Strategy, Structure, and Managerial Skills*. New York: Free Press.

Burgelman, R. A. and Grove, A. S. (2007). Let chaos reign, then rein in chaos — repeatedly: Managing strategic dynamics for corporate longevity. *Strategic Management Journal,* **28**(10): 965–979.

Cameron, K. S. and Freeman, S. J. (1991). Cultural congruence, strength, and type: Relationships to effectiveness. *Research in Organizational Change and Development*, **5**: 23–58.

Cooper, R. G. (2006). Managing technology development projects. *Research Technology Management,* **49**(6): 23–31.

Courpasson, D., Dany, F. and Martí, I. (2016). Organizational entrepreneurship as active resistance: A struggle against outsourcing. *Entrepreneurship Theory and Practice*, **40**(1): 131–160.

Criscuolo, P., Salter, A. and Ter Wal, A. L. J. (2014). Going underground: Bootlegging and innovative performance. *Organization Science*, **25**(5): 1287–1305.

Drazin, R., Glynn, M. A. and Karanjian, R. K. (1999). Multilevel theorizing about creativity in organizations: A sensemaking perspective. *Academy of Management Review*, **24**(2): 286–307.

Eisenberger, R. and Aselage, J. (2009). Incremental effects of reward on experienced performance pressure: Positive outcomes for intrinsic interest and creativity. *Journal of Organizational Behavior*, **30**(1): 95–117.

Eisenhardt, K. M. (1985). Control: Organizational and economic approaches. *Management Science,* **31**(2): 134–149.

Feldman, L. P. (1996). The role of salary and incentives in the new product function. *Journal of Product Innovation Management*, **13**: 216–228.

George, J. M. (2007). Creativity in organizations. *Academy of Management Annals*, **1**:439–477.

Ghasemzadeh, K., Bunjak, A., Bortoluzzi, G. and Černe, M. (2020). Efficaciously smuggling ideas: Untangling the relationship between entrepreneurial self-efficacy, creative bootlegging and embedded lead users. *International Journal of Innovation Management*. Available from: https://doi.org/10.1142/S1363919621500328.

Gist, M. E. and Mitchell, T. R. (1992). Self-efficacy: A theoretical analysis of its determinants and malleability. *Academy of Management Review*, **17**(2): 182–211.

Globocnik, D. (2015). Does user-innovation theory explain employees' bootlegging behavior? An empirical investigation of a novel theoretical approach. In *Proceedings of the 22nd IPDMC Innovation and Product Development Management Conference* (pp. 1–30).Globocnik, D. (2019). Taking or avoiding risk through secret innovation activities — The relationships among employees' risk propensity, bootlegging, and management support. *International Journal of Innovation Management*, **23**(3), 1950022.

Globocnik, D. and Salomo, S. (2015). Do formal management practices impact the emergence of bootlegging behavior? *Journal of Product Innovation Management*, **32**(4): 505–521.

Globocnik, D., Peña Häufler, B. and Salomo, S. (2020). Opportunities for radical innovation through bootlegging — An investigation of antecedents and outcomes. In *Proceedings of the 27th IPDMC Innovation and Product Development Management Conference* (pp. 1–21).

Goodale, J. C., Kuratko, D. F., Hornsby, J. S. and Covin, J. G. (2011). Operations management and corporate entrepreneurship: The moderating effect of operations control on the antecedents of corporate entrepreneurial activity in relation to innovation performance. *Journal of Operations Management*, **29**(1–2): 116–127.

Griffin, A. (1997). PDMA research on new product development practices: Updating trends and benchmarking best practices. *Journal of Product Innovation Management*, **14**: 429–458.

Hornsby, J. S., Kuratko, D. F. and Zahra, S. A. (2002). Middle managers' perception of the internal environment for corporate entrepreneurship: Assessing a measurement scale. *Journal of Business Venturing*, **17**(3): 253–273.

Howell, J. M. and Higgins, C. A. (1990). Champions of technological innovation. *Administrative Science Quarterly*, **35**(2): 317–341.

Jaworski, B. J. (1988). Toward a theory of marketing control: Environmental context, control types, and consequences. *Journal of Marketing*, **52**(3): 23–39.

Jaworski, B. J. and Macinnis, D. J. (1989). Marketing jobs and management controls — Toward a framework. *Journal of Marketing Research*, **26**(4): 406–419.

Judge, W. Q., Gryxell, G. E. and Dooley, R. S. (1997). The new task of R&D management: Creating goal-directed communities for innovation. *California Management Review*, **39**(3): 72–85.

Kanter, R. M. (2000). When a thousand flowers bloom: Structural, collective, and social conditions for innovation in organization. In Swedberg, R. (Ed.), *Entrepreneurship: The Social Science View* (pp. 167–210). Oxford: Oxford University Press.

Keltner, D., Gruenfeld, D. H. and Anderson, C. (2003). Power, approach, and inhibition. *Psychological Review*, **110**: 265–284.

Kirsch, L. J. (2004). Deploying common systems globally: The dynamics of control. *Information Systems Research*, **15**(4): 374–395.

Kirsch, L. J., Ko, D.-G. and Haney, M. H. (2010). Investigating the antecedents of team-based clan control: Adding social capital as predictor. *Organizational Science*, **21**: 469–489.

Klein, K. J. and Knight, A. P. (2005). Innovation implementation overcoming the challenge. *Current Directions in Psychological Science*, **14**(5): 243–246.

Koch, R. and Leitner, K. H. (2008). The dynamics and functions of self-organization in the fuzzy front end: Empirical evidence from the Austrian semiconductor industry. *Creativity and Innovation Management*, **17**(3): 216–226.

Krueger, N. F. (2000). The cognitive infrastructure of opportunity emergence. *Entrepreneurship Theory and Practice*, **24**(3): 5–23.

Krueger, N. F. and Dickson, P. R. (1994). How believing in ourselves increases risk taking: Perceived self-efficacy and opportunity recognition. *Decision Sciences*, **25**: 385–400.

Kuratko, D. F., Hornsby, J. S. and Bishop, J. W. (2005). An examination of managers' entrepreneurial actions and job satisfaction. *International Entrepreneurship and Management Journal*, **1**:275–291.

Lee, M. and Ofshe, R. (1981). The impact of behavioral style and status characteristics on social influence: A test of two competing theories. *Social Psychology Quarterly*, **44**: 73–82.

Lin, B., Mainemelis, C. and Kark, R. (2016). Leaders' responses to creative deviance: Differential effects on subsequent creative deviance and creative performance. *The Leadership Quarterly*, **27**(4): 537–556.

Lopes, L. L. (1987). Between hope and fear: The psychology of risk. *Advances in Experimental Social Psychology*, **20**(1): 255–295.

Luchsinger, V. and Bagby, D. R. (1987). Entrepreneurship and intrapreneurship: Behaviors, comparisons, and contrasts. *SAM Advances Management Journal*, **52**(3): 10–13.

Mainemelis, C. (2010). Stealing fire: Creative deviance in the evolution of new ideas. *Academy of Management Review*, **35**(4): 558–578.

Martin, F. F. and Ismail, R. (2019). The role of openness to experiences, conscientiousness and creative self-efficacy in predicting creative deviance. In *E-Proceedings of UKM-GSB I c-Rise 2019* (pp. 76–89).

Marvel, M. R., Griffin, A., Hebda, J. and Vojak, B. A. (2007). Examining the technical corporate entrepreneurs' motivation: Voices from the field. *Entrepreneurship Theory and Practice*, **31**(5): 753–768.

Masoudnia, Y. and Szwejczewski, M. (2012). Bootlegging in the R&D departments of high-technology firms. *Research Technology Management*, **55**(5): 35–42.

Michalik, C. (2003). *Innovatives Engagement, Eine empirische Untersuchung zum Phaeanomen des Bootlegging*. Weisbaden: Deutscher Universitäts-Verlag.

Mitchell, J. R. and Shepherd, D. A. (2010). To thine own self be true: Images of self, images of opportunity, and entrepreneurial action. *Journal of Business Venturing*, **25**(1), 138–154.

Mohammed, S. and Billings, R. S. (2002). The effects of self-efficacy and issue characteristics on threat and opportunity categorization. *Journal of Applied Social Psychology*, **32**(6): 1253–1275.

Moorman, C. and Miner, A. S. (1998). The convergence of planning and execution: Improvisation in new product development. *Journal of Marketing*, **62**(3): 1–20.

Morrison, E. W. and Phelps, C. C. (1999). Taking charge at work: Extra-role efforts to initiate workplace change. *Academy of Management Journal*, **42**: 403–419.

Mumford, M. D., Scott, G. M., Gaddis, B. and Strange, J. M. (2002). Leading creative people: Orchestrating expertise and relationships. *The Leadership Quarterly*, **13**(6), 705–750.

Nijhof, A., Krabbendam, K. and Looise, J. K. (2002). Innovation through exemptions: Building upon the existing creativity of employees. *Technovation*, **22**(11): 675–683.

O'Connor, G. C. and Veryzer, R. W. (2001). The nature of market visioning for technology-based radical innovation. *Journal of Product Innovation Management*, **18**(4): 231–246.

Oldham, G. R. and Cummings, A. (1996). Employee creativity: Personal and contextual factors at work. *Academy of Management Journal*, **39**(3): 607–634.

Ouchi, W. G. (1979). A conceptual framework for the design of organizational control mechanisms. *Management Science*, **25**(9): 833–848.

Parker, S. K., Williams, H. M. and Turner, N. (2006). Modeling the antecedents of proactive behaviour at work. *Journal of Applied Psychology*, **91**(3): 636–652.

Pearce, J. A., Kramer, T. R. and Robbins, D. K. (1997). Effects of managers' entrepreneurial behavior on subordinates. *Journal of Business Venturing*, **12**(2): 147–160.

Pearson, A. (1997). Innovation management - Is there still a role for "bootlegging"? *International Journal of Technology Management*, **1**(2): 191–200.

Pinchot, G. (1985). Intrapreneuring: Why you don't have to leave the corporation to become an entrepreneur. New York, NY: Harper and Row.

Rindova, V., Barry, D. and Ketchen, D. J., Jr. (2009). Entrepreneuring as emancipation. *Academy of Management Review*, **34**(3): 477–491.

Roussel, P. A., Saad, K. N. and Erickson, T. J. (1991). *Third Generation of R&D: Managing the Link to Corporate Strategy*. USA: Arthur D. Little Inc.

Schultz, C., Globocnik, D., Kock, A. and Salomo, S. (2019). Application and performance impact of stage–gate systems — The role services in the firm's business focus. *R&D Management*, **49**(4): 534–554.

Scott, S. G. and Bruce, R. A. (1994). Determinants of innovative behavior: A path model of individual innovation in the workplace. *Academy of Management Journal*, **37**: 580–607.

Sitkin, S. B. and Pablo, A. L. (1992). Reconceptionalizing the determinants of risk behavior. *Academy of Management Review*, **17**(1): 9–38.

Speier, C. and Frese, M. (1997). Generalized self-efficacy as a mediator and moderator between control and complexity at work and personal initiatives: A longitudinal field study in East Germany. *Human Performance*, **10**: 171–192.

Tenzer, H. and Yang, P. (2019). Personality, values, or attitudes? Individual-level antecedents to creative deviance. *International Journal of Innovation Management*, **23**(2): 1950009.

Tenzer, H. and Yang, P. (2020). The impact of organizational support and individual achievement orientation on creative deviance. *International Journal of Innovation Management*, **24**(2): 2050020.

Tesluk, P. E., Farr, J. L. and Klein, S. R. (1997). Influences of organizational culture and climate on individual creativity. *Journal of Creative Behavior*, **31**(1): 27–41.

Tierney, P., Farmer, S. M. and Graen, G. B. (1999). An examination of leadership and employee creativity: The relevance of traits and relationships. *Personnel Psychology*, **52**(3): 591–620.

Turner, K. L. and Makhija, M. V. (2006). The role of organizational controls in managing knowledge. *Academy of Management Review*, **31**(1): 197–217.

Tushman, M. L. and O'Reilly, C. A. (1999). Building ambidextrous organizations: forming your own 'skunk works'. *Health Forum Journal*, **42**(2): 20–24.

von Hippel, E. (1986). Lead users: A source of novel product concepts. *Management Science*, **32**(7): 791–805.

Wood, R. and Bandura, A. (1989). Social cognition theory of organizational management. *Academy of Management Review*, **14**(3): 361–384.

Zahra, S. A. and Covin, J. C. (1995). Contextual influences on the corporate entrepreneurship-performance relationship: A longitudinal analysis. *Journal of Business Venturing*, **10**(1): 43–58.

Zhou, J. and George, J. M. (2001). When job dissatisfaction leads to creativity: Encouraging the expression of voice. *Academy of Management Journal*, **44**(4): 682–696.

Zhou, J. and Hoever, I. J. (2014). Research on workplace creativity: A review and redirection. *Annual Review of Organizational Psychology and Organizational Behavior*, **1**: 333–359.

https://doi.org/10.1142/9781800612266_0007

Chapter 6

Which Factors Enable Self-Organized Product Innovations? The Diverse Effects of Formal Management Systems

Rudolph Koch* and Karl-Heinz Leitner†
FH JOANNEUM, Graz, Austria
*rk@rudolphkoch.com
†karl-heinz.leitner@ait.ac.at

Abstract

This chapter investigates which organizational and managerial factors foster or hamper self-organized or autonomous innovation activities within firms. Based on a case study approach and on a theoretical framework, which is rooted in the complexity science and innovation literature, the informal bottom-up NPD projects of six Austrian electronics companies are examined. The analysis focuses mainly on the role of an open communication culture that delivers autonomy for experimentation, the impacts of financial incentives systems, the rigidity of organizational structures and, finally, the formalism of control systems. The authors deliver evidence how classical formal management systems affect self-organized innovation activities and how they can be designed deliberately to promote and harness such bottom-up activities.

6.1. Introduction

In the innovation literature as well as organizational practice, many models and instruments have been developed and implemented to manage innovation by structuring, planning, and ordering the innovation process (e.g., Cooper, 1990). These models heavily rely on anticipation and control and a certain level of formal control is also seen as conducive to manage radical innovation. Nixon (1998), for instance, claimed that formal management control systems have positive effects on facilitating learning and that the pressure to meet milestones and deadlines enhances creative problem solving, discussion, and coordination among project teams and across different levels of the organization. However, the awareness of the open and networked characteristics of innovation processes and the increasingly complex and dynamic environments make the formalization and routinization of the R&D and new product development process more difficult and have questioned the effectiveness of strongly formalized control approaches for innovation.

In the last 20 years, innovation phenomena such as user innovations, open-source software development, crowdsourcing, Web 2.0, and collaborative innovation arrangements among others have been thoroughly discussed and are seen as new ways to realize innovations that go far beyond what can be managed in the traditional, rather formal sense (Leitner and Weber, 2019). These phenomena can be interpreted as reaction and response to the prevailing formal and rigid activities in companies. Classical customer surveys, for instance, were replaced by activities to support user innovations, patenting encouraged open-source software development, and narrowly focused innovation strategies often led to adopting open innovation strategies. Such rather informal and networked innovation activities harnessing swarm intelligence can be regarded as self-organizational processes that often occur and emerge beyond formal innovation processes, outside the core business or outside the firms' boarders.

In addition, hidden innovation activities often called bootlegging behavior have been identified and investigated as important organizational phenomena (e.g., Augsdorfer, 2005; Criscuolo *et al.*, 2016; Sakhdar and Bidakhavidi, 2016). Although empirical literature about factors supporting self-organizational innovation activities has grown, it is still fragmented and rare (e.g., Globocnik and Salomo, 2015). Due to this empirical gap, the aim of this chapter is to explore which organizational factors and which elements of formal management control systems facilitate or harm self-organizing behavior in the fuzzy front of the new product development (NPD) process.

While we analyzed the process of self-organizational activities in a previous paper (Koch and Leitner, 2008), in this chapter, we will focus on the organizational and managerial factors that foster or hamper self-organized or autonomous innovation activities within firms. Only a limited number of studies have analyzed in more depth how the management can promote self-organizational activities (e.g., Sakhdari and Bidakhavidi, 2016). Autonomous innovation activities do not happen in an organizational vacuum and we thus analyze how management deliberately supports or why it tolerates such behavior. While phenomena such as open-source development and innovation activities of networks or user groups can be considered as self-organizational activities as well, we only focus on innovation activities embedded in firms. In addition, it is not dealt with strategies to support corporate incubation and entrepreneurship (e.g., Ayatse *et al.*, 2017) even though they somehow are related to the subject.

Our study is based on a case study approach investigating the informal bottom-up NPD projects of six Austrian electronics companies focusing on the fuzzy front end. Based on a framework that integrates the influencing factors rooted in findings from complexity science and innovation literature, it is explored to what extent these factors enable or harm bottom-up innovation activities. Therefore, the characteristics of typical purely bottom-up innovation projects are examined, and it is analyzed how the management copes with such activities. Hence, we aim to better understand how classical formal management systems for innovation affect such activities and how they may be designed by the management to promote and harness self-organized NPD activities.

The chapter is organized as follows. First, the theoretical framework for the study that rests on findings of the complexity science is presented. Afterward, the study design will be described and finally the empirical findings and their implications will be presented.

6.2. Innovation as Self-Organized Process

Despite the vast literature that stresses that planning, structuring, and ordering the innovation process are crucial elements of successful NPD processes, some researchers have generally taken a critical view on these classical approaches. They especially argue against a too strongly structured, planned, and ordered innovation process, particularly for managing and promoting radical innovations. Such studies, for instance, have been carried out in line with organizational theories (Perrow, 1986; Amabile, 1997) or sociological theories (Akrich *et al.*, 2001), criticizing that traditional linear models are neither supporting learning nor creative problem-solving but rather are means of control through standardization. Some authors claim that innovation requires not only a sequence of planned actions and tight structures, but also some level of disorder, improvisation, and self-directed teams (Nonaka, 1991; Brown and Eisenhardt, 1997; Miner *et al.*, 2001). These views are underpinned by empirical studies that have shown that the NPD process does not necessarily follow idealistic models and, for instance, decisions are not always taken at stage-meetings in the case of an implemented stage-gate process (Christiansen and Varnes, 2007) or that innovations even often emerge outside the strategically defined core areas, teams, or formal processes (Kanter, 1988; Robinson and Stern, 1997; Christensen, 1997). Moreover, authors (e.g., Brown and Eisenhardt, 1997) also stressed that such classical models lose effectiveness in an increasingly complex organizational and competitive environment — especially in times of open innovation and collaboration, and swarm intelligence. In this context, a specific literature strand stresses that especially informal engagements, bottom-up initiatives, and self-organization are key features of many innovation activities. Such types of NPD activities are labeled, for instance, as skunkwork (Kanter, 1988), bootlegging (Augsdorfer, 2005) or autonomous innovation activities (Burgelman, 1983).

Bootlegging is one term used within the innovation literature to investigate innovation activities that secretly start within the firm. Augsdorfer (2005), for instance, studied the role of bootlegging in NPD and stresses that many innovations have their origins in the corporate underground, which is seemingly valuable for the firm too. Another notion used to describe innovation activities that happen apart from formal and official routines is so called skunkwork, which is usually deliberately managed and supported by the management (Kanter, 1988).

The literature of product champions also stresses the role of informal activities. It is emphasized that champions contribute to overcoming organizational barriers, linking R&D and marketing by informal contacts or their power function to support innovations. Although some authors stress that product champions can be selected by the top management (e.g., Cooper, 2006), self-organized early NPD activities as investigated in this chapter correspond to the bottom-up emergent view of championing as identified by Day (1994). However, the question on whether champions' activities are more formal or informal is not always investigated explicitly in the product champion literature.

Another recently growing research stream is taken by some authors who adopt a complexity science perspective to study innovation (e.g., Brown and Eisenhardt, 1997; Dooley, 2002; Gomes and Cunha, 2003; McCarthy *et al.*, 2006; Akgün *et al.*, 2014). This complexity science perspective on NPD interprets organizations as complex systems and stresses that self-organization and emergence are important elements for developing new products refusing the assumptions of classical management approaches.

Self-organization in the light of complexity science means that new structures, patterns, or properties emerge spontaneously without being externally imposed on the system. Neither imposed top-down nor controlled by a central, hierarchical command-and-control center, self-organization is usually distributed throughout the system (Dooley, 2002: 5020). Emergence can be defined as a process whereby novel and coherent structures, patterns, or properties arise on the global level out of the local interactions of the agents (Goldstein, 1999: 49). These interactions lead to something new that has not been there before and cannot be explained by analyzing the local interactions.

Brown and Eisenhardt (1997: 1) studied the innovation processes in the computer industry with its high demand for continuous change and innovation. Their study is influenced by the complexity science and the idea that the organizational structures and processes are "neither so structured that change cannot occur nor so unstructured that chaos ensues." Based on six case studies, they found that successful firms combined limited structure (e.g., with respect to responsibility) with extensive interaction and freedom to create improvisation within current projects. They call these structures and processes "semistructure," which, according to them, is a balanced state between order and disorder proposing that the NPD process of successful firms is neither too structured nor too loosely organized. In terms of complexity science, this condition is termed as "bounded instability," meaning a state that is far from equilibrium and where systems are constantly poised at the edge between order and chaos (Burnes, 2005: 79). The aim for organizations is to "dance" on the edges without falling out of the emergent complexity zone (McMillan and Carlisle, 2006: 7).

Similarly, Cunha and Gomes (2003: 182) proposed an NPD model — termed the "improvisational model" — which refers to the temporal convergence of planning and execution, with action viewed as improvised when it "constitutes a deliberate, real-time response to a problem or opportunity." Innovation processes are hence characterized by complexity and emergence requiring partially disordered processes. The challenge for management is to somehow use disorder productively, so to overcome the constraints of traditional linear and sequential innovation models such as Cooper's (1990) prominent stage-gate model.

McCarthy *et al.* (2006) perceive NPD as a complex adaptive system of decisions. They present some propositions on how decision-making is influenced by nonlinearity, self-organization, and emergence. Based on a case study, McCarthy *et al.* reported, for instance, that in one case a significant product idea emerged amid intensive interaction during a social event, where a spontaneously formed group was able to cooperatively solve problems apart from usual bureaucratic constrains. Besides, they referred to a case where a radical new innovation emerged simply because the project team disregarded the process rules and procedures, a finding that is in line with Olin and Wickenberg's (2001) observations on rule breaking.

6.3. What Enables Self-Organizational Innovation Activities?

While literature on self-organization is growing, there is only little literature about what type of conditions enable self-organizational activities in organizations. In general, the findings in this field are very fragmented. So far, scholars — mainly from the complexity science — have only delivered insights about the conditions for self-organization either from a very generic and abstract level or for a very concrete and focused situation. In the first case, scholars delivered mainly meta-variables that do not relate to the principles of a specific context and its self-organizing process, but rather to the underlying relationships that form the process, regardless of the situation (e.g., Eoyang, 2001; Clippinger, 1999; Lichtenstein, 2000; Coleman, 1999). In this case, some common features and elements (like interaction, diversity, autonomy, etc.) can be identified, but — due to their broad level of generalization — they do not deliver concrete implications for innovation processes. In the second case, however, scholars focus on very specific situations where every context demands a completely different setting — for example, change management (Olson and Eoyang, 2001), self-organizing strategies (Stacey, 1993), entrepreneurship (Lichtenstein and Jones, 2004), or team building (Anderson and McMillan, 2003).

Complexity theory offers a theoretical pillar for this study. It enables us to derive the most common and generally accepted generic features and factors from literature and integrate them into a coherent framework and operationalize them in a more detailed way on an organizational context. Based on this operationalization from the abstract principles, it is expected that especially the following factors strongly influence the bottom-up behavior of employees in the NPD process.

6.3.1. Open culture allowing autonomy for experimentation

Open culture and shared values are key requisites for innovations as they establish an environment supportive of and conducive to learning. If organizations want to capitalize on their collective human capital, then culture must be open and tolerate conflicts and failures as well as people who are provocative (Tetenbaum, 1998: 31). Besides the hierarchical structure and the distribution of power, especially this open culture sets the boundaries, around which self-organizing processes emerge (Stacey, 1996: 459). These boundaries are fostered by common values acting as a bonding glue that keeps a fluid organization from evolving beyond recognition and allows for coordination without control and for experimentation and adaptation without lawlessness (Tetenbaum, 1998: 28). Within these boundaries, it is possible and preferable to grant employees a high level of autonomy.

This autonomy fosters creativity as granting people freedom in how they approach their work, it increases both their intrinsic motivation and their sense of ownership (Amabile, 1998: 82). For Coleman (1999: 40), this relatively high degree of autonomy within boundaries works according to a system of "loose–tight" controls: The shared values of corporate culture provide tight control as a form of protocol or a kind of implicit code of conduct and create intrinsic motivation in employees and, hence, provide the context for empowerment to pursue entrepreneurial initiatives. These findings go in line with the above noted "semistructure" (Brown and Eisenhardt, 1997) as an enabler of self-organizing activities. In order to pursue these entrepreneurial initiatives, it is necessary for employees to experiment — that means that besides their daily work they have the opportunity to pursue issues within their theme scope. Since innovation depends significantly on chance (Stacey, 1993), vast experimenting enhances the probability that employees identify an interesting opportunity. But emphasizing experimenting also involves an iterative and dynamic process and a mindset of trial-and-error (Nonaka and Takeuchi, 1986: 145). Summing up the abovementioned facts, we assume plenty of opportunities to experiment, enabled by an open culture with a high degree of autonomy, fuels self-organizing activities.

6.3.2. Financial incentive systems

One means of promoting the idea creation of employees in organizations are incentive systems, mostly in form of financial rewards. Thus, these rewards should foster the extrinsic motivation. However, literature about incentive systems provides different findings whether they support or harm the product innovativeness. While some authors, such as Davila (2003), found that financial incentives should motivate, others, in contrast, such as Katz and Allen (1982) and Osterloh and Frey (2000), stress that intrinsic motivation is the prime driving force for creative and innovative work. The later authors argue that formal management systems may be counterproductive and have unintended effects, and, as a result, are often ignored or bypassed by organizational members. The partly contradicting findings within the incentive literature stem from the fact that every setting and context (e.g., scientific work versus problem solving in a blue-collar environment) has different underlying and nonlinear dynamics and triggers. Thus, making a generalization is not possible. We follow Amabile's claim (1998: 79) and propose that especially financial reward systems do not have a positive impact on bottom-up innovation activities.

6.3.3. Organizational structure and formal control systems

While Stacey (1996: 332) claims that self-organization in general may occur in bureaucratic organizations and even in a dictatorship (e.g., revolutions may be a form of self-organization and that is how dictatorships are overthrown), its conditions and impacts are different when it comes to the innovation process. On the one side, too much bureaucratic procedures, paperwork, and formalism are seen as an impassable barrier to bottom-up activities. On the other side, organizational constraints that are too loose are not seen as fruitful either. Therefore, appropriate organizational structures are key. One important condition that generates self-organizing behavior clearly is the right balance between a tight and structured organization on the one side and informal organizing on the other side. In relation to NPD, this means that the organizational structure and processes are neither too bureaucratic nor too loose, which is in line with the concept of "semistructure" by Brown and Eisenhardt (1997) and with the "loose–tight" controls by Coleman (1999: 40), both mentioned above. Consequently, rather simple rules are essential as they move the company to the edge of chaos, providing just enough structure to allow taking the best opportunities (Eisenhardt and Sull, 2001: 110).

Based on the abovementioned propositions, we assume that organizational structures and processes that neither are too bureaucratic nor too loose stimulate self-organizing activities.

6.3.4. Instabilities

One factor that might be a major part in explaining self-organized innovation activities is the role of instabilities. Many authors, both within innovation literature as well as within complexity science, claim that especially instabilities in form of crises and turbulences can spur self-organizing behavior and creativity and thus lead to innovation (e.g., Monks, 1998; Nonaka and Takeuchi, 1986). From a complexity science view, the authors stress that if a system moves away from the equilibrium to the state referred to as "far from equilibrium," the ability to self-organize is the greatest.

While in highly settled orderly conditions, learning is rather reduced to a limited process of testing, in "the edge of chaos" conditions are favorable for both single and double loop learning and for radical innovation (McMillan and Carlisle, 2006: 4). Nonaka (1988), who also refers to complexity theory, stresses that managers should, therefore, deliberately provoke crises in order to generate innovations. Hence, for Nonaka (1988: 66) "a crisis can often stimulate the creative activities of an organization or even rejuvenate the organization itself. [...] Some form of crisis is needed to generate an entirely new, innovative product concept or to abolish a company's existing patterns and replace them with a new order. This reasoning leads to the conclusion that one of the important functions of top management is to create an active, creative crisis."

In a similar vein, Anderson (1999b: 139) proposes: "By setting aggressive goals, managers create a perceived mismatch between the performance presently achieved and the performance required. If agents accept the objectives, the gap motivates a self-organizing network to redouble its search efforts." Additionally, Nixon (1998) notes that the pressure to meet milestones and deadlines enhances creative problem solving, discussion, and coordination among project teams and across different levels of the organization. Based on these arguments, we assume that companies that are in a change process or faced by instabilities and tensions (also on a top-down imposed pressure on a project level) show a higher level of self-organized innovation activities.

6.4. Methods

The NPD practices of six Austrian companies in the electronics industry focusing on manufacturing of semiconductors and medical equipment were examined as a means to study the types, impacts, functions, and conditions of self-organization. We chose this industry with its high dynamics, velocity, and demand for continuous innovation, as we expected that self-organization was crucial to compete successfully. The enterprises analyzed were Austrian companies as well as Austrian subsidiaries of international firms.

The companies were Supertec with nearly 1,000 employees, Chipcom employing about 1,500 employees, Microwaver with approximately 2,500 employees, Silicius engaging around 700 people, and finally NewCo, a startup company with 120 employees whereas the numbers of employees refer only to the Austrian subsidiaries. Medicaltronics is a subsidiary of an international firm with more than 600 employees working in the unit in Austria specialized in developing and manufacturing medical products.

The case study approach is considered as an appropriate methodology in order to study the dynamics of self-organizational innovation activities in-depth. We combined multiple data collection methods and included semistructured interviews, which lasted between 40 and 90 minutes and were conducted in a narrative way, that is, personal and subjective impressions were gathered and relevant artifacts (e.g., mission statements, arrangement of offices) observed. The interviewees were the six heads of the R&D departments of each firm as well as employees of the

R&D departments. Based on the interviews with the R&D directors, two to three NPD teams were selected in each company for further investigation of initiatives, in which self-organizing activities played a significant role in the NPD process. Two developers from each team were interviewed subsequently to investigate the role, effects, and motivation for self-organizational activities from the employees' point of view. In total, 25 people of 13 NPD teams were interviewed. These interviews were conducted with a semistructured questionnaire covering a set of common questions and some specific questions for the R&D directors as well as the team members. Asking management and employees nearly the same questions contrasted their different perceptions of the activities and organizational processes. Each examined self-organizing activity was seen as a separate case and considered relevant for further observation.

Based on these settings, the collected cases were analyzed in an iterative process. This was mainly done by combining within-case analysis and cross-case analysis. Hence, first of all, the typical patterns and characteristics of each case were analyzed, afterwards, in the cross-case analysis, these findings were compared with findings of other cases.

6.5. Results

Our investigation revealed the following evidence: firstly, self-organizing dynamics strongly occur in the fuzzy front end of innovation in the electronics industry, and, secondly, these dynamics are heavily influenced by certain conditions. Focusing in particular on: (1) organizational structure and formal control systems, (2) open culture allowing autonomy for experimentation, (3) financial incentive systems, and (4) instabilities, we found that especially certain instances of these factors strongly influence the bottom-up behavior of employees in the NPD process, while some instances only have little or no impacts or even hindered the behavior, as will be presented in this chapter.

6.5.1. The role of experimentation

A main factor for a high innovation output is the possibility for employees to experiment. All interviewed developers confirmed that an open culture allowing and promoting experimentation was a necessary prerequisite for identifying bottom-up issues and that they used their leeway for pursuing their issues. Also, the top management of all examined companies considered experimenting as very important and, therefore, granted leeway as well as incentives and the required infrastructure and resources (e.g., simulation tools) for these activities. But the ranges of leeway offered differed within the companies. Whereas Silicius allowed their employees to experiment only within their scope of activities, all other companies allowed and even endorsed their employees also to experiment outside as long as the main deliverables were not threatened. In these companies, the top management was convinced that employees will not experiment too far outside the firm's scope and that findings in the adjacent areas would also fertilize the formal innovation activities. And here we found evidence that this was the case — nearly all emerged bottom-up activities took place within or at least near the firms focus scope and also fruitfully influenced official innovations. Medicaltronics has introduced a stage-gate process to manage incremental innovations, but at the same time has created a 15% rule to promote completely new ideas.

6.5.2. The impacts of financial incentives on spurring motivation

As already mentioned, the top management of all examined companies was aware that the experimental activities of the employees cross-fertilized the innovation process. But the willingness and quality of employees' initiatives and experiments heavily depend on their motivation. Thus, as Amabile (1998: 84) claims, it is necessary to install appropriate systems or procedures and emphasize values that make it clear that creative efforts are a top priority. Also, the examined companies were aware of this important motivation aspect and, therefore, offered appropriate incentive systems where employees were financially rewarded for ideas, patents, scientific publications, inventions, and so on. Thus, extrinsic motivators are used to positively stimulate the workforce's willingness and creativity to search for ideas. But these incentives are also used for the purpose, to spot, trace, and process the employees' ideas already at a very early stage as the innovation manager of Microwaver describes: "With this system we also encourage our engineers to quickly report their findings so that we can intervene for the further development at a very early stage."

Although these extrinsic incentives were appreciated by the employees, we found out that they even played a more important role for official, top town-imposed experiments, and idea searching. For the motivation to pursue own ideas, they rather play a subordinate role as one developer of Microwaver stated: "From my point of view inspiration, passion and internal desire to do something are much more important than incentives." In view of this context, we, therefore, revealed evidence that extrinsic motivators — especially in form of financial rewards — hardly are a trigger for bottom-up innovations. We found out that bottom-up innovations in fact emerge mainly from passion, inspiration, challenge, and the internal desire to make an impact. Our findings here are also underpinned by Anderson (1999b: 139f) who explored the generic conditions for self-organization and who notes the following: "Because people are motivated by factors other than money, management must do more than align incentives with market forces. They must energize agents by providing inspiration and challenges [...] Incentives alone do not explain why people go above and beyond their job descriptions." Also, Amabile (1998: 79) who explored the impacts of incentives on creativity supports our results: "money by itself doesn't make employees passionate about their jobs. A cash reward can't magically prompt people to find their work interesting..."

Our findings are additionally supported by the fact that employees often work for a very long time secretly and unofficially on their own innovations and, as a consequence, deliberately abandon incentives, which they normally would have gotten if they had reported their idea. Instead, they rather decide to pursue their innovation secretly on their own and in this context often perform extraordinary tasks and engage with fields for which they do not get paid.

None of these activities are based on external motives but — also already stated above — are rather driven by their own stimuli and individual motives. Thus, intrinsic motivation plays a crucial role in context of self-organizing innovations. Therefore, it is important that these individual motives and stimuli are facilitated by the propriate infrastructure and the right work environment (Amabile, 1998: 79). Here, as Amabile notes, it is important that the company acknowledges the innovative efforts of its employees and does not greet them with skepticism and criticism, because in many companies "new ideas are met not with open minds but with time-consuming layers of evaluation — or even with harsh criticism" (Amabile, 1998: 83). This fact was empirically identified by us in some cases as well. To be more specific this means, for example, that the top management shows too little interest or the procedures are too bureaucratic or simply take too long from the perceptions of the inventors, as a developer from Silicius claims: "For me the whole things with filing patents are so cumbersome because the processes are so bureaucratic, time-consuming and long lasting." Especially with respect to patents, our case study also revealed that they often were not welcomed by certain inventors either, as companies often file them only for the reason to thwart competitors but without the intention to further pursue the invention. Thus, filing a patent may be associated with the risk that the innovation may not be developed for strategic reasons. All the abovementioned aspects are crucial aspects why very often inventors abandon these bonuses since they prefer to pursue their intentions secretly. Therefore, the well-intentioned incentive systems, which should spur official innovation activities often act oppositely and rather lead to underground activities. Our results show clearly that intrinsic motivation is the prime force for self-organized innovations and that it is not facilitated by formal financial incentive systems. Instead of financial rewards, the incentive systems should rather focus on granting employees more leeway and the right infrastructure for experimenting.

6.5.3. Suitable organizational structures and processes

As already mentioned in the theoretical background, the right organizational structures and processes — especially in context of innovation processes — are not only a key requisite for high innovative performance but also for self-organizational behavior (Coleman, 1999). Therefore, they should not be too structured so that change cannot occur but on the other hand, also not too unstructured so that chaos ensues (Brown and Eisenhardt, 1997: 1). Our empirical research showed that all companies had innovation processes that were not so tightly structured and where loose structures dominated. The only exception was Silicius, where the process was a bit more structured in contrast to the other companies, but still relatively loose. Therefore, the innovation processes of all examined companies exhibit exactly those structures, which Brown and Eisenhardt (1997) label as "semistructure" — the right state balanced between order and disorder. While this is a quite vague and abstract term, in context of an organizational setting in the NPD process this means the following: All examined companies had a rather tight formal innovation process according to official company policies. In reality, however, and especially at the beginning of the process, rather loose structures and high degrees of freedom and leeway dominated, as a developer of Supertec quotes: "Especially at the beginning there are hardly any formal proceedings, even if they are normally required." That means that the factual proceedings differ very much from the ones that were officially planned. Here we observed that especially the innovation managers play a crucial role, since they are responsible for the process and, therefore, not only tolerate these loose structures, but also — in contrary to the officially required policies — deliberately promote them. This means that also the formal organization is not only aware of these occurrences and tolerates them, but also lets them deliberately happen. Hence, the formal organization relies on the dynamics and virtues of the informal system, which is heavily present in this stage.

In general, this informal organization plays a very crucial role in companies as it especially enables the fine tuning as well as the seamless interlocking of the formal structures and procedures and, as a consequence, overcomes the inherent deficits of the formal organization with its rigid structures and processes (Niggl, 1998: 71). For Stacey (1996: 377) the activities taking place in the shadow system are often inevitably subversive of the legitimate system, in that they replace some parts of it with more useful alternatives. And in particular in the early stages of the innovation process, the informal organization is an important factor. Due to the flexibility and adaptiveness, the informal organization enables more rapid responses to unforeseen changes and also provides an important psychological and social relief to individuals who have to operate in a bureaucratic system or are confronted with great ambiguity and uncertainty, resulting that they are more motivated and psychologically capable to operate effectively (Stacey, 1996: 453).

We also identified that with the further advancement and in the later stages the process gets tighter and more structured. Finally, as soon as the first feasibility tests or the first agreements with the customers are made, the structures and processes are so tight that they corresponded to the officially required ones and a deviation from them is neither possible nor allowed anymore. This is because, first, concrete obligations to the customer exist and second, the investment of resources is already so high that a deviation from the plan would be very risky. As already mentioned, Silicius was the only company where also at the beginning the structures and procedures were not so loose compared to the other companies, as the innovation manager quotes: "The top management eagerly tries to keep the process very structured and tight throughout all phases, since we are a very big corporation and, therefore, they want to control and plan everything very exactly."

Due to the fact that the top management of Silicius wants to exactly control the innovation process it — compared to the other companies — often interferes with the process. But this interference is first of all extremely annoying for the developers and secondly — as developers claimed — reduces their leeway for experiments, which results in decreased bottom-up activities. Summing up the role of the organizational structures and processes, it can be argued that especially loose conditions at the beginning of the innovation process enhance experimenting in adjacent fields and, consequently, stimulate self-organizing behavior.

Although Medicaltronics has an official stage-gate process, it has also a semiofficial project route that is tolerated by the management. Hence, the company is aware of informal activities that are called "black op projects" in reference to secret military operations. Within the scope of such projects, technicians and resourceful tinkerers find the corresponding creative freedom, which is also granted to them or their actions are condoned. The company has found that informal networks are necessary to give innovative projects the status they need to be accepted within the organization. Nevertheless, such informal network-oriented work runs counter to the stage-gate idea to a certain extent. At the same time, Medicaltronics is aware that an "underground project" mostly makes it to the proof-of-concept stage, but after that the commitment of management is needed, especially to be able to raise the resources for product development and to explicitly secure budgets. At the latest then, an informal project becomes a formal project.

Although the organizational structures of the studied companies were generally not perceived as highly bureaucratic, we found some evidence that apart from organizational structures, certain procedures, policies, or mechanisms were perceived as a barrier and, hence, hampered self-organizing activities. To be more specific, these were the formal reporting procedures, the security policies, and the internal transfer prices.

The formal reporting procedures that must be obeyed within the innovation process — especially for experiments or for the request of assessment of an idea — resulting in vast formalism, are seen as very hindering for pursuing own ideas. From the developers' viewpoint, they do not only consume a lot of time, but also shorten the leeway as one developer claims: "Due to the required reporting mechanisms, the freedom for experiments suffers much."

The high-security regulations that prevail within the companies studied in this chapter are also perceived as an obstacle for pursuing own ideas, because many formalities have to be fulfilled for being compliant with these strict standards. Especially the access to necessary infrastructure and resources (e.g., laboratory, test equipment, simulation tools), which often gets restricted by these regulations is seen as very hindering, as an engineer of Supertec claims: "When I have an idea and quickly want to try something but, therefore, have to file an application, it gets very complicated and time-consuming." At Silicius, it was even the case that due to the high-security standards of certain projects (which dealt about cryptography), the access to some areas was suddenly restricted to only those employees who were directly involved in the project. All the other employees who also had used these areas before were not allowed to access those anymore, which was also seen as a blockade for pursuing own ideas as one engineer claims: "If you want to implement something but you are not allowed to access certain areas, it gets very hard. In such cases you can only rely on your connections and pull the strings."

This statement perfectly reflects our findings, how strong self-organizing activities work, and that the intrinsic stimulus and desire to make an impact are much stronger than any extrinsic motivators like financial rewards. Even arising barriers will not stop self-motivated employees to work on their ideas. Also, in this context the importance of the shadow organization becomes again evident, as inventors deliberately bypass formal procedures and policies by harnessing their personal network within the organization, according to Stacey (1996: 377), acting inevitably subversive of the legitimate system.

We also identified that internal transfer prices are perceived as a barrier within the innovation process. In detail that means that the interactions between different departments within the organization are based on contracts and therefore valued in money. How this badly affects the interactions and, thus, learning and bottom-up activities was observed at Silicius, where one business unit was divided into two separate units that henceforth only interacted upon contract and transfer prices as one engineer claims: "We were split up into two cost departments. If you now need any cross departmental knowledge or resources, you have to make contracts and calculate prices. Before, under one cost unit, it was all very easy and convenient, but now this does not work anymore and, therefore, many ideas cannot be pursuit, since you often don't get official budget."

These observed aspects not only considerably affect the possibilities and motivations for experiments, they also have negative consequences for the interactions and communications, which are both very important factors for self-organization (Mitleton-Kelly, 2003; Anderson, 1999a). As already pointed out above, we also observed in this context that with the existence of barriers self-organizational activities tend to occur on a subversive level in the underground — a fact that is also supported by Knowles (2001). This specially becomes evident in the case that employees master and deliberately bypass formal procedures and obstacles by using their informal networks or work for quite a long time secretly and in the underground on their innovations to avoid formalism and bureaucracy. Noticeable with regard to underground activities is also the fact that at the startup NewCo, where neither any fully developed structures nor procedures existed, the subversive activities did not occur very often as one developer reported: "Fortunately, we are not stuck in such strict structures which have to be broken first or where you have to act only subversively to pursue your ideas. Here you can act very open minded."

6.5.4. Evoking instabilities in form of pressure and turbulences

Whereas this proposition may be the case in other self-organizing contexts — like emergency events or company bankrupts (Lichtenstein, 2000) — we could not find any evidence in relation to bottom-up innovations processes. In our context, where self-organization refers to employees who intrinsically pursue their own ideas within the organizational innovation management, we identified rather the opposite of the above claimed propositions. We found evidence that any kind of crises, turbulences, or similar events that result in a high time pressure act as an obstacle for self-organizing behavior in the innovation process.

Applied to the context of innovation processes, this means that when projects are supplied with only scarce resources and when deliverables are so challenging and demanding that these circumstances permanently result in a shortage, an overload with work and time pressure as an engineer of Silicius claims: "If the schedule is permanently too scarce and the workload so high, there is absolutely no time for searching for new ideas — not to mention looking for the right optimum." In this context we identified that the possibilities for experimenting are very little. Especially at Silicius, where in recent times the project pressure increased so enormously resulting in very high workloads, this became very evident as one engineer complained: "Own ideas emerged very scarcely in the last time, since all of us have heavily been overloaded with work." But not only are the possibilities for experimenting limited by the perceived stress and pressure, the motivation to pursue own ideas also decreases tremendously as one developer of Silicius mentions: "... under such circumstances there is absolutely no motivation to additionally invest time to pursue own ideas, do small simulations or prototyping — these activities are likely to fall by the wayside." These facts coincide with the findings of Amabile *et al.* (2002) that pressure simply does not spur creativity.

But the willingness to pursue own ideas also decreases, because the employees do not want to threaten the progress of the official innovation project if the time frame is very scarce. While studying these impacts of turbulences and tensions, we found evidence that they also severely affect the willingness of employees to cooperate. As described in the bottom-up innovation process model (Koch and Leitner, 2008), in the phase of coalition building and networking, the inventors try to draw the attention of other individuals to their issue for getting support for the further pursuit. But with the decreased willingness to cooperate due to the tensions, it is getting extremely hard for the inventors to attract people who are considered important for the implementation.

The tensions and turbulences evoked by the principles of internal competition and countercultures may have negative impacts too. As proposed by several authors, establishing countercultures or having two or more groups of employees pursuing the same target in a competition encourages looking at topics from a variety of perspectives and, thus, spurs creativity and learning (e.g., Nonaka, 1988, 1991; Stacey, 1996). But in the context of bottom-up innovations, we found evidence that this approach turned out as contra productive. Because here, where especially the informal networks and interpersonal relations are important, this approach leads to the emergence of competing parties and often to a long-lasting dispute as the innovation manager of Chipcom describes very well: "Having two teams pursuing the same project with different approaches often results in enduring animosities, which are very difficult to remove afterwards." But this approach also leads to intraorganizational competitiveness and to knowledge egoism. Therefore, all the mentioned aspects of this approach harness the transfer and sharing of knowledge.

Summing up the impacts of crises, turbulences, and instabilities, it can be argued that they negatively impact the bottom-up dynamics in the innovation process.

6.6. Conclusion

We found that informal networks, autonomy, and openness were important enabling conditions for self-organization and emergence. Experimentation and large discretion given by the management as well as minimal structures are thus the key pillars of innovation in this development path. This shadow organization not only acts as a corrective to overcome the deficits of the formal innovation process, but moreover enables inventors to master organizational barriers or deliberately bypass formal procedures and policies by harnessing their personal network. Our empirical study also reveals evidence that the evoking of instabilities, which is often claimed as prerequisite for fostering self-organization in the complexity science literature, negatively impacts the bottom-up dynamics in the innovation process. When interpreting the results of this study, limitations need to be considered. We have studied innovation in the electronics industry and thus generalizations have to be made with caution since the conditions and organizational factors such as leadership style, extent of hierarchy or culture that facilitate or harm self-organizational activities, were not examined in more detail whereas in another study they are (Koch, 2007).

The case studies deliver evidence that formal systems such as stage-gate-systems, financial incentive schemes or patenting policies were bypassed or even ignored by the teams in order to push their own ideas and projects. Our findings are hence in line with some literature stressing that intrinsic motivation is the prime driving force and stimulus for creative and innovative work and that formal systems may be counterproductive and have unintended effects, and are, thus, often ignored or bypassed by organizational members (e.g., Katz and Allen, 1982; Osterloh and

Frey, 2000; Mainemelis, 2010) even if they were financially awarded. The empirical findings also deliver lessons on how to design management systems that explicitly aim to promote corporate entrepreneurship and incubation, which has become popular in industrial practice in the most recent years (e.g., Ayatse *et al.*, 2017).

We conclude that in addition to formal management processes, managers should pay attention to informal innovation activities, and steer them in an orderly manner, so to avoid that too extensive secret innovation activities undermine the effectiveness and efficiency of the entire process. Innovation management should provide space for discussion away from formal meetings, foster an open communication culture, and provide feedback on ideas in early development stages to facilitate informal activities' (later) path into the organizational hierarchy. Consequently, a certain amount of attention, resources, and time should be allocated to support self-organized bottom-up activities. To this end, separate budgetary resources should be used specifically for innovative developments.

References

Akgün, A., Keskin, H. and Byrne, J. (2014). Complex adaptive systems theory and firm product innovativeness. *Journal of Engineering and Technology Management*, **31**: 21–42.

Akrich, M., Callon, M. and Latour, B. (2002). The key to success in innovation. Part I: The key to interessement. *International Journal of Innovation Management*, **6**(2): 187–206.

Amabile, T. M. (1997). Motivating creativity in organizations: On doing what you love and loving what you do. *California Management Review*, **40**(1): 39–58.

Amabile, T. M. (1998). How to kill creativity. *Harvard Business Review*, (5): 77–87. September-October 1998.

Amabile, T. M., Hadley, C. N. and Kramer, S. J. (2002). Creativity under the gun. Special issue on the innovative enterprise: Turning ideas into profits. *Harvard Business Review*, **80**(8): 52–61. August 2002.

Anderson, C. and McMillan, E. (2003). Of ants and men: Self-organized teams in human and insect organizations. *Emergence*, **5**(2): 29–41.

Anderson, P. (1999a). Complexity theory and organization science. *Organization Science*, **10**(3): 216–232.

Anderson, P. (1999b). Seven levers for guiding the evolving enterprise. In Clippinger, J. H. (Ed.), *The Biology of Business: Decoding the Natural Laws of the Enterprise* (pp. 113–152). Jossey-Bass: San Francisco.

Augsdorfer, P. (2005). Bootlegging and path dependency. *Research Policy*, **34**(1): 1–11. Elsevier.

Ayatse, F., Kwahar, N. and Iyortsuun, A. (2017). Business incubation process and firm performance: An empirical review. *Journal of Global Entrepreneurship Research*, **7**(2): 1–17.

Brown, S. L. and Eisenhardt, K. M. (1997). The art of continuous change: Linking complexity theory and time-paced evolution in relentlessly shifting organizations. *Administrative Science Quarterly*, **42**(1): 1–34.

Burgelman, R. A. (1983). A process model of internal corporate venturing in the diversified major firm. *Administrative Science Quarterly*, **28**: 223–244.

Burnes, B. (2005). Complexity theories and organizational change. *International Journal of Management Reviews*, **7**(2): 73–90.

Christensen, C. M. (1997). *The Innovator's Dilemma: When New Technologies Cause Great Firms to Fail*. Boston, MA: Harvard Business School Press.

Christiansen, J. K. and Varnes, C. J. (2007). Making decisions on innovation: Meetings or networks? *Creativity and Innovation Management*, **16**(2): 82–98.

Clippinger, J. H. (1999). Order from bottom up: Complex adaptive systems and their management. In Clippinger, J. H. (Ed.), *The Biology of Business: Decoding the Natural Laws of the Enterprise* (pp. 1–30). San Francisco: Jossey-Bass.

Coleman, H. (1999). What enables self-organizing behavior in business. *Emergence: Complexity and Organization*, **1**(1): 33–48.

Cooper, R. G. (1990). Stage gate systems: A new tool for managing new products, *Business Horizons*, **33**(3): 44–53.

Cooper, R. G. (2006). The seven principles of the latest stage-gate method add up to a streamlined, new-product idea-to-launch process. *Product Development Institute*. March/April.

Criscuolo, P., Salter, A. and Ter Wal, A. L. (2014). Going underground: Bootlegging and individual innovative performance. *Organization Science*, **25**(5): 1287–1305.

Davila, A. (2003). Short-term economic incentives in new product development. *Research Policy*, **32**(8): 1397–1420.

Day, D. L. (1994). Raising radicals: Different processes for championing innovative corporate ventures. *Organization Science*, **5**(2): 148–172.

Dooley, K. (2002). Organizational complexity. In Warner, M. (Ed.), *International Encyclopedia of Business and Management* (pp. 5013–5022). London: Thompson Learning.

Eisenhardt, K. M. and Sull, D. N. (2001). Strategy as simple rule. *Harvard Business Review*, **79**(1): 106–116.

Eoyang, G. (2001). *Conditions for Self-Organization in Human Systems*. Dissertation, Union Institute, Cincinnati, Ohio.

Globocnik, D. and Salomo, S. (2015). Do formal management practices impact the emergence of bootlegging behavior? *Journal of Product Innovation Management*, **32**(4): 505–521.

Goldstein, J. (1999). Emergence as a construct: History and issues. *Emergence: Complexity and Organization*, **1**(1): 49–72.

Gomes, J. F. S. and Cunha M. P. (2003). Order and disorder in product innovation models. *Creativity and Innovation Management*, **12**(3): 174–187.

Kanter, R. M. (1988). When a thousand flowers bloom: Structural, collective, and social conditions for innovation in organization. In Swedberg, R. (Ed.), *Entrepreneurship: The Social Science View* (pp. 67–210). Oxford: Oxford University Press.

Katz, R. and Allen, T. J. (1982). Investigating the not-invented-here (NIH) syndrome: A look at the performance, tenure and communication patterns of 50 R&D project groups. *R&D Management*, **12**(1): 7–19.

Knowles, R. N. (2001). Self-organizing leadership: A way of seeing what is happening in organizations and a pathway to coherence. *Emergence: Complexity and Organization*, **3**(4): 112–127.

Koch, R. (2007). *Wirkung, Funktion und Determination von Selbstorganisation im Innovationsprozess*. PhD thesis, Vienna University of Economics and Business Administration, Vienna.

Koch, R. and Leitner, K.-H. (2008). The dynamics and functions of self-organization in the fuzzy front end: Empirical evidence from the Austrian semiconductor industry. *Creativity and Innovation Management*, **17**(3): 216–226.

Leitner, K.-H. and Weber, M. (2019). Research and innovation futures: Challenging the dominant innovation paradigm. *e&i elektrotechnik und informationstechnik, Special Issue on Innovation Management*, **136**(3): 226–233.

Lichtenstein, B. (2000). Emergence as a process of self-organizing: New assumptions and insights form the study of non-linear dynamic systems. *Journal of Organizational Change Management*, **13**(6): 526–546.

Lichtenstein, B. and Jones, C. (2004). A self-organization theory of radical entrepreneurship. In *National Academy of Management Best-Paper Proceedings*, New Orleans, LA.

Mainemelis, C. (2010). Stealing fire: Creative deviance in the evolution of new ideas. *Academy of Management Review*, **35**(4): 558–578.

McCarthy, I. P., Tsinopoulos, C., Allen, P. and Rose-Anderssen, C. (2006). New product development as a complex adaptive system of decisions. *Journal of Product Innovation Management*, **23**(5): 437–456.

McMillan, E. and Carlisle, Y. (2006). Innovation in organizations from a complex adaptive systems perspective. *Emergence*, **8**(2): 2–9.

Miner, A. S., Bassoff, P. and Moorman, C. (2001). Organizational improvisation and learning: A field study. *Administrative Science Quarterly*, **46**: 304–337.

Mitleton-Kelly, E. (2003). Ten principles of complexity & enabling infrastructures. In *Complex Systems and Evolutionary Perspectives of Organisations: The Application of Complexity Theory to Organisations*. Oxford: Pergamon.

Monks, R. (1998). *The Emperor's Nightingale: Restoring the Integrity of the Corporation*. Oxford: Capston Publishing Limited.

Niggl, M. (1998). *Unternehmenssteuerung im Spannungsverhältnis zwischen Selbst- und Fremdorganisation — Eine strukturationstheoretische Untersuchung*. München: Shaker Verlag.

Nixon, B. (1998). Research and development performance measurement: A case study. *Management Accounting Research*, **9**(3): 329–355.

Nonaka, I. (1988). Creating organizational order out of chaos: Self-renewal in Japanese firms. *California Management Review*, **38**(3): 57–73.

Nonaka, I. (1991). The knowledge-creating company. *Harvard Business Review*, **69**(6): 96–104.

Nonaka, I. and Takeuchi, H. (1986). The new product development game. *Harvard Business Review*, **64**(1): 137–146.

Olin, T. and Wickenberg, J. (2001). Rule breaking in new product development — Crime or necessity? *Creativity and Innovation Management*, **10**(1): 15–25.

Olson, E. and Eoyang, G. (2001). *Facilitating Organization Change: Lessons from Complexity Science*. San Francisco: Jossey-Bass/Pfeiffer.

Osterloh, M. and Frey, B. (2000). Motivation, knowledge transfer, and organizational forms. *Organization Science*, **11**(5): 538–550.

Perrow, C. (1986) *Complex Organizations* (3rd edn.). New York: Random House.

Robinson, S. and Stern, B. (1997). Corporate creativity: How innovation and improvement actually happen. Oakland: Koehler Publishers.

Sakhdari, K. and Bidakhavidi, E. J. (2016). Underground innovation: How to encourage bootlegging employees to disclose their good ideas. *Technology Innovation Management Review*, **6**(3): 5–12.

Stacey, R. D. (1993). Strategy as order emerging from chaos. *Long Range Planning*, **26**(1): 10–17.

Stacey, R. D. (1996). Strategic management and organisational dynamics (2nd edn.). London: Pitman.

Tetenbaum, T. J. (1998). Shifting paradigms: From Newton to chaos. *Organizational Dynamics*, **26**(4): 21–32.

https://doi.org/10.1142/9781800612266_0008

Chapter 7

A Spatio-Political Approach to Bootlegging: Empowerment Within Third Spaces

Amadou Lô* and Pauline Fatien Diochon†
Grenoble Ecole de Management, Grenoble, France
**amadou.lo@tbs-education.fr*
†pauline.fatien@grenoble-em.com

Abstract

While bootlegging is often reduced to an individual equation, Chapter 7 opens to a spatio-political approach to bootlegging. It depicts how a third space (here a Fab Lab) supports' low power actors' bootlegging through three dimensions of transgression (namely cognitio-cultural, material, and socio-political). In doing so, this bootlegging enables them to empower themselves through a triple control of meaning, resources, and processes. It builds on a case study we conducted in the Fab Lab of the French car manufacturer Renault.

7.1. A Need for a Spatio-Political Perspective in Bootlegging

While bootlegging is often reduced to an individual equation, this chapter opens to a spatio-political approach to bootlegging. It depicts how a third space (here a Fab Lab) supports low power actors' bootlegging, through three dimensions of transgression (namely cognitio-cultural, material, and socio-political). In doing so, this bootlegging enables them to empower themselves through a triple control of meaning, resources, and processes. It builds on a case study we conducted in the French Fab Lab of the car manufacturer Renault (Lô and Fatien, 2018).

7.1.1. Beyond individual-centric perspectives in bootlegging

Bootlegging has long been reduced to individual initiatives where the success of new actions is based on isolated providential actors whose entrepreneurial capacities enable them to circumvent the organization and develop creative projects on the margins of the established order (Hatchuel *et al.*, 2009). This makes bootlegging a process highly dependent on people's abilities and willingness and therefore uncertain for organizations. It might, however, be possible to reduce such dependency and uncertainty by offering organizational spaces that might stabilize bootlegging while still maintaining their key features supportive of underground innovation. What is at stake then is an ability to offer a space that is inherently ambivalent, that combines both formality and informality, authorization, and transgression, overt and covert actions. This is precisely a key feature of third spaces, defined as in-between flexible work settings that derive from their hybridity a few social and political features (Oldenburd, 1989; Bhabha, 1994).

7.1.2. A focus on third spaces

Originally, third spaces or "places" (Oldenburg, 1989) designate concrete places beyond the home (the first place) and work (the second place), covering "a great variety of public places that host the regular, voluntary, informal, and happily anticipated gatherings of individuals beyond the realms of home and work" (Oldenburg, 1989: 15). While often associated with cafés, coffee shops, community centers, general stores, and bars, they increasingly penetrate organizations to constitute new third workspaces (Kingma, 2016). Such flexible "workscape" (Felstead *et al.*, 2005: 16–18) includes workspaces at home, at clients' sites, at companies, and/or mobile workspaces. Too rarely, third spaces have been studied in connection to innovation and entrepreneurship, probably reflective of a lack of consideration of the spatial and material equations in these disciplines (Kornberger and Clegg, 2005; Taylor and Spicer, 2007).

In this context of a scarcity of research on the spatial dimension of innovation, our study explores how a third space can support bootlegging, and uncovers the associated political dimensions.

7.2. Renault's Fab Lab: An Emerging Space for Bootlegging

7.2.1. Context of study

The Fab Lab we studied belongs to the French car manufacturer Renault, part of the world's leading automotive alliance Renault–Nissan. The Fab Lab is located in Renault's Technocenter, in Guyancourt, France. This site has more than 10,000 employees whose jobs range from vehicle conception and fabrication (research, design, product engineering, etc.). These employees evolve in a highly competitive and fast-evolving industry, which confronts them to an urge for innovation to face insider and outsider competitors (such as Google). However, Renault has struggled over the past few decades with innovation processes, in particular to convert innovations into mature projects. And central to Renault's overall innovation strategy, though challenging, is the tension between R&D and manufacturing that has been addressed until recently through a structural separation of innovation processes. R&D activities were located within "research" units while manufacturing activities were physically separated, in "technological" units. In this context of structural separation, where innovation processes are relatively stable and standardized, the implementation of a Fab Lab, as we describe later in the chapter, does not go unnoticed. Indeed, in September of 2013, while Fab Labs were multiplying in civil society, Renault implemented a corporate Fab Lab. A Fab Lab, or Fabrication-Laboratory, is a technical prototyping platform for innovation and invention, initially developed within the Massachusetts Institute of Technology (MIT) by Professor Neil Gershenfeld in the years 2000 (Gershenfeld, 2012). It has been conceived as a freedom space, supportive of exchanges that occur within a democratic culture of lightness, openness, and trial-and-error (Lô, 2017). It is a place to play, learn, mentor, create, and invent (Getting Started with Fab Labs; fabfoundation.org). The implementation of such a space within Renault triggered our research interest and our decision to explore what was happening in this emerging innovation structure.

Specifically, Renault's Fab Lab has been designed as a space of circulation and exchange. A 65 m^2-space, it is centrally located within Renault, with easy access from the main entrance, 7 minutes walking distance from the research department and 5 minutes from the development department. It has been designed and organized in a circular way to nurture relaxed and open discussions. This culture of openness is sustained by an absence of hierarchy and the free access to a variety of both simple tools and machines (such as a soldering iron) and more sophisticated ones (3D printer and a laser cutter). Several multicolored objects, models, card games, and toys are available and are part of the supplies. While the space is closed, it opens on the outside thanks to large glass walls that run all around the perimeter of the Fab Lab.

7.2.2. A contested implementation

The implementation of the Fab Lab first results from a conquest won by two visionary and rebel engineers. As they were themselves suffocating in Renault's rigid, standardized, and shy innovation culture, they decided to lead a "cultural revolution" and create a "Gallic village" of innovation. They notably intended to foster flexibility and inclusiveness into the existing innovation processes. Their ambitious projects were not an easy task since they initially struggled to gather the resources necessary for Renault's Fab Lab to become a legitimate structure. On their road, they faced the opposition from several employees and managers who perceived the potential arrival of an alternative structure as either *detrimental* (an impediment to the proper functioning of the innovation routines already in place), *useless* (redundant with processes already in place), or *costly* (which explains the founders' difficulties in assembling financial, human and material resources). Fortunately, countering this opposition, they received the support from a key stakeholder, the manager of the Innovation Direction subunit who would later agree to host the Fab Lab, as well as from early adopters who informally engaged in the Fab Lab to conduct exploration activities.

7.3. Bootlegging in a Third Space: From Transgression to Empowerment

7.3.1. Bootlegging in a third space: A triple transgression

Once implemented, the Fab Lab allowed low power actors to circumvent traditional and standardized innovation processes to engage in fruitful exploration activities. Through this space, these actors engaged in a triple transgression. First, *a Cognitivo-Cultural Transgression Through the Destabilization of Existing Order.* Renault's Fab Lab constituted a unique opportunity for employees usually excluded from exploratory activities to not only dream about this innovation utopia, but also to make it come true. Their usual frustration progressively diminished as they realized that they indeed had an actual possibility of changing the innovation processes. A new innovation discourse emerged around what innovation meant and how to conduct it. Second, a Material Transgression Through Access to Resources. In itself, as a bubble within the established structure, the Fab Lab constitutes a transgressive place. This transgression is furthered materialized by the tools and technologies offered (such as 3D printers), the setting and decoration of the space (a very colorful place where coffee and cakes are freely served), the design methods offered to participants. Finally, and Third, *a Socio-Political Transgression Through a Systematization of Autonomous Initiatives.* Through its establishment, the Fab Lab allowed for the systematization of autonomous initiatives, that is, the integration of initiatives back into the traditional innovation processes. In fact, the Fab Lab acted as a parallel structure offering a new path for employees to engage in the innovation processes of their large organization, despite the constraints of a rigid and exclusive structure. Rather, the Fab Lab offered flexibility and inclusiveness. This transgression is political insofar as it circumvents and transforms preexisting and culturally anchored innovation processes, thus countering established interests.

7.3.2. From transgression to empowerment within a third space

Each of the above-described transgressions correspond to a dimension of empowerment, which we can define as the power (or powers) given or gained to accomplish something. Indeed, Hardy and Leiba-O'Sullivan (1998) encourage us to conceptualize empowerment as made of several power(s); there are powers behind empowerment. They emphasize notably the control of *meaning* (which corresponds to what we have identified above as the cognitive-cultural dimension of transgression), the control of *resources* (the material dimension of transgression), and the control of *processes* (socio-political dimension of transgression). We next detail this three dimensions of empowerment in connection with the above-identified transgression.

First, the *Control of Meaning*, refers to "how we think" and corresponds to the ability to shape others' lives (Hardy and Leiba-O'Sullivan, 1998). This type of control occurred as employees who founded the Fab Lab, and those who used it, managed to offer a counter narrative about innovation at Renault. Aside from standardized processes, this space legitimized informal, underground innovation in making clear that another path was possible.

Second, the *Control of Resources*, refers to the mobilization of scarce valuable assets (Hardy and Leiba-O'Sullivan, 1998). In the Fab Lab, it took place through the access to critical spaces, methodologies, tools, and technologies. This equipment of transgression emphasizes the materiality of bootlegging, necessary to challenge the status quo.

Third, the *Control of Processes*, refers to the control of decision-making processes (Hardy and Leiba-O'Sullivan, 1998). Here, employees managed to systematize their autonomous initiatives within the Fab Lab by reintegrating and stabilizing their own innovations within the larger innovation process at Renault. It was key to leverage the innovation developed within the Fab Lab.

In sum, we see the multifaceted dimension of empowerment through which low power employees engage within this Fab Lab. While the control of resources refers to a more explicit and visible form of empowerment, the control of meaning and processes is more intangible.

7.3.3. Conditions for empowerment through bootlegging within a third space

Additionally, these results open promising avenues for bootlegging by helping us identify supportive conditions for empowerment. While, as pointed out by Hardy and Leiba-O'Sullivan (1998), empowerment often fails to deliver on its promises, and sadly too often remains an empty shell, when not generating resentment, we can build on our case study to delineate two conditions that seem to have been beneficial to empowerment through bootlegging, namely inclusion and hybridity.

First, the Fab Lab is an inclusive space where employees can engage freely into bootlegging. Indeed, by offering a permissive social context enabling informal activities such as exploration and free exchange, the Fab Lab offers psychological comfort, leveling differences in support of inclusiveness, which is a key feature of third spaces according to Oldenburg (1989). A second key feature is hybridity. We demonstrated, especially through the systematization of processes, that the Fab Labs manages to combine the best of two worlds. It is a liminal in-between space (Van Gennep, 1909; Turner, 1967), between a dominant rigid organization with its traditional innovation processes and an emerging space with informal unstructured interactions. This liminality is liberating, energizing, and stimulating for innovation (Prashantham and Floyd, 2019).

7.4. Conclusion

The intention of this chapter is to contribute to bootlegging literature by opening a conversation on a spatio-political approach to transgression. More specifically, we showed how a space, here a Fab Lab acting as a third space, allows low power actors to engage in bootlegging, which in turn allows them to be empowered thanks to a triple control of meaning, resources, and processes. We therefore intend to make two major contributions.

First, the focus on space in bootlegging expands the mostly individual-centric literature on bootlegging to a dimension too often ignored, as if innovation happened in vacuum. Spaces are not neutral containers (Taylor and Spicer, 2007), but rather enable action; this chapter is therefore an encouragement to reconsider the spatial dimension of bootlegging.

Second, we showed that what happens between walls and among space is empowerment. This political dimension is key, and our study provides promising avenues in an empowerment era where employees, more than ever, seek self-fulfillment in their work. Our case suggests that inclusiveness and hybridity are key features of productive empowerment.

References

Bhabha, H. K. (1994). *The Location of Culture*. London & New York: Routledge.

Criscuolo, P. Salter, A. and Ter Wal, A. L. J. (2014). Going underground: Bootlegging and individual innovative performance. *Organization Science*, **25**(5): 1287–1305.

Felstead, A. Jewson, N. and Walters, S. (2005). *Changing Places of Work*. Basingstoke: Palgrave MacMillan.

Gennep, A. V. (1909). *Les Rites de Passage: Etude Systématique des Rites*. Paris: Librairie Critique.

Gershenfeld, N. (2012). How to make almost anything. *Foreign Affairs*, **91**(6): 43–57.

Kingma, S. F. (2016). The constitution of 'third workspaces' in between the home and the corporate office. *New Work, Employment, Society*, **31**(2): 176–193.

Kornberger, M. and Clegg, S. R. (2004). Bringing space back in: Organization the generative building. *Organization Studies*, **25**(7): 1095–1114.

Lô, A. (2017). Un FabLab d'Entreprise Pour Favoriser l'Ambidextrie des Salariés. Étude de cas Chez Renault. *Revue Française de Gestion*, **43**(264): 81–99.

Lô, A. and Fatien Diochon, P. (2019). Unsilencing power dynamics within third spaces. The case of Renault's Fab Lab. *Scandinavian Journal of Management*, **35**(2): 1–9.

Oldenburg, R. (1989). *The Great Good Place: Cafes, Coffee Shops, Community Centers, Beauty Parlors, General Stores, Bars, Hangouts, and How They Get You Through the Day*. New York: Paragon House.

Prashantham, S. and Floyd, S. W. (2019). Navigating liminality in new venture internationalization. *Journal of Business Venturing*, **34**(3): 513–527.

Taylor, S. and Spicer, A. (2007). Time for space: A narrative review of research on organizational spaces. *International Journal of Management Reviews*, **9**(4): 325–346.

Turner, V. (1967). Betwixt and between: The liminal period in rites de passage, in *The Forest of Symbols*. Ithaca, NY: Cornell University Press.

https://doi.org/10.1142/9781800612266_0009

Chapter 8

Creative Bootlegging as a Catalyst Between Job Design (Mis)fit and Innovative Work Behavior

Tomislav Hernaus[*,‡], Matej Černe[†,§], and Miha Škerlavaj[†,¶]

[*] *Faculty of Economics and Business, University of Zagreb, Zagreb, Croatia*
[†] *School of Economics and Business, University of Ljubljana, Ljubljana, Slovenia*
[‡] *thernaus@efzg.hr*
[§] *matej.cerne@ef.uni-lj.si*
[¶] *miha.skerlavaj@ef.uni-lj.si*

Abstract

Previous meta-analytic evidence has shown several job-design characteristics to be crucial predictors of employee innovativeness. The reality is, however, that many individuals are likely to be in misfit with the experienced characteristics of their jobs. Discrepancy in job-design characteristics (actual versus wanted) has (paradoxically) the potential to explain employee innovative work behavior. In particular, we focused on task identity and entertain the possibility that employee engagement in creative bootlegging interacts with incongruent situations between actual- and wanted-task identity, thereby increasing their creative and innovative performance. The results of moderated polynomial regression analyses from the multisource field study of 233 working professionals and 62 direct supervisors employed by a European bank suggest several interesting findings. First, congruence in actual–wanted task identity at high levels (a high-fit situation) leads to higher levels of innovative work behavior than congruence achieved at low levels (a low-fit situation). Second, we found empirical evidence that task–identity incongruence is driving innovative work behaviors more than congruence does. Finally, incongruence in actual–wanted task identity interacts with creative bootlegging in positively predicting innovative work behavior when employees self-report higher levels of underground innovation activities.

8.1. Experienced (Actual) Versus Expected (Wanted) Task Identity

Business performance improvements are often fueled by employee innovativeness. Creative and innovative actions of working individuals occur when one or more of the following conditions are present: transformational leadership, risk-taking climate, creative personality, or high-involvement HR practices. The latter includes design of jobs, which has been recognized as a critical individual-level antecedent of a plethora of beneficial work outcomes, including innovative work behavior (IWB). In other words, the actual content and structure of tasks that employees perform (i.e., job design; Oldham and Fried, 2016) may create or diminish a favorable work environment for stimulating higher levels of employees' idea generation (creativity), idea promotion (championing), and subsequent implementation (realization) activities (i.e., IWB; de Jong and den Hartog, 2010).

Job design — as a useful human resource management (HRM) tool that intrinsically motivates individual (and team) working practices — is commonly operationalized through numerous employee-perceived job characteristics (e.g., work autonomy, job complexity, task variety, task interdependence, and others) reflecting their subjective experience of formal (present or actual) job requirements. Nevertheless, to get a complete picture about the motivating potential and gain an understanding of subsequent behavioral responses to a particular job setting, we should also take into account personal expectations of job incumbents. Wanted (preferred or desired) job design represents an anchor for evaluating the appropriateness of existing job characteristics for each individual. By simultaneously considering employees' job attribute preferences (needs) and work position requirements (supplies), organizational decision makers might take an advantage of a person–job fit perspective to generate more straightforward, performance-optimizing, and risk-averse job-design decisions.

Among many job characteristics recognized in the literature, we find task identity (i.e., the scope of task activities an individual handle within his or her job position; Hacker, 2003) to be specifically intriguing for studying microinnovation performance patterns. This core job/task dimension represents a horizontal dimension of job scope that is a consequence of the division of the labor and task specialization within an organization. A high degree of task identity means that all phases (from goal setting to implementation and checking the process and results) are represented in a task and all modes of mental regulation (intellectual and experience based) are involved. On the other side of the continuum, a low degree of task identity encompasses a fragmented, narrowly defined (specialized, even routine) piece of work that does not require conscious problem-solving.

Enlarged or enriched task identity (i.e., making a whole product/service, running the entire workflow, or managing end-to-end customer experience) is nowadays a desired job attribute across occupations and industry sectors. However, there is no consensus achieved on whether having complete (multitask) or partially (task-specialized) designed work is optimal for employees' IWB. A higher degree of actual-task identity might not provide creative and innovative outcomes in each occasion; it might be a pleasant experience only for those individuals who prefer to take responsibility and control over the entire work process or product development/improvement. Other employees, who do not search for perceived wholeness, may respond differently to the given task challenge, finding it stressful and being not so meaningful at all.

If we approach task identity by addressing both perspectives (i.e., actual- and wanted-task identity), four respective different fit–misfit situations emerge: (1) high-fit, (2) low-fit, (3) under-fit, and (4) over-fit. A *high-fit* situation means that actual- and wanted-task identity are matched at a high level. Employees have a strong need to execute complete tasks with identifiable outcomes, and they are indeed formally responsible for managing the entire workflow of interdependent activities. Similarly, a *low-fit* situation represents a match, although at the low level of task identity, such as employees who prefer doing a small, either simplified or specialized (deep structure) pieces of the work and are supposed to do so. Furthermore, going beyond the optimal level may lead to an *over-fit* situation, where an oversupply of task identity exists, thus creating extra job demands. In this scenario, employees have jobs that encounter an increased level of clearly identifiable work results, although they prefer to deal with fragmented, more specialized tasks. Finally, an *under-fit* situation is another form of discrepancy where employees' needs are unfulfilled because the existing (assigned) level of actual-task identity is below the expected (wanted) level. Their personal attributes are greater than environmental attributes, or their job design offers less challenge than job incumbents need or prefer (van Vianen, 2018).

The key focus of the chapter is to examine how different task identity fit–misfit situations lead to more or less frequent IWB, and to explore the boundary condition of creative bootlegging (i.e., a bottom-up, non-programmed activity of motivated individuals that secretly organize the corporate innovation process without official authorization from the relevant management; Augsdorfer, 2005). To provide field evidence and thus move beyond theorizing, we sampled 233 non-R&D individuals (clerical and professional staff) and 62 direct supervisors from a European bank in a time-lagged study.[1] Both basic (means, correlations, cross-tabulations) and advanced (polynomial regression analysis and response surface modeling; moderation analysis using the block variable approach) statistical techniques are employed to test our research model (see Fig. 8.1).

Means, standard deviations, and Pearson's correlations between four main study variables are reported in Table 8.1. On average, sampled employees desire substantially more complete tasks ($M = 4.26, SD = 0.63$) than currently assigned ($M = 3.42$, $SD = 0.87$). Direct supervisors noted

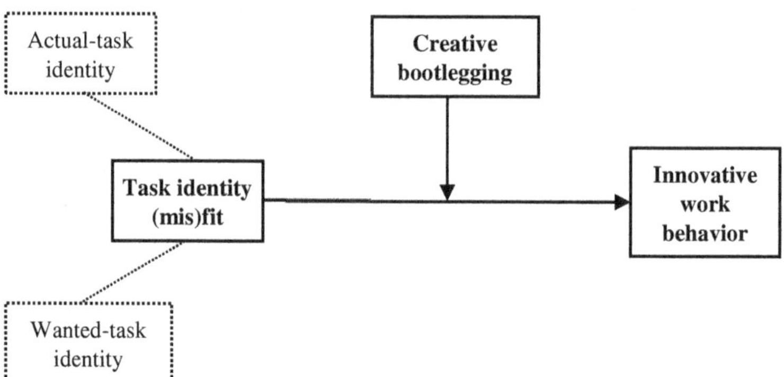

Fig. 8.1. Research model.

[1]A response rate was 62.63%. The average employee age was 38.64 years ($SD = 9.09$), with an average job tenure of 6.14 years ($SD = 5.69$). A total of 78 were men, and 155 were female. The majority of supervisor respondents had received a university bachelor's degree education (43.97%), followed by 40.95% of the subordinate respondents who had received a high school education, 11.21% who had higher diploma education, and 3.88% with master's degrees.

Table 8.1. Descriptives and correlations between main study variables.

		Mean	SD	1	2	3	4
1	Actual-task identity (E)	3.42	0.87	(0.87)	—	—	—
2	Wanted-task identity (E)	4.26	0.63	0.40**	(0.86)	—	—
3	Creative bootlegging (E)	2.85	0.66	−0.08	0.03	(0.60)	—
4	Innovative work behavior (S)	3.00	0.89	0.09	0.13*	0.14*	(0.96)

Notes: Cronbach's alphas are shown in parentheses on the diagonal.
*Correlation is significant at the 0.05 level; **Correlation is significant at the .01 level.
E — employee-reported; S — supervisor-reported.

their employees practiced IWB sometimes ($M = 3.00$, $SD = 0.89$), while job incumbents self-reported about their creative bootlegging efforts ($M = 2.85$, $SD = 0.66$). Furthermore, a correlation matrix revealed that both wanted-task identity ($r = 0.13$, $p < 0.05$) and creative bootlegging ($r = 0.14$, $p < 0.05$) are positively related to IWB, while such an association is missing for actual-task identity. Obviously, the interplay between actual- and wanted-task identity, as well as creative bootlegging, should be considered in more detail to understand what drives microinnovation processes.

Next, we grouped and assigned our employee respondents to four clusters according to the respective modality of the actual–wanted task identity relationship. A mean split was used for making cluster grouping decisions and a 2 × 2 matrix has been created (see Fig. 8.2). The majority of the sampled workforce where either in the *low-fit* (33.05% of the sample) or *high-fit* situation (30.47% of the sample). However, a notable difference has been revealed across two task–identity fitted situations. Specifically, while innovative work behavior is most frequently practiced by employees who are in a *high-fit* situation ($M = 3.12$, $SD = 0.79$), their *low-fit* counterparts operate in the least stimulating work environment for employee innovativeness ($M = 2.89$, $SD = 0.91$). Levels of IWB were similar in *over-fit* and *under-fit* situations. In terms of creative bootlegging, it appears that such an underground innovative effort is more often present when employees experience a low amount of experienced (actual-)task identity ($M = 2.90$, $SD = 0.68$ for a *low-fit* situation; $M = 2.91$, $SD = 0.57$ for an *under-fit* situation), no matter the preferred (wanted) level of task identity.

Actual-task identity \ Wanted-task identity	Low	High
High	**OVER-FIT cluster** (22.32%) IWB = 3.03 Creative bootlegging = 2.80	**HIGH-FIT cluster** (30.47%) IWB = 3.12 Creative bootlegging = 2.79
Low	**LOW-FIT cluster** (33.05%) IWB = 2.89 Creative bootlegging = 2.90	**UNDER-FIT cluster** (14.16%) IWB = 2.99 Creative bootlegging = 2.91

Fig. 8.2. IWB and creative bootlegging practices across task–identity clusters.

8.2. Employee Innovativeness Within the Task–Identity Fit Situations

Jobs should match or fit with other personal or organizational features (Toh *et al.*, 2008) to promote performance, development, positive attitudes, and well-being (Daniels and de Jonge, 2010). A person–job fit should also play a significant role in influencing whether employees occupying non-R&D positions engage in IWB (Afsar *et al.*, 2015); employees with better P–J fit are satisfied with their tasks and are thus intrinsically motivated to display creative and innovative outputs (de Jong and den Hartog, 2007).

Nevertheless, the congruence achieved between employee needs and job supplies is possible at different levels of the task–identity scale, that is, a continuous line of fits between actual- and wanted-task identity exists, along which employees may manifest different levels of innovative work behavior. To operationalize this Cartesian approach (see Donaldson, 2001), we introduce a *high-fit* (a high degree of actual-task identity and a high degree of wanted-task identity) and a *low-fit* situation (a low degree of actual-task identity and a low degree of wanted-task identity) and assert that need fulfillment at higher level of task identity ends in more intense employee innovativeness than such occurrence at the lower levels of the actual–desired task–identity fit line.

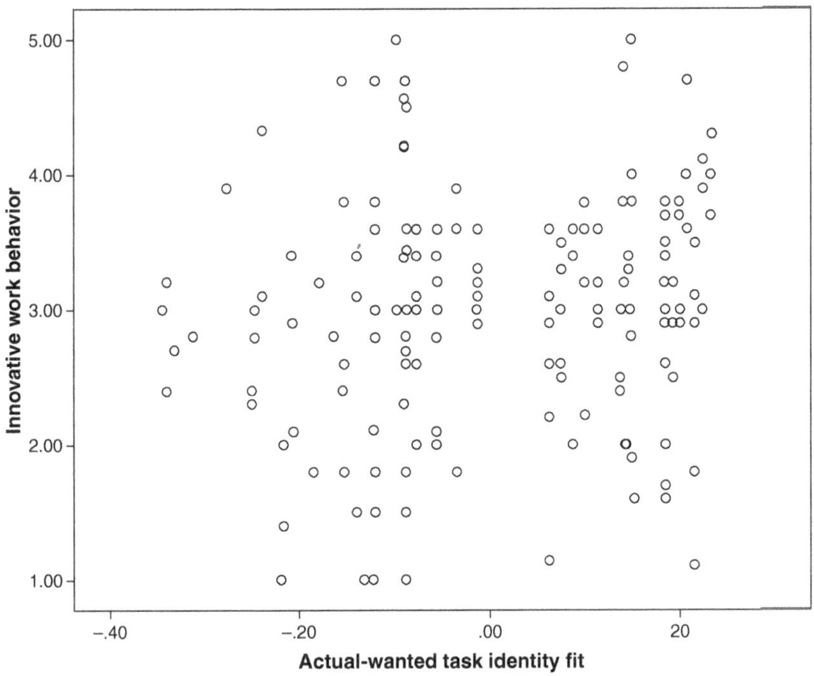

Fig. 8.3. A scatter plot of the relationship between task–identity fits and IWB.

A scatter plot in Fig. 8.3 indicates assumed linear-shaped relationship between actual–wanted task identity fit and employee IWB.[2] Moreover, polynomial regression analysis and related response surface modeling (see Fig. 8.4) clearly show that the linear slope along the actual–wanted congruence line was positive and significant ($a_1 = 0.32$, $p < 0.05$). Specifically, the lowest level of IWB is found at the front corner at the right of the slope graph, where actual- and wanted-task identity are low (a *low-fit* situation). Increasingly higher levels of IWB are found toward the (left) back of the graph, where actual- and wanted-task identity are in balance and high (a *high-fit* situation). In other words, we evidenced that employee

[2]The graph shows 159 subsampled cases/respondents from high-fit and low-fit situations. Actual–wanted task identity fit represents a block variable or weighted composite (consisted of the five polynomial terms related to actual- and wanted-task identity perceptions: $b_1X + b_2Y + b_3X^2 + b_4XY + b_5Y^2$).

innovativeness is higher when actual- and wanted-task identity perceptions are present at a similarly high level (*a high-fit* situation) compared to when they are present at a similarly low level (a *low-fit* situation).

Such reasoning is in line with the general premise of P–J fit theory and is made possible because high-task identity situations can be considered as a fertile ground for workplace innovation (Loher *et al.*, 1985). For instance, employees with an enlarged or enriched job design can visualize and be responsible for the entire workflow, which in turn increases their intrinsic motivation to engage in IWB. However, a downward spiral applies in the case of aligned but impaired jobs. Less enriched job attributes and contraction of work roles (i.e., low actual-task identity), despite of the reached balance between formal requirements and personal expectations, promote negative affect, which in turn likely discourages employees from innovative actions (Searle and Parker, 2013).

8.3. Employee Innovativeness Within the Task–Identity Misfit Situations

A significant number of individuals is imperfectly matched with the characteristics of their jobs. In terms of task identity, this would mean that some employees handle more complete tasks than desired (an *over-fit* situation in which actual-task identity overrules wanted-task identity), while others have fragmented tasks despite of their strivings toward more complete ones with an identifiable outcome (an *under-fit* situation where wanted-task identity is higher than the level of actual-task completeness). Both *over-fit* (actual > wanted) and *under-fit* (wanted > actual) task identity situations at the workplace are not so rare. For instance, the present research indicates that every third employee respondent is experiencing a task–identity misfit (36.48% of the sample).

Certain problems may arise from partialized actions where job incumbents have a low regulation level (e.g., a lack of conscious problem-solving activities; not being required to develop personal plans and goals), such as a reduced level of competence and a diminished ability to deal with problems from more than one perspective (Frese and Zapf, 1994). On the other hand, the potential stress of an elevated task identity is another extreme that has been overlooked to a large extent (Xie and Johns, 1995). Few studies have examined a too-much-of-a-good-thing effect (Lam *et al.*, 2014;

Pierce and Aguinis, 2013), that is, the possibility that job characteristics that are usually thought to have positive effects can provoke stress when present at high levels. Such evidence still does not exist for task identity.

While misfit situations might and usually do result in dissatisfaction, they can also present an opportunity for increased diversity in priorities and perspectives within an organization, which can lead to increased creativity/innovation (e.g., Hoever *et al.*, 2012; Vogel *et al.*, 2016). Dissatisfied "creators" seemed to get engaged in idea generation as a constructive expression of voice (Lee *et al.*, 2019) and put an additional effort to implement their innovative ideas.

Specifically, when dealing with a more partial set of tasks than desired (an *under-fit* situation), individuals might strive to gain comprehensiveness of their job, which could enable them to take "a bird's eye view" into the existing situation at work, increase job meaningfulness, and thereby exercise thinking outside of the box and idea implementation behaviors (e.g., Coelho and Augusto, 2010; Frese *et al.*, 1996). On the other hand, the oversupply of task identity (an *over-fit* situation) should benefit employee innovativeness because it is viewed as a buffer or reservoir of task–identity supply that can be applied in the future (e.g., Edwards, 1996; Shipp and Jansen, 2011). Furthermore, having to deal with a complete set of tasks (which could over exceed his or her role expectations and job preferences), an employee might feel overwhelmed and experience a high level of job strain and stress, resorting to IWB as an effective way of dealing with stressors (e.g., Bunce and West, 1994; Janssen, 2004).

Our polynomial regression results confirmed that the level of IWB is higher when the levels of actual- and wanted-task identity perceptions are dissimilar. The linear slope along the incongruence line was not significant ($a_3 = 0.06$, n.s.), while the curvature was indeed positive (convex) and significant ($a_4 = 0.75$, $p < 0.01$). The response surface graph (Fig. 8.4) shows that when we follow the incongruence line from the midpoint of the response surface to the left-hand (upper) corner, the degree of wanted-task identity increases, and we move away from the point where actual-task identity matches wanted-task identity (the state of fit). When employees experience an *under-fit* (high-wanted and low-actual task identity) situation, IWB is higher than when there is a task–identity fit. Furthermore, when we move along the incongruence line from the center to the right-hand (upper) corner of the response surface, the amount of actual-task identity surpasses

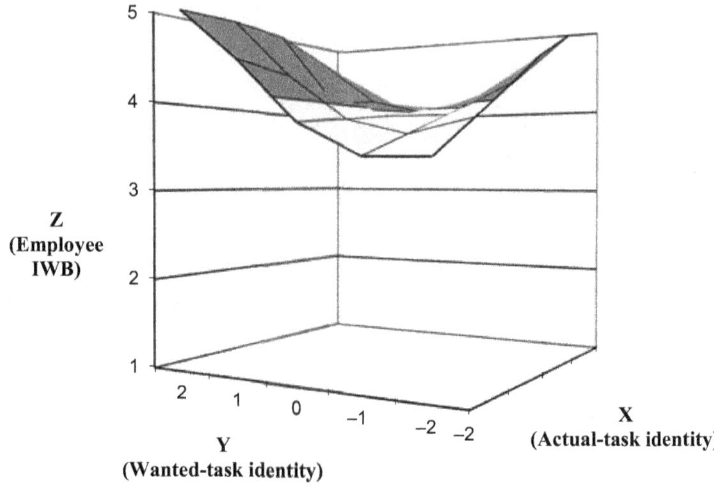

Fig. 8.4. Response surface analysis for actual–wanted task identity (in)congruence predicting innovative work behavior.

the amount of wanted-task identity, leading to an *over-fit* (low-wanted and high-actual task identity) situation. In other words, employees' IWB becomes more frequent as their task–identity misfit increases signaling that incongruence in actual–wanted task identity is driving innovative work behaviors more than congruence does.

8.4. Creative Bootlegging as a Catalyst Condition

Creative bootlegging refers to intrinsically motivated individuals who secretly — without receiving the official permission and support from top management — pursue their creative and innovative ideas (Augsdorfer, 2005) with the aim to ultimately benefit the organization (Umphress and Bingham, 2011). Such behavioral response occurs extensively across organizations (Augsdorfer, 2012; Eicher, 2021) and should not be either ignored or taken negatively. Contrary, bootlegged projects frequently lead to product or process innovations (Masoudnia and Szwejczewski, 2012) and enable nurturing unconventional ideas until they are reasonably developed to be revealed. They also have the entrepreneurial element of building competencies for the future innovation potential of the organization (Pavitt, 1988), and are associated with achievement of high levels of innovative performance for R&D personnel (Criscuolo *et al.*, 2014).

On one hand, covert innovations might not be necessary or prevalent (although such behavioral patterns occur frequently) in organic structures with a transparent and organized innovation management efforts. Nevertheless, leading organizations such as 3M, Virgin, or Google have still been known to induce "creative freedom" of their workforce, either directly through job innovation requirements (e.g., number of reported ideas), or more indirectly by introducing autonomy-stimulating initiatives (e.g., task ownership and part of work time devoted for personal pet projects) or heavily emphasizing the trial-and-error climate (providing high levels of psychological safety). On the other hand, several highly differentiated and bureaucratic structures (e.g., Volvo Cars, Xerox), succeeded to launch innovative breakthroughs thankfully to individuals who strived to develop innovations and were likely to favor covert, bootlegged (creative and innovative) activities without having formal organizational support (Criscuolo *et al.*, 2014).

We find particularly interesting to analyze how creative bootlegging as nonmanagerially planned activities intervene the relationship between motivational job design and discretionary employee innovativeness. The basic premise of the current study is that underground innovation strengthens the relationship between incongruence in actual–wanted task identity perceptions and IWB. The background logic for such reasoning originates from the most recent finding that the absence of work autonomy does not eliminate yet facilitate creative bootlegging (Eicher, 2021). Translated to our focal job characteristic, among employees who experience either oversupply or undersupply of task identity, especially those individuals who are more likely to ignore formal structures, ready to bypass formal rules and to avoid bureaucracy will also provide more frequent and continuous efforts to elaborate their ideas' potential and promoting subsequent implementation (Globocnik and Salomo, 2015). In other words, we predicate that creative bootleggers, when experiencing a person–job misfit in terms of discrepancy between actual- and wanted-task identity, are more likely to exhibit higher levels of IWB.

The results of our moderated polynomial regression analyses confirmed this assertion. In terms of the interaction between task–identity incongruence and creative bootlegging, for high levels of creative bootlegging (+1 SD above the mean), the conditional effect size was 0.40, with a p-value of less than 0.01. At low levels of the moderator (−1 SD below the mean), no such moderation could be claimed, as the conditional effect was

−0.35 and remained nonsignificant. Obviously, employees who experience task–identity misfit (actual < wanted, or wanted > actual) yet follow a formal innovation system and simultaneously do not show interest to engage in informal (deviant) innovative actions miss the opportunity to add their two cents to IWB. These individuals do not recognize bootlegging efforts as an important source of innovation (Eicher, 2021).

8.5. Concluding Remarks

It is an unfortunate fact of organizational reality that not all employees are congruent with their jobs. How this person–job incongruence might affect employees' innovative work behavior practices was the focus of our field research. Specifically, the present chapter examined the interplay among task identity (in) congruence (actual- and wanted-task identity perceptions), creative bootlegging, and employee innovativeness within the case-studied financial organization. Interestingly, we revealed that in the case of this particular core job dimension, the misfit is not that much unfortunate and detrimental; it actually helps stimulating IWB in reaching higher levels of that specific type of extra-role performance than in certain task–identity fit situations.

Creative bootlegging is further boosting the focal relationship by offering an alternative, informal way of achieving innovative objectives. Apparently, at times turning a blind eye to underground practices of employee self-engagement in creative and innovative processes without reporting to formalized structures shows that formal and informal innovation systems can work hand in hand. Such bottom-up non-programmed innovation activities occur more regularly when employees are supplied with fragmented tasks (i.e., low-actual task identity), no matter the level of their personal expectations and preferences (i.e., low- and high-wanted task identity). While our findings are indicative, it remains open to see whether other job characteristics and/or job design bundles make a difference in boosting creative and innovative outputs of the (non-) R&D workforce.

References

Afsar, B., Badir, Y. and Khan, M. M. (2015). Person–job fit, person–organization fit and innovative work behavior: The mediating role of innovation trust. *The Journal of High Technology Management Research,* **26**(2): 105–116.

Augsdorfer, P. (2005). Bootlegging and path dependency. *Research Policy*, **34**(1): 1–11.

Augsdorfer, P. (2012). A diagnostic personality test to identify likely corporate bootleg researchers. *International Journal of Innovation Management*, **16**(1): 1250003–1250021.

Bunce, D. and West, M. (1994). Changing work environments: Innovative coping responses to occupational stress. *Work & Stress*, **8**(4): 319–331.

Coelho, F. and Augusto, M. (2010). Job characteristics and the creativity of frontline service employees. *Journal of Service Research*, **13**(4): 426–438.

Criscuolo, P., Salter, A. and Ter Wal, A. L. (2014). Going underground: Bootlegging and individual innovative performance. *Organization Science*, **25**(5): 1287–1305.

Daniels, K. and Jonge, J. (2010). Match making and match breaking: The nature of match within and around job design. *Journal of Occupational and Organizational Psychology*, **83**(1): 1–16.

de Jong, J. and den Hartog, D. (2007). How leaders influence employees' innovative behaviour. *European Journal of Innovation Management*, **10**(1): 41–64.

de Jong, J. and den Hartog, D. N. (2010). Measuring Innovative work behaviour. *Creativity and Innovation Management*, **19**(1): 23–36.

Donaldson, L. (2001). *The Contingency Theory of Organizations*. Thousand Oaks: Sage Publications.

Edwards, J. R. (1996). An examination of competing versions of the person-environment fit approach to stress. *Academy of Management Journal*, **39**(2): 292–339.

Eicher, S. (2021). *Uncovering Covert Innovation: Bootlegging, Illegitimacy, and Management's Attitude*. Nürnberg: Springer Gabler.

Frese, M. and Zapf, D. (1994). *Action as the Core of Work Psychology: A German Approach*. In Triantis, H. C., Dunnette, M. D. and Hough, L. M. (Eds.), *Handbook of Industrial and Organizational Psychology* (pp. 271–340). Palo Alto: Consulting Psychologists Press.

Frese, M., Kring, W., Soose, A. and Zempel, J. (1996). Personal initiative at work: Differences between east and west Germany. *Academy of Management Journal*, **39**(1): 37–63.

Globocnik, D. and Salomo, S. (2015). Do formal management practices impact the emergence of bootlegging behavior? *Journal of Product Innovation Management*, **32**(4): 505–521.

Hacker, W. (2003). Action regulation theory: A practical tool for the design of modern work processes? *European Journal of Work and Organizational Psychology*, **12**(2): 105–130.

Hoever, I. J., van Knippenberg, D., van Ginkel, W. P. and Barkema, H. G. (2012). Fostering team creativity: Perspective taking as key to unlocking diversity's potential. *Journal of Applied Psychology*, **97**(5): 982–996.

Janssen, O. (2004). How fairness perceptions make innovative behavior more or less stressful. *Journal of Organizational Behavior*, **25**(2): 201–215.

Lam, C. F., Spreitzer, G. and Fritz, C. (2014). Too much of a good thing: Curvilinear effect of positive affect on proactive behaviors. *Journal of Organizational Behavior*, 35(4): 530–546.

Lee, Y. S. H., Nembhard, I. M. and Cleary, P. D. (2019). Dissatisfied creators: Generating creative ideas amid negative emotion in health care. *Work and Occupations*, **47**(2): 200–227.

Loher, B. T., Noe, R. A., Moeller, N. L. and Fitzgerald, M. P. (1985). A meta-analysis of the relation of job characteristics to job satisfaction. *Journal of Applied Psychology*, **70**(2): 280–289.

Masoudnia, Y. and Szwejczewski, M. (2012). Bootlegging in the R&D departments of high-technology firms. *Research-Technology Management*, **55**(5): 35–42.

Oldham, G. R. and Fried, Y. (2016). Job design research and theory: Past, present and future. *Organizational Behavior and Human Decision Processes*, **136**: 20–35.

Pavitt, K. (1988). International patterns of technological accumulation. Strategies in global competition. In Hood, N. and Vahlne, J.-E. (Eds.), *Strategies in Global Competition* (pp. 126–157). London: Routledge.

Pierce, J. R. and Aguinis, H. (2013). The too-much-of-a-good-thing effect in management. *Journal of Management*, **39**(2): 313–338.

Searle, B. J. and Parker, S. K. (2013). Work design and happiness: An active, reciprocal perspective. In David, S. A., Boniwell, I. and Conley Ayers, A. (Eds.), *Oxford Handbook of Happiness* (pp. 711–732). Oxford: Oxford University Press.

Shipp, A. J. and Jansen, K. J. (2011). Reinterpreting time in fit theory: Crafting and recrafting narratives of fit in medias res. *The Academy of Management Review*, **36**(1): 76–101.

Toh, S. M., Morgeson, F. P. and Campion, M. A. (2008). Human resource configurations: Investigating fit with the organizational context. *Journal of Applied Psychology*, **93**(4): 864–882.

Umphress, E. E. and Bingham, J. B. (2011). When employees do bad things for good reasons: Examining unethical pro-organizational behaviors. *Organization Science*, **22**(3): 621–640.

van Vianen, A. E. M. (2018). Person-environment fit: A review of its basic tenets. *Annual Review of Organizational Psychology and Organizational Behavior*, **5**: 75–101.

Vogel, R. M., Rodell, J. B. and Lynch, J. W. (2016). Engaged and productive misfits: How job crafting and leisure activity mitigate the negative effects of value incongruence. *Academy of Management Journal*, **59**(5): 1561–1584.

Xie, J. L. and Johns, G. (1995). Job scope and stress: Can job scope be too high? *Academy of Management Journal*, **38**(5): 1288–1309.

https://doi.org/10.1142/9781800612266_0010

Chapter 9

Creative Bootlegging: A Transitional Space for Employees Toward Innovating

Khatereh Ghasemzadeh
University of Bologna, Bologna, Italy
khatereh.ghasemzadeh@unibo.it

Abstract

This chapter discusses the role of creative bootlegging as a bridge between individuals' self-efficacy characteristics and individuals' tendency to become the lead users. Analyzing the mechanism of bootlegging activities among working employees of small and medium enterprises (SMEs) in the blue sector, this chapter shows that bootlegging is a transitional space between individuals' self-beliefs in their abilities and their willingness to and generate innovative ideas by providing the opportunity for identity play among employees. The chapter contributes to the bootlegging concept by shedding light on the individuals' self-exploration characteristics, namely self-efficacy that triggers them to perform bootleg activities through which achieve enough confidence and autonomy to participate in the innovation-related activities.

9.1. Introduction

For a long time, scholars have scrutinized the different angles of the user innovation (UI) phenomenon, not to mention the behavioral and motivational characteristics that trigger individuals to contribute to UI. The emphasis here is on the pivotal role of the users in the innovation process to primarily fulfill their own unmet needs (von Hippel, 1976). However, users are not similar, and some users can play a more crucial role than others in the UI process called lead users. Generally, so-called lead users are ahead of the other users and even the market to sense the problem and benefit from the innovation of a product or service to a large extent (von Hippel, 1986). During the last almost 40 years, many studies endeavored to elucidate the reason behind the free innovation by users and so-called lead users and mainly discussed the self-rewarding in terms of gaining experience and fun as well as helping others as the main motivational constructs.

Embedded lead users (ELUs) are a specific group of lead users defined as "employees who are lead users of their employing firms' products or services" (Schweisfurth and Herstatt, 2015: 2). A number of arguments make it plausible that ELUs own different cognitive structures compared to external lead users as a consequence of their double identity of being external users and internal employees. This group of lead users has shown to put themselves in the shoes of the users and confront the current and future problems that users may face (Schweisfurth and Herstatt, 2016). What shapes the motive of conducting this chapter is to illuminate the less researched angle of the topic that is the inner characteristics of such internal (to the firm) lead users. We discuss the peculiar attitudes, beliefs, and behaviors that drive ELUs to act as they do in particular the self-efficacy characteristics and the creative bootlegging and the interplay between these two constructs to trigger employees to act as lead users within their organization. The chapter is grounded on the social cognitive theory, which is about the perception employees have about themselves (Bandura, 1991) and the concept of "identity play" at the workplace (Ibarra and Obodaru, 2016) though creative deviance and bootleg activities.

9.2. Creative Bootlegging Plays a Transitional Space Self-efficacy and ELU

Social cognitive theory is founded on self-regulatory mechanisms indicating that understanding one's own behavior affects the individual himself and the environment and, in turn, triggers future behavior (Bandura and Walters, 1977). Individuals' thoughts, motivations, and routines are affected by the manipulation of self-control and self-motivation proactively (Bandura, 1991). Social cognitive theory implies that individuals with self-exploration characteristics are willing to learn things about themselves and scrutinize and enhance their own identity (Berzonsky, 2004). The self and the identity interact constantly in such a way that the self gets cognitive, emotional, behavioral, and social boundaries from identity (Petriglieri *et al.*, 2019).

One manifestation of self-regulatory behaviors is self-efficacy that concerns with one's confidence about his or her ability to perform a specific task (Bandura, 1989; Bandura and Cervone, 1986). Entrepreneurial self-efficacy is a particular type of self-efficacy that refers to the individuals' beliefs connected to carrying out entrepreneurial tasks (Stajkovic and Luthans, 1998). The result of our study on 554 employees in 41 Italian and Croatian firms in the shipbuilding and boat-building sector (such as engines, furniture, industrial design services, etc.) revealed that entrepreneurial self-efficacy has a positive impact on embedded lead userness (Ghasemzadeh *et al.*, 2020). To examine the entrepreneurial self-efficacy, we asked employees to declare how confident they were in successfully creating new products, thinking creatively, and further commercializing an idea or new development.

On the other hand, the embedded lead userness has been measured by understanding to what extent employees are dissatisfied with the current products and their associated unresolved problems and how much they sense the void of unmet needs and try to put themselves in the shoes of the users. Individuals with high level of entrepreneurial self-efficacy show more self-confidence toward thinking creatively, creating new ideas (Newman *et al.*, 2018). An important reason is that individuals with the higher level of self-efficacy characteristics always try to find the opportunities for identity work meaning craft who they are and what they do (Caza *et al.*, 2018). Another important reason why employees with entrepreneurial self-efficacy are more likely become the lead users of their performing firm is because they have high level of confidence to take part in creative thinking and innovation-related activities. This is due to the fact that employees' identities grow in a steady process from a sense of self toward cultivating one's own values, norms, and commitments (Ibarra and Obodaru, 2016).

The question that arises here is whether having a relatively high level of self-efficacy attributes are enough to trigger creative thinking to perform innovation-related activities. The answer to this question is that even when individuals are confident enough to perform the innovation-related activities corresponding to ELUs' portfolio, they may lack some sort of proactive creativity. In this vein, employees with belief in themselves to have the necessary abilities for entrepreneurial tasks illustrate the motivation for bootlegging and subsequently begin bootleg activities (Globocnik and Salomo, 2015). Bootlegging counts as a kind of secret, bottom-up, non-programmed proactive activity (Criscuolo *et al.*, 2013). Employees take on bootlegging activities to increase their knowledge about the overall viability of their idea (Masoudnia and Szwejczewski, 2012) to verify legitimacy for the idea within an organization and to acquire the needed resources to further develop such idea (Kannan-Narasimhan, 2014).

As discussed earlier, self-efficacious employees always inspect their own self and what they do at work and look for opportunities to perform "identity play." Creative bootlegging activities enable these individuals to discover the various, often heterogeneous, and variable nature of their self, as well as the process of exploration and intuition for creating new identities. Thus, bootleg activities provide a transitional space for employees to participate in identity play and experiment with their work identity and further grow their identity. Exerting bootlegging behavior, employees gain more autonomy by themselves in their efforts to develop innovations through unconventional paths in favor of their own interests meaning that employees deviate from formal job requirements and show proactive creativity to generate innovative outcomes (Criscuolo *et al.*, 2013). To do so, employees often bypass formal rules and everyday routines (Kanter, 1988) and get involved in pre-development activities in the absence of official control (Harding, 1997).

Devoting time on bootleg activities in the form of pet projects, hobbies, and preferred projects, employees learn new things to boost the quality of their performance and decrease the uncertainty associated with their ideas to be accepted by manager (Criscuolo *et al.*, 2013; Masoudnia and Szwejczewski, 2012). Consequently, employees boost their entrepreneurial attitude through creative bootlegging, which result in showing more characteristics associated with leading-edge users. Admittedly, individual employees showing self-motivation and conviction in entrepreneurial activities enjoy working around their personal ideas and take more time and risks to work on their favorite projects through which they become more concerned about the *status quo* of products and services in current markets. This way they become more willing to think of the frustrations and problems associated with the products and services of their working firm and to engage in articulating and providing ideas and solutions.

9.3. Encourage Creative Bootlegging in Firms

As discussed in the previous section, bootleg activities provide the opportunity for identity play among employees to improve their entrepreneurial attitude, which led to generating more innovative outcomes. More specifically, employees with self-efficacy characteristics tend to find more time and freedom to play between the usual routine tasks and what is assumed to be work out of love through unconventional and informal paths (Globocnik and Salomo, 2015). Bootlegging as a self-regulating element on innovation is "long-run," meaning employees find freedom and time both secretly and with permission and devote it to obtain more expertise on technological domain and market. This chapter emphasizes on the importance of unofficial freedom that individuals provide themselves or sometimes is provided by firms to leverage their creativity and curiosity: leading-edge status. Firms more than ever should provide a flexible and supportive climate in which employees feel confident — and over time, gain even more confidence — in behaving entrepreneurially and, at the same time, are not afraid of "stealing" some official working time to follow their own intuitions. These days, in leading companies like Google, employees are given a percentage of their working hours to let them work freely on their ideas and personal projects.

Decreasing the tight control over employees especially on those who show a good entrepreneurial attitude and encouraging them to try out what they have passion about benefit both the employees and firms.

9.4. Summary

The chapter investigates the role of bootlegging creativity as a transitional space between individuals' self-beliefs in their abilities and their willingness to become embedded leas users and generate innovative ideas by providing the opportunity for identity play among employees. From a practical point of view, to benefit from internal lead users and their leading ideas in relation to firms' products and services, firms should create a climate in which employees feel confident — and gain over time even more confidence — in behaving entrepreneurially and, at the same time, are not afraid of "stealing" some official working time to follow their intuitions.

References

Bandura, A. (1989). Human agency in social cognitive theory. *American Psychologist*, **44**(9): 1175.

Bandura, A. (1991). Social cognitive theory of self-regulation. *Organizational Behavior and Human Decision Processes*, **50**(2): 248–287.

Bandura, A. and Cervone, D. (1986). Differential engagement of self-reactive influences in cognitive motivation. *Organizational Behavior and Human Decision Processes*, **38**(1): 92–113.

Bandura, A. and Walters, R. H. (1977). *Social Learning Theory* (Vol. 1). Prentice Hall: Englewood Cliffs, NJ.

Berzonsky, M. D. (2004). Identity processing style, self-construction, and personal epistemic assumptions: A social-cognitive perspective. *European Journal of Developmental Psychology*, **1**(4): 303–315.

Caza, B. B., Vough, H. and Puranik, H. (2018). Identity work in organizations and occupations: Definitions, theories, and pathways forward. *Journal of Organizational Behavior*, **39**(7): 889–910.

Criscuolo, P., Salter, A. and Ter Wal, A. L. (2013). Going underground: Bootlegging and individual innovative performance. *Organization Science*, **25**(5): 1287–1305.

Ghasemzadeh, K., Bunjak, A., Bortoluzzi, G. and Černe, M. (2020). Efficaciously smuggling ideas: Untangling the relationship between entrepreneurial self-efficacy, creative bootlegging and embedded lead users. *International Journal of Innovation Management*, 2150032.

Globocnik, D. and Salomo, S. (2015). Do formal management practices impact the emergence of bootlegging behavior? *Journal of Product Innovation Management*, **32**(4): 505–521.

Harding, R. (1997). Forbidden fruit: An analysis of bootlegging, uncertainty and learning in corporate R& D. *Technovation*, **11**(17): 734–735.

Ibarra, H. and Obodaru, O. (2016). Betwixt and between identities: Liminal experience in contemporary careers. *Research in Organizational Behavior*, **36**: 47–64.

Kannan-Narasimhan, R. (2014). Organizational ingenuity in nascent innovations: Gaining resources and legitimacy through unconventional actions. *Organization Studies*, **35**(4): 483–509.

Kanter, R. M. (1988). When a thousand flowers bloom: Structural, collective, and social conditions for innovation in organizations. *Knowledge Management and Organisational Design*, **10**: 93–131.

Masoudnia, Y. and Szwejczewski, M. (2012). Bootlegging in the R&D departments of high-technology firms. *Research-Technology Management*, **55**(5): 35–42.

Newman, A., Herman, H., Schwarz, G. and Nielsen, I. (2018). The effects of employees' creative self-efficacy on innovative behavior: The role of entrepreneurial leadership. *Journal of Business Research*, **89**: 1–9.

Petriglieri, G., Ashford, S. J. and Wrzesniewski, A. (2019). Agony and ecstasy in the gig economy: Cultivating holding environments for precarious and personalized work identities. *Administrative Science Quarterly*, **64**(1): 124–170.

Schweisfurth, T. G. and Herstatt, C. (2015). Embedded (lead) users as catalysts to product diffusion. *Creativity and Innovation Management*, **24**(1): 151–168.

Schweisfurth, T. G. and Herstatt, C. (2016). How internal users contribute to corporate product innovation: The case of embedded users. *R&D Management*, **46**(S1): 107–126.

Stajkovic, A. D. and Luthans, F. (1998). Social cognitive theory and self-efficacy: Going beyond traditional motivational and behavioral approaches. *Organizational Dynamics*, **26**(4): 62–74.

von Hippel, E. (1976). The dominant role of users in the scientific instrument innovation process. *Research Policy*, **5**(3): 212–239.

von Hippel, E. (1986). Lead users: A source of novel product concepts. *Management Science*, **32**(7): 791–805.

https://doi.org/10.1142/9781800612266_0011

Chapter 10

Bootlegging and Individual Innovation Performance: The Joint Effect of Status and Creativity

Wei Huang*, Guopeng Xiang*,§, Yunzhou Du†, and Yang Liu‡
*School of Business Administration, Zhejiang Gongshang University, Zhejiang, China
†School of Economics and Management, Southeast University, Nanjing, China
‡School of Business Administration, South China University of Technology, Guangzhou, China
§pmx2018@163.com

Abstract

This chapter discusses the relationship between bootlegging and individual innovation performance, and considers the joint moderating effect of status and creativity. It has been found that bootlegging contributes to the improvement of individual innovation performance on the whole, and individuals with high creativity and high status benefit from bootlegging. In addition, when and only when individual creativity and status (formal or informal) are high, bootlegging will have a significant positive impact on individual innovation performance. This chapter discusses the function boundary of bootlegging, how it enriches and improves the concept of contingency relationship between bootlegging and individual innovation performance, and also explains the complex mechanism of individual level variables on the effect of bootlegging.

10.1. Introduction

There is a paradox in innovation practice where organizations usually encourage employees to innovate, but at the same time institute a set of formal procedures and rules to restrict employees' innovation behavior. When an individual's innovation plan is rejected by the organization, the individual may continue to carry out the innovation behavior secretly if the individual believes that the innovation plan is valuable. This is called bootlegging.

Can bootlegging improve employee innovation performance? There are two conflicting schools of thought in the existing studies: the destructive deviant school (Robinson and Benett, 1995; Bennett and Robinson, 2000) and the constructive deviant school (Warren, 2003; Mainemelis, 2010). The former thinks that deviant behavior deviating from the current system of the organization is harmful, while the latter thinks that deviant behavior deviating from the current system of the organization for a reasonable purpose is beneficial. Existing literature reviews suggests that the majority of scholars support the latter. It is generally believed that bootlegging, once successful, can significantly improve individual innovation performance. Even if it fails, this trial-and-error learning process is beneficial to bootlegging activities in the future.

The key to solving this paradox is to thoroughly understand the characteristics of bootlegging behavior and clarify its functional boundaries. Based on this, Guopeng Xiang and Wei Huang, and other people published a paper in *Nankai Business Review*, titled "Bootlegging and Individual Innovation Performance: The Joint Effect of Status and Creativity" in 2017. This paper mainly discusses the mechanism of bootlegging, the status of employees in the organization and the contingency influence of their own creativity, and makes an empirical test with the survey data of 456 employees and 78 superiors in 10 high-tech enterprises in five cities in China (see Fig. 10.1).

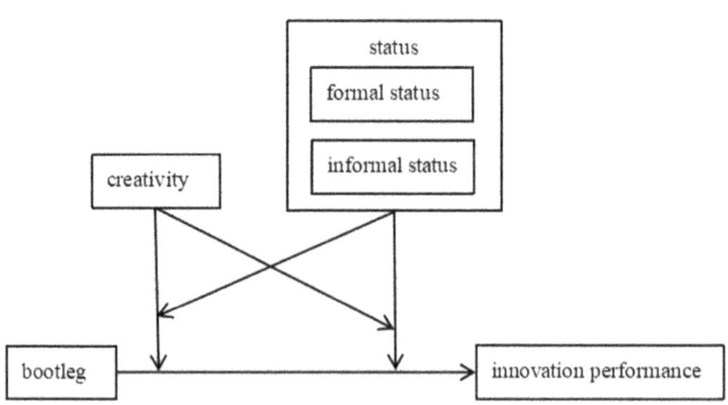

Fig. 10.1. The research framework of the relationship between bootlegging and individual innovation performance.

The emergence of bootlegging results from the conflict between the individual's pursuit of innovation autonomy and the organization's accountability to the innovation process. Due to the limitations of the organization's R&D funds or other better choices under the same conditions (Mowery, 2009), some immature and high-risk R&D ideas proposed by individuals are likely to be rejected in the process of hierarchical inspection of the organization (O'Connor and DeMartino, 2006). As a result, individuals violate the rules by privately developing innovative ideas that they believe are valuable to the organization. When the time is right, it will be submitted to the decision makers for review. In addition, when an individual thinks that there is not enough evidence at the current stage to make the organizational decision makers agree with their innovation assumption, the individual will also resort to bootlegging behavior. It would not be disclosed to the organization until the evidence is sufficient, so as to increase the possibility of the innovation idea being included in the formal R&D plan by the organization (Augsdorfer, 2005; Masoudnia and Szwejczewski, 2012).

The characteristics of bootlegging are summarized into three aspects: (1) Concealment: Since the bootlegging is not authorized by any formal or official authority and will occupy the individual's daily working time and organizational resources, the individual will choose to keep up the concealment of this behavior in order to avoid punishment (Masoudnia and Szwejczewski, 2012). (2) Bottom-up rather than project-based: Bootlegging is a kind of employee's spontaneous out-of-role behavior, and it is an individual's voluntary violation of the organizational system to carry out innovation activities conducive to the development of the organization (Unsworth, 2001). This behavior is fundamentally different from top-down brainstorming and project-based pilot experiments with innovation. (3) Duality: Bootlegging is illegal in terms of violation of organizational rules. However, in terms of serving as an orientation activity it is legitimate (Augsdorfer, 2005; Criscuolo, Salter and Ter Wal, 2014).

Due to the complex characteristics of bootlegging and different research perspectives, existing scholars still hold differences on the mechanism of bootlegging on individual innovation performance. Scholars with a positive outlook believe the following: (1) Bootlegging ideas usually show marginality, advance, and difficulty (Criscuolo, Salter and Ter Wal, 2014), but such pioneering and aggressive attempts can enable the bootlegger to obtain exploratory advantages in some blank research areas, thus transforming them into high innovation performers in the later period of individuals. (2) Individuals can avoid the imbalance between the R&D investment in innovation performance and the time to seek for the recognition of innovative ideas by the organization. In addition, individuals can also carry out more in-depth exploration in a relatively relaxed environment. Based on the above viewpoints of exploratory advantages and innovation proposition of delayed disclosure of advantages, the researchers proposed the following hypothesis:

H1a: Individual bootlegging behavior positively affects individual innovation performance.

Scholars holding the opposite view believe the following: (1) Institutional rigidity and bootlegging irregularities are likely to leave the individuals subjected to punishment by the organization, such as demotion or deprivation of R&D autonomy, which will seriously affect the improvement of individual innovation performance. (2) The innovation behaviors that deviate from organizational norms, formal research and development plans will distract individuals' work attention. Coupled with the dual characteristics of bootlegging, it is difficult for individuals to openly seek the help of other members of the organization (Masoudnia and Szwejczewski, 2012). Based on this, the researchers proposed a competitive hypothesis:

H1b: Individual bootlegging behavior negatively affects individual innovation performance.

In order to further understand the contingency influence of individual creativity and status on the relationship between bootlegging and innovation performance, researchers believe the following: (1) Highly creative individuals are more effective in promoting bootlegging and achieving success and also more effective in avoiding the external supervision of organizations on bootlegging. (2) Individuals with high formal status have more innovation time, indirect access to resources, and lower pressure, thus contributing more to the improvement of individual innovation performance. In addition, individuals with high informal status have advantages in acquiring information and resources and are more likely to get support and recognition from other members of the organization, thus contributing to the advancement of the bootlegging process. Based on the above analysis, the researchers proposed three hypotheses:

H2: The higher the individual creativity is, the stronger (weaker) the positive (negative) influence of individual bootlegging behavior on innovation performance will be.

H3a: The higher the formal status of an individual is, the stronger (weaker) the positive (negative) influence of individual bootlegging behavior on innovation performance will be.

H3b: The higher the informal status of an individual is, the stronger (weaker) the positive (negative) influence of individual bootlegging behaviors on innovation performance will be.

What is the influence of the combination of individual creativity and status on the relationship between bootlegging and innovation performance? Researchers believe that individual creativity, status, and bootlegging may have a combined effect on individual innovation performance, and that only if individual creativity, status, and deviant innovation are properly combined can higher performance output be achieved. In addition, individual creativity also affects the regulating effect of status on bootlegging and individual innovation performance. Accordingly, the researchers proposed the following hypothesis:

H4a: When both individual creativity and formal status in the organization are high, bootlegging behavior will (not) have a positive (negative) impact on performance.

H4b: When both individual creativity and informal status in the organization are high, bootlegging behavior will (not) have a positive (negative) impact on performance.

In order to avoid the social approval problems caused by common method deviation and self-report, the research adopts the matching survey method. The superior questionnaire mainly evaluates the performance and informal status of subordinates, while the subordinate questionnaire mainly evaluates the individual demographic characteristics, formal status creativity, internal and external motivation, team innovation atmosphere, bootlegging behavior, performance, and other variables.

The results show the following: (1) In view of exploratory advantage and delayed disclosure advantage of innovation proposition, bootlegging is generally conducive to the improvement of individual innovation performance. (2) The positive effect of bootlegging is context-dependent. Individuals with high creativity and high status are easy to benefit from bootlegging.

(3) Creativity and status have a joint regulating effect on the relationship between bootlegging and innovation performance. If and only if the creativity and status of individuals (formal or informal) are high, bootlegging will have a significant positive impact on individual innovation performance.

This chapter contributes to the existing literature in the following three aspects: firstly, it discusses the functional boundary of bootlegging, enriches the existing research results of bootlegging, and harmonizes the existing arguments about the advantages and disadvantages of bootlegging. Secondly, it is found that the positive effect of bootlegging on individual bootlegging performance depends on the individual's status and creativity in the organization, so as to further enrich and improve the contingent relationship between bootlegging and individual innovation performance. Finally, it is found that the combined effect of individual status and creativity in the organization jointly determines the influence of bootlegging on individual innovation performance and reveals the complex mechanism of individual variables on bootlegging effectiveness.

References

Augsdorfer, P. (2005). Bootlegging and path dependency. *Research Policy*, **34**(1): 1–11.

Bennett, R. J. and Robinson, S. L. (2000). Development of a measure of workplace deviance. *Journal of Applied Psychology*, **85**(3): 349–360.

Criscuolo, P., Salter, A. and Ter Wal, A. L. J. (2014). Going underground: Bootlegging and individual innovative performance. *Organization Science*, **25**(5): 1287–1305.

Mainemelis, C. (2010). Stealing fire: Creative deviance in the evolution of new ideas. *Academy of Management Review*, **35**(4): 558–578.

Masoudnia, Y. and Szwejczewski, M. (2012). Bootlegging in the R&D departments of high-technology firms. *Research-Technology Management*, **55**(5): 35–42.

Mowery, D. C. (2009). Plus Ca change: Industrial R&D in the "Third Industrial Revolution". *Industrial & Corporate Change*, **18**(1): 1–50.

O'Connor, G. C. and DeMartino, R. (2006). Organizing for radical innovation: An exploratory study of the structural aspects of RI management systems in large established firms. *Journal of Product Innovation Management*, **23**(6): 475–497.

Robinson, S. L. and Bennett, R. J. (1995). A typology of deviant workplace behaviors: A multidimensional scaling study. *Academy of Management Journal*, **38**(2): 555–572.

Unsworth, K. (2001). Unpacking creativity. *Academy of Management Review*, 26(2): 289–297.

Warren, D. E. (2003). Constructive and destructive deviance in organizations. *Academy of Management Review*, **28**(4): 622–632.

Part 3

Bootlegging Disclosure Processes

https://doi.org/10.1142/9781800612266_0012

Chapter 11

Overcoming the Initial Illegitimacy of Ideas

Stephan Eicher
Siltronic AG, Munich, Germany
stephan.eicher@outlook.de

Abstract

This chapter presents how bootleggers uncover their underground projects to their organizations and overcome the initial illegitimacy of their ideas. This study seems to be the first attempt to link bootlegging research with legitimacy research to explain this endeavor. We find that bootleggers just as other innovators need to win legitimacy for their projects. To overcome initial illegitimacy, we find that they follow several known but also several new patterns. Consequently, this chapter expands the knowledge on legitimacy seeking behavior of innovators and closes the research gap of how bootleggers successfully uncover their clandestine projects. Our collection of cases furthermore highlights that managers should listen carefully when being confronted with such projects. Innovations that may appear illegitimate at first can turn into important assets for their firms.

11.1. Introduction

This chapter presents how bootleggers uncover their underground projects to their organizations and overcome the initial illegitimacy of their ideas. This study seems to be the first attempt to link bootlegging research with legitimacy research to explain this endeavor. We find that bootleggers just as other innovators need to win legitimacy for their projects. To overcome initial illegitimacy, we find that they follow several known but also several new patterns. Subsequently, this chapter expands the knowledge on legitimacy-seeking behavior of innovators and closes the research gap of how bootleggers successfully uncover their clandestine projects. Our collection of cases furthermore highlights that managers should listen carefully when being confronted with such projects. Innovations that may appear illegitimate at first can turn into important assets for their firms.

11.2. Theoretical Framework

11.2.1. Bootlegging

Secrecy is an essential element of bootlegging. Existing bootlegging research shows various ways how innovation projects are kept secret from the sight of the organization (e.g., Shepard, 1967; Brown, 1991; Augsdorfer, 1996). Bootleg projects are often not pursued by only one researcher but in teams and can also involve direct managers (Masoudnia, 2012). Often bootlegging is also informally tolerated by management (Augsdorfer, 1996), but it is usually kept secret from senior management and decision makers (Criscuolo, Salter and Ter Wal, 2013).

At some stage, underground projects need to surface and be unveiled to the organization. If underground projects are to become successful, they need the support of their organizations and management approval (Koch and Leitner, 2008). Without organizational support, they cannot become an innovation for the firm. Little is known on how bootleggers unveil their work. In his research, Masoudnia (2012) identifies a two-step process that bootleggers use. The initial step is to informally approach their direct manager. With their support, decision makers are then contacted in the second step. This process appears plausible because skipping the direct manager would jeopardize the relationship. On the other hand, however, excluding the direct manager may be necessary if he/she opposes to the idea or presents in any other way a threat to its acceptance. Furthermore, this simple process does not appear to deal with the delicate nature of uncovering bootlegging. Burgelman and Grove (2007) and Koch and Leitner (2008) underline that revealing bootlegging is case dependent and very political. It involves making alliances and seeking promoters. Burgelman and Grove (2007) describe a bootlegging case at Intel in the 1980s. At the time, Intel had strategically decided to not engage in the reduced instruction set computer (RISC) processor business. A young engineer nevertheless developed such a processor clandestinely, and even identified a new market to avoid cannibalization arguments. Convincing top management was still anything but easy. By uniting supporters for the architecture, he nevertheless managed to drive top management to change corporate strategies and support his processor. Similarly, Koch and Leitner (2008) find that innovators themselves — and not only through their superiors — try to convince managers and often use one-sided information to accomplish that. The findings of Burgelman and Grove (2007) as well as Koch and Leitner (2008) stand in contrast to the simple two-step process as Masoudnia (2012) identifies it. Subsequently, our research question is to clarify these opposing views and identify how the transition into the official world works.

> Research Question: How do bootleggers reveal their secret projects to the organization to make them successful?

11.2.2. Legitimacy

In our context, legitimacy "is a generalized perception or assumption that the actions of an entity are desirable, proper, or appropriate within some socially constructed system of norms, values, beliefs, and definitions" (Suchman, 1995). This means that innovations in pursuit of legitimacy need to appear desirable, proper, or appropriate to the organization and its decision makers. Legitimacy research has frequently also focused on the external perspective, which grants organizations legitimacy in front of external stakeholders (e.g., Meyer and Rowan, 1977). In this study, we focus on the internal perspective.

It is clear that bootlegging is a special form of innovative activity. Nevertheless, the task that is at the heart of any bottom-up innovation is to gain organizational support. Accordingly, the pursuit of support should also play a major role in how bootleggers reveal their projects. This is why we have chosen a legitimacy approach for our purpose. Legitimacy authors argue that legitimacy is a prerequisite for innovators to access resources (Brown, 1998; Zimmerman and Zeitz, 2002; Diez-Martin *et al.*, 2013). When innovators gain legitimacy, they gain organizational support and access to resources that are required to advance their initiatives. At some stage, bootleggers also need further resources, since their access to slack resources or their ability to divert funds from official projects is no longer possible. It is important to add that legitimacy lies in the eye of the beholder (Zimmerman and Zeitz, 2002). In firms, it is therefore the management that grants legitimacy. We find strong parallels in how Burgelman and Grove (2007) and Koch and Leitner (2008) describe the process of bootleggers going public with legitimacy research. Legitimacy literature provides an understanding of how innovators win organizational support for their ideas. The findings of Burgelman and Grove (2007) and Koch and Leitner (2008) can be described with several elements of legitimacy research, which will be outlined in the following paragraphs.

Types of legitimacy: Several publications have identified different typologies of legitimacy (e.g., Scott, 1995; Suchman, 1995; Zimmermann and Zeitz, 2002). We find that for our internal innovator perspective, the types of legitimacy proposed by Suchman (1995) are most suitable. Suchman (1995) identified three types of legitimacy, namely cognitive, moral, and pragmatic legitimacy. He describes cognitive legitimacy as either based on comprehensibility or taken-for-grantedness. Comprehensibility refers to the plausibility and predictability with regards to the content of an innovation proposal. Taken-for-grantedness means that others do not question the rightfulness of a proposal to start with and accept it as a given (Suchman, 1995). According to Suchman (1995), moral legitimacy answers if something is "the right thing to do." It is therefore related to the moral compass of people. An important subtype is personal legitimacy. Personal legitimacy stems from a person itself and not primarily from the content of the innovative proposal. This legitimacy can, for instance, be the result of the track record and reputation of an innovator. Another important subtype of moral legitimacy is consequential legitimacy. Consequential legitimacy is based on the accomplishments of an organization. This can refer to superior products, for instance, which facilitate the legitimacy of companies. Lastly, pragmatic legitimacy arises from the self-interest of people within the organization. An innovation gains pragmatic legitimacy based on its expected value to the organization itself (Suchman, 1995).

Legitimacy strategies: Our explanation of legitimacy strategies is again focused on the internal perspective. In pursuit of the different types of legitimacy, innovators can choose from several strategies. According to Suchman (1995), there are three strategies to achieve legitimacy, namely conformity, selection, and manipulation. A conforming strategy accepts the existing boundaries within the organization and does not challenge them. In our context, this can, for instance, refer to the bootlegger's conformity with innovation management frameworks and their requirements upon surfacing.

A selection strategy chose the environment that is most likely to provide legitimacy (Suchman, 1995). In this case, bootleggers select the most promising environment for their case, instead of simply following the predetermined path. If conformity or selection are not sufficient, actors can also choose a manipulation strategy. Here they actively manipulate the environment in a way that will make their concern appear legitimate (Suchman, 1995).

Legitimacy mechanisms: Besides the types of legitimacy and the strategies to achieve it, legitimacy research has recently added another very interesting perspective, which is highly relevant for this study. Bunduchi (2017) identifies three basic mechanisms that innovators use within known strategies. Mechanisms describe practical actions that innovators apply in pursuit of legitimacy. They are on a more tactical level than strategies. In this study, these mechanisms will be applied to explain how bootleggers go public. Bunduchi (2017) describes the three mechanisms of lobbying, building relationships, and seeking feedback. Lobbying describes activities to influence the assessment of innovation proposals by decision makers, such as technical demonstrations and product demonstrations. By building relationships, innovators build informal networks internally to achieve a critical mass of supporters or collaborate externally to build on the legitimacy of these partners. Seeking feedback applies internal tests and external customer studies. This allows innovators to learn about the standards required to achieve legitimacy and to adjust accordingly. Furthermore, it also allowed them to learn about who is in favor of their proposal.

In summary, the legitimacy types and strategies put forward by Suchman (1995) as well as the legitimacy mechanisms proposed by Bunduchi (2017) will be used in this study to identify how bootleggers reveal their covert projects to their organizations. In this context, bootlegging represents a special form of bottom-up creativity. Because it is in itself an illegitimate activity, gaining legitimacy must be a particular challenge for bootleggers. It is therefore the question if the mechanisms identified by Bunduchi (2017) suffice for bootleggers or if they draw from a more sophisticated set of mechanisms. Therefore, our second research question is:

> What strategies and mechanisms do employees apply to win legitimacy for their bootleg projects when disclosing them to their corporate decision makers?

11.3. Results

11.3.1. Legitimacy types

Bootleggers pursue moral, cognitive, and pragmatic legitimacy to surface and promote their projects. In all 26 cases, bootleggers in the end answered all the dimensions (moral and/or cognitive and/or pragmatic) of illegitimacy that they were exposed to. No type of illegitimacy was left unanswered in the end. In some cases, bootleggers temporarily bypassed or ignored illegitimacy. In case 6, for instance, bootleggers implemented their ideas without the knowledge of anyone by adding the desired feature to the medical tool. Nobody else in their company realized what they were doing. Also, in case 2, the bootlegger implemented the product in production without knowledge of the organization. So, bootlegging helped them to secretly bypass and ignore illegitimacy for some time. But in the end and for their products and features to become official, they needed legitimacy. Bootleggers chose to pursue legitimacy at different stages and in different order. We did not observe two identical sequences of events. If, for instance, initial illegitimacy was of moral, cognitive, and pragmatic nature, bootleggers in the end resolved them by gaining moral, cognitive, and pragmatic legitimacy. But some bootleggers chose to directly tackle all sources of illegitimacy at once, while others focused on only one or two dimensions in the beginning. However, in the end all were addressed and sometimes bootleggers playfully orchestrated their parallel attempts to gain legitimacy. This is highlighted by case 2, where bootleggers disguised their development of a new product as efficiency enhancement of an existing product, at the same time informally approached an important customer, and with their support gained legitimacy before anyone internally realized that this efficiency enhancement was fake. The style and sequence in which the bootleggers in all cases approached the different types of legitimacy was very much driven by their personality and preference. Some bootleggers strongly focused on the cognitive viability of their ideas, others also strongly considered the pragmatic nature of the task at hand, while yet others also took care of the moral dimension from the beginning.

In all cases, cognitive legitimacy played a vital role. This was because in all cases the technical feasibility as well as the financial and market potential contributed fundamentally to decisions in innovation selection. Personal legitimacy facilitated cognitive legitimacy in cases 2, 4, 5,

7, 9, 10, 11, 17, 20, and 25. It helped to bridge uncertainty inherent to these innovations. Frequently bootleggers drew personal legitimacy from customers. When customers voiced interest in the idea, this helped bootleggers to reduce market uncertainty and convince their companies of their ideas (e.g., case 20). To get there, bootleggers either waited for a suitable customer inquiry (e.g., case 17), used existing personal customer contacts (e.g., case 19), or got access to customers via colleagues (e.g., case 2). Personal legitimacy also originated from bootleggers themselves, because of their own professional reputation (e.g., case 11). In this case, management trusted their reasoning, because of a good personal track record of successful innovations. Personal legitimacy also stemmed from others within their informal network or a management promotor. In case 5, the bootlegger personally knew a head of R&D and convinced him to promote his idea. In case 4, the bootlegger accidently met a higher ranked manager and used the opportunity to convince him of his ideas. From then on, this manager supported him and helped to promote his idea. Lastly, personal legitimacy also originated from the credibility of a responsible department. In case 7, the business development department was convinced of the idea, which in return put it on their agenda as a valuable business opportunity. The principle was the same in case 10, where product management helped the bootlegger by promoting his idea.

In 24 cases, bootleggers pursued moral legitimacy to give their innovation the stamp of "it is the right thing to do." Usually, the highest authority in firms that grants moral legitimacy is the management. Pragmatic legitimacy played a considerable role in 14 cases.

In our analysis, we also found that sometimes legitimacy was not actively pursued but the mere consequence of another type of legitimacy. If, for instance, management takes the decision for a new product (moral legitimacy), it is most pragmatic for other members of the organization to adopt and give up potential resistance (e.g., case 14). Sometimes personal legitimacy can be so strong that cognitive legitimacy is a mere product of it. This occurred in case 17 when a big customer inquired about a product. In case 14, a management decision superseded the moral issue that a bootlegger was working against his colleagues and against company strategies (moral legitimacy). As pointed out in the literature section, the original idea of consequential legitimacy is legitimacy, which is based on the accomplishments of organizations. The original intention of the concept is, however, so similar to what we observed in our data that we borrowed the term consequential legitimacy for this purpose.

11.3.2. Legitimacy strategies

Legitimacy strategies explain how the different types of legitimacy are sought. They therefore also illustrate how bootleggers surface. It is not surprising that our cases were dominated by selection and manipulation strategies and not by conformity. This is not surprising because bootlegging in itself is not a conforming phenomenon and a manipulation strategy. Selection gives bootleggers the opportunity to reveal their secret ideas to the environment that promises the highest chance for gaining legitimacy. A selection strategy was present when bootleggers did not merely take the predetermined way within their environment or conform to the requirements imposed on them, which would characterize a conformity strategy. We saw bootleggers include their ideas in strategy projects to tackle their strategic illegitimacy (case 4), sneak them into management meetings that promised success (case 1), address it to higher management that was suspected to be potentially supportive (case 5), publish reports in forums likely to be visited by potential internal supporters (case 10), informally notify customers to get their support (e.g., case 19). In all cases with a selection strategy, bootleggers consciously chose the most promising environments. A selection strategy makes sense since by taking their ideas into the underground they left the conformity path already. Some bootleggers, however, returned to conformity later on. In case 9, the bootlegger after having developed the concept and a prototype in secrecy went through the regular innovation process of his firm with the support of a management promoter. In case 6 where bootleggers have not gained final legitimacy yet, they are waiting for the regular process to select their idea. So, a return to conformity, even in the underground phase, appears to be possible. As discussed, manipulation strategies alter environments to win legitimacy. This strategy was frequently chosen by bootleggers. In cases 2, 5, 6, 15, and 18, bootleggers disguised their idea as something else (e.g., as improvement of an existing product instead of development of a new product) or gave improper information. Giving improper information included lying about the progress or purpose of an idea (e.g., case 5). In cases 3 and 19, resistance from the organization was so heavy that extensive work was required to change perceptions. In cases 7 and 8, pragmatic legitimacy was achieved by bribing others with potential rewards. In cases 22, 23, and 24, bootleggers showed potential internal users and decision makers the benefits of their innovation to change their perception.

11.3.3. Legitimacy mechanisms

In this section, we look at what mechanisms bootleggers used within their chosen strategies. This explains on the most practical level how bootleggers go public with their clandestine ideas. It furthermore answers our second research question of how bootleggers use existing mechanisms and whether they use others that are new. Bunduchi (2017) identified the three mechanisms lobbying, building relationships, and seeking feedback, which lead to legitimacy. In our cases, bootleggers heavily used all three mechanisms, but we also observed new mechanisms. A list and description of the mechanisms we observed is provided as follows.

(i) *Lobbying* for their ideas played a crucial role in bootleggers' attempts to win legitimacy. In the simplest form, lobbying meant for bootleggers to be the public relations voice for their idea. This included praising its benefits and showing convincing data in conversations, meetings, or workshops. Lobby work greatly benefits from available evidence in the form of prototypes or mock-ups that help to illustrate the idea (e.g., case 14). Showing the pragmatic benefits also included demonstrations in which colleagues and managers could grasp these benefits themselves. This was, for instance, crucial in case 22, where the demonstration of an automation script proved just how much manual work it could eliminate and therefore showed its pragmatic value. When pragmatic legitimacy was sought for internal process innovations, some of these innovations went viral (cases 22 and 23 greatly facilitated internal processes). The benefit to colleagues and managers was so great that the innovation spread without further efforts from the bootlegger and eventually earned legitimacy. Bootleggers also spread rumors concerning their ideas. In case 7, for instance, the bootlegger spread rumors about his idea and its potential benefits to colleagues who he thought to be likely to spread the rumor further. By doing so, curiosity within the organization was stimulated. Lobbying also includes to position the innovation well.

In cases 25 and 26, close attention was paid to how the idea was sold to others. What can it do and how it is better than alternatives? This also includes to speak the language of your audience. Lobbying also refers to reaching out to customers to get them on board. Meetings with customers were abused to do side presentations of underground ideas and how they could be beneficial for them (e.g., case 20). In some cases, colleagues in sales reached out to customers to present ideas (e.g., case 2). An important aspect in lobbying is also to extend the lobbying network. Internal workshops were used to convince colleagues of one's concepts, who in turn started promoting them to possible applications, markets, or customers (e.g., case 17).

(ii) *Seeking feedback* was crucial for bootleggers to increase the viability of their projects. Because of initial illegitimacy, a very strong case for their ideas was vital in most cases. Bootleggers often sought feedback within their existing community and by building new relationships. In case 7, an engineer used his informal network to advance his ideas surrounding the application of 3D printing. The informal network was important to give input and feedback in order to generate a viable concept. After all, he had only very little experience with 3D printing. Building new relationships to seek feedback included testing prototypes with customers and presenting specifications to see if they were in line with customer expectations (case 19). In case 8, the bootleggers collaborated for about one year with marketing to align their idea to market requirements. In case 17, the bootleg engineer needed some measurement data for his optical sensor to see if it sufficiently measured light waves. Since his company had no such measurement tool, he sent the sensor to customers engineers who then provided the relevant measurement data. In case 4, the team of bootleggers worked with five customers in the underground phase to get their feedback and do testing on their software product. Also, in case 16, collaboration with an external partner was applied to get feedback on their requirements.

(iii) *Building relationships* in most of our cases was done by bootleggers if the existing relationship did not suffice. Building new relationships was not as easy as walking into a trusted colleague's office. When existing relationships were not good enough, then bootleggers started reaching out and worked on building the needed relationships. Management is very important in the context of legitimacy. Bootleggers used accidental meetings (case 4), poster shows (case 7), or conferences to present their ideas to higher managers (case 7). They cold called their offices to get the opportunity for a meeting (case 24). With these direct contacts to decision makers, they tried to talk them into their ideas and get their support. But not all bootleggers had the courage to address higher ranking managers directly. Some chose a more classical way and started to build up relationships at their level. In case 10, the bootlegger identified the responsible product manager and convinced him of the technical superiority of his medical tool. He got him excited about the new applications this could generate. In return, the product manager helped promoting his concept and prototype to management. In the end, it was finally turned into an official development project. In case 7, the bootlegger called the business development department, hoping that if he could convince them, these colleagues could support his 3D printing application in front of management and declare it to a viable business even though the market potential was still completely unclear. If the market potential is unclear, bootleggers also reached out to the marketing department (e.g., case 8). In case 11, it was also critical for the engineer to learn about the customer's perspective on his idea. He therefore used the opportunity to have a beer with a customer engineer to discuss his idea and get feedback.

(iv) *Exploiting existing relationships* is a means used more frequently by bootleggers than establishing new relationships. We identified this as an additional mechanism, since Bunduchi (2017) does not mention the exploitations of existing informal networks as a mechanism to win legitimacy. Exploiting existing relationships is also easier than establishing new ones. An established relationship bridges many issues. It was much easier for bootleggers to convince people who they had an established relationship with. Such people can also be asked for personal favors and when being management members, they tend to turn a blind eye on one's underground activities. Very crucial in this context is that bootleggers use their relationships to gain informal support from their network. This was the key success factor in cases 5, 10, 12, 15, 17, 22, 24, and 25. People from their network were ready to take the time to listen to their ideas and provide valuable feedback. They could also give advice on what steps to take next and open new doors. In the end, legitimacy is granted by higher management and the easiest way to get there is through your personal network. The personal network opens doors. It was also easier for them to include people from their personal network into their lobbying network. Bootleg projects can be subject to heavy opposition. Supporters from your network can help to overcome opposition. Bootleggers also reported that making an idea successful is not only about praising it potential but also about establishing a strong coalition of supporters (e.g., case 14). Existing relationships can also go beyond company borders. In case 18, an engineer used relations to a customer to get measurement data for which their own company had no tools for.

(v) *Managing opponents* was a new mechanism we observed. While lobbying has the aim to promote an idea, managing your opponents tries to limit negative influences on it. As a consequence of initial illegitimacy, bootleggers were frequently confronted with partially heavy opposition that tried to kill their projects. In case 1, for instance, large parts of senior management tried to stop the project, because it was in violation to a fundamental strategy and jeopardized the legacy of several managers. The company considered itself a high-quality manufacturer and this group of engineers tried to introduce inferior raw material on a very large scale. For several long-serving managers, this would have meant the question as to why they have not had this idea in decades of service. Others saw their duty in making sure that such a jump into complete uncertainty would never happen. Case 3 had the decision openly challenged by some top managers. As a result, some of these managers were heavy opponents. Bootleggers therefore need to actively manage their opponents and not only rely on positive lobby work. Within their underground projects, they have a great asset at their side. Their projects are often not or only partially known to their opponents. From this protected space, they can control the information flow and manage their opponents as needed. Opponents that are unlikely to have the power to destroy projects can be simply ignored. These opponents can be left in the dark until a decision has been taken (e.g., case 15). Another example of ignoring opponents is case 2. In this case, the marketing department, who did not support the new product being proposed was simply left out of any following communication. The bootlegger directly worked with a big customer to prove the existence of a market and marketing only learned about it when everything was settled. Bootleggers can also choose to withhold critical information from opponents and rather provide such information to individuals that are supportive. In case 4, the bootlegger took care that his sales colleagues were left out of any communication, because he was afraid that these colleagues would not like the fact that that this new product would lead to a temporary loss in sales. Opponents who are critical to achieve legitimacy, however, need to be convinced and confronted however. If the chief technology officer (CTO) or important members of management of your company dislike your idea, you have no other choice but to convince him/them (cases 1, 19). Also, in case 15, an engineer had a radical idea concerning cryptography where he expected fierce opposition from colleagues. He was convinced that he could not work against them. But instead of actively attacking the issue, he decided to give his colleagues the necessary time to grasp the benefits for themselves. By that time his ideas would also not challenge their current work. Once they understand the pragmatic benefits it could provide to them, they will give up their opposition and turn into supporters.

(vi) *Waiting for the window of opportunity* was a mechanism that we started to observe soon in our data. On the one hand, side waiting in itself sounds like a very passive activity. But on the other hand, it was a very smart activity in several cases. It was smart because bootleggers were conscious about the fact that an innovation is not worth much without a window of opportunity. A highly illegitimate innovation may face overwhelming opposition and turn the bootlegger into Don Quixote tilting at windmills. If, for instance, in case 4 the young bootlegger would have approached his organization with his idea that questioned the decision of top management to spend millions on externally buying the source code and furthermore was in clear violation of company strategies, it is very easy to imagine what would have happened. With some ideas, it was smarter to wait for things to change within the company. In case 4, it was important to wait for the management decision to be largely forgotten. Only then was it possible to present the idea without management being threatened of losing face and instantly refusing it. As another bootlegger mentioned, the decisions that are taken today are not that present anymore in two years from now. In other cases, a window of opportunity opened with changing technological and organizational trends. In case 22, due to an organizational change, the idea was all the sudden perfectly morally legitimate, which it had not been before. In case 23, the rise of a new trend in IT also opened a window of opportunity for moral legitimacy to use the desired IT tool. For product innovations, if you cannot identify a potential market for your idea, it may be smart to wait for a market to reveal itself when a bigger customer enquires for a related product (cases 17, 19, and 20). Windows of opportunity can also close. In case 24 legitimacy seeking attempts were brought to a halt, because IT security considerations challenged the very nature of the idea. Moral illegitimacy overturned all attempts to gain legitimacy. As a consequence, the proposal was dismissed.

(vii) *Lying and bribing* are also mechanisms used by bootleggers to gain legitimacy. Lying to management was relatively easy in cases 5 and 15, because management could never identify the lie. In both cases, this provided moral legitimacy. In case 5, management was told that the innovation project was already 90% done and that it would therefore make no sense to stop it now. In reality it was about 50% done but management could only find out if they followed up on future progress. But for small projects like the development of a training tool in this case, management never spent the time to do so. When in case 15 the bootlegger had to justify upon revealing his project why he was working on it at all, he plainly claimed that it was required as part of an external cooperation, which was of course not true. When in case 2 the underground project needed funds to go into production, the team simply disguised it as an efficiency improvement to an existing product, which provided cognitive legitimacy. It is also very simple to claim to be working on something totally different (e.g., case 18). Bribing grants pragmatic legitimacy. In cases 7 and 8, this was referred to as the fact that people will not support you if they have no benefit from it. After all bootlegging means to be doing something illegitimate and going the extra mile beyond of what is formally expected of you. The bootleg engineer overcame this problem by praising the great opportunities of his ideas. If it turns into a successful innovation, rewards would be split equally. Rewards included to be attached to an outstanding innovation, which is beneficial to get recognition, pay raises, or promotions. Furthermore, allies were promised that the patent and associated rewards would be shared equally. By promising such rewards, people had clear pragmatic benefits and in turn supported bootleggers.

11.3.4. Summary of legitimacy types, strategies, and mechanisms

Below we summarize the strategies and mechanisms used by bootleggers when surfacing in our cases to win moral, cognitive, and pragmatic legitimacy (Table 11.1).

Table 11.1. Overview of legitimacy types, strategies, and mechanisms.

Strategies Mechanisms	Moral Legitimacy	Cognitive Legitimacy	Pragmatic Legitimacy
manipulation	lobbying(3, 5, 18) manage opponents(2, 3, 18) exploit relationships(2, 3, 5, 8) wait for window(18) lying & bribing(2, 6, 15, 18)	lobbying(18, 24) exploit relationships(3) build relationships(22) seek feedback(3, 18, 22) wait for window(18, 22)	lobbying(22, 23, 24) manage opponents(22) exploit relationships(22) wait for window(23) lying & bribing(5, 7, 8)
selection	lobbying(7, 13) manage opponents (13) exploit relationships(7) build relationships(9, 11) wait for window(4)	lobbying(1, 4, 10, 12, 13, 14, 15, 16, 17, 18, 20, 25) manage opponents(1, 4, 12, 13, 14, 15) exploit relationships(1, 11, 12, 14, 15, 17, 18) build relationships(4, 8, 10, 14, 25, 26) seek feedback(4, 7, 8, 11, 14, 15, 17, 18, 20, 21, 25, 26) wait for window(15, 17, 20)	lobbying(26) exploit relationships(26) build relationships(26)
conformity		lobbying(6, 9) manage opponents(9) seek feedback(9) wait for window(6)	wait for window(6)

Note: Numbers refer to cases in the sample.

We observe a strong emphasis on winning cognitive legitimacy via selection strategies. Bootleggers were very selective and cautious of the environments they expose their ideas to. We therefore classified such attempts to choose the best environment as selection strategies even though they may also contain manipulating elements. Within this selection strategy, they applied all mechanisms, except lying and bribing. Not surprisingly, lying and bribing is mostly a mechanism used within a manipulation strategy to gain moral and pragmatic legitimacy. We find lobbying to be an essential part of selection and manipulation strategies. Lobbying can be even part of an overall conformity strategy, in which innovators, for instance, follow predetermined internal processes and conform to their requirements. In these cases, lobbying was applied to emphasize the conformance to requirements. Furthermore, and not surprisingly in none of our cases it could be observed that conformity strategies were applied to win moral legitimacy.

11.4. Discussion

In answer to research question 1, we find that the majority of bootlegging cases we studied were uncovered to their organizations in a nonlinear fashion at different points in the company. Related activities cannot be described as a clear or linear process. Little of this was executed in a planned fashion. Revealing bootlegging is also not free of setbacks. Nevertheless, all successful bootleggers had the persistence to overcome such barriers. Our findings in answer to research question 1 are very much in line with the ones of Burgelman and Grove (2007) and Koch and Leitner (2008). Burgelman and Grove (2007) and Koch and Leitner (2008) describe it as a political bargaining process in which innovators try to persuade management to support their ideas. We did not find exclusive evidence that supports Masoudnia and Szwejczewski's (2012) results of a simple two-stage process, in which they at first inform their direct manager and then with their support the greater public. We found cases where bootleggers intentionally ignored their direct manager until the last minute (e.g., case 9).

We find that when surfacing, bootleggers pursue legitimacy for their clandestine projects. Legitimacy types, strategies, and especially mechanisms explain how bootleggers go public with their ideas. Legitimacy mechanisms represent the practical actions they undertake and therefore give an answer to the "how" in combination with types and strategies. We find that bootlegging itself is a manipulation strategy that innovators apply when their ideas are subject to severe organizational constraints, which we refer to as initial illegitimacy. Without bootlegging as an alternative to take ideas into the corporate underground, such ideas could never be developed to a level where legitimacy can be sought. Bootlegging overcomes organizational obstacles and alters the internal environment so that illegitimate ideas can become legitimate. As such bootlegging represents a manipulation strategy (Suchman, 1995). Within this overall manipulation strategy of bootlegging, bootleggers chose from further manipulation, selection, or even conformity strategies. At the heart of underground projects lies complex initial illegitimacy, which causes these projects to go underground. By doing so bootleggers can work on their projects from a protected space and also steer the information flow to the outside. Many of our analyzed cases would have been eliminated by their organizations otherwise. Factors like challenging management decisions or company strategies often generate complex illegitimacy barriers for innovators. To explain how bootleggers overcome these barriers, we also found that illegitimacy always has a moral, cognitive, and pragmatic dimension, which is in line with Suchman (1995). In pursuit of legitimacy, bootlegging helps to temporarily bypass illegitimacy and, in the end, to overcome these barriers. Bootleggers primarily used selection and manipulation strategies to gain moral, pragmatic, and cognitive legitimacy. We observe a strong emphasis on winning cognitive legitimacy via selection strategies, which is an aspect that should be confirmed by future research, since our limited data does not allow for generalizations. Bootleggers were very selective of the environments they expose their ideas to. While we frequently also observed manipulating elements within these selection strategies, we identified selection as the dominant strategic element. Legitimacy research, for instance, could argue that especially lobbying should be part of a manipulation strategy. After all, lobbying aims to shape perceptions of audiences. However, we found lobbying to also be an essential mechanism within strategies that were dominated by selection and sometimes even conformity. Conformity strategies played a minor role, because bootlegging itself is already a nonconforming activity. We discovered that the findings of Burgelman and Grove (2007) as well as

Koch and Leitner (2008) on how innovators reveal their ideas to the public have strong parallels to legitimacy research. Their findings outline the importance of lobbying and building relationships.

In answer to research question 2, we find that bootleggers extensively use known and unknown legitimacy mechanisms. In pursuit of legitimacy, bootleggers use the mechanisms of lobbying, managing opponents, exploiting existing relationships, building new relationships, seeking feedback, waiting for the window of opportunity, and lying and bribing. Bunduchi (2017) identifies three mechanisms that innovators apply. We extend this list to seven mechanisms. Some of these mechanisms may be more prone to bootlegging, because of the particular initial illegitimacy of bootlegging. Nevertheless, the mechanisms may be used by innovators in general. This is also a subject that future research should look into. Using the described strategies and mechanisms, bootleggers answered all dimensions of initial illegitimacy, even though they may have temporarily bypassed illegitimacy issues (research question 3). In the end, all initial illegitimacy was resolved. We also found that some types of legitimacy can be the mere consequence of other legitimacy types. Sometimes, for instance, pragmatic legitimacy is the mere consequence of moral legitimacy. A management decision that grants moral legitimacy makes it most pragmatic for others to also support the innovation. Borrowing from Suchman (1995), we refer to this aspect as consequential legitimacy.

Literature touching on bootlegging is indecisive whether bootlegging predominantly leads to radical or incremental innovation. Authors argue in different directions (compare Augsdorfer, 2005; Abetti, 2004; Mainemelis, 2010). One of our findings, however, is that also innovations that at first appeared incremental in our study can face substantial illegitimacy that forces innovators into the corporate underground. This may be because they are in conflict with managerial orders, because they may appear as a waste of time and resources and some improvements even have the potential to violate strategies. We therefore find that the radicalness of innovations in this context is also substantially driven by initial illegitimacy.

References

Abetti, P. A. (2004). Informal corporate entrepreneurship: Implications from the failure of the concord alloy foundry and the success of the Toshiba laptop. *International Journal of Entrepreneurship and Innovation Management*, **4**(6): 529–545.

Augsdorfer, P. (1994a). Taxonomy of management attitudes bootlegging and uncertainty. In Oakey, R. (Ed.), *New Technology-Based Firms in the 1990s*. London: Sage.

Augsdorfer, P. (1994b). The manager as pirate: An inspection of the gentle art of bootlegging. *Creativity and Innovation Management*, **3**(2): 91–95.

Augsdorfer, P. (1996). *Forbidden Fruit — An Analysis of Bootlegging, Uncertainty and Learning in Corporate R&D*. Aldershot: Avebury.

Augsdorfer, P. (2005). Bootlegging and path dependency. *Research Policy*, **34**(1): 1–11.

Augsdorfer, P. (2008). Managing the unmanageable. *Research — Technology Management*, **51**(4): 41–47.

Brown, J. S. (1991). Research that reinvents the corporation. *Harvard Business Review*, 101–111. August 2002.

Bunduchi, R. (2017). Legitimacy-seeking mechanisms in product innovation: A qualitative study. *Journal of Product Innovation Management*, **34**(3): 315–342.

Burgelman, R. A. (1983). A process model of internal corporate venturing in the diversified major firm. *Administrative Science Quarterly*, **28**: 223–244.

Burgelman, R. A. and Grove, A. S. (2007). Let chaos reign, then rein in chaos — Repeatedly: Managing strategic dynamics for corporate longevity. *Strategic Management Journal*, **28**: 965–979.

Criscuolo, P., Salter, A. and Ter Wal, A. (2013). Going underground: Bootlegging and individual innovative performance. *Organization Science*, 1287–1305. Oct 2013.

Diez-Martin, F., Prado-Roman, C. and Blanco-Gonzalez, A. (2013). Beyond legitimacy: Legitimacy types and organizational success. *Management Decision*, **51**(10): 1954–1969.

EETimes. (2001). Available from: https://www.eetimes.com/document.asp?doc_id=1143754.

Globocnik, D. and Salomo, S. (2015). Do formal management practices impact the emergence of bootlegging behavior? *Journal of Product Innovation Management*, **32**(4): 505–521.

Koch, R. and Leitner, K. H. (2008). The dynamics and functions of self-organization in the fuzzy front end: Empirical evidence from the Austrian semiconductor industry. *Creativity and Innovation Management*, **17**(3): 216–226.

Mainemelis, C. (2010). Stealing fire: Creative deviance in the evolution of new ideas. *Academy of Management Review*, **35**(4): 558–578.

Masoudnia, Y. (2012). *Bootlegging in High Technology R&D Departments: From Initiation to Disclosure*. Dissertation at Cranfield University. Available from: https://dspace.lib.cranfield.ac.uk/handle/1826/7919.

Masoudnia Y. and Szwejczewski, M. (2012). Bootlegging in the R&D departments of high-technology firms. *Research Technology Management*, **55**(5).

Meyer, J. W. and Rowan, B. (1977). Institutionalized organizations: Formal structure as myth and ceremony. *American Journal of Sociology*, **83**(2): 340–363.

Scott, W. R. (1995). Institutions and organizations. Ideas, interests and identities. *Management*, **17**(2): 136–140.

Shepard, H. A. (1967). Innovation-resisting and innovation-producing organizations. *The Journal of Business*, **40**(4): 470–477.

Suchman, M. C. (1995). Managing legitimacy: Strategic and institutional approaches. *Academy of Management Review*, **20**(3): 571–610.

Yin, R. K. (2003). *Case study research: Design and methods*. Thousand Oaks, CA: Sage.

Zimmerman, M. A. and Zeitz, G. J. (2002). Beyond survival: Achieving new venture growth by building legitimacy. *Academy of Management Journal*, **27**(3): 414–431.

https://doi.org/10.1142/9781800612266_0013

Chapter 12

Bootlegging Behavior: From Underground to Disclosure

Erfan Jalali Bidakhavidi* and Kamal Sakhdari
University of Tehran, Tehran, Iran
**erfanjb65@gmail.com*

Abstract

Research on bootlegging shows that individuals, as the origin of corporate entrepreneurship and innovation, often resort to undercover activities to develop and elaborate their initial ideas. Although reasons behind such behavior are well documented in the extant literature, less is known about what drives bootleggers to reveal their ideas. Drawing on field data from in-depth interviews with innovators in R&D departments in different industries of Iran, this research identified five groups of factors at the individual, managerial, firm, industrial, and idea level, which are at play in the revealing stage of bootlegging behavior.

12.1. Introduction

Individuals are the drivers of innovation within established firms. In many cases, successful corporate entrepreneurship projects and new product development projects are commenced by employees who operate at lower levels, following a bottom-up pattern (Burgelman, 1983). The extant literature emphasizes the importance of employees' innovative behavior and entrepreneurial activities in promoting corporate entrepreneurship (Kanter, 2000; Amabile, 1988; Turner and Pennington, 2015); however, innovative employees do not always enjoy formal support from their organizations. They might face denial from top managers or encounter other organizational obstacles when they come up with new ideas, put them forward, and want to implement them.

Previous studies show that, in such cases, individuals might resort to underground activities to continue developing their ideas and strive to implement them (Aram, 1973). Working secretly on ideas without top managers' permission is a form of creative deviance (Mainemelis, 2010) and is referred to as "bootlegging" (Augsdorfer, 1996). According to Augsdorfer (2005), bootlegging is the process of employees clandestinely working on and elaborating their ideas, which are not formally supported by the organization.

What drives individuals to pursue their ideas clandestinely is well studied in the bootlegging literature. Reducing uncertainty associated with vague ideas (Masoudnia and Szwejczewski, 2012), proving the technological and market potential of unelaborated ideas (Criscuolo and Ter Wal, 2014), and establishing legitimacy for the acquisition of resources (Kannan-Narasimhan, 2014) are some examples of causes of bootlegging behavior. Yet, why and when bootleggers make their hidden ideas and activities public is still an unanswered question in this domain.

The importance of answering this question is twofold. Firstly, based on bootlegging literature, elaborating underground ideas and bootlegging behavior is beneficial for firms (Augsdorfer, 1996; Criscuolo and Ter Wal, 2014; Ryan, 2006), so identifying the factors encouraging bootleggers to reveal their ideas is of value. Secondly, prior research is confined to developed countries' context, while contextual factors in emerging countries may affect bootlegging behavior, thus needs to be investigated.

To address these gaps, this study draws on the data from in-depth interviews with bootleggers working in R&D departments in Iran, a country with a developing context. Therefore, this study makes at least two contributions. Firstly, while the existing literature is mainly focused on the causes of underground activities (Augsdorfer, 2005; Masoudnia and Szwejczewski, 2012), this study sheds light on the back-end of bootlegging behavior; the disclosure stage. Secondly, this study investigates bootlegging behavior in an emerging setting, considering the effects of context-specific factors.

12.2. Research Background

Despite the secretive and unauthorized nature of bootlegging behavior, it is intended to benefit the firm and fulfill the top managers' expectations about innovation and creativity. As Augsdorfer (1996) defines, bootlegging is a deviant behavior hidden from the top management team, in which innovative employees use organizational time and resources to elaborate their new ideas that are mainly in line with organizational goals and benefits. When innovative employees elaborate their ideas without their senior managers' permission, they are circumventing obstacles and formal hindrances to achieve what is demanded of them. That is to say, going underground is an unofficial way of undertaking innovative activities when facing barriers to meet the official goals of the organization (Knight, 1968).

Three important characteristics should be considered to distinguish bootlegging from other types of deviant and secret activities in organizations. Firstly, bootlegging is secret and without senior managers' knowledge, but sometimes other colleagues and line managers might be aware of it. Secondly, bootlegging consists of bottom-up and non-programmed activities and is initiated by employees at the organization's lower levels. Those who work in R&D departments are a perfect example. Finally, although deviant, bootlegging is constructive; its ensuing goals and innovations are legitimate while the means used may be illegitimate (Criscuolo and Ter Wal, 2014).

Drivers of bootlegging behavior can be explained by structural strain theory, introduced by Merton (1968). Based on this theory, organizations have valuable internalized goals that should be achieved by their members. If an organization provides its members with legitimate means needed for achieving the goals, the members will conform to the organizational rules and standards and do not violate or circumvent them. However, when legitimate means are not available, but there is pressure on members to achieve the goals, members resort to other options and may use illegitimate means to fulfill the goals. Organizations that place a high value on their goals and push their members to realize the goals but do not provide legitimate means will face the structural strain. In turn, structural strain leads to members showing deviant behavior such as bootlegging and hiding their activities from senior managers. The structural strain is common in many firms as resources are generally limited, while there is overpromotion of innovation and creativity, leading to an imbalance between these two sides (Mainemelis, 2010).

There are also empirical studies on the reasons behind bootlegging behavior. Burgelman (1983), for example, argues that if employees come up with ideas that are out of the firm's core business, they will undertake "hidden innovative activities" to elaborate their ideas. Likewise, suppose employees consider the firm's strategic and structural conditions inappropriate and not supportive of new ideas. In that case, they will go underground to develop and elaborate their ideas secretly until the idea reaches the point that it can prove its value to the senior decision makers. Augsdorfer (1996) also posits that ideas' immaturity motivates employees to bootleg and put back the revelation. Bootlegging is a way of elaborating and developing ideas whose economic justification and feasibility are vague; therefore, the bootlegging process continues until the idea's feasibility can be proved. Whether an organization supports experimental trials for new ideas and the level of flexibility in firms' R&D planning and budgeting are also at play in the occurrence of bootlegging (Augsdorfer, 1996, 2008).

Bootlegging can also be seen as an effective way of escaping rigid and time-consuming processes, avoiding managers' interference (Abetti, 1997), and a smart approach to protecting undeveloped ideas from early rejection (Koch and Leitner, 2008). Undertaking bootlegging can also reduce the uncertainty associated with new ideas (Masoudnia, 2012), establish legitimacy, and acquire resources for elaborating them (Kannan-Narasimhan, 2014). Formal management practices, such as strategic autonomy and rewards, and employees' level of self-efficacy (Globocnik and Salomo, 2015), and creativity (Augsdorfer, 2012) can explain why employees undertake bootlegging activities.

The findings mentioned above mainly focus on the earlier phases of bootlegging behavior, while factors and conditions that stimulate bootleggers to terminate their hidden activities and reveal their clandestine projects are neglected. Besides, there is an allusion in Abetti's (1999) research to the cultural and institutional factors that can affect bootlegging, which has not received attention thus far. As he has found, bootlegging behavior is more common among Japanese employees than their American counterparts. Abetti (1999) believes that this difference ensues from the fact that Japanese culture places greater value on long-term employment and loyalty to the firm. Thus, cultural and institutional factors, which have been neglected in the literature, can also explain bootlegging behavior. These two gaps provide the opportunity for this research to contribute to our body of knowledge about bootlegging behavior.

This study aims to gain a deep understanding of the bootlegging phenomenon and identify the factors encouraging bootleggers to reveal their ideas, so a case study strategy is appropriate (Yin, 2014). Data was gathered through 33 in-depth interviews with 18 employees from 15 companies operating in information technology, software, and pharmaceutics industries as prior research indicates that bootlegging behavior is more common in such settings (Masoudnia and Szwejczewski, 2012).

Following Corbin and Strauss (2014), we used open and axial coding to identify first- and second-order codes. Then, peer and expert briefing was used to validate the identified codes.

12.3. Discussion

The literature on bootlegging has clarified why employees resort to underground activities to elaborate their ideas, but why such employees end their clandestine activities and reveal their hidden ideas is still unknown. As such, the aim of this research identifying the factors affecting the uncovering stage of bootlegging behavior. Using field data from in-depth interviews, this study identified five categories of factors, namely individual, manager, organization, idea, and industry level.

The first category is the individual-level factors. Many of these factors cannot be controlled by firms, but human resources practices can manipulate some of them (Augsdorfer, 2012). An important factor at this level is persistence, which can enable employees to find many ways and try all possible options to elaborate and realize their ideas. A low level of self-confidence, however, impedes employees from publicizing their ideas, so less self-confident people will postpone uncovering. Extroverted employees who are more comfortable speaking up are also more likely to uncover their ideas sooner than introverted ones.

Last but not least, morality, ethics, and religious beliefs can impact individuals' decisions about disclosure. We found that if morality is important for an employee, they may make public their idea earlier since activities that are hidden from the employer would be against their ethical and religious beliefs. It is noteworthy that the role of ethical and religious beliefs in bootlegging behavior has not received any attention so far; thus, this is a compelling avenue for future research on bootlegging behavior.

The second category is related to the way managers treat their subordinates. These factors consist of a trust-based relationship between managers and employees, managers' relational skills, and employees' perception of their managers' approach to new ideas. These factors play an important role in creating a proper strategic context for uncovering clandestine activities. For example, the perception that a manager or supervisor has full control over the situation makes bootleggers uncover their hidden activities as soon as possible. Likewise, the perception that the manager or supervisor embraces new ideas and listens to employees' voices encourages employees to end their hidden activities sooner and share it with senior managers. Moreover, if bootleggers feel that top managers might steal their idea, they will postpone uncovering it until the conditions are favorable and they are sure that top managers acknowledge their contribution to the idea. Managers' relational skills are also at play in this stage. If managers can establish mutual trust, employees feel motivated to reveal their hidden ideas.

Organizational factors can affect bootlegging behavior. One of these factors is the focus on goals compared to the focus on the means to achieve the goals. In organizations with a greater emphasis on goals than means, bootleggers are more motivated to publicize their hidden ideas. This finding is in line with Mainemelis's (2010) argument explaining creative deviant behavior. As he contends, strict normative enforcement can hinder bootlegging actions. Additionally, our study indicates that cultural factors such as the importance of transparency, clarification of organizational values, and the encouragement of teamwork predispose bootleggers to make their ideas public.

As to industrial-level factors, type of business and the business environment affect bootlegging behavior in the revealing stage. The more the business setting is competitive and fast-changing, the earlier bootleggers will uncover their hidden ideas. For example, in a competitive industry, bootleggers will unveil their ideas sooner because creativity and idea presentation are highly valued and encouraged, or in the information technology industry, which has a rapid pace of changes, revealing ideas happens earlier.

Idea-related factors can also explain the revealing of hidden activities. Factors such as immaturity, low level of relatedness to the firm's core business, and being far from the implementation stage can postpone the revelation of hidden ideas. Failing to support such ideas can negatively affect firms' venturing activities and innovativeness as it confines the firm to planned ideas and formal channels of idea generation (Covin and Miles, 2006).

References

Abetti, P. A. (1997). Underground innovation in Japan: The development of Toshiba's word processor and laptop computer. *Creativity and Innovation Management*, **6**(3): 127–139.

Abetti, P. A. (1999). Underground innovation in USA, Europe, and Japan. In *PICMET'99: Portland International Conference on Management of Engineering and Technology*. Proceedings Vol. 1, Book of Summaries (IEEE Cat. No. 99CH36310), *IEEE*.

Amabile, T. M. (1988). A model of creativity and innovation in organizations. *Research in Organizational Behavior*, **10**(1): 123–167.

Aram, J. D. (1973). Innovation via the R&D underground. *Research Management*, **16**(6): 24–26.

Augsdorfer, P. (1996). *Forbidden Fruit: An Analysis of Bootlegging, Uncertainty and Learning in Corporate R&D*. Avebury: Aldershot, UK.

Augsdorfer, P. (2005). Bootlegging and path dependency. *Research Policy*, **34**(1): 1–11.

Augsdorfer, P. (2008). Managing the unmanageable. *Research-Technology Management*, **51**(4): 41–47.

Augsdorfer, P. (2012). A diagnostic personality test to identify likely corporate bootleg researchers. *International Journal of Innovation Management*, **16**(1): 1250003.

Burgelman, R. A. (1983). A process model of internal corporate venturing in the diversified major firm. *Administrative Science Quarterly*, **28**(2): 223–244.

Corbin, J. and Strauss, A. (2014). *Basics of Qualitative Research: Techniques and Procedures for Developing Grounded Theory*. Sage Publications: Newbury Park, California, USA.

Covin, J. and Miles, M. (2006). Corporate entrepreneurship and the pursuit of competitive advantage. *Entpreneurship Theory and Practice*, spring 1999, 47–63.

Criscuolo, P. A. Salter, and Ter Wal, A. L. (2014). Going underground: Bootlegging and individual innovative performance. *Organization Science*, **25**(5): 1287–1305.

Globocnik, D. and Salomo, S. (2015). Do formal management practices impact the emergence of bootlegging behavior? *Journal of Product Innovation Management*, **32**(4): 505–521.

Kannan-Narasimhan, R. (2014). Organizational ingenuity in nascent innovations: Gaining resources and legitimacy through unconventional actions. *Organization Studies*, **35**(4): 483–509.

Kanter, R. M. (2000). When a thousand flowers bloom: Structural collective and social conditions for innovation in organizations. *Knowledge Management and Organisational Design*, **10**: 93–131.

Knight, K. E. (1967). A descriptive model of the intra-firm innovation process. *The Journal of Business*, **40**(4): 478–496.

Koch, R. and Leitner, K. H. (2008). The dynamics and functions of self-organization in the fuzzy front end: Empirical evidence from the Austrian semiconductor industry. *Creativity and Innovation Management*, **17**(3): 216–226.

Mainemelis, C. (2010). Stealing fire: Creative deviance in the evolution of new ideas. *Academy of Management Review*, **35**(4): 558–578.

Masoudnia, Y. and Szwejczewski, M. (2012). Bootlegging in the R&D departments of high-technology firms. *Research-Technology Management*, **55**(5): 35–42.

Merton, R. (1968). *Social Theory and Social Structure*. Simon and Schuster: New York.

Ryan, B. (2006). The Problematic Nature of Organizational Culture and a Changing Control Context. *Strategic Direction*, **22**(8): 431–440.

Turner, T. and Pennington, W. W. (2014). Organizational networks and the process of corporate entrepreneurship: How the motivation, opportunity, and ability to act affect firm knowledge, learning, and innovation. *Small Business Economics*, **45**(2): 447–463.

Yin, R. K. (2014). *Case Study Research: Design and Methods (Applied Social Research Methods)*. Sage Publications: Thousand Oaks, CA.

Part 4

Psychology of Bootlegging

https://doi.org/10.1142/9781800612266_0014

Chapter 13

The Individual in Bootlegging Innovation*

Alexander Krueger† and Arne Buchwald‡
EBS, Wiesbaden, Germany and Arne Buchwald,
Vlerick Business School, Gent, Belgium
†*alexander.krueger@ebs.edu*
‡*arne.buchwald@vlerick.com*

Abstract

One key source of innovation is the individual employee, who can develop innovations either with or without the official authorization by management. Previous research about bootlegging focused mostly on structural determinants while little is known about individual determinants of bootlegging behavior. We relate two research streams that address deviance and motivation to develop a conceptual model that explains bootlegging behavior in the workplace. Based on the assumption that an innovating agent can simultaneously engage in compliant and in deviant innovative behavior (i.e., bootlegging), we conceptualize these distinctly different types of behavior as two dependent variables and derive intrinsic and extrinsic motivational sources as independent variables. Our conceptual model contributes to existing literature on individual-level determinants of bootlegging and offers a basis to further study workplace innovation.

13.1. Introduction

Successful innovations ultimately benefit organizations as a whole. However, the driving factor behind innovations is the individual employee

*This chapter is a secondary publication of an article that was previously presented at The ISPIM Innovation Conference 2019 and included in its conference proceedings (Krüger, A. and Buchwald, A. (2019). *Motivation as Determinant of Bootlegging Innovation*, The ISPIM Innovation Conference, June 16–19, Florence, Italy).

(Krueger Jr., 2000). Individually driven innovation can occur in two distinctly different ways: within the structural boundaries created for this purpose (Aram, 1973) and outside of them (Burgelman, 1983; Kanter, 2000). Thus, innovators inevitably find themselves at crossroads where they chose either the official or the in-official innovation route.

The first conduct takes place within managerially designated structures. In such a setting, space for innovation is opened up through a top-down decision by the management and subsequently implemented by the individual employee (Wheelwright and Clark, 1992) as a form of innovative work behavior (Cooper, 1990). Innovative work behavior is defined as "all individual actions directed at the generation, introduction and or application of beneficial novelty at any organizational level" (Kleysen and Street, 2001: 285), compliant with the structures and processes of the individual organization.

In contrast, the noncompliant variation of an innovation process is the development and pursuit of ideas without managerial consent (Burgelman, 1983; Kanter, 2000). This mostly uncharted phenomenon, termed as "bootlegging" (Knight, 1967), is defined as "an R&D activity in which motivated individuals secretly engage in bottom-up, nonprogrammed innovation efforts not officially authorized by management but which are for the benefit of the company" (Criscuolo *et al.*, 2014: 1290).

Previous scientific literature on bootlegging has mostly focused on structural factors to explain why individual innovation endeavors were taken "underground" and secretly realized (Abetti, 1997; Augsdorfer, 2005). Recent research, however, starts to also acknowledge determinants of bootlegging on the individual level (Globocnik and Salomo, 2015). This comprises studies on the relationship of bootlegging and creativity (Augsdorfer, 2012), intrapreneurial self-efficacy (Globocnik and Salomo, 2015), psychological empowerment (Buchwald *et al.*, 2015), and risk propensity (Globocnik, 2018). While several scholars link creative output (i.e., innovation) to motivation (Amabile, 1997; Amabile and Pratt, 2016; Globocnik, 2018), the effect of motivational factors on the decision which innovation road to take, the official or the unofficial one, has not yet been investigated. Accordingly, our research question is:

> Which motivational factors determine the behavior of compliant or noncompliant individual innovation?

We systematically address this question by introducing individual-level determinants to the bootlegging literature. To close the existing research gap, we derive propositions and develop a conceptual model as a basis for future empirical work.

The chapter is structured as follows: Section 13.2 provides a brief sketch of previous literature on innovation management and bootlegging; Section 13.3 introduces the concepts of motivation and deviance from a theoretical perspective; Section 13.4 includes the development of our propositions on the theoretical accounts, and Section 13.5 concludes the chapter, acknowledges limitations, and provides suggestions for future research.

13.2. Literature Review

13.2.1. Innovation in organizations

There is an ample body of literature on innovation in organizations (Anderson *et al.*, 2014). One important determinant of organizational innovation is the creative actions of individual employees (Krueger Jr., 2000). They are a significant basis for continuous innovation and improvement in companies (Amabile, 1988; De Jong and Den Hartog, 2010). Based on this premise, companies try to leverage individual power by designing official structures that encourage and allow innovative initiatives (Janssen and Huang, 2008). But structured innovation processes also tend to hinder problem solving (Amabile, 1997; Augsdorfer, 2008) since a certain degree of disorder, improvisation, and self-control are indispensable elements for successful innovation processes (Amabile and Pratt, 2016). This dynamic is at odds with official innovation structures, also referred to as front-end formality, with which companies make an attempt to ensure that coincidences are minimized and creativity is channeled in an efficiency-oriented manner (Aram, 1973; Globocnik and Salomo, 2015).

13.2.2. Bootlegging: Noncompliant innovation

Bootleggers innovate outside of official structures and do so often in secret (Aram, 1973). Nevertheless, this behavior rarely remains hidden from other team members and — in some cases — they are even drawn in as active contributors (Abetti, 1997). The element of secrecy thus refers primarily to the interaction between the innovator and the upper management level (Augsdorfer, 2005), while direct supervisors may even know about the bootleg attempts of their subordinates. Bootleggers don't strive for management approval (Augsdorfer, 2008), but are aware that their side projects must be treated as secondary to official projects in order to deflect unwanted attention, which would put the implementation of the bootlegging activity at risk and might jeopardize the job (Masoudnia and Szwejczewski, 2012). The limited previous research on bootlegging focused largely on structural and organizational factors that determine bootlegging behavior, such as bureaucratic barriers (Abetti, 1997), lack of autonomy, or formal processes and management practices (Masoudnia and Szwejczewski, 2012). In most studies, bootlegging efforts are framed as productive processes that lead to positive effects, such as improvements, new products, successful troubleshooting, or learning (Augsdorfer, 2005; Masoudnia and Szwejczewski, 2012) or a higher innovation output (Criscuolo *et al.*, 2014). However, adverse effects of bootlegging have also been researched and documented. They include resource diversion, time consumption, disobedience, spill-over effects to the broader team (Abetti, 1997; Augsdorfer, 2005; Masoudnia and Szwejczewski, 2012), and negative influence on an individual's ability to innovate in a formal setting (Criscuolo *et al.*, 2014).

13.3. Theoretical Foundation

13.3.1. Deviant behavior

A well-established theoretical approach frames bootlegging as a form of positive deviance, which some authors also refer to as creative deviance (Buchwald *et al.*, 2015; Criscuolo *et al.*, 2014; Globocnik and Salomo, 2015; Mainemelis, 2010). It is triggered by a self-initiated and proactive creative process (Mainemelis, 2010; Masoudnia and Szwejczewski, 2012; Unsworth, 2001) and inevitably violates current organizational norms (Criscuolo *et al.*, 2014; Globocnik and Salomo, 2015). Bootleggers thus disregard formal work requirements in favor of following their creative impulses. However, their guiding principle remains the objective to achieve positive goals for the company (Augsdorfer, 2005; Spreitzer and Sonenshein, 2004) and to actively solve problems following their innate creative drive (Unsworth, 2001). Innovation through bootlegging is evaluated based on the benefits for the organization and not based on the means by which these benefits were achieved (Mainemelis, 2010).

13.3.2. Motivation

The second theoretical component of our study refers to motivation. The degree to which a company motivates its employees to develop new ideas is the most important prerequisite for creative output (Amabile *et al.*, 1996) and, thus, for organizational innovation (Amabile, 1988). The higher the levels of motivation are, the higher is the creative performance of employees (Amabile and Pratt, 2016). Conceptually, motivation can be divided into extrinsic and intrinsic factors (Amabile, 1993; Deci, 1976): On one hand, intrinsic motivation is positively linked to creative performance (Amabile, 1993). Individuals with a high level of intrinsic motivation put in more effort and dedication in tasks and thus are likely to use multiple approaches to find solutions. They tend to go beyond their comfort zone in conducting tasks (Amabile, 1990). On the other hand, extrinsic motivation is negatively linked to creative performance as it neutralizes the effects of intrinsic motivation (Amabile *et al.*, 1996; Deci and Ryan, 1985).

Initial empirical evidence seems to suggest that internal motivational factors, such as respect, positive recognition, or personal satisfaction play a more decisive role for the innovating agent than external incentives such as, for example, financial benefits (Unsworth, 2001). Previous research proposed an integrative meta-theory of work motivation that further differentiates external and internal sources of motivation (Leonard *et al.*, 1999). Subsequent studies implicitly proposed single motivational determinants that can be assigned to our framework of internal as well as external motivational sources to bootlegging behavior (Augsdorfer, 2008; Augsdorfer, 2012; Criscuolo *et al.*, 2014; Globocnik and Salomo, 2015).

13.4. Conceptual Development

We develop the propositions to explain bootlegging behavior as the behavioral outcome of motivational factors based on the research on employee motivation (Leonard *et al.*, 1999). The unit of analysis is the individual employee. In order to gain a better understanding of the different factors in innovative behavior we contrast compliant innovative behavior with its noncompliant counterpart, bootlegging, in a dual-factor approach.

At first glance, the two dependent variables seem to be the reverse of the other. However, in our conceptual model, the internal and external motivational sources could possibly influence the dependent variables in a different, noncontrary way. For the independent variables we draw on the salient model of Leonard *et al.* (1999), which contains five sources of work motivation, three extrinsic sources [goal internalization, self-concept external and instrumental motivation] and two intrinsic sources [intrinsic process and self-concept internal motivation]. This particular framework is suitable for our study because it focuses explicitly on workplace motivation.

13.4.1. Goal internalization motivation

Goal internalization motivates individuals to "accept group goals because the attainment of such goals is important to the individual" (Leonard *et al.*, 1999, p. 991). It refers to the compatibility of an employee's individual value system with the company's general value system (Barbuto Jr. *et al.*, 2004; Ryan, 2011). While individual values overlap with overarching goals, it is not important whether the individual fully agrees with the company's mission (Barbuto and Story, 2011). A high degree of goal internalization motivation facilitates an effective formulation and accordingly more consequent realization (Ryan, 2011) in accordance [i.e., compliant] with the objectives of the company (Riketta and Van Dick, 2005). On the other hand, an orientation toward nonofficial standards could cause conflicts with those goals and, therefore, drive noncompliant behavior. Yet, we propose:

P1a: A higher level of goal internalization motivation leads to a higher level of compliant innovative behavior.
P1b: A higher level of goal internalization motivation leads to a lower level of bootlegging.

13.4.2. Self-concept external motivation

Self-concept external motivation refers to individuals with "a high, weak, ordinal self-concept" (Leonard *et al.*, 1999: 989), which translates to a highly external determined orientation. These individuals base their self-awareness and motivation on perceptions by others (Barbuto and Scholl, 1998; Yang and Lai, 2011). Employees motivated this way aim for positive feedback, recognition, external confirmation, and finally status in this regime. Consequently, the resulting behavior depends on the expectations of the reference group or a higher authority (Barbuto and Story, 2011; Ryan, 2011). On one side, external expectations are a natural part of an employment relationship that work toward a role-conform accomplishment of a certain task. On the other side, however, bootleg research also refers to recognition and admiration of colleagues as strong motives for hiding the results until such a mature state is reached that ensures the successful revelation of the secret project (Augsdorfer, 2008). We therefore propose:

P2a: A higher level of self-concept external motivation leads to a lower level of compliant innovative behavior.
P2b: A higher level of self-concept external motivation leads to a higher level of bootlegging.

13.4.3. Instrumental motivation

Instrumental motivation relates to the mechanism that "attainment of group goals leads to a greater level of extrinsic rewards" (Leonard *et al.*, 1999: 989). In this case, employees associate their behavior with the particular motivation-linked outcomes. These include, for example, bonuses, promotions, or salary increases. These instruments transform the relationship toward a direct transaction (Barbuto and Scholl, 1998; Ryan, 2011). Employees who are influenced by instrumental motives will strive for an optimal balance between input and output (Barbuto Jr. *et al.*, 2004). It is therefore important to link the compensation system with the company's objectives to ensure that employees act accordingly (Globocnik and Salomo, 2015). When it comes to creative performance, rewards increase the commitment and performance pressure of employees and can, therefore, lead to a departure from routines and well-functioning norms (Eisenberger and Aselage, 2009). At the same time, it is established that external motivational instruments — if used improperly — block creativity (Amabile, 1990; Augsdorfer, 2008), the nucleus of any innovative output. In this case, the overall innovation output decreases independently of its realization path. Nevertheless, a relatively higher level of bootlegging activity also seems reasonable. Given the effects of external motivational instruments, a prolonged protection of the idea allows for a higher probability of success and therefore favors unofficial innovation behavior:

P3a: A higher level of instrumental motivation leads to a lower level of compliant innovative behavior.
P3b: A higher level of instrumental motivation leads to a higher level of bootlegging.

13.4.4. Self-concept internal motivation

Self-concept internal motivation is present when "an individual has a high, weak, fixed self-concept" (Leonard *et al.*, 1999: 990). This source of motivation comes from inside the innovative individual and is commonly known as the classic intrinsic motivation that is based on satisfaction derived from the achievement of goals or tasks (Barbuto Jr. *et al.*, 2004). Driven by this specific motivation, the individual optimizes his internal standards, values, and competencies and thus his ideal self through his distinct behavior, whereas external factors such as recognition or rewards fail to trigger the desired outcome (Barbuto and Scholl, 1998; Leonard *et al.*, 1999; Ryan, 2011; Yang and Lai, 2011). Employees pursue their goals by proving to themselves that they are equipped to meet the specific challenge. In bootleg literature, this is recognized as a driving force for innovative behavior (Augsdorfer, 2012). Since success is their predominant objective, we argue that those individuals, if necessary, disappear into hidden activity to protect their ideas. On the contrary, more convenient and safer perceived conditions let individuals openly strive for achievement. This leads to the following proposition:

P4a: A higher level of self-concept internal motivation leads to a higher level of compliant innovative behavior.
P4b: A higher level of self-concept internal motivation leads to a higher level of bootlegging.

13.4.5. Intrinsic process motivation

Intrinsic process motivation will lead individuals to "only engage in activities which they consider fun" (Leonard *et al.*, 1999: 989). Pure, inherent pleasure in the task itself [process], not the result of the task

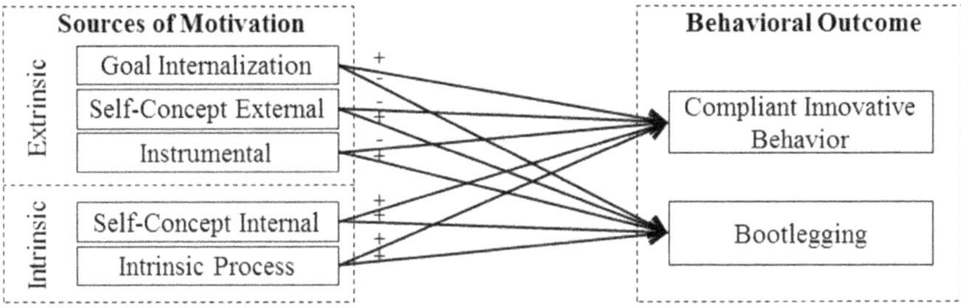

Fig. 13.1. Conceptual model of compliant innovative behavior and bootlegging.

[achievement], is the central motive (Barbuto and Scholl, 1998; Ryan, 2011). This translates to immediate gratification (Barbuto Jr. *et al.*, 2004), which is likely to result in more innovative action and, thus, creative output. The process focus distinguishes this variable from the classical understanding of intrinsic motivation (Barbuto and Scholl, 1998; Barbuto Jr. *et al.*, 2004; Deci, 1976; Hackman and Oldham, 1976). Hence, a possible link to bootlegging is implied by the fact that the work itself is experienced as exciting (Augsdorfer, 2012). Employees motivated in this way will not let themselves be held back from any external constraints and bootleg to further enjoy their activity.

P5a: A higher level of intrinsic process motivation leads to a higher level of compliant innovative behavior.
P5b: A higher level of intrinsic process motivation leads to a higher level of bootlegging.

Finally, we synthesize our propositions in the conceptual model in Fig. 13.1.

13.5. Conclusion

In this chapter, we aimed at developing a conceptual model to explain the decision of an individual innovator, to bootleg instead of using official innovation channels. While previous research had mostly focused on structural factors (Abetti, 1997; Augsdorfer, 2005), our research brings the individual level into focus. We synthesize different streams of literature on motivation, deviance, and innovation to explain bootlegging behavior with a particular focus on motivational factors. Our conceptual model contributes to the recently emerging discourse of individual-level determinants of bootlegging literature.

From a practical perspective, this research provides managers with a more thorough understanding of the phenomenon of bootlegging and its individual-level determinants. As a result, organizations will be in a better position to maximize their internal innovation resources, which will make them more competitive on the global marketplace.

We acknowledge the following limitations: First, while we developed the model on theoretical accounts, the validation of it remains for future work. Second, the explanatory power of our model in a later full paper could be further increased by integrating additional moderating variables between independent and dependent variables, such as willingness to take risk (Amabile, 1988; Deci and Ryan, 1985) or the need for cognition (Wu *et al.*, 2014).

References

Abetti, P. (1997). The birth and growth of Toshiba's laptop and notebook computers: A case study in Japanese corporate venturing. *Journal of Business Venturing*, **12**: 507–529.

Amabile, T. (1988). A model of creativity and innovation in organizations. *Research in Organizational Behavior*, **10**: 123–167.

Amabile, T. (1990). Within you, without you: The social psychology of creativity, and beyond.

Amabile, T. (1993). Motivational synergy: Toward new conceptualizations of intrinsic and extrinsic motivation in the workplace. *Human Resource Management Review*, **3**: 185.

Amabile, T. (1997). Motivating creativity in organizations: On doing what you love and loving what you do. *California Management Review*, **40**: 39–58.

Amabile, T. and Pratt, M. (2016). The dynamic componential model of creativity and innovation in organizations: Making progress, making meaning. *Research in Organizational Behavior*, **36**: 157–183.

Amabile, T., Conti, R., Coon, H., Lazenby, J. and Herron, M. (1996). Assessing the work environment for creativity. *Academy of management journal*, **39**: 1154–1184.

Anderson, N., Potočnik, K. and Zhou, J. (2014). Innovation and creativity in organizations: A state-of-the-science review, prospective commentary, and guiding framework. *Journal of management*, **40**: 1297–1333.

Aram, J. D. (1973). Innovation via the R&D underground. *Research Management*, **16**: 24–26.

Augsdorfer, P. (2005). Bootlegging and path dependency. *Research Policy*, **34**: 1–11.

Augsdorfer, P. (2008). Managing the unmanageable. *Research-Technology Management*, **51**: 41–47.
Augsdorfer, P. (2012). A diagnostic personality test to identify likely corporate bootleg researchers. *International Journal of Innovation Management*, **16**: 1250003-1–1250003-18.
Barbuto, J. E. and Scholl, R. (1998). Motivation sources inventory: Development and validation of new scales to measure an integrative taxonomy of motivation. *Psychological Reports*, **82**: 1011–1022.
Barbuto, J. E. and Story, J. (2011). Work motivation and organizational citizenship behaviors. *Journal of Leadership Studies*, **5**: 23–34.
Barbuto, J. E., Jr., Trout, S. K. and Brown, L. L. (2004). Identifying sources of motivation of adult rural workers. *Journal of Agricultural Education*, **45**(3): 11–21.
Buchwald, A., Urbach, N. and Mähring, M. (2015). Understanding employee engagement in un-official projects–A conceptual model based on psychological empowerment and constructive deviance. In *International Conference on Information Systems (ICIS)*.
Burgelman, R. A. (1983). A process model of internal corporate venturing in the diversified major firm. *Administrative Science Quarterly*, **28**(2): 223–244.
Cooper, R. G. (1990). Stage-gate systems: A new tool for managing new products. *Business Horizons*, **33**: 44–54.
Criscuolo, P., Salter, A. and Ter Wal, A. (2014). Going underground: Bootlegging and individual innovative performance. *Organization Science*, **25**: 1287–1305.
De Jong, J. P. and Den Hartog, D. N. (2010). Measuring innovative work behaviour. *Creativity and innovation management*, **19**: 23–36.
Deci, E. (1976). Notes on the theory and metatheory of intrinsic motivation. *Organizational Behavior and Human Performance*, **15**: 130–145.
Deci, E. and Ryan, R. (1985). The general causality orientations scale: Self-determination in personality. *Journal of research in personality*, **19**: 109–134.
Eisenberger, R. and Aselage, J. (2009). Incremental effects of reward on experienced performance pressure: Positive outcomes for intrinsic interest and creativity. *Journal of Organizational Behavior: The International Journal of Industrial, Occupational and Organizational Psychology and Behavior*, **30**: 95–117.
Globocnik, D. (2019). Taking or avoiding risk through secret innovation activities—The relationship among employees' risk propensity, bootlegging, and management support. *International Journal of Innovation Management*, 1950022.
Globocnik, D. and Salomo, S. (2015). Do formal management practices impact the emergence of bootlegging behavior? *Journal of Product Innovation Management*, **32**: 505–521.
Hackman, J. and Oldham, G. (1976). Motivation through the design of work: Test of a theory. *Organizational Behavior and Human Performance*, **16**: 250–279.
Janssen, O. and Huang, X. (2008). Us and me: Team identification and individual differentiation as complementary drivers of team members' citizenship and creative behaviors. *Journal of Management*, **34**: 69–88.
Kanter, R. M. (2000). When a thousand flowers bloom: Structural, collective, and social conditions for innovation in organizations. In Staw, B. and Sutton, R. (Eds.), *Research in Organizational Behavior* (Vol. 22). Amsterdam: Elsevier Science.

Kleysen, R. F. and Street, C. T. (2001). Toward a multi-dimensional measure of individual innovative behavior. *Journal of Intellectual Capital*, **2**: 284–296.
Knight, K. E. (1967). A descriptive model of the intra-firm innovation process. *The Journal of Business*, **40**: 478–496.
Krueger, N. F., Jr. (2000). The cognitive infrastructure of opportunity Emergence. *Entrepreneurship Theory and Practice*, **24**: 5.
Leonard, N. H., Beauvais, L. L. and Scholl, R. W. (1999). Work motivation: The incorporation of self-concept-based processes. *Human Relations*, **52**: 969–998.
Mainemelis, C. (2010). Stealing fire: Creative deviance in the evolution of new ideas. *Academy of Management Review*, **35**: 558–578.
Masoudnia, Y. and Szwejczewski, M. (2012). Bootlegging in the R&D departments of high-technology firms. *Research-Technology Management*, **55**: 35–42.
Riketta, M. and Van Dick, R. (2005). Foci of attachment in organizations: A meta-analytic comparison of the strength and correlates of workgroup versus organizational identification and commitment. *Journal of Vocational Behavior*, **67**: 490–510.
Ryan, J. (2011). Development of a measure of work motivation for a meta-theory of motivation. *Psychological Reports*, **108**: 743–755.
Spreitzer, G. and Sonenshein, S. (2004). Toward the construct definition of positive deviance. *American Behavioral Scientist*, **47**: 828–847.
Unsworth, K. (2001). Unpacking creativity. *Academy of Management Review*, **26**: 289–297.
Wheelwright, S. C. and Clark, K. B. (1992). *Revolutionizing Product Development: Quantum Leaps in Speed, Efficiency, and Quality*. New York: Simon and Schuster.
Wu, C.-H., Parker, S. K. and De Jong, J. P. (2014). Need for cognition as an antecedent of individual innovation behavior. *Journal of Management*, **40**: 1511–1534.
Yang, H.-L. and Lai, C.-Y. (2011). Understanding knowledge-sharing behaviour in Wikipedia. *Behaviour & Information Technology*, **30**: 131–142.

https://doi.org/10.1142/9781800612266_0015

Chapter 14

Innovative Engagement in Bootlegging Projects: How to Manage the Rise of the Innovation Rebel

Claudia C. Michalik
Independant Consultant, London, England
inspim@gmx.net

Abstract

This chapter explores the innovative engagement in bootlegging projects and some of the many questions coming up when covert commitment leads to innovation against the odds. The author develops a model of innovative engagement that identifies character traits of innovation rebels and the environment they need to thrive in an organization. Based on an empirical study in the chemical and pharmaceutical industry, this chapter presents two specific types of innovation rebels — the ambitious bootlegger and the creative bootlegger — and discusses how to manage their innovative engagement to create ground-breaking innovation.

14.1. The Innovation Rebel at Work

Organizations are reluctant to admit bootlegging activities. But bootlegging is everywhere. In many organizations, it is standard day-to-day R&D behavior.[1]

Many groundbreaking innovations have been the sole result of the enthusiasm and overly dedicated innovative commitment of individual researchers who continued to tinker with their ideas in secrecy when things got challenging. Although these so-called bootlegging projects were

[1]Anonymous quote from one of the initial interviews.

often carried out against the will of superiors and sometimes even top management, some amounted to outstanding innovation successes for the organization, contributing to significant growth and revenue.

Well-known everyday products such as 3M's post-it notes, Bayer's Aspirin, or Nespresso's coffee capsules are the result of passionate and determined individuals in successful bootlegging activities, defying a variety of obstacles along the way.

Let's take a look at a few of these success stories, their main driving force and the hurdles they had to overcome:

- Hughes Aircraft engineer and physicist Theodore Maiman constructed the first functional laser, despite funding being axed by R&D management.
- Carl Zeiss researcher Meinrad Mächler developed an industrial simultaneous spectrometer for color analysis, which, despite being abandoned by the board due to financial difficulties, has turned into one of the company's most important achievements.
- Bayer chemist Felix Hoffmann, encouraged by his rheumatic father, produced a medicine devoid of the unpleasant effects of sodium salicylate on his own initiative. Despite secretly using nonproject-allocated resources, the resulting product Aspirin has been a household name for Bayer ever since.
- Hewlett Packard engineer Charles House was eager to build a large-screen display monitor in the 1960s, when company founder David Packard told him it was a stupid idea. House built it anyway and the device became a big hit with customers. Packard, swallowing his pride, eventually awarded him the Medal of Defiance, "in recognition of extraordinary contempt and defiance beyond the normal call of engineering duty."
- Bayer's polymer chemist Dieter Freitag was the driving force in the development of the plastics industry. Freitag and his research team adapted Makrolon polycarbonate to the needs of the electronics industry, creating disks that were stable and readable, and had a high capacity for data storage. When skeptical superiors postponed the scheduled test production, Freitag produced his samples in a top-secret overnight mission.
- In 1980, neither a serious illness nor a decision by the company's pharma division to halt work on quinolones prevented Bayer chemist Klaus Grohe from using his Grohe process to synthesize ciprofloxacin

just a year later. This resulted in a broad-spectrum antibiotic used to treat bacterial infections and is one of the top-selling antibiotics worldwide (Bayer, 2020).

Quite a few success stories for projects abandoned by the organization but fought for and eventually brought to life by the notwithstanding innovative engagement of a dedicated researcher.

All these bootlegging activities are characterized by one common denominator — the innovative engagement of individual researchers who bypass all barriers and accept consequences in order to realize their ideas.

Wouldn't it be good to know what exactly makes up such extraordinary innovative engagement so that an organization can lead it to further success in a targeted manner? Or do bootlegging activities exist precisely because of their secret mission and would not succeed in a permitted and controlled environment?

This study explores some of the many questions coming up when covert commitment leads to innovation against the odds: What distinguishes innovative engagement within R&D? How does one recognize such commitment? And who exactly are these innovation rebels? How are they to be identified? What makes them stand out? What drives them? Is it even possible to measure innovative engagement? And how can it be managed in order to steer this innovative strength in a productive direction? Let's try to answer at least a few of them.

14.2. Getting to Know the Innovation Rebel

The exploration of innovative commitment in bootlegging projects is still in its infancy. Empirical studies are sparse due to the defined nature of bootlegging. There is currently no cohesive theory about innovative commitment within R&D, let alone bootlegging innovations. However, a few existing case studies enable potential factors that need to be considered when analyzing personality traits of bootleggers and identifying how to measure and manage their displayed innovative commitment.

In order to shed some light on the previously scientifically unexplored properties of innovative engagement, a conceptual model of innovative engagement has been developed and empirically proven in a study with 32 individual researchers in the chemical and pharmaceutical industry who were involved in bootlegging activities.

This chapter assumes bootlegging as an expression of innovative engagement. Even if the phenomenon of bootlegging is by no means new, the outstanding importance of above-average commitment of individual personalities has been largely neglected by human resources management.

First and foremost, organizations need to understand what characterizes a bootlegger and what motivates them to direct their innovative engagement into hidden innovation activities. Additionally, organizations are keen to understand how to best manage and promote innovative engagement in a targeted manner to use it for their own purposes.

14.2.1. How to identify the innovation rebel inside?

14.2.1.1. *Dimensions of innovative engagement*

The innovative engagement in organizations depends on various aspects and is determined by whether an innovator

- *can* produce certain innovative achievements according to his or her technical abilities;
- *wants* to deal with a new area of expertise after all;
- *dares* to take certain risks when implementing his or her idea; and
- *may* allow an above-average innovative engagement based on the situational conditions of his or her environment.

These behavioral dimensions only gain importance when they are linked to specific levels of the individual innovative personality. These relate to the innovator

- in his or her individual personality (*personal level*);
- as a result of an innovative environment within the organization (*organizational level*);
- who is an actor in an innovative climate that is subject to situational conditions (*situational level*).

Linking the central dimensions with these specific levels of the individual innovative personality leads to the matrix provided as Fig. 14.1.

Initial research into the identified fields of the matrix is necessary for a more detailed description of innovative engagement. Further research

Innovative Levels / *Behavioral Dimensions*	**Innovative Personality**	**Innovative Environment**	**Innovative Climate**
Want / Dare	Passion and drive for innovative engagement		
Can / Know	Capabilities and Know-How as prerequisite		
May / Permit	Creativity and freedom to explore own ideas		

Fig. 14.1. Dimensions of innovative engagement.
Source: Own illustration based on Schlicksupp (1991) and Michalik (2003).

is then needed to analyze the respective incentives that can be aimed at strengthening and promoting the development of innovative engagement.

The dimensions of *can* and *know* are relatively easily to be influenced as they are part of the conscious mind and therefore not too strongly anchored within the individual.

The dimensions of *want* and *dare* are, on the other hand, firmly anchored within the subconscious of the individual and therefore more difficult to influence (Nieder and Zimmermann, 1992).

Finally, the dimensions of *may* and *permit* are primarily influenced by the scope of the organizations and can be changed accordingly.

14.2.1.2. *Bearers of innovative engagement*

The properties of the innovative personality are not individually displayed features that are isolated from one another but rather a combination of features that are linked by complex structures. Innovative engagement and high innovation performances are most likely if the following properties of the innovative personality are particularly pronounced:

- Creative
- Performance-motivated
- Independence-driven
- Non-conformist
- Cosmopolitan.

14.2.2. Model of innovative engagement

14.2.2.1. *Theoretical framework*

The theoretical research to develop a model of innovative engagement is based on three main theoretical approaches: institutional-economic theories, personality-related theories, and motivational theories. The following descriptions provide a rough overview of the specific aspects of each theory used (Michalik, 2003).

Within the framework of institutional-economic theories, innovative behavior is considered from a principal–agent perspective. Attempts are made to create appropriate incentives in order to control and promote innovative engagement.

Personality-related theories attribute that specific personality traits are responsible for an engaged and motivated display of behavior. Research of individual key personalities helps to identify innovative personalities and allows the management to make a decision regarding promotion of their innovative engagement.

Motivational theories see behavior resulting from the interaction of task-related characteristics, individual personality traits, and situational aspects. In other words, motivation always arises when an individual perceives certain incentives in a certain situation that lead to a certain behavior through the activation of motives. The differentiation between hygiene factors and motivators forms the basis to answer questions on how to reach high motivation and performance in individuals (Herzberg, 1968).

14.2.2.2. *Designing a model of innovative engagement*

The aim is to develop a model of innovative engagement that helps to explain the extraordinary innovation performance of individual innovative personalities within R&D.

Figure 14.2 introduces the model of innovative engagement as a conceptional framework for the following empirical study. It can be interpreted as an explanatory model to research the innovative engagement of individual personalities in an organization.

The model highlights the individual variables that are believed to have an impact on innovative engagement. The arrows represent the postulated interdependencies between individual variables and their direction of impact.

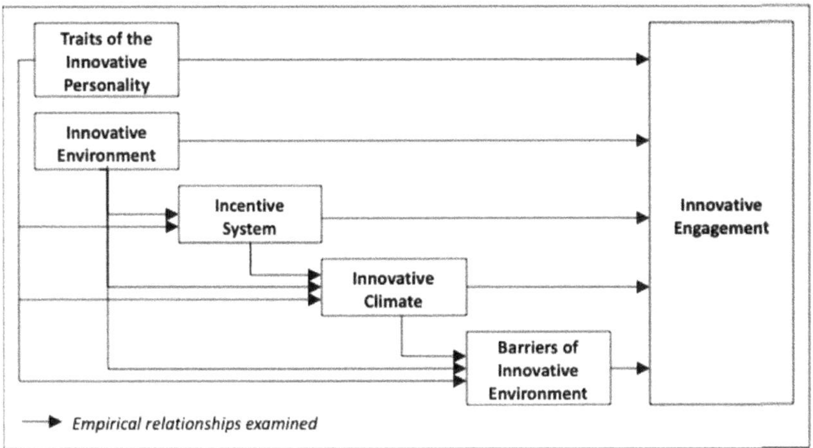

Fig. 14.2. Model of innovative engagement.
Source: Own illustration based on Michalik (2003).

The model implies different interactions of the individual variables on the innovative engagement. Furthermore, it assumes multivariate correlations between the respective variables instead of just singular influences. The variable *innovative engagement* represents the only exclusively dependent variable in this model.

On a high-level view, the model highlights that innovative engagement is mainly dependent on two direct factors: *characteristics of the innovative personality* and the *innovative environment.* In addition, innovative engagement is indirectly dependent on the *incentive system* within the organization, the *innovative climate* within the R&D departments, and existing *barriers within the innovation process.*

A further operationalizational design of the model is dispensed with at this point, as this would go beyond the scope of this contribution (Michalik, 2003).

14.2.3. Empirical study

14.2.3.1. *Methodology of data collection*

The aim of this empirical study is to reduce the previously existing "blank spot" in the research landscape and to provide an initial picture of the relevant attributes of innovative engagement within R&D.

The present study is limited to the consideration of innovative engagement in bootlegging projects. Due the nature of bootlegging projects, face-to-face expert interviews followed by a subsequent written survey were chosen as the methodology for data collection.

14.2.3.2. *Identification of bootleggers*

The study requires to identify active bootleggers within R&D functions of organizations. Identifying eligible bootleggers proved difficult at the beginning and was very much dependent on specific insider knowledge. However, once the first individual was recommended by word of mouth, the famous Pandora's box literally opened. It felt a bit like opening a well-hidden door to a secret member's club of active bootleggers.

One of the participating bootleggers states: "It is more difficult to find researchers who have never been involved in bootlegging projects."[2]

14.2.3.3. *Sample characteristics and first findings*

A total of five expert interviews were initially conducted as prerequisite for the design of the questionnaire. The data sample was limited to the chemical and pharmaceutical industry in Germany.

The empirical study identified a total of 54 bootleggers, out of which 32 contributed to the provided questionnaire. This return rate of about 60% is seen as a rather satisfying result given the secretive nature of the study topic.

The participating 32 bootleggers have a combined experience of a total of 174 bootlegging projects. With 32 questionnaires returned, this order of magnitude indicates the presence of an above-average level of innovative engagement.

In 92 out of the 174 bootlegging projects, the bootlegger acted as the initiator while playing the role of a supporter in the remaining 82 projects. This result confirms that about half of the bootlegging projects considered in the present study were not conducted single-handedly.

14.2.4. First high-level results and conclusions

The following study results provide only a small snapshot of the extensive findings of the original work. As a full empirical examination of the

---

[2] Anonymous quote resulting from one of the interviews.

model in its individual components would go beyond the scope of this contribution. Nonetheless, the following "breadcrumbs" already give first empirical results to verify the model of innovative engagement and how it can be used to promote innovative activity in an organization. Some information about 32 bootleggers and their activities.

14.2.4.1. *What kind of bootlegging experience do they have?*

Almost all of the 32 participating bootleggers have experience in both successful and unsuccessful bootlegging projects. Only three bootleggers did not show any successful bootlegging activities at the time of the study. However, this doesn't keep them from displaying innovative engagement and pursuing their own innovative ideas.

This clearly indicates that the drive to follow up on innovative ideas is bigger than the risk of failure or barriers. As most of the participating bootleggers have seen their secretive efforts resulting in successful bootlegging projects and therefore indirectly creating revenue for their organization, this is a first indication that such innovative engagement adds value to an organization.

14.2.4.2. *Are they all high up the hierarchy?*

The hierarchical position of the respondents is considered under the following aspects: their hierarchical position at the time of the study and their position at the time of their bootlegging projects. We distinguished between successful and unsuccessful bootlegging projects to determine if innovative engagement in bootlegging activities might have a negative impact on the future career progression of a researcher.

Table 14.1 provides an insight into the distribution of hierarchy levels.

Table 14.1. Hierarchical position of bootleggers.

Hierarchical Position	Laboratory Assistant	Group/ Team Lead	Department Project Lead
At Time of Study	3.1%	31.3%	65.6%
At Time of Successful Bootlegging Projects	13.8%	58.6%	27.6%
At Time of Unsuccessful Bootlegging Projects	16.1%	64.5%	19.4%

A few interesting findings here. Firstly, the results lead us to believe that the majority of bootlegging activities happen at group or team lead level. An explanation could be that junior researchers might neither have sufficient know-how nor the required access to resources. Senior researchers in contrast might often be too engrossed in their managerial duties to free up enough time for bootlegging activities. During the initial interviews, it was highlighted that there is often little or even no time at all for bootlegging activities in higher positions.

This leaves the hierarchical level of group and team leads as most likely to engage in bootlegging activities. They have amassed sufficient expertise to build a supporting network, are authorized to manage resources, and have a junior team to perform tasks. An almost perfect combination.

Secondly, it is worth comparing the hierarchical position of the participating bootleggers at the time of study to the time of both successful and unsuccessful bootlegging projects. The results indicate that the majority of our bootleggers qualified for a management position regardless of the success of their covert innovation activities.

14.2.4.3. *Are they all super-experienced?*

The analysis of our bootleggers' work experience goes hand in hand with findings about their hierarchical position in the organization. The study confirms that over half of the respondents have 15–29 years of work experience and have been with their current organization for a similar amount of time (Augsdorfer, 1996). Once again, the study proves that a certain level of professional experience, organizational knowledge, and a well-established network act as prerequisite for innovative engagement in bootlegging projects.

In addition, it appears that a certain longevity of commitment to a single organization is given within R&D. Most of our bootleggers have been with their organization for an average of 22.38 years.

14.2.4.4. *Do they have more time than others?*

Out of the participating bootleggers, 54.8% state that their organization offers free space for their own research interests while the remaining 45.2% complain that there is no support for such ambitions.

The study results show that the majority of bootleggers (70%) have less than five hours per week to scratch the individual innovation itch.

This finding is consistent with statements in literature that allocate roughly 10% of the weekly working hours as free time for individual innovative activities.

Only 18% confirm that they have five to ten hours per week at their disposal for bootlegging activities. As much as 12% are in the lucky position to have above 10 hours at hand for their own innovative interests.

14.2.4.5. *Do they network?*

The findings suggest that bootlegging is a team effort. Impulses for new innovation activities often arise from a lively exchange of ideas with peers outside the organization. In our study, 72% of the participating bootleggers state that they maintain regular contacts. The remaining 28% forego such an exchange of ideas with peer groups.

The most frequent contacts seem with members of institutions in the same industry. However, there are bootleggers who regularly take up innovation-specific discussions with peers outside their own industry. One bootlegger mentions that sometimes it is an "out-of-the-box" perspective that provides the impulse for innovation.[3]

14.2.4.6. *Do they multi-task?*

The study confirms that the majority of bootleggers (nearly 70%) engage in multiple bootlegging projects at the same time rather than focusing on one specific project. One-third of them concentrate their covert efforts on one bootlegging project at a time.

This result suggests that the participating bootleggers show a generally high interest in bootlegging activities and therefore display an above-average level of innovative engagement.

14.2.4.7. *How often do they bootleg?*

We wanted to understand whether bootleggers engage in secretive innovation activities on a regular basis or whether their innovative engagement is displayed on an ad-hoc basis.

Nearly two-thirds of the respondents (64.5%) claim that their innovative engagement in bootlegging activities occurs on a regular basis.

[3]Anonymous quote from one of the initial interviews.

Two researchers say that for them it has become a daily activity.[4] Once they are hooked on an innovative idea or challenge, a certain fascination and passion automatically drives toward a significantly higher level of innovative engagement (Augsdorfer, 1996).

14.2.4.8. *What makes them quit?*

The definition of bootlegging implies the overcoming of obstacles. Therefore, it is all the more important to understand what exactly drives bootleggers to ultimately abandon their covert projects.

Figure 14.3 highlights the main reasons why bootlegging efforts are potentially being abandoned by the researcher.

The findings highlight that the two main reasons to abandon innovative engagement in their bootlegging projects are insufficient results and the lack of risk readiness. It is worth noting that these two reasons are purely driven by the bootlegger's evaluation of their perceived project success. This leads us to believe that the bootleggers have a fairly realistic view on how successful their innovative engagement will turn out going forward.

The lack of time to experiment and dedicate to own innovative ideas was another noticeable reason for abandoning bootlegging efforts. This was

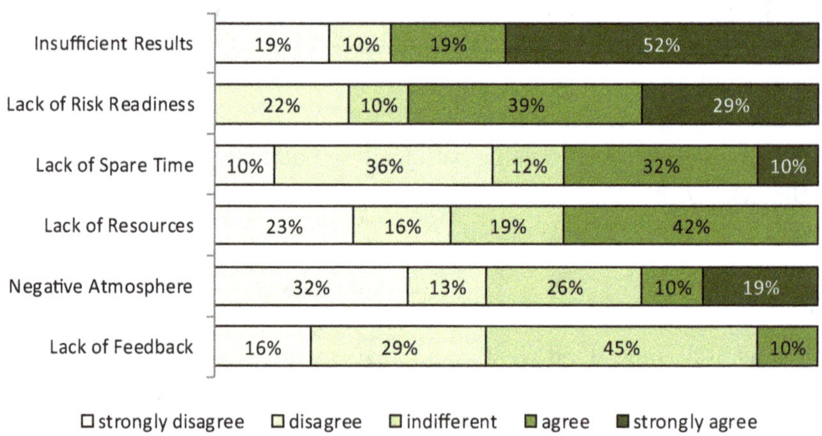

Fig. 14.3. Reasons to quit bootlegging projects (Michalik, 2003).

[4] Anonymous quote from one of the initial interviews.

confirmed by over half of the sample. It ties in with our previous findings in Section 14.2.4.4. Furthermore, for 42% of our respondents, lack of access to required resources such as time, material, machinery, and expertise is a significant factor that contributes to abandoning their bootlegging activities.

A few bootleggers give up on their bootlegging activities because they perceive a negative atmosphere within their R&D departments. This section elaborates further on this as the envy of colleagues and superiors in particular is seen as a consequence of bootlegging and might help to create such negative atmosphere in the first place.

Unsurprisingly, the lack of feedback is rarely considered a reason to abandon bootlegging activities. This is due to the nature of "true bootlegging" where feedback is not sought as a matter of fact; in case of an unsuccessful bootlegging effort, feedback is simply not needed (Greller and Parsons, 1992).

14.2.4.9. *What happens if they get caught?*

The study results show that our respondents did not face serious consequences for their bootlegging projects, independent of whether they were successful or not (Augsdorfer, 1996). The following consequences were probed:

- Notice of termination
- Notice of warning
- Lack of salary progression
- Tougher controls
- Budget constraints
- Envy of colleagues and superiors
- Acknowledgment of innovative engagement
- More spare time for own innovative ideas
- No consequences.

Overall, sanctions and punishments by management play a rather subordinate role when it comes to managing innovative engagement in bootlegging projects. They do not prevent such potentially undesirable behavior and most bootleggers carry on with the development of their ideas regardless.

Neither the acknowledgment of outstanding bootlegging performance nor an increase in free time trigger a positive consequence. Merely in the case of successful bootlegging projects, bootleggers might get some form of praise or acknowledgment from their direct superiors or even top management, but even this is not always the case.

It is worth noting that envy of colleagues and superiors is seen as negative consequence of innovative engagement in bootlegging activities. As mentioned in the previous section, such envy might create a negative mood within R&D and prevent researchers from showing their true potential.

Despite being great networkers and actively seeking out communication with peers, bootleggers are not immune to envy. Several bootleggers raised the issue of such peer envy during the pre-study interviews. In some isolated cases, envious superiors actively tried to jeopardize the bootleggers' career progression.

14.2.5. Two types of innovation rebels? Implications on how to manage innovative engagement

The study confirms that innovative engagement in bootlegging activities is extremely valuable for the innovation success of an organization. In most cases, the bootlegger displays character traits and capabilities that identify them as important driver for innovative success. This is an important finding with regards to human resource management in organizations.

Firstly, it is of utmost importance for human resources management to identify such outstanding innovative talents within an organization. Then, they will have to follow up with appropriate incentives to motivate further innovative engagement (Narin and Geitzman, 1995). This sounds logical, but the devil is in the detail.

The study analyzes, among other aspects, the influence of specific personality traits on the innovative engagement, the incentive system, and the innovative climate. Table 14.2 highlights some revealing findings.

Looking at different personality traits and their impact, it appears that we can identify two different types of bootleggers. Let's call them *the ambitious bootlegger* and *the creative bootlegger*. Both types bear a combination of all four properties. They are typified by the dominance of their outstanding direct and indirect properties on their innovative engagement, incentives, and innovative climate.

Table 14.2. Effects of existing personality traits (Michalik, 2003).

Influence on:	Innovative Engagement		Incentive System				Innovative Climate	
Character Traits	Direct	Indirect	Flexibility Incentives	Material Incentives	Development Incentives	Status Incentives	Relationship with Colleagues	Relationship with Superiors
Strength of Purpose	−	−1.217	+	+	o	+	−	−
Non-Conformity	−	+1.069	o	o	+	−	+	+
Creative Ideas	−	+1.315	o	o	+	−	+	+
Performance Motivation	+0.814	+2.099	+	o	+	−	+	+

Notes: +: positive influence; −: negative influence; o: no influence.

While the first type is predominantly characterized by a pronounced strength of purpose and determination, the latter's innovative drive is dominated by creative flow, nonconformity, and performance-motivated innovation behavior.

14.2.5.1. *The ambitious bootlegger*

The ambitious type shows a negative indirect influence on the innovative engagement. This leads to believe that such bootlegger, although highly motivated, primarily pursues personal innovation goals without regard for colleagues or the organization. This often leads to "bad" innovative engagement, which could be associated with high costs for companies but without necessarily delivering a corresponding output.

Interestingly, the ambitious type is predominantly driven by flexibility, material, and status-related incentives. Development incentives do not seem important to them. Additionally, they have a negative influence on colleagues and superiors. Maybe their drive for solely personal goals is what worsens the innovative climate in such a way that it leads to envy and a toxic atmosphere.

14.2.5.2. *The creative bootlegger*

On the contrary, the creative type records a consistently and positive influence on innovative engagement, both directly and indirectly. All three personality traits positively influence the innovative climate to both colleagues and superiors. They seem a joy to work with; the players you'd want on your team.

Interestingly, the creative type is motivated by more or less the opposite incentives to the ambitious type. Only flexibility-related incentives seem to show a positive influence for performance motivation, but no influence on creative flow and nonconformity.

In our study, the creative type is positively motivated by development-related incentives. They are not motivated at all by material incentives; even more interestingly they seem repelled by status-related incentives. This finding indicates that the two bootlegger types seem to have rather different motives for their innovative engagement and are therefore motivated by opposing incentives.

The creative type's efforts tend to lead to "good" innovative engagement that supports the organization with innovative creativity. We now know that creative bootleggers are motivated by development-related and repelled by status-related incentives.

This result suggests that creative bootleggers are less interested in traditional career paths within R&D. Their passion is creativity and innovation, not people management and company politics.[5] A parallel hierarchy, which is established alongside the traditional hierarchy, might be a good way forward for organizations to promote career progression for the creative bootlegger type. With such parallel hierarchy, they could continue to climb up the career ladder without losing the fun of using their outstanding innovative engagement. This is confirmed by the findings highlighted in Section 14.2.4.2.

14.3. Conclusion

The study confirms that innovation rebels are characterized by an extraordinary innovative engagement. They possess an "innovative itch." Their innovative itch needs to be scratched, whether the organization offers an adequate outlet or not. A passionate and driven bootlegger will always find a way out of the organizational dead end, with or without permission.

---

[5]This aspect was highlighted by all five bootleggers during the initial interviews.

We have learned that individual character traits of an innovative personality are the decisive factor for innovative engagement within R&D. But it is not just down to these personality traits to disperse innovative engagement.

The innovative rebels need more for their covert activities to flourish. Some of them require a specific innovative climate within their own organization; others thrive on the extra pressure of having to overcome obstacles on the way. Some bootleg for the praise; others couldn't care less about accolades. Some are keen to prove their point; others simply are a bit of a Gyro Gearloose, Walt Disney's genius inventor cartoon character.

With this in mind, a well-functioning human resources management needs to understand that there is no one-size-fits-all incentive system to promote innovative engagement and manage their individual innovative personalities. An incentive system is required that is tailored to the individual needs of each researcher. This seems the only way to steer innovative engagement in the desired direction, if at all.

Until then, innovative engagement in bootlegging projects will remain innovation against the odds.

References

Augsdorfer, P. (1996). *Forbidden Fruit — An Analysis of Bootlegging and Uncertainty and Learning in Corporate R&D*. Aldershot: Avebury.

Bayer (2020). *The Grohe Method and Quinolone Antibiotics*. Company Research Brochure.

Greller, M. M. and Parsons, C. K. (1992). Feedback and feedback inconsistency as sources of strain and self-evaluation. *Human Relations*, **45**: 601–620.

Herzberg, F. (1968). One more time: How do you motivate employees? *Harvard Business Review*, **46**(1): 53–62.

Michalik, C. C. (2003). *Innovative Engagement — An Empirical Study on the Phenomenon of Bootlegging* (in German). Gabler.

Narin, F. and Beitzman, A. (1995). Inventive productivity. *Research Policy*, **24**: 507–519.

Nieder, P. and Zimmermann, E. (1992). Obstacles to innovation within the company (in German). *Betriebswirtschaftliche Forschung und Praxis*, (4): 374–387.

Schlicksupp, H. (1991). Incentives to develop creativity (in German). In Schanz, G. (Ed.), *Handbuch Anreizsysteme* (pp. 525–545). Stuttgart.

https://doi.org/10.1142/9781800612266_0016

Chapter 15

TSD-Z, a Creativity Test to Identify Bootleggers

Peter Augsdorfer
Technical University of Ingolstadt, Ingolstadt, Germany
peter.augsdorfer@thi.de

Abstract

The purpose of this chapter is to show that potential bootleg entrepreneurs can be identified beforehand, maybe already during the job interview. This can be interesting for two reasons. First, a firm might not want the "hassle" of having to deal with illicit activity and can then prevent with this test those people from joining their organization. Second, the reverse is the case. As bootleggers are particularly creative, a company might want a creative force in its laboratory and can identify them beforehand with this test.

15.1. Introduction

"The entrepreneur gets things done!" wrote Schumpeter about one of the main forces of technological change (1989). Schumpeter, in his book *Theorie der wirtschaftlichen Entwicklung* (1912), introduced the central figure of the entrepreneur gifted with initiative, creativity, and motivation. However, nearly 30 years later, he asks, "In the large-scale corporation of today, the question that is never quite absent arises with vengeance, namely, who should be considered the entrepreneur?" (Schumpeter, 1947).

Bootlegging is an innovation organized in secret by motivated corporate individuals (Augsdorfer, 1996). If the definition of entrepreneurship is taken more broadly, for example, as suggested by Pavitt, bootlegging has the entrepreneurial element of building competencies for the future innovation potential of the firm (Pavitt, 1988). So, not only on the personality level of "getting things done," but also on the corporate level there are similarities between the bootlegger and Schumpeter's entrepreneur.

The purpose of this chapter is to show that potential bootleg entrepreneurs can be identified before a firm experiences their activity. This can be interesting for two reasons. One, a firm might not want the "hassle" of having to deal with illicit activity and can then prevent those people from joining their organization. Bootleg researchers are frequently considered to be a "pain in the neck" for organizations (Duncan *et al.*, 1990). Unsurprisingly, with their "entrepreneurial genes," they disrupt the established system by challenging it and experiment with new ways of doing things. Or, the second reason, which is the reverse. As bootleggers are particularly creative, a company might need a creative force in its laboratory.

Ekvall and others have shown that the corporate organizational context determines the level of individual creativity (Ekvall, 1996, 1997; Hrncir and MacTurk, 1990). While management and the organization can enhance or stop innovation, ultimately, it is the individual who is the source of a new idea. A number of authors have shown that individuals who take on specific roles can play an important part in the innovation process (Sayles, 1964; Schon, 1973; Witte, 1973; Rothwell, 1975; Pinchot, 1988).

Corporate R&D members come with different qualities, but creative individuals in particular represent the "life force" for any change through technical innovation. Their initiative, commitment, creativity, and persistence are key to corporate R&D and the transition from an abstract idea to the physical artifact. This is not new knowledge. Most good textbooks have some basic description of these individuals (Bessant and Tidd, 2013). Several sources allude to different types of research personalities within the laboratory team. Allan (1966) as well as Roussel *et al.* (1991) distinguish between the personality types "engineer" and "scientist." The Nobel laureate Gerd Binnig, who developed the tunneling electron microscope at IBM in Zürich, distinguishes between "analytic" and "synthetic" persons (1989). Quinn similarly found "experts" and "fanatics" (1979). Very clearly, literature refers to two different types of research personality. On the one hand, there seems to be a kind of individualistic and "actively creative" researcher with a broad attention span, and on the other hand, more guided, "reactively creative" researchers, who are in the majority. The active-creative researcher may contribute to more in the earlier phase of creative problem-solving efforts, when new ideas need to be generated, while the reactively creative person may be more effective in later phases, when new ideas and understanding has to be implemented and refined (Puccio *et al.*, 1995).

> "It is not difficult to see that bootleg researchers are part of the active-creative group. Knight wrote that creative people appear to have a detached devotion to their work; they have a deep commitment to the problem they are trying to solve, yet they are not so deeply immersed that they are unable to see the problem in a broader perspective. Creative people are receptive to all kinds of ideas. They will consider them and judge them on their own merits. Creative people rely on free exploration in that they actively go out and search for new alternatives, advice, ideas, and opinions from a wide variety of sources. Creative individuals appear to commit themselves to a specific solution to their problems later than their less-creative counterparts. Creative people tend to be non-conformists and question authority and existing problem solutions" (Knight, 1967).

A study by Amabile throws more light on the qualities of creative individuals (1988). In her findings, 40% of the researchers mentioned self-motivation as a factor, excitement generated by the work itself, the challenge of a problem, and a belief in or commitment to the idea. Forty-one percent of them said that persistence, curiosity, energy, enthusiasm, and intellectual honesty are necessary requirements for creativity. Thirty-eight percent thought it was important for the creative researcher to have special talents in their field and problem-solving abilities. Social skills, a high level of general intelligence, and sophistication were considered less important. It seems that actively creative people are "born with intrinsic motivation, self-esteem, dignity and curiosity" for creative learning (Senge, 1990).

In fact, many of the characteristics of creative people are consistent with common stereotypes of creative personalities. Their motivation seems to be less based on financial incentives than on intrinsic needs, such as self-interest and achievement of personal goals (Rothwell and Zegveld, 1982; Pinchot, 1988; Morris *et al.*, 1993; Tsui, 1993; Feist, 1998).

In 1996, Augsdorfer carried out comprehensive research on the character of bootleg researchers (1996). The study provided answers to questions such as: is everybody at one time or another a bootleg entrepreneur, or are bootleg entrepreneurs always the same type of person? If they are always the same type of person, how do companies describe them? Have they any characteristics in common across firms? Then it looked into what prompts the bootleg entrepreneur. Are they tempted by extrinsic, financial incentives or is bootlegging an outlet for intrinsic needs? Fifty-seven European firms from different industries and more than 120 interviews revealed the following: it is always the same type of person who initiates bootleg projects. The elements of this character are described in Table 15.1.

Similar findings were reported by Michalik (2003). In contrast, reactive researchers are described as being better at "solving problems than creating ideas" and their creativity can therefore be described as "adaptive." In general, these researchers "prefer a guiding organizational structure" and planning. They seem to be "more pragmatic and inflexible" in their work style. One company named them "bits and bytes types" (Augsdorfer, 1996).

Table 15.1. Personality traits of bootleg researchers (Augsdorfer, 1996).

• Super interest for technology and scientific phenomena • Steadfast ambition to improve technological parameters • Highly motivated • Intrinsic motivation • Natural drive • Workaholics • Cannot be stopped anyway • Stay after five o' clock • Very self-motivated • Regard their work less in terms of hours than results • Questioning mind • Lateral thinkers	• Have a unique way of seeing things, very analytical and prepared to step out of the norm • More likely to be found among scientists • The best, brightest and most innovative people • Mavericks • Genius • Quick understanding • Behavior cannot always be explained rationally • High degree of idiosyncratic identification with their ideas • Obsessed by their ideas	• Would not give up an idea easily, try to pursue it until they accept that it is useless • Failure is regarded as personal failure • Strong belief in what they are doing • Can be recognized by their hobbies (interest in aircraft, car maintenance, or a hobby based on practical skills) • Unconventional • Anticonformist • Managers report problems and unease in supervising them

The objective of this research study was to find out whether it is possible to identify bootleg researchers with the help of the well-known TSD-Z creativity test. The hypothesis is that it is possible. The test is a proven test, developed by psychologists Urban and Jellen in 1995 (Urban and Jellen, 1995).[1] More information about the test can be found at the end of this chapter.

15.2. Findings

In this section, the results of the TSD-Z tests are matched with the information about who is a bootlegger and who is not a bootlegger.[2] In Fig. 15.1 it is clear that the average score of a bootlegger is higher than that of their peers.

The highest creativity score was 53 from a possible 72. The size of the sample was $N_{\text{total}} = 51$. Two respondents were not interested in the psychological drawing test and were dropped from the sample. Nine bootleg researchers were identified [$N_{\text{bootleg}} = 9$ and $N_{\text{non-bootleg}} = 40$].

Figure 15.1 shows the test-persons and their score, separated according to bootleg and non-bootleg researchers.

---

[1] After comparing several tests, the TSD-Z test was found to be preferable for two reasons. Its sole focus is on creativity and it is simple to use. Moreover, the TSD-Z test meets all the quality factors required for a psychological test as defined by Lienert and Raatz (1998): objectivity, reliability, validity, and standardization. All such tests are compared and their qualities described in Brickenkamp's *Handbook for Psychological and Pedagogical Tests*, Volume 1 (Brähler *et al.*, 2002) and the homepage of the Testzentrale. The TSD-Z test attempts to estimate the degree of creativity as the capacity to produce new, unconventional products that are comprehensible to others. It covers aspects such as openness, curiosity, other personality traits and cognitive models of creativity such as risk awareness and divergent thinking (Urban and Jellen, 1995). It is a predominantly qualitative test in which participants have to complete a drawing giving it a coherent purpose (i.e., tell a story).

[2] The sample size is small. Only 49 corporate researchers took part in the survey. However, carrying out psychological tests in firms is not easy in Germany and Switzerland. Stringent law is applied to the protection and generation of personal data (e.g., in Germany: Bundesdatenschutzgesetz (BDSG)). Corporate organizations are obliged to comply with this law. Generally, no psychological testing is allowed without the consent of the Workers Council and which is usually not given. In Germany, written consent to the test, its further processing, and use is required from participants (§13 (2)). The situation is similar in Switzerland. So, all testing had to be done applying the bootleg method; in other words, secretly. The author was happy to at least have this small sample.

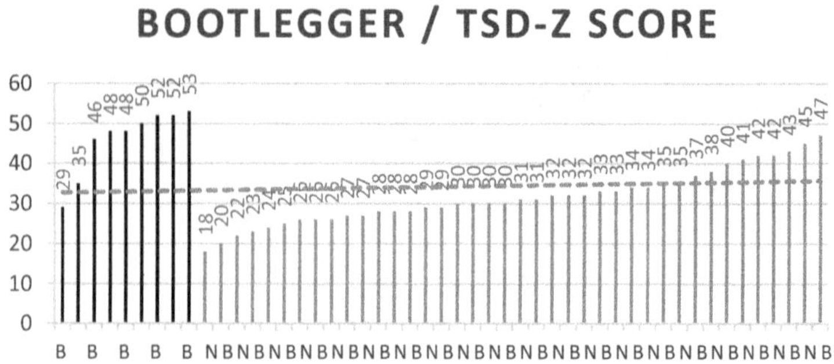

Fig. 15.1. Creativity score (B = Bootlegger; NB = Non-Bootlegger).

The average value is: $\bar{x}_{\text{total}} = 34.20$, $\bar{x}_{\text{bootlegger}} = 45.\overline{8}$, $\bar{x}_{\text{non-bootlegger}} = 31.575$.

At this stage, it is already possible to say that the hypothesis is found to be true. Bootleggers can be identified with the help of a creativity test as their average score is higher than their peers.

In order to identify random failures, the median might be a better indication of the average creativity factor. The difference between the two groups (bootlegger and non-bootlegger) using the more robust median is even more significant.

The average median is: $\tilde{x}_{\text{total}} = 32$, $\tilde{x}_{\text{bootlegger}} = 48$, $\tilde{x}_{\text{non-bootlegger}} = 30.5$

Considering variance, the standard deviation is calculated as:

$$V_{(x)-\text{total}} = 79.1420245$$

$$V_{(x)-\text{bootlegger}} = 61.654321 \quad V_{(x)-\text{non-bootlegger}} = 45.444375$$

$$s_{\text{total}} = 8.89618033$$

$$s_{\text{bootlegger}} = 7.85202655 \quad s_{\text{non-bootlegger}} = 6.74124432$$

It is evident that variance between the groups is lower than the total variance. Similarly, this is true for the standard deviation. This is another indication of the different creativity potentials of the two groups. The creativity score can be translated into the following grades of creativity. This was done following the classification given in the TSD-Z test manual.

A = far below average, B = below average, C = average,
D = above average, E = far above average,
F = extremely above average, G = phenomenal.

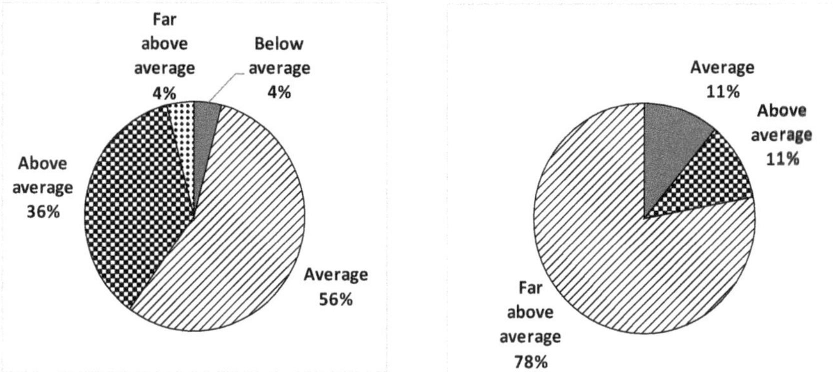

Fig. 15.2. TSD-Z score NB (left pie chart) and B (right pie chart).

Figure 15.2 shows the classification for non-bootleg and for bootleg staff. In the group of non-bootleg staff, the average creativity level is 56% with 36% above average. In the group of bootleg staff, the classifications are almost exclusively "average," "above average," and "far above average." It is particularly remarkable that 78% of bootleg people show a creativity level "far above" the average.

The result is only valid if the two variables "bootlegger" and "non-bootlegger" are stochastically independent. Due to the difficulties encountered in obtaining data, the sample size of our study is small. In order to see how confidently the results of this research can be interpreted, a test for equality of means between the series with the null hypothesis that bootlegger and non-bootlegger have the same mean of creativity index was applied. The pre-condition for the application of such tests is that the populations of bootleggers and non-bootleggers are normally distributed and that there is equality of variances in both populations.

This was carried out with a Jarque Bera test (Figs. 15.3 and 15.4). As the probability of both variables is close to 0.5, it points toward the assumption of a normal distribution of non-bootlegger (NBL) and bootlegger (BL) being valid.

In a second step, a test for the equality of variances (F-test) was carried out. All tests, with exception of the Siegel–Tukey test, showed that the variances of both variables were neither equal nor different (Table 15.2). In other words, the null hypothesis of equal variances cannot be rejected.

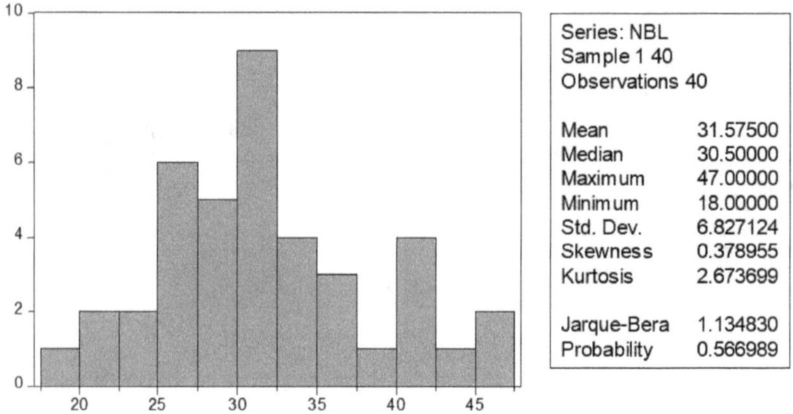

Fig. 15.3. Jarque Bera test for non-bootlegger.

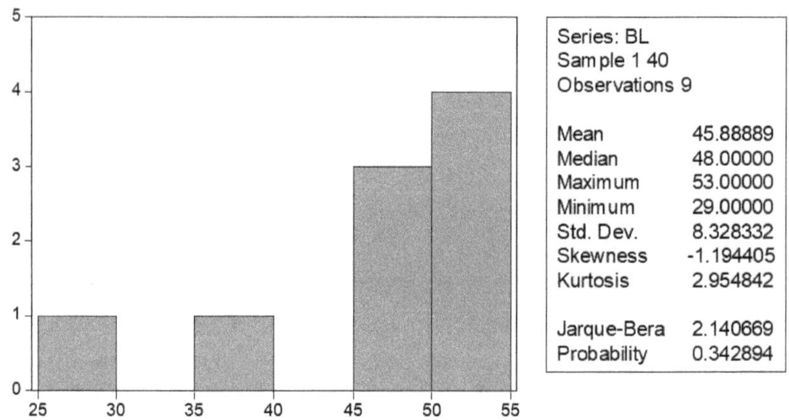

Fig. 15.4. Jarque Bera test for bootlegger.

Table 15.2. Equality of variance test (F-test).

Test for Equality of Variances Between Series
Date: 02/12/09 Time: 17:59
Sample: 1 40
Included observations: 40

Method	df	Value	Probability
F-test	[39, 8]	1.488129	0.5744
Siegel–Tukey		2.674884	0.0075
Bartlett	1	0.547500	0.4593
Levene	[1, 47]	0.273275	0.6036
Brown-Forsythe	[1, 47]	0.009187	0.9240

As can be seen, all tests indicate that null hypothesis — that the creativity indices of bootleggers and non-bootleggers have the same mean — can be rejected with statistical significance (Table 15.3). As both samples have a statistically significant different mean value and bootleggers have a statistically significant higher creativity score, the test results of the TSD-Z test are valid despite the small sample size (Tables 15.4 and 15.5).

Table 15.3. Equality of means.

Test for Equality of Means Between Series
Date: 02/12/09 Time: 18:01
Sample: 1 40
Included observations: 40

Method	df	Value	Probability
T-test	47	5.460616	0.0000
Satterthwaite-Welch T-test	10.55254	4.805584	0.0006
Anova F-test	[1, 47]	29.81833	0.0000
Welch F-test	[1, 10.5525]	23.09363	0.0006

Table 15.4. T-test (assumption of equal variance).

Paired samples T-Test under the assumption of equal variances

	Variable 1	Variable 2
Mean	31.575	45.8888889
Variance	46.6096154	69.3611111
Sample	40	9
Pooled variance	50.4822104	
Hypothetical difference of mean value	0	
Degrees of freedom (df)	47	
t-statistic	−5.46061642	
$P(T <= t)$ one sided	0.0001%	
Critical T-value at single-sided T-test	1.67792678	
$P(T <= t)$ double-sided	0.0002%	99.9998%
Critical T-value at double-sided T-test	2.01173862	

Interpretation: BL is more creative than NBL with a probability of 99.9998%

Table 15.5. T-test (assumption non-equal variance).

Paired samples T-Test under the assumption of non-equal variances

	Variable 1	**Variable 2**
Mean	31.575	45.8888889
Variance	46.6096154	69.3611111
Sample	40	9
Pooled variance	0	
Hypothetical difference of mean value	11	
Degrees of freedom (df)	−4.80558351	
t-statistic	0.03%	
$P(T <= t)$ one sided	1.79588369	
Critical T-value at single-sided T-test	0.05%	99.95%
$P(T <= t)$ double-sided	2.20098627	

Interpretation: BL are more creative than NBL with a probability of 99.95%

15.3. Conclusions

In conclusion, the hypothesis is found to be true. Managers should be able to identify bootleg researchers prior to appointment with the help of a TSD-Z test. The majority of all people tested in the classification "far above average" and higher were identified as bootleggers.

Further descriptive elements of the personality of bootleg people were collected. They can be found in Table 15.6. They are very similar to the findings of Augsdorfer (1996) and Michalik (2003) and provide only minor additional elements.

This chapter looked at the creativity level of bootleg researchers. More specifically, it looked at whether it is possible to identify bootleggers by their creativity level. The results very clearly confirmed that the psychological test TSD-Z can identify potential bootleg staff with a high degree of significance. Of the researchers in the sample, 87.5% could have been identified in advance by their exceptionally high creativity score.

It has to be pointed out that the character description of researchers remains more or less at the level of human stereotypes. As such, there is a risk of type casting. However, a comparison with other research investigating creative and entrepreneurial activity in companies shows that a number of renowned investigators used a similar level to describe their

Table 15.6. Personality traits of bootleg researchers.

• Risk takers	• Interest in learning something non-job specific	• Questioning
• Mavericks	• Hunger for new tasks and projects	• Enthusiastic
• Curiosity	• Loyal	• Bored with routine
• Open-mindedness	• Motivated	• Unconventional
• Low tolerance of frustration	• Erratic	• Difficult to manage
• Passionate	• Often feel unloved	• Self-confident
• Nonconformist	• Like to communicate	• Critical of the firm
• Chaotic work attitude	• Self-confident	• Chaotic
• Not punctual	• Jovial	• Agile
• Unstructured work mode	• Interested	• Good transfer capacities
• Too many projects at the same time	• Not very analytical at times	• Do not obey the rules
• Can never say "no" to new jobs	• Pursuit of an idea defended strongly even at a vague stage	• Need for free space
• Ability to connect with others who are like-minded	• Wide range of interests	• Difficult characters
• Ability to translate something from another industry to their own industry	• Unconventional approaches	• Strong self-belief
• Ability to present material or ideas in creative ways	• Pursue multiple things at once	• Self-promoting
	• Focused on the end-user not just the idea	• To them the solution is obvious and they struggle to see why no-one else can see it
		• Lots of energy

findings (Quinn, 1979; Kanter, 1983; Burgelman, 1986; Allan, 1988). This level of analysis is commonly considered as "broadly useful" despite its shortcomings (Roussel *et al.*, 1991).

A major unifying characteristic found in bootleg entrepreneurs is restlessness in active creativity. This seems to be fueled by permanent curiosity. However, generally, companies are collectivist institutions and offer no formal space for the needs of such individuals. Actively creative researchers make use of bootlegging as an outlet for their creativity. Furthermore, the bootleg entrepreneur, due to his creative spirit, is probably the most important source of bottom-up impulses for innovations in R&D. In this sense, the result of this research can help companies to understand the different needs of their employees and to balance their skills that are needed for the innovation process.

These elements remind us of Schumpeter's entrepreneur. However, the bootleg researcher's entrepreneurial behavior takes only place within the R&D department as opposed within the whole firm.

References

Allan, T. (1966). *Managing the Flow of Scientific and Technological Information.* Doctoral dissertation, M.I.T., Sloan School of Management, Cambridge, US.

Allan, T. (1988). Distinguishing engineers from scientists. In Katz, R. (Ed.), *Managing Professionals in Innovative Organizations.* Cambridge, Mass.: Ballinger.

Amabile, T. (1988). From individual creativity to organizational innovation. In Grønhaug, K. and Kaufmann, G. (Eds.), *Innovation: A Cross-Disciplinary Perspective* (p. 139).

Augsdorfer, P. (1994). The manager as pirate, an inspection of the gentle art of bootlegging. *Creativity and Innovation Management*, **3**(2): 91–95.

Augsdorfer, P. (1996). *Forbidden Fruit: An Analysis of Bootlegging, Uncertainty, and Learning in Corporate R&D.* Aldershot: Avebury.

Augsdorfer, P. (2005). Bootlegging and path dependency. *Research Policy*, **34**: 1–11.

Berthon, P. R. (1993). Psychological type and corporate culture: Relationship and dynamic. *OMEGA*, **21**(3): 329–344.

Binnig, G. (1989). *Aus dem Nichts.* München: R. Piper GmbH & Co.

Brähler, E., Holling, H., Leutner, D. and Petermann, F. (2002). *Brickenkamp Handbuch psychologischer und pädagogischer Tests, 3. Auflage.* Göttingen: Hogrefe Verlag für Psychologie.

Burgelman, R. A. (1986). *Inside Corporate Innovation.* New York: Free Press.

Duncan, W. J., Ginter, P. M., Rucks, A. C. and Jacobs, T. D. (1990). Intrapreneurship and the reinvention of the corporation. *IEEE*, **17**(3): 77 ff.

Ekvall, G. (1996). Organisational climate for creativity and innovation. *European Journal of Work and Organizational Psychology,* **5**(1): 105–123.

Ekvall, G. (1997). Organizational conditions and levels of creativity. *Creativity and Innovation Management,* **6**(4). December.

Feist, G. (1998). A meta-analysis of personality in scientific and artistic creativity. *Personality and Social Psychology Review*, **2**(4): 290–309. November.

Gratton, L. (1987). How can we predict management potential in research scientists. *R&D Management*, **17**(2): 87.

Griffin, A. (2005). *Organizationally Coping with Product Visionaries.* Working paper 98, University of Illinois, Urbana-Champaign.

Guilford, J. P. (1986). *Creative Talents — Their Nature, Uses and Development, 1. Auflage.* Buffalo, New York: Bearly Limited.

Hauschildt, J. and Kirchmann, E. (2001). Teamwork for innovation - The 'troika' of promotors. *R&D Management*, **31**(1): 41.

Howell, J. and Higgins, C. (1990). Champions of technological innovation. *Administrative Science Quarterly*, **35**: 317–341.

Hrncir, E. and MacTurk. R. H. (Eds.). (1990). Models of mastery motivation and development. *Early Education and Development*, **5**: 317–393.

Kanter, R. M. (1983). *The Change Masters: Innovation and Entrepreneurship in the American Corporation*. London: Unwin.

Knight, K. E. (1967). A descriptive model of the intra-firm innovation process. *The Journal of Business*, **40**: 478–496.

Lienert, K. and Raatz, L. (1998). *Testaufbau und Testanalyse, 6. Auflage*. Weinheim: Beltz Psychologie Verlags Union.

Maidique, M. (1980). Entrepreneurs, champions, and technological innovation. In Roberts, E. B. (Ed.). (1987). *Generating Effective Corporate Innovation*.

Mansfeld, M., Hölzle, K. and Gemünden, H.-G. (2010). Personal characteristics of innovators - An empirical study of roles in innovation management. *International Journal of Innovation Management,* **14**(06): 1129–1147.

Michalik, C. (2003). *Innovatives Engagement, Eine empirische Untersuchung zum Phänomen des Bootlegging*. Wiesbaden: Deutscher Universitäts-Verlag.

Morris, M. H., Avila, R. A. and Allen, J. (1993). Individualism and the modern corporation: Implications for innovation and entrepreneurship. *Journal of Management,* **19**(3): 595–612.

Pimmer, H. (1995). *Kreativitätsforschung und Joy Paul Guilford 1897-1987. 1.Auflage*. München: Akademischer Verlag.

Pinchot, G. (1988). Innovation through intrapreneuring. In Katz, R. (Ed.), *Managing Professionals in Innovative Organizations* (pp. 121–129). Cambridge, Mass: Ballinger.

Puccio, G. J., Treffinger, D. J. and Talbot, R. J. (1995). Explanatory examination of the relationship between creative styles and creative products. *Creative Research Journal*, **8**: 157–172.

Quinn, J. B. (1979). Technological innovation, entrepreneurship and strategy. *Sloan Management Review*, **20**(1): 15–26.

Rothwell, R. (1975). Intracorporate entrepreneurs. *Management Decision*, **13**(3): 142–154.

Rothwell, R. and Zegveld, W. (1982). *Innovation in the Small and Medium Sized Firm*. London: Pinter.

Roussel, P. A., Saad, K. N. and Erickson, T. J. (1991). *Third Generation of R&D*. USA: Arthur D. Little, Inc.

Sayles, L. R. (1964). *Individualism and Big Business*. New York: McGraw Hill.

Schilling, M. (2005). *Strategic Management of Technological Innovation*. New York: McGraw-Hill.

Schon, D. A. (1973). Champion for radical new inventions. *Harvard Business Review*, March/April.

Schumpeter, J. A. (1912). *Theorie der wirtschaftlichen Entwicklung*. Leipzig.

Schumpeter, J. A. (1947). The creative response in economic history. *Journal of Economic History*, 149–159. November.

Schumpeter, J. A. (1989). *Essays - On Entrepreneurs, Innovations, Business Cycles and the Evolution of Capitalism*. Brunswick, U.S.: Transaction Publishers.

Senge, P. M. (1990). The leader's new work: Building learning organizations. *Sloan Management Review*, **32**(1): 7–23.

Shepard, H. A. (1967). *Innovation-Resisting and Innovation Producing Organizations*. Chicago: University of Chicago Press.

Smith, D. (2007). The politics of innovation: Why innovations need a godfather. *Technovation*, **27**: 95–104.

Tsui, A. S. (1993). *Reputational Effectiveness, Research in Organisational Behavior* (Vol. 16, pp. 257–307). London: JAI-Press.

Urban, K. and Jellen, H. (1995). *Test zum schöpferischen Denken, Zeichnerisch (TSD-Z): Manual.* Frankfurt: Swets Test Service.

Witte, E. (1973). *Organisation für Innovationsentscheidung*. Göttingen: Verlag Otto Schwartz & Co.

Appendix

TSD-Z. In the Fig. 15A.1 only the starting figure is shown to give an idea about the nonverbal test. The test including the manual is available online: https://www.pearsonclinical.de/tct.html.

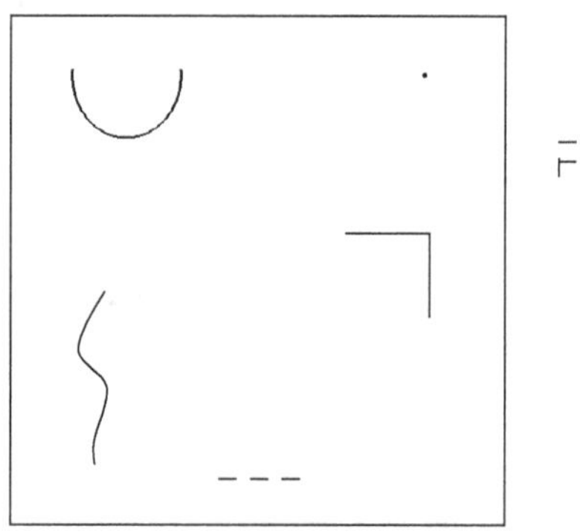

Fig. 15A.1. Nonverbal TSD-Z test.

https://doi.org/10.1142/9781800612266_0017

Chapter 16

Extreme Bootlegging: Individual-level Antecedents to Creative Deviance

Helene Tenzer* and Philip Yang†
Tübingen University, Tübingen, Germany
**helene.tenzer@uni-tuebingen.de*
†philip.yang@uni-tuebingen.de

Abstract

The final chapter is dedicated to hardcore bootlegging or creative deviance and complements prior research on the organizational-level determinants of bootlegging by discussing its individual-level antecedents. Analyzing survey data from 457 employees in a German high-tech corporation, Tenzer and Yang demonstrate that risk propensity as a personality trait is positively related, whereas allocentrism as a personal value orientation and organizational commitment as a personal attitude are negatively related to creative deviance. Risk propensity emerged as the strongest predictor, as it affects hardcore bootlegging or creative deviance both directly and indirectly through allocentrism and commitment.

16.1. Introduction

Defined as a secret activity, which is typically conducted out of supervisors' sight (Augsdorfer, 2005), bootlegging describes the behavior of employees who pursue innovations without any formal authorization to do so. Colleagues and sometimes superiors may be aware of this activity and refrain from intervening, as it is intended for their company's benefit (Criscuolo *et al.*, 2013). In extreme cases, however, individuals even continue to work on projects, which have been formally terminated by management. Mainemelis (2010: 558–559) labels these particular instances of bootlegging as *creative deviance*, defined as "the violation of a managerial order to stop working on a new idea."

Early research on this phenomenon has conceptualized deviance as a function of the overarching social structure (see, for example, Coleman and Ramos, 1998; Staw and Boettger, 1990) and focused on the organizational conditions producing deviant behavior. In a recent article published in the *International Journal of Innovation Management* (Tenzer and Yang, 2019), we complemented this perspective with a closer look at the psychological underpinnings of creative deviance. This chapter summarizes our key findings.

16.2. Creative Deviance: A Matter of Personality, Values, and Attitudes?

Individual personality traits, values, and attitudes are considered the most important psychological determinants of behavior (Ajzen, 2005; Bilsky and Schwartz, 1994). From each of these three categories, we selected one exemplary construct and studied its influence on creative deviance. We investigated risk propensity as an individual personality trait, allocentrism as a personal value orientation, and organizational commitment as an individual attitude. Based on a survey of 457 employees working in a German technology corporation, we found a positive association of risk propensity and negative associations of allocentrism and organizational commitment with creative deviance. Risk propensity emerged as the strongest predictor, affecting creative deviance, both directly and indirectly through allocentrism and organizational commitment.

16.2.1. Deviant personalities: The influence of risk propensity

As personality traits were shown to influence individual innovators' success in realizing their project ideas (Stock *et al.*, 2016), Lin, Mainemelis, and Kark (2016) conjectured that personality may also affect employees' proclivity for creative deviance. We selected *risk propensity*, defined as "the extent to which a person is willing to knowingly take risks" (Zhang and Arvey, 2009: 437), as an exemplary personality trait to empirically test this proposition.

An association of risk propensity with creative deviance is highly plausible, as deviant behaviors entail substantial personal risk for the perpetrator (Mainemelis, 2010). Illustrating just how much risk creative deviants may incur, the inventor of the LED lighting technology, Shuji Nakamura, violated his superior's orders to stop working on his ambitious project and experimented with the only substances available in his laboratory, causing several explosions. He could have failed spectacularly, but ultimately succeeded, founded a multibillion-dollar industry and even received the Nobel Prize for Physics in 2014 (Johnstone, 2015). Risk-seekers are drawn to such creative deviance, because they overestimate the likelihood of success and strive for the insecure, but possibly high rewards of transgressing the boundaries set by the supervisor.

We studied the impact of individual risk propensity on creative deviance by surveying 457 employees from a large German multinational engineering and electronics company, who reported to regularly feel constrained by the organization in pursuing their ideas. Capturing creative deviance by asking "Did you have to pursue innovative activities even against organizational resistance?" and using a four-item scale to measure general risk propensity as a personality trait, we found that creative deviance was positively associated with risk propensity (Tenzer and Yang, 2019).

16.2.2. Conformist value orientations: The influence of allocentrism

Whereas personality traits refer to "what persons are like" regardless of their intentions, values express a person's intentional life goals (Bilsky and Schwartz, 1994: 165), that is, "what is important to them." As values are known to guide individual behaviors (Bilsky and Schwartz, 1994), we also studied them as possible antecedents of creative deviance. Considering that creative deviance, if gone wrong, may be socially harmful (Warren, 2003) and subject the deviant to punishment from the social group (Morrison, 2006; Zhang and Arvey, 2009), employees' values regarding their involvement in the group are likely to influence deviant behavior. We therefore investigated *allocentrism*, a value indicating high group orientation (Triandis, 1989), as a potential antecedent to creative deviance. Whereas the frequently studied construct of "collectivism" represents a general attribute of a given culture (Hofstede, 2001), the term "allocentrism" refers to an individual's value orientation independent of his or her society's dominant culture (Chen *et al.*, 2007).

Allocentrics see themselves as embedded in social contexts, are loyal to their in-group, and concerned with interpersonal harmony (Chen *et al.*, 2007). They are unlikely to defy managerial orders, given that rule breaking is defined as the failure to comply with the group's normative expectations (Zhang and Arvey, 2009) and would strain the supervisor–subordinate relationship. Allocentrics are particularly sensitive to rejection and punishments from in-group members (Yamaguchi *et al.*, 1995), so they are less prone to exposing themselves to such treatment by defying managerial directives.

In our study, we measured allocentrism using two items based on Kim, Triandis, Kagitcibasi, Choi, and Yoon (1994) and Triandis (1993). As expected, our results imply a negative association between allocentrism and creative deviance (Tenzer and Yang, 2019).

16.2.3. Conformist attitudes: The impact of organizational commitment

Besides personality traits and values, social psychologists often draw on attitudes to explain human behavior (Ajzen, 2005). These psychological tendencies are "expressed by evaluating a particular entity with some degree of favor or disfavor" (Eagly and Chaiken, 2007: 582) and influence their holders' behaviors toward that entity (Mulki *et al.*, 2006). We studied employees' attitudes toward the organization, captured in the concept of organizational commitment (Meyer *et al.*, 2002), as a potential antecedent to creative deviance.

Whereas prior research portrays highly committed employees as very creative (Ng *et al.*, 2010), there is ample evidence that they will not become creative *deviants*. According to Meyer *et al.*'s (2002) meta-analysis of commitment research, committed employees' emotional attachment to their organization and their strong identification with it make them adhere to organizational policy. Both Liao, Joshi, and Chuang (2004) and Tepper, Henle, Lambert, Giacalone, and Duffy (2008) found that affective commitment correlated negatively with workplace deviance. These findings are intuitive for general deviance, which carries negative connotations. *Creative* deviance might be different, as it results from employees' intention to benefit their corporation. However, we argue that emotionally committed individuals will still be less likely to antagonize their superiors, whom they often perceive as surrogates for the organization (Mulki *et al.*, 2006), by disregarding their directives.

Deviant behavior is also discouraged by organizational commitment, which arises from a rational assessment of the costs associated with changing one's employer (Meyer *et al.*, 2002). One may expect that employees, who calculate that remaining in their current organization will be the least costly option, will act in ways that maximize their chances of maintaining their positions. Disobeying their leaders' orders in order to pursue innovations would not be a rational choice in this context, as their superiors may punish them (Lin *et al.*, 2016) or even discontinue their contracts.

Finally, deviant behavior is reduced by organizational commitment, which rests on employees' feeling of obligation that they ought to stay with their employer (Meyer and Allen, 1997). Such feelings develop if an organization invests in the employee and honors its part of the psychological contract, that is, the mutual obligations between employer and employee (Meyer and Allen, 1991). In these cases, the individual will feel indebted and motivated to behave appropriately and to do what is right for the organization (Erdheim *et al.*, 2006). Although there is little empirical evidence on this relationship, it is plausible to assume that individuals wanting to reciprocate their organization's favors will be less likely to disregard directives from their superiors.

In line with other studies that have empirically analyzed commitment in the context of creative deviance (e.g., Mulki *et al.*, 2006), we measured organizational commitment by capturing its affective, rational, and obligation-based components using three items. Supporting our theoretical reasoning, we found that organizational commitment in our sample was negatively associated with creative deviance (Tenzer and Yang, 2019).

16.2.4. The relative strength of risk orientation, allocentrism, and organizational commitment in predicting creative deviance

Raising the question of which antecedent will influence creative deviance most profoundly, we found that risk propensity as a deeply engrained personality trait was a stronger predictor of creative deviance than allocentric values and organizational commitment attitudes. This dominance manifested so strongly that no significant relationship between allocentrism and creative deviance or between commitment and creative deviance could be detected, which prevailed irrespective of risk. As soon as risk propensity, allocentrism, and organizational commitment were included in the same regression, only risk propensity remained significant.

Our analyses also revealed that risk propensity influences creative deviance indirectly through allocentric values and organizational commitment, that is, the higher an individual's risk propensity, the less (s)he will display allocentric values and the less (s)he will be committed to the organization (Tenzer and Yang, 2019).

16.3. Theoretical Implications

Whereas early research focused on organizational framework conditions triggering deviant behavior, our study built on Mainemelis' (2010: 574) proposition that "individual differences can explain why some people are more likely than others to engage in creative deviance under the same contextual conditions." It established how particular personality traits, value orientations, or attitudes toward the organization may influence an individual's proclivity for pursuing innovative ideas despite managerial orders to stop. Our study thus shed first light on the psychological underpinnings of creative deviance. We argue that this extreme form of bootlegging needs to be better understood, as its impact on organizational outcomes is highly ambivalent. On the one hand, creative rule-breakers take unauthorized risks (Warren, 2003) and may waste valuable resources that way (Mainemelis, 2010). On the other hand, they may also enable breakthroughs in product development if successful (Johnstone, 2015). Anecdotes about famous creative deviants such as the designer of Pontiac's successful Fiero model, who was repeatedly ordered to stop working on the prototype, or about the creator of HP's large and highly profitable electrostatic displays, who was instructed by David Packard himself to abort the project (Mainemelis, 2010), illustrate the potential benefit of creative deviance for disruptive innovation.

Studying individual tendencies to innovate against the employer's resistance also advances research about the basis of entrepreneurial behavior in corporations (see e.g., Kuratko *et al.*, 2014). Personality traits have been investigated as predictors of entrepreneurship constructs such as entrepreneurial alertness or business planning (Brandstätter, 2011; Frese and Gielnik, 2014), but mostly among startup founders, who are less constrained by top-down orders to stop working on their pet projects. Studying the bottom-up innovation of employees in large corporations, we advance our understanding of the drivers of intrapreneurship (Subramanian, 2005).

16.4. Managerial Implications

Given today's fast-paced technological change (Manso, 2017), innovation-oriented corporations frequently seek individuals "who will put extraordinary thought and effort into achieving things previously not done in the organization" (Kuratko and Goldsby, 2004: 19). Risk-seeking personalities are valuable candidates in that sense, as they will be more proactive regarding business opportunities (Kuratko and Goldsby, 2004). Our study has demonstrated, however, that these individuals are also more prone to pursuing ideas against their superiors' mandates to stop. In industries facing high pressures for innovation, risk-seeing employees' innovative potential may outweigh the drawbacks of their deviance, whereas more stable industry environments may require stricter conformity. Consequently, recruiters are well advised to include personality assessments into their hiring decisions to increase person–organization fit (Morley, 2007), that is, the fit of an applicant's personality, values, and attitudes with the organization's culture, values, and priorities.

Our study's findings also have leadership implications. To harness their employees' creativity, corporate leaders need to encourage employees to generate numerous and diverse ideas. Due to scarce budget, materials, and time (Globocnik and Salomo, 2015), however, they must exercise judgment on which of their proposals to act (Wiklund *et al.*, 2018) and reject many ideas. To strike this balance, leaders need to create an enabling climate for initiative while simultaneously setting standards for how employees should behave. Extending Lin *et al.*'s (2016) work on leaders' responses to their subordinates' creative deviance, our study suggests that superiors should differentiate their leadership measures depending on their subordinates' individual dispositions and tendencies. Risk-averse, allocentric, and highly committed employees may need encouragement to propose new ideas but will gravitate toward rule conformity. More risk-seeking, idiocentric, and less committed individuals will need little incentive to innovate but require more active monitoring to keep them aligned with organizational directives.

16.5. Conclusion

To adapt to changing conditions and keep astride in today's dynamic business environment (Shepherd *et al.*, 2010), businesses need to nurture an entrepreneurial spirit among their workforce. Employees are encouraged to suggest product and process innovations, but only a small proportion of these innovative ideas can be sponsored due to scarce resources. This tension between leaders supporting idea generation but curbing idea implementation may result in creative deviance — an understudied and highly ambivalent flipside to the organizational pursuit of innovation. Our study in the *International Journal of Innovation Management* (Tenzer and Yan, 2019) has elucidated some psychological predicators of creative deviance, but further empirical work on its contingencies is needed.

References

Ajzen, I. (2005). *Attitudes, Personality, and Behavior*. UK: McGraw-Hill Education.

Augsdorfer, P. (2005). Bootlegging and path dependency. *Research Policy*, **34**: 1–11. Available from: https://doi.org/10.1016/j.respol.2004.09.010.

Bilsky, W. and Schwartz, S. H. (1994). Values and personality. *European Journal of Personality*, **8**: 163–181. Available from: https://doi.org/10.1002/per.2410080303.

Brandstätter, H. (2011). Personality aspects of entrepreneurship: A look at five meta-analyses. *Personality and Individual Differences*, **51**: 222–230.

Chen, X.-P., Wasti, S. A. and Triandis, H. C. (2007). When does group norm or group identity predict cooperation in a public goods dilemma? The moderating effects of idiocentrism and allocentrism. *International Journal of Intercultural Relations*, **31**: 259–276.

Coleman, J. W. and Ramos, L. L. (1998). Subcultures and deviant behavior in the organizational context. *Research in the Sociology of Organizations*, **15**: 3–34.

Criscuolo, P., Salter, A. and Ter Wal, A. L. J. (2013). Going underground: Bootlegging and individual innovative performance. *Organization Science*, **25**: 1287–1305. Available from: https://doi.org/10.1287/orsc.2013.0856.

Eagly, A. H. and Chaiken, S. (2007). The advantages of an inclusive definition of attitude. *Social Cognition*, **25**: 582–602.

Erdheim, J., Wang, M. and Zickar, M. J. (2006). Linking the big five personality constructs to organizational commitment. *Personality and Individual Differences*, **41**: 959–970.

Frese, M. and Gielnik, M. M. (2014). The psychology of entrepreneurship. *Annual Review of Organizational Psychology and Organizational Behavior*, **1**: 413–438. Available from: https://doi.org/10.1146/annurev-orgpsych-031413-091326.

Globocnik, D. and Salomo, S. (2015). Do formal management practices impact the emergence of bootlegging behavior? *Journal of Product Innovation Management*, **32**: 505–521. Available from: https://doi.org/10.1111/jpim.12215.

Hofstede, G. (2001). *Culture's Consequences: Comparing Values, Behaviors, Institutions and Organizations Across Nations*. Thousand Oaks: Sage Publications.

Johnstone, B. (2015). *Brilliant! Shuji Nakamura and the Revolution in Lighting Technology* (Updated edn.). Amherst, New York: Prometheus.

Kim, U. E., Triandis, H. C., Kâğitçibaşi, Ç. E., Choi, S.-C. E. and Yoon, G. E. (1994). *Individualism and Collectivism: Theory, Method, and Applications*. Thousand Oaks: Sage Publications, Inc.

Kuratko, D. F. and Goldsby, M. G. (2004). Corporate entrepreneurs or rogue middle managers? A framework for ethical corporate entrepreneurship. *Journal of Business Ethics*, **55**: 13–30.

Kuratko, D. F., Hornsby, J. S. and Covin, J. G. (2014). Diagnosing a firm's internal environment for corporate entrepreneurship. *Business Horizons*, **57**: 37–47.

Liao, H., Joshi, A. and Chuang, A. (2004). Sticking out like a sore thumb: Employee dissimilarity and deviance at work. *Personnel Psychology*, **57**: 969–1000.

Lin, B., Mainemelis, C. and Kark, R. (2016). Leaders' responses to creative deviance: Differential effects on subsequent creative deviance and creative performance. *The Leadership Quarterly*, **27**: 537–556.

Mainemelis, C. (2010). Stealing fire: Creative deviance in the evolution of new ideas. *AMR*, **35**: 558–578. Available from: https://doi.org/10.5465/amr.35.4.zok558.

Manso, G. (2017). Creating incentives for innovation. *California Management Review*, **60**: 18–32. Available from: https://doi.org/10.1177/0008125617725287.

Meyer, J. P. and Allen, N. J. (1991). A three-component conceptualization of organizational commitment. *Human Resource Management Review*, **1**: 61–89. Available from: https://doi.org/10.1016/1053-4822(91)90011-Z.

Meyer, J. P. and Allen, N. J. (1997). *Commitment in the Workplace: Theory, Research, and Application*. Thousand Oaks: Sage.

Meyer, J. P., Stanley, D. J., Herscovitch, L. and Topolnytsky, L. (2002). Affective, continuance, and normative commitment to the organization: A meta-analysis of antecedents, correlates, and consequences. *Journal of Vocational Behavior*, **61**: 20–52.

Morley, M. (2007). Person-organization fit. *Journal of Managerial Psychology*, **22**: 109–117.

Morrison, E. W. (2006). Doing the job well: An investigation of pro-social rule breaking. *Journal of Management*, **32**: 5–28. Available from: https://doi.org/10.1177/0149206305277790.

Mulki, J. P., Jaramillo, F. and Locander, W. B. (2006). Emotional exhaustion and organizational deviance: Can the right job and a leader's style make a difference? *Journal of Business Research*, **59**: 1222–1230.

Ng, T. W., Feldman, D. C. and Lam, S. S. (2010). Psychological contract breaches, organizational commitment, and innovation-related behaviors: A latent growth modeling approach. *Journal of Applied Psychology*, **95**:744.

Shepherd, D. A., Patzelt, H. and Haynie, J. M. (2010). Entrepreneurial spirals: Deviation–amplifying loops of an entrepreneurial mindset and organizational culture. *Entrepreneurship Theory and Practice*, **34**:59–82. Available from: https://doi.org/10.1111/j.1540-6520.2009.00313.x.

Staw, B. M. and Boettger, R. D. (1990). Task revision: A neglected form of work performance. *Academy of Management Journal*, **33**: 534–559.

Stock, R. M., von Hippel, E. and Gillert, N. L. (2016). Impacts of personality traits on consumer innovation success. *Research Policy*, **45**: 757–769. Available from: https://doi.org/10.1016/j.respol.2015.12.002.

Subramanian, N. (2005). The economics of intrapreneurial innovation. *Journal of Economic Behavior & Organization*, **58**: 487–510. Available from: https://doi.org/10.1016/j.jebo.2004.03.006.

Tenzer, H. and Yang, P. (2019). Personality, values, or attitudes? Individual-level antecedents to creative deviance. *International Journal of Innovation Management*, (IJIM) **23**: 1–30.

Tepper, B. J., Henle, C. A., Lambert, L. S., Giacalone, R. A. and Duffy, M. K. (2008). Abusive supervision and subordinates' organization deviance. *Journal of Applied Psychology*, **93**: 721.

Triandis, H. C. (1989). The self and social behavior in differing cultural contexts. *Psychological Review*, **96**: 506.

Triandis, H. C. (1993). Collectivism and individualism as cultural syndromes. *Cross-Cultural Research*, **27**: 155–180.

Warren, D. E. (2003). Constructive and destructive deviance in organizations. *Academy of Management Review*, **28**: 622–632. Available from: https://doi.org/10.5465/amr.2003.10899440.

Wiklund, J., Yu, W. and Patzelt, H. (2018). Impulsivity and entrepreneurial action. *Academy of Management Perspectives*, **32**: 379–403. Available from: https://doi.org/10.5465/amp.2016.0177.

Yamaguchi, S., Kuhlman, D. M. and Sugimori, S. (1995). Personality correlates of allocentric tendencies in individualist and collectivist cultures. *Journal of Cross-Cultural Psychology*, **26**: 658–672.

Zhang, Z. and Arvey, R. D. (2009). Rule breaking in adolescence and entrepreneurial status: An empirical investigation. *Journal of Business Venturing, Special Issue Ethics and Entrepreneurship*, **24**: 436–447. Available from: https://doi.org/10.1016/j.jbusvent.2008.04.009.

https://doi.org/10.1142/9781800612266_bmatter

Index

F

G

H

I

J

K

L

M

N

O

P

R

S

T

U

V

W

Series on Technology Management

(Continuation of series card page)

Vol. 31 *Innovation Heroes: Understanding Customers as a Valuable Innovation Resource*
by Fiona Schweitzer (Grenoble École de Management, France & University of Applied Sciences Upper Austria, Austria) & Joe Tidd (University of Sussex, UK)

Vol. 30 *Innovation Discovery: Network Analysis of Research and Invention Activity for Technology Management*
edited by Tugrul Daim (Portland State University, USA) &
Alan Pilkington (University of Westminster, UK)

Vol. 29 *Exploiting Intellectual Property to Promote Innovation and Create Value*
edited by Joe Tidd (University of Sussex, UK)

Vol. 28 *Promoting Innovation in New Ventures and Small- and Medium-Sized Enterprises*
edited by Joe Tidd (University of Sussex, UK)

Vol. 27 *The Role of Creativity in the Management of Innovation:State of the Art and Future Research Outlook*
edited by Alexander Brem (University of Southern Denmark, Denmark),
Rogelio Puente-Diaz (University Anáhuac, Mexico) &
Marine Agogué (HEC Montréal, Canada)

Vol. 26 *Total Value Development: How to Drive Service Innovation*
by Frank M Hull (Cass Business School, UK & Fordham University, USA) &
Chris Storey (University of Sussex, UK)

Vol. 25 *Small Firms as Innovators: From Innovation to Sustainable Growth*
by Helena Forsman (University of Tampere, Finland)

Vol. 24 *The Knowledge Enterprise: Innovation Lessons from Industry Leaders (Second Edition)*
by Edward Huizenga (University of Amsterdam, The Netherlands &
Benthurst & Co, The Netherlands)

Vol. 23 *Open Innovation Research, Management and Practice*
edited by Joe Tidd (SPRU, University of Sussex, UK)

Vol. 22 *Discontinuous Innovation: Learning to Manage the Unexpected*
by Peter Augsdörfer (Technische Hochschule Ingolstadt, Germany),
John Bessant (University of Exeter, UK),
Kathrin Möslein (Universität Erlangen-Nürnberg, Germany),
Bettina von Stamm (Innovation Leadership Forum, UK) &
Frank Piller (RWTH Aachen University, Germany)

Vol. 21 *Workbook for Opening Innovation: Bridging Networked Business, Intellectual Property and Contracting*
by Jaakko Paasi (VTT Technical Research Centre of Finland, Finland), Katri Valkokari (VTT Technical Research Centre of Finland, Finland), Henri Hytönen (VTT Technical Research Centre of Finland, Finland), Laura Huhtilainen (University of Eastern Finland, Finland) & Soili Nystén-Haarala (University of Eastern Finland, Finland)

Vol. 20 *Bazaar of Opportunities for New Business Development: Bridging Networked Innovation, Intellectual Property and Business*
by Jaakko Paasi (VTT Technical Research Centre of Finland, Finland), Katri Valkokari (VTT Technical Research Centre of Finland, Finland), Tuija Rantala (VTT Technical Research Centre of Finland, Finland), Soili Nystén-Haarala (University of Eastern Finland, Finland), Nari Lee (University of Eastern Finland, Finland) & Laura Huhtilainen (University of Eastern Finland, Finland)

Vol. 19 *From Knowledge Management to Strategic Competence: Assessing Technological, Market and Organisational Innovation (Third Edition)*
edited by Joe Tidd (University of Sussex, UK)

Vol. 18 *Perspectives on Supplier Innovation: Theories, Concepts and Empirical Insights on Open Innovation and the Integration of Suppliers*
edited by Alexander Brem (University of Erlangen-Nuremberg, Germany) & Joe Tidd (University of Sussex, UK)

Vol. 17 *Managing Process Innovation: From Idea Generation to Implementation*
by Thomas Lager (Grenoble Ecole de Management, France)

Vol. 16 *Perspectives on User Innovation*
edited by Stephen Flowers (University of Brighton, UK) & Flis Henwood (University of Brighton, UK)

Vol. 15 *Gaining Momentum: Managing the Diffusion of Innovations*
edited by Joe Tidd (SPRU, University of Sussex, UK)

Vol. 14 *Innovation and Strategy of Online Games*
by Jong H Wi (Chung-Ang University, South Korea)

Vol. 13 *Building Innovation Capability in Organizations: An International Cross-Case Perspective*
by Milé Terziovski (University of Melbourne, Australia)

Vol. 12 *Project-Based Organization in the Knowledge-Based Society*
by Mitsuru Kodama (Nihon University, Japan)

Vol. 11 *Involving Customers in New Service Development*
edited by Bo Edvardsson (Karlstad University, Sweden), Anders Gustafsson (Karlstad University, Sweden), Per Kristensson (Karlstad University, Sweden), Peter Magnusson (Karlstad University, Sweden) & Jonas Matthing (Karlstad University, Sweden)

Vol. 10 *Open Source: A Multidisciplinary Approach*
by Moreno Muffatto (University of Padua, Italy)

Vol. 9 *Service Innovation: Organizational Responses to Technological Opportunities & Market Imperatives*
edited by Joe Tidd (University of Sussex, UK) &
Frank M Hull (Fordham University, USA)

Vol. 8 *Digital Innovation: Innovation Processes in Virtual Clusters and Digital Regions*
edited by Giuseppina Passiante (University of Lecce, Italy),
Valerio Elia (University of Lecce, Italy) &
Tommaso Massari (University of Lecce, Italy)

Vol. 7 *Innovation Management in the Knowledge Economy*
edited by Ben Dankbaar (University of Nijmegen, The Netherlands)

Vol. 6 *Social Interaction and Organisational Change: Aston Perspectives on Innovation Networks*
edited by Oswald Jones (Aston University, UK),
Steve Conway (Aston University, UK) & Fred Steward (Aston University, UK)

Vol. 5 *R&D Strategy and Organisation: Managing Technical Change in Dynamic Contexts*
by Vittorio Chiesa (Università degli Studi di Milano-Bicocca, Milan, Italy)

Vol. 4 *Japanese Cost Management*
by Yasuhiro Monden (University of Tsukuba, Japan)

Vol. 3 *From Knowledge Management to Strategic Competence: Measuring Technological, Market and Organizational Innovation (Second Edition)*
edited by Joe Tidd (SPRU, University of Sussex, UK)

Vol. 3 *From Knowledge Management to Strategic Competence: Measuring Technological, Market and Organizational Innovation*
edited by Joe Tidd (SPRU, University of Sussex, UK)

Vol. 2 *The Knowledge Enterprise: Implementation of Intelligent Business Strategies*
by J Friso den Hertog (MERIT, Maastricht University & Altuïtion bv,
's Hertogenbosch, The Netherlands) &
Edward Huizenga (Altuïtion bv, 's Hertogenbosch, The Netherlands)

Vol. 1 *Engines of Prosperity: Templates for the Information Age*
by Gerardo R Ungson (University of Oregon, USA) &
John D Trudel (The Trudel Group, USA)

www.ingramcontent.com/pod-product-compliance
Lightning Source LLC
LaVergne TN
LVHW010330220926
848484LV00004BB/873